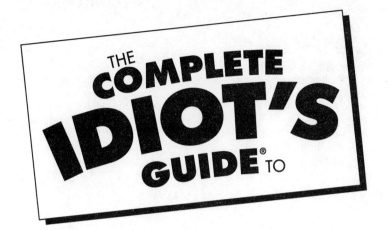

THE **COMPLETE IDIOT'S GUIDE®** TO

# Poker

*By Andrew N.S. Glazer,*
*"The Poker Pundit"*

## ALPHA

A member of Penguin Group (USA) Inc.

International Standard Book Number: 1-59257-257-x
Library of Congress Catalog Card Number: 2004106745

06   05   04       8   7   6   5   4   3   2   1

Interpretation of the printing code: The rightmost number of the first series of numbers is the year of the book's printing; the rightmost number of the second series of numbers is the number of the book's printing. For example, a printing code of 04-1 shows that the first printing occurred in 2004.

*Printed in the United States of America*

**Note:** This publication contains the opinions and ideas of its author. It is intended to provide helpful and informative material on the subject matter covered. It is sold with the understanding that the author and publisher are not engaged in rendering professional services in the book. If the reader requires personal assistance or advice, a competent professional should be consulted.

The author and publisher specifically disclaim any responsibility for any liability, loss, or risk, personal or otherwise, which is incurred as a consequence, directly or indirectly, of the use and application of any of the contents of this book.

Most Alpha books are available at special quantity discounts for bulk purchases for sales promotions, premiums, fund-raising, or educational use. Special books, or book excerpts, can also be created to fit specific needs.

For details, write: Special Markets, Alpha Books, 375 Hudson Street, New York, NY 10014.

**Publisher:** *Marie Butler-Knight*
**Product Manager:** *Phil Kitchel*
**Senior Managing Editor:** *Jennifer Chisholm*
**Senior Acquisitions Editor:** *Mike Sanders*
**Development Editor:** *Ginny Bess Munroe*
**Senior Production Editor:** *Billy Fields*
**Copy Editor:** *Sara Fink*
**Illustrator:** *Chris Eliopoulos*
**Cover/Book Designer:** *Trina Wurst*
**Indexer:** *Heather McNeil*
**Layout/Proofreading:** *Ayanna Lacey, Mary Hunt*

*To my sister, Donna Hall, and my brother-in-law/de-facto brother, Ken Hall, who have always offered unconditional faith, support, and love, but who have a special knack for bestowing these gifts when I need them most and deserve them least.*

# Contents at a Glance

# Contents

## Appendixes

# Foreword

I first met Andrew N.S. Glazer in May 2000, when I arrived in Las Vegas to write a story for *Harpers Magazine*. Editor Lewis Lapham had given me a fair advance to write an article about two big events that were happening simultaneously: the sensationalistic Ted Binion murder trial and the World Series of Poker, which was, as it always has been, to be held at a venue called Binion's Horseshoe.

Of course I took the assignment: How often does a novelist and poet get the chance to write about murder, sex, drugs, and poker for a hoity-toity literary magazine? My only problem was that the very highest ranks of poker society are something of a private club, that clique that we all wanted to want us back in high school, and I neither knew them nor had the kind of access that I knew I'd want.

When I asked around, I kept getting the same story. "Talk to Andy Glazer," they said. "He writes a weekly gambling column for *The Detroit Free Press*, he covers these tournaments for *Card Player* (the definitive poker magazine), he plays as well as he writes, he's taught for universities and law schools, and despite that "Andrew N.S." stuff, he's a regular guy who takes his work seriously without taking himself seriously. If anyone can get you inside, it's him. He's the only reporter they respect and trust. The other reporters can't play very well and the other players can't write very well."

Actually, Andy did a lot more than introduce me around. I became part of the story instead of just its author. I combined my own experience, a lot of time reading poker books and practicing with poker software, and frequent tips from Andy (who quickly became an informal coach) into a run at the title. I wound up finishing fifth, winning a quarter of a million dollars, and writing not just the *Harpers* piece, but a book, *Positively Fifth Street*. My book has hung around *The New York Times* best-seller list long enough to give my wife Jennifer a chance to forgive me for spending so much time "researching" it.

My friendship with and knowledge of Andy has continued to grow and I can now state with conviction that in *The Complete Idiot's Guide to Poker*, Andy Glazer has written the best introductory poker book of all time.

This doesn't surprise me, because he's such a gifted teacher, writer, and player. (He just finished winning two major tournaments at the 2004 *Australasian Poker Championships* and you've seen him on TV playing at a *World Poker Tour* final table.) I thank my lucky stars that *The Complete Idiot's Guide to Poker* wasn't around when I started playing because I'd have done so much better so much sooner that I might not have stayed with my life's ambition. I'm very happy being a writer who plays poker, instead of a poker player who wonders what kind of a writer he might have been.

Come to think of it, I might not have fallen into that trap because Andy convinces his students that while poker can be a fun and profitable hobby or even second job, it isn't a good primary occupation for most.

I'm told the cover price for *The Complete Idiot's Guide to Poker* is going to be under $20. I'll guess it will save or earn the *casual* reader a hundred times that much and the serious nonprofessional reader more like a thousand times that in the course of a lifetime. Actually, anyone who is serious about poker will eventually consider it priceless, and even though the book was designed with the beginner in mind, if you haven't won a World Series tournament or two, you'll probably learn more than you believe possible.

Whether you daydream about extra pocket money, impressing your friends, or playing at a *World Poker Tour* final table, the road starts here.

James McManus
Chicago, Illinois
February, 2004

# Introduction

We all play poker, even if we don't realize it.

You're playing poker when you tell the boss you need a raise or you'll have to start looking elsewhere. (If you're bluffing, hope he doesn't call.)

You're playing poker when, upon learning your girlfriend's ex has asked her to dinner, you decide to propose. (The ex-boyfriend bet and you raised.)

You're playing poker when you decide not to buy the TV you want on December 23, hoping that its price will go down during the post-Christmas sales. (You're waiting for a better hand.)

Poker, that card game you first encountered in the kitchen, the army, or in college, is actually a "people game." It just so happens that one of its more popular variations employs cards and chips.

Sometimes when you play the cards and chips variation, you're focused entirely on trying to win money; sometimes, you hardly notice that money is involved at all!

You might be trying to understand what they're doing on all those televised poker shows. You might be trying to impress people in a game you've joined or simply trying to become friends or acquaintances with them. You might not care about winning, but you don't want to play so poorly that your hosts feel they're taking advantage
of you if they invite you back. You also might want to ensure your inadequate poker skills aren't sending messages about your skills in other aspects of life. This book will help you achieve all these goals.

Most people's attitude will fall somewhere in-between caring only about money and caring about it not at all: Even if you're playing "just to have fun," most people find that winning is more fun than losing!

Because poker is so intertwined with philosophy, history, friendship, politics, psychology, communication skills, and emotions, it will be difficult for you to read *The Complete Idiot's Guide to Poker* without learning something about each of those subjects. But make no mistake—you're not here to learn philosophy. You're here to learn that a flush beats a straight, how to extract every possible dollar out of your opponents when you do catch that flush, and how to cheaply rid yourself of the worst possible poker hand: the one that comes in second.

As with all *Idiot's Guides*, this is *not* a book for idiots. It is a book for beginners and intermediates, and you're not an idiot if you don't know poker—we all had to start somewhere.

Actually, I would be hugely surprised if almost everyone who thinks of himself as "advanced" won't pick up many valuable ideas here. Indeed, because advanced players tend to play for high stakes, the book may be worth more to them than to the novice in the short term.

Nonetheless, because I'm not merely an experienced poker player, but also an experienced teacher (I've taught hundreds of classes to thousands of students in colleges, law schools, and adult education centers) you won't need to know one darned thing about poker to learn from this book. My teaching experience also means the advanced reader won't be bored to tears.

You may, though, wind up reevaluating your self-assessed status as an advanced or expert player. Ten years ago, I thought I was a star because I regularly ripped fairly high stakes private games populated by intelligent people. Then I moved to California and found out what a truly great player was.

Fortunately, the native talent that had enabled me to beat those private games worked in concert with information I learned in great books and experience I gained playing against true stars, and today I actually *can* play a little.

I remember what it was like to be a novice competing against intermediates in my first high school poker games, what it was like being an intermediate competing against advanced players when I first moved up to higher stakes, and what it was like being an advanced player first battling world champions.

More to the point, I remember what I wish I had known at each of those stages and can differentiate between what I wish I'd known and what I needed to know because you just can't absorb everything at once. If you could, the game would be easy and it isn't.

One of the truly great things about poker, though, is that you don't have to be great to succeed. There's the luck factor, of course, but that's not what I refer to. As long as you can find the right class of opponent, you can succeed practically the first time you play. An intermediate will make more money against beginners than a world champion will make against experts.

Read *The Complete Idiot's Guide to Poker* and you'll not only be able to pick the right games, you'll be well on your way to learning what you'll need to beat the games you'll try tomorrow. In short, you'll soon be a feared and respected opponent. If you can avoid letting that go to your head, you'll stay that way.

# How to Use This Book

*The Complete Idiot's Guide to Poker* is divided into six parts and six appendixes (most of which focus on methods and resources you can use to further your never-ending poker education).

**Part 1, "An Introduction to Poker,"** starts you on the journey that makes poker so fascinating and deceptively difficult: the intermixture of people and card skills, and of social and monetary motivations. It debunks common myths and misunderstandings, teaches you about your opponents, and begins not merely to teach you strategy, but to show you why the learning process never ends. Perhaps most importantly, it shows you why the information you'll learn in the rest of the book will be so useful, no matter what your motivation for playing might be.

Part 1 also walks you through the etiquette of what can at first seem an intimidating process and gets into the rules, odds, and strategies necessary to beat the twenty-first century's most commonly-played forms of poker.

**Part 2, "Home Game Poker,"** may feel the most familiar to those of you who have played a hand or two around the kitchen table. Home poker games vary in size and shape even more than kitchen tables do, though. Part 2 walks you through potential opportunities and classic errors in joining or starting your own game. It also offers its share of strategic tips, money management considerations, and solutions for practical problems that plague poorly planned home games.

**Part 3, "Internet Poker,"** will open your eyes to the fastest-growing segment of the fast-growing poker industry: real money Internet poker played in real-time against players from around the globe. You'll learn etiquette, how to pick a good site, how to benefit from industry competition, and how to use Internet poker to improve not just your Internet results, but your home and/or casino results, too.

**Part 4, "Tournament Poker,"** explains the ins and outs of the most exciting and fame-attracting form of poker. You'll learn about a wide variety of tournaments and how you can turn a relatively small investment into fame and fortune. Tournaments allow you to take a legitimate shot at winning big money without risking big money, something not possible in money poker, and success requires its own unique brand of strategy.

**Part 5, "The Psychological Side of Poker,"** teaches you why mere mathematicians or those gifted with perfect memories stand very little chance at poker unless they can bring something else to the table. You'll learn why honesty with yourself is a powerful weapon and why learning how to understand how your opponents think can be even more important than an illegal glance at their cards!

## Extras

*The Complete Idiot's Guide to Poker* also features little hoards of informational ammunition in boxed sidebars sprinkled through each chapter. These sidebars provide you with insider tips, definitions of key terms, warnings about potentially dangerous plays, and moments from poker history that you will probably find helpful and often amusing. (You don't have to have a sense of humor to be a poker player, but it can help in more ways than one!) We call these sidebars:

> **The Inside Straight**
>
> These sidebars contain money-making or money-saving tips on the current topic. They often provide you with a quick and easy way of remembering the most important lessons in a chapter.

> **Perilous Play**
>
> The wrong move in a poker game can cost you not only money, but also psychological disadvantages and considerable enjoyment. You'll make your own mistakes: There's no need to make "the classics."

> **Table Talk**
>
> Like any subculture, poker has its own language and it helps to learn it quickly, both to avoid mistakes and the psychological disadvantage at which apparent "rookie" status can place you.

> **Poker Lore**
>
> Poker occupies a unique place in American history and many stories from poker's past are both amusing and instructive. The author also shares amusing, profitable, and painful moments from his own games.

## Acknowledgments

I mentioned Sir Isaac Newton's famous quote, "If I have seen further it is because I have stood on the shoulders of giants" in my first gambling book, *Casino Gambling the Smart Way*, and it seems appropriate to mention it again. I've had so many important teachers in life that I don't really know where to begin, so I'll take the age-old advice of trying the beginning. My fourth grade teacher, Nina Kimball, told our class that "If you can't explain something to someone else, you don't really understand it yourself." I took that advice to heart and almost always used it as my gauge in studying.

As a result, I became a pretty good teacher and not just in poker. I'm not sure how much I know, but what I do know, I can explain to you. Mrs. Kimball probably would have been horrified to learn that I used her advice to become a poker teacher, but there are risks inherent in shaping young minds.

Although our opponents are often our best teachers, because only they will show us our weaknesses, I think the best of those teachers have already been compensated, so they'll get no mention here. Just try to make sure you pay these teachers as little as possible and to use their "lessons" to "teach" others.

You can find the names of most of my best poker teachers in Appendix A. I didn't list any books that didn't teach me at least something. Therefore, in a sense, all of those authors rate an acknowledgment.

A few poker teachers stand out, though. Phil Hellmuth, who never gave me actual lessons because he didn't want to reveal anything I might use against him, still taught me much through idle chatter and by letting me follow him closely as I worked on his long-threatened biography, *Poker Brat*. I owe Hellmuth more than my understanding of why I must throw certain hands away, though. As we worked on the book's early stages (which will, some decade, most certainly be finished), Hellmuth took me into his family and let me live in my own wing of his house for a number of months. Hellmuth is far luckier to have a good relationship with his wife, Kathy, than he is to have won the 1989 World Championship, a statement that is also true of his sons Phillip and Nick.

Other great champions who have been willing to explain their thought processes (often in the wake of tournament victories when I was writing the reports that will serve as the core for *Tournament Poker with the Champions)* include John Juanda, Chris "Jesus" Ferguson, Jennifer Harman, Diego Cordovez, Erik Seidel, Mike Matusow, "Miami" John Cernuto, and T. J. Cloutier.

Providing special help with this book were Michael Wiesenberg, who helped with the draw and lowball material (those games were popular "before my time"), as well as with the glossary; John Hoernemann, a nonplayer who nonetheless pushed and pulled me through my deadlines; George Hacker, whose late night availability (it's easy to call someone at 2:00 A.M. when it's 10:00 A.M. his time) helped focus me during my favorite writing hours; and my agent, Jessica Faust, who first told the Alpha Books people I was the right guy for the job and who reassured them I'd get them to the church on time when some unexpected surgical complications got me behind schedule.

Special thanks have to go to Michael Konik, who is not merely a close friend but who also set the modern standard for excellence in combining writing ability with gambling knowledge. It's also hard to imagine writing a poker book without thanking

Linda Johnson, who recognized so quickly at the 1999 World Series of Poker that I seemed able both to write about and play poker. Five minutes after reading my first tournament report, she gave me carte blanche to sell as many World Series of Poker reports to *Card Player Magazine* (then hers) as I wanted to write.

I grew up more or less idolizing Mike Caro as a poker writer. While his books and musings have earned me a lot of money, he did me a bigger favor by accepting me as an equal and contemporary after I'd been around big-time poker for what seemed to me a relatively short while. Just imagine yourself a young baseball player to whom Barry Bonds warmly says "Of course you belong on the all-star team with me, kid," and you'll get the idea of what Caro's acceptance meant to me. Caro might not have accepted me so readily had not Wendeen Eolis vouched for me, so for that and for much other advice, she, too, deserves acknowledgment.

Theresa Lina, Jessica Forbes, Howard Ring, and Donn Johnson also deserve special mention for the way they supported me when I got this crazy notion of combining all the things I love to do (writing, teaching, playing poker, and speaking) into a career.

I've left many important names out, in part because I have to leave room for actual poker instruction, and in part because I have three more books I'm now writing and I need to leave room to thank a few people there, too. I know I have left out a good many poker-playing friends, to say nothing of the nonpoker players. I'm sorry. Your time will come.

I hope my good health lasts a very long time because I believe in the old saying "what you do speaks so loudly that I cannot hear what you say." Until fairly recently, I haven't *done* nearly enough to thank so many of the people that, without whom, I not only would not have been successful, but I would also have had little reason to keep trying. Money is very useful and self-respect as important as oxygen, but without close friends and companions, life is empty.

My life's cup, thanks to all the friends mentioned above and to the many more not mentioned here, is not merely empty: It runneth over. If I can give a little back by teaching you something occasionally useful or giving you a chuckle, don't thank me. Thank the people who put me in a position to do so.

## Trademarks

All terms mentioned in this book that are known to be or are suspected of being trademarks or service marks have been appropriately capitalized. Alpha Books and Penguin Group (USA) Inc. cannot attest to the accuracy of this information. Use of a term in this book should not be regarded as affecting the validity of any trademark or service mark.

# Part 1

# An Introduction to Poker

Part 1 debunks common myths and misunderstandings, teaches you about your opponents, and begins not merely to teach you strategy, but to show you why the learning process never ends. Perhaps most important, it shows you why the information you'll learn in the rest of the book will be useful no matter what your motivation for playing might be.

Your first trip into public poker can leave the unprepared player feeling like a fish out of water so this part also walks you through the casino poker process step-by-step. After reading this section, you'll not only know etiquette and how to play the most important casino games, but you'll also know how to look like a pro when you're playing them.

**1**

# Understanding Poker's Nature

## In This Chapter

- ◆ The basic rules
- ◆ Why poker is both a card game and a people game
- ◆ Why poker is both a money game and a social game
- ◆ Poker is a game of incomplete information
- ◆ How to learn to play poker

Although poker has now arrived in the rest of the world, in many ways it is the quintessential American game. During the Cold War, it was often said that you could explain the difference between the American way of thinking and the Russian way of thinking by noting that "Russian generals play chess, and American generals play poker."

It's not just American generals who play poker. Quite a few American presidents have played the game, and more than 50 million Americans have played poker at least once. We find poker games throughout our literature, television, and movies, and an astonishing amount of poker terminology has become part of our daily lives. You'll learn that statement isn't a bluff as you follow through the text. Poker stays with us to the very end: When we die, we're said to have "cashed in our chips."

You will learn a lot about the history of poker and the nature of the people who play it throughout this book. I'm going to start with some very basic material, though.

Because so many people have played at least a *little* poker, I'm not going to stop and define every single poker concept immediately. For example, the first time the poker game "hold'em" is mentioned, I don't explain how it is played; that comes later. If you are a complete novice, and don't know some basic basics, remember that the glossary and Appendix F include definitions of a list of hand rankings, such as what constitutes a straight or a flush, and whether or not a straight beats a flush. Just flip to the back of the book if you need to start with more basic material.

# A Few Important Definitions

Even though you'll find most definitions in the glossary, a few are too important to ignore this early. These are:

- ◆ **Pot.** The money (or, more usually, chips) in the center of the table that players have bet and are trying to win.

- ◆ **Betting Round.** Most forms of poker involve at least two betting rounds, which are opportunities to bet. In the poker form probably most familiar to movie-goers, "five-card draw," there are two betting rounds: one after everyone has received his first five cards, and then a second one after players have discarded the cards they don't want to keep and have been dealt replacements. Most poker forms use more betting rounds, as you'll see when we discuss those games— hold'em has four rounds and seven-card stud has five rounds of betting.

- ◆ **Bet.** To start the action in a hand by being the first one to place money into the pot in a betting round. Although you are in a sense betting whenever your money goes into the pot, your action is called a bet only if you are the first person to place money in the pot during a round.

- ◆ **Call.** When someone else has already made a bet, and you decide to match the size of that bet, you have called.

- ◆ **Raise.** When someone else has already made a bet, and you decide to bet more, you have raised. If no one else calls or re-raises, the hand is over and you win immediately, regardless of your hand's strength.

- ◆ **Fold.** When someone else bets and you opt not to call or raise, but instead you save your money for a better opportunity, you end your participation in a hand by folding. You don't literally fold your cards (destruction of cards is frowned upon), but you turn your cards face down and gently push them to the dealer.

◆ **Check.** If no one else has bet yet, you need not bet to remain in the hand. You can say "check," (sometimes players rap the table with their knuckles to indicate a check) and this passes the betting opportunity along to the next player, clockwise. If no one bets on that betting round, the next card is dealt; if this happens on the final betting round, hands are exposed to determine the winner. If you check and someone else bets, you can then opt either to call, raise, or fold. Many beginning players forget about the checking option and automatically fold if they don't want to bet. Hold onto your cards until/unless someone else bets.

# Basic Poker Rules and Concepts

Poker is an umbrella term for a collection of many different games, such as five-card draw, hold'em, seven-card stud, and many more. You will learn much more about rules for specific games in later chapters. Right now, let's go over some of the basic rules and concepts that underlie most, if not all, forms of poker.

Two to ten players can play simultaneously at one table; the maximum practical number varies a bit from game to game, depending on the rules and how many cards each player gets.

A standard 52-card deck is employed, usually without a joker. There are 13 *ranks* in such a deck, which from lowest value to highest are 2, 3, 4, 5, 6, 7, 8, 9, 10, J (jack), Q (queen), K (king), and A (ace). Each rank comes in one of four *suits*: clubs, diamonds, hearts, and spades. Although it can be very helpful to be dealt a hand where all your suits match (this would be either a flush or a straight flush), it's usually no better to hold cards in one suit than another; that is, spades aren't inherently stronger than hearts, or vice versa (with some very minor exceptions that you'll learn in Chapter 8). If you and your opponent hold cards of equal rank, you have an equal claim to the pot and would therefore split it.

For example, if you and an opponent each hold a five-card hand of 4-7-9-10-Q, and your cards are all spades while his are all diamonds, your hands have equal value. Assuming that no one else holds a better hand, you would split the pot.

**The Inside Straight**

By keeping track of all exposed or folded cards—both their ranks and their suits—you'll be able to calculate everyone's chances of making a particular hand. Once you know that, you'll be able to make an informed decision about whether you want to invest more money in a pot.

In standard poker games, a complete poker hand always consists of five cards. If you own, or have access to, more than five cards, you select which five cards will act as your hand: even though in a game like seven-card stud you might own three pairs, there is no such hand as "three pair," because that hand would require six cards to create.

Similarly, if you happen to hold 4-5-6-7-8-9, you have a *straight*, but it is no stronger as a high hand than if it were 5-6-7-8-9. This is because only five cards count. (If your cards were all in the same suit, such as 5♥-6♥-7♥-8♥-9♥, you would have one of the most rare and powerful hands possible: a straight flush.) If you are unfamiliar with hand rankings like a flush or straight flush, please jump ahead to Appendix F and familiarize yourself with them.

### Perilous Play

You need to have five cards in your hand to collect a pot and you should insist that your opponents do, too. Even though someone who shows three kings can beat your two pair, he must show his other two cards. This rule was developed to help protect players from cheaters who might have concealed cards up their sleeves: A cheat who slipped an extra ace of spades into his hand won't want to show it if you hold the ace of spades in yours!

If you play a poker variation that employs *community cards*, it is possible and even quite common for several players to use the same community cards in their final hand. If the board in a hold'em game is A♠-A♥-A♦-8♠-9♠, every player who is still in the hand at the end has at least three aces! In such situations, the value of the other two cards determines the winner.

### Table Talk

**Community cards**, also known as "the board," are dealt face up in the middle of a table and are shared by all players in a game. Community cards are used mainly in hold'em and Omaha; in these games, players use a combination of their own private *hole cards* and some number of community cards to make their five-card hand.

In this scenario, someone whose hole cards are both spades has a flush because there are three spades on board; however, if anyone has either an eight or a nine in his hand, that player has a full house (as does anyone whose hole cards are a pair). If no one has one of these powerful hands, the winner is the player whose hole cards are highest in rank. This is one of the many reasons why, all else equal, you should prefer to play cards with high ranks over cards with low ranks.

# Poker Is a Card Game and a People Game

It is difficult to imagine a game in which context is more important than it is in poker—where the right decision against Jeff may be the wrong decision against Phil, or where the right decision against a player who has been winning for the last 20 minutes would be the wrong decision against someone who has been losing heavily during that time.

Although many decisions are clear-cut—for example, you would not want to fold the strongest possible hand in poker, a royal flush—just how you should bet with your royal flush to maximize the amount you will win isn't at all clear-cut.

Some players will be intimidated by an early bet and may drop out; if you're up against such a player, you're much better off checking and hoping that he catches some good cards and becomes the aggressor himself. The amount you will win with this hand can vary dramatically depending on how well you understand your opponents' tendencies and personalities.

**The Inside Straight**

Winning poker players know that while luck can intervene in the short run, luck evens out over the long haul; the players who make the most correct decisions will eventually take the money. The more information you have available to you, the better your decisions will be. Sometimes "information" is about cards; other times, it's about people.

When you first learn the rules, poker may not seem too different from blackjack, if you are familiar with that; however, the games are similar only in that they each use a standard 52-card deck and they are both popular ways to gamble. Indeed, if you do like your games and your world in black and white blackjack would probably be a better way for you to gamble than poker; there is always a correct choice in blackjack. Concepts like opposing player tendencies and skill levels don't matter. In blackjack, you face a *dealer* who must operate like a machine. He must hit until he has at least 17 and he can't take an extra card if he thinks he's losing. In poker, if the dealer is playing, he's free to play as well or as badly as he is able.

**Table Talk**

The **dealer** is the person who is responsible for fairly shuffling and distributing the cards to all players in the game. The dealer is also responsible for managing the game. This includes making sure that all bettors actually put their money into the pot and settling rule disputes (although in a casino, a serious dispute might require the presence of a supervisor called a floorman). In home games, the dealer usually plays; in casino games, he only deals.

Generally, the higher the stakes become, the more poker becomes a people game, and the less it resembles a card game. At low stakes—which is what you should almost certainly be playing for as a beginner—many poker decisions are fairly straightforward. If you have a strong hand, you bet or raise, and if you have a weak hand, you check or fold.

# Poker Is Both a Money Game and a Social Game

Although most of this book is designed to help you improve your monetary results in poker, it's important not to lose sight of the fact that many (if not most) of the people who play poker—even those who are playing for what appear to be fairly substantial stakes—are not playing solely for the money they can win. The more you learn about the other motivations people have for playing poker, the easier you will find it to beat them.

Among the nonfinancial reasons people play poker are:

- **Social bonding.** Time with your friends, or people you hope to become friendly with.

- **Adrenaline rush.** Some people get a thrill out of gambling, win or lose. Although the pure gamblers tend to play other games, because they lose too quickly at poker, you still find them here.

- **Ego.** Poker presents terrific opportunities to get an ego boost. When a player wins, he can claim (to himself and/or to others) that it was skill; when he loses, he can blame the cards, even if his play was actually the true reason he lost.

- **Analytical opportunity.** Some people enjoy solving riddles, puzzles, or mysteries. Poker has elements of each of these, and many people enjoy it just as an intellectual exercise.

---

### Poker Lore

You might think that a poker competition's thrill pales in comparison to the adrenaline levels produced by professional athletic competitions, but Monday morning quarterbacks aren't the only folks who find poker filling a role in their lives. I was playing in a $1,000 buy-in tournament in Los Angeles when a fellow player said, "You play this better than you play baseball, Lenny," to the hitherto unrecognized player on my left. It turned out I was seated next to Lenny "Nails" Dykstra, the former major league baseball star for the Mets and Phillies. "It's not as exciting as the baseball World Series," Dykstra later said of the poker event bearing the same name, "but it comes pretty close."

Poker also provides an opportunity for recreational competition that many people found in sports during their youth.

By providing not only an excuse to get out of the house, but also a format conducive to conversation and bonding, poker helps fill an important void in many people's lives. There are certainly other ways to fill this gap that don't require gambling, and I wouldn't for a moment suggest that poker is the highest and best use of an individual's free time. But if you enjoy the hours spent at a poker table, you don't need to win money for the evening to be a success.

If a player's conversation makes it clear that he looks at his night of card playing as a social activity, it's a pretty good bet that he is getting involved in more hands than a cash-focused player would: He's out to have fun, after all, and folding isn't fun.

### The Inside Straight

It's unrealistic to think you're going to play poker like a machine. You don't conduct other aspects of your life that way, so why should poker be different? You'll enjoy the game more if you improve and succeed, but don't think yourself inferior to professionals just because you enjoy what you're doing. If you can find a balance between poker's social and monetary aspects, you'll probably thrive in both areas.

There's nothing inherently wrong with playing poker primarily for social reasons, as long as you understand the price you're paying for doing so. It costs money to travel, shop, go to the theatre or sporting events, or collect trinkets. Most people's hobbies cost money, and few think there is anything wrong with that. The key for a social poker player is to understand how much his hobby is actually costing him and, as long as it's a reasonable price to pay for entertainment, that he isn't doing anything harmful.

Most players, of course, find that winning is more entertaining than losing, so even socially-oriented players try to improve their play. Remember, though, that even someone who is focused primarily on money can enjoy his time playing poker, and probably does. With very few exceptions, even successful poker players could make more money doing something else with the time they devote to poker. For all but the most successful of pros, it's not logical to play poker unless you enjoy it, too. If you *are* hugely successful, you're probably enjoying what you're doing.

# Poker Is a Game of Incomplete Information

Although games like chess and backgammon may be difficult to master, there's no mystery to them: All the information you need to succeed is sitting out in the open.

You don't have to try to estimate where your opponent's queen is in a chess game, and you don't have to be worried about a hidden piece attacking you in a backgammon game. The difficulty in mastering these games and others like them comes in learning how best to use your out-in-the-open armies to overwhelm your opponent.

Poker is quite different. Poker would be dull and pointless if everyone knew what cards everyone else had. You could gamble on it, but there would be no more point to the gamble than there is in betting on who can cut a higher card out of a deck, or in who can win a child's card game like War.

However, we don't know what cards our opponents hold in poker and it is the attempt to succeed in the face of this incomplete information that makes the game difficult. What cards does our opponent have in the hole? Is he bluffing, or does he really have the goods? Does he have a very good hand already, or is he on a draw?

Because the answers to these questions dictate how you should bet or fold your own hand, anything you can do to gain additional information is likely to help your chances of making a correct decision, and anything you can do to deny information to your opponents is likely to make it harder for them to make correct decisions. Because luck evens out over the long haul, if you make more good decisions than your opponents, you'll probably be a winning player.

## The Least You Need to Know

- ◆ Poker is both a card game and a people game
- ◆ Poker is both a money game and a social game.
- ◆ Poker is a game of incomplete information.
- ◆ Poker is best learned through a combination of reading and practice.

# Chapter 2

# Texas Hold'em: The Biggest Game in the World

## In This Chapter

◆ Learning the rules

◆ Learning the starting hand values

◆ Understanding the odds

◆ Selecting strategies

Forget what you've seen in the movies, unless you've seen *Rounders*.

Forget what you've seen on television, unless you've watched *The World Poker Tour (WPT)*, *The World Series of Poker (WSOP)*, or the occasional other televised tournament.

Draw poker and five-card stud are nice vehicles for movies and TV because it's so easy for the viewer to follow what the players have. In modern casino poker, though, the action is mainly confined to three games. You'll learn about the second- and third-biggest games, seven-card stud and Omaha, in the next two chapters. Here, you'll learn about the biggest, most widely dealt, and most important game in the modern poker world: Texas Hold'em.

# The Rules

Hold'em is a simple game to learn: You can begin playing five minutes after someone has explained the game to you. Mastering it takes a lifetime, though. Fortunately, because the game is so simple to learn, you will often find yourself opposing players who think an understanding of the rules is enough to compete. It isn't, but it is where we'll begin.

---

### Poker Lore

Because movies are designed to entertain rather than to educate, most movie poker scenes are hysterically funny to poker veterans. Usually several rules are violated, everyone has a powerhouse hand, and one or more supposed experts plays horribly.

That wasn't the case in the 1998 film *Rounders*. This Matt Damon/Edward Norton flick did a surprisingly good job of representing modern poker, with the only purist complaint being too much emphasis on card cheating.

---

The game can be played by two to ten players, with nine being the most commonly-dealt full game. Assume, for purposes of discussion, the following situation:

- A professional dealer is distributing the cards but not playing. (It is possible to play the game at home with the players taking turns dealing the cards.)

- There are nine players in the game

- The stakes are $10-20 (where all bets and raises are in $10 increments for the first two betting rounds and in $20 increments for the final two betting rounds).

### Table Talk

The **button** is a small plastic puck, which is commonly white with the word "dealer" written on it. The dealer button's purpose is to determine who acts first on each hand. After each hand is completed, the dealer moves the button one position to the left. The player who owns the button is also called "the button."

The game begins by the dealer giving each player one card. The person who receives the highest card receives the *button*.

When the button's position has been established, the dealer collects the single cards, shuffles again, and now deals two cards (called the hole cards) to each player.

Before play begins, the first two players to the left of the button must post the *blinds*. Blinds serve a purpose similar to *antes* in stud games: They put something into the pot for the other players to shoot at.

Without some starting money in the pot, there would be little or no incentive to enter a hand without the best possible starting cards. Why risk being the first player in when your bet can't win anything? It only sits out there as a target.

Using blinds eliminates this problem. The first player to the button's left posts the *small blind* and the second player posts the large, or *big blind*.

With the blinds in place, the player sitting three seats to the button's left is first to act. He is already facing a bet: The person sitting in the big blind has "bet" $10. The third player can now call the $10, decide that his hand is too weak and fold, or decide that he likes his hand and wants to *raise* another $10.

> **Table Talk** _____
>
> The size of the **small blind** and the **big blind** is determined by a game's betting structure. In a $10-20 game, the small blind is $5 and the big blind is $10. That's a typical ratio, although some betting limits require slightly different ratios to avoid using small chips. In a $15-30 game, for example, the small blind is $10, rather than $7.50; the big blind is the expected $15.

Each player, in clockwise rotational order, faces the same decision. If the third player has folded or called, the next player faces a $10 bet. If the third player has raised, it is now "$20 to go," and later players must decide if they want to call $20, fold, or raise to $30. Once the action increases to a higher dollar figure because of a raise, it stays that high; by raising to $20, the third player has eliminated the fourth player's opportunity to participate at the $10 level.

Let's assume that the third player has raised to $20 and that the fifth and ninth players call (the ninth player, the button, gets to act last in all betting rounds *after* the first one). In the first round only, the action (opportunity to bet) comes back past the button to the blinds, who now must decide what they want to do with their hands.

The small blind already has $5 invested in the pot. If he wants to call, he has to put an additional $15 in. The big blind already has $10 invested in the pot. If he wants to call, he has to put an additional $10 in. Each of these players also has an option to raise.

(*If* no one had raised, that is, if we'd changed the example so that there had only been callers to this point, the small blind would have had to put another $5 in to call or $15 to raise. Assuming no raise, the big blind could have checked or raised. Normally, a player cannot raise his own bet, and theoretically, the big blind is the person who made the first $10 bet. However, because the big blind had no option about betting that first $10, he is given the option to raise if no one else does.)

Let us suppose that the small blind decides to fold and the big blind decides to call. The pot has $85 in it: $20 from players three, five, nine, and two (the big blind), and $5 from player one (the small blind, who is no longer in the hand).

With betting on the first round complete, the dealer now burns a card (disposes of it face down, so that if it had been marked, no one could have benefited from seeing it) and then deals the next three cards simultaneously face up in the center of the table. These three community cards are called *the flop* and like all *board* cards, they belong to all players equally.

Because player two is the first player to the button's left still in the hand, he acts first after the flop. He can check or bet and if he checks, the next player's options are the same. Let's assume that players two and three check, but player five bets. His bet must be $10. Let's assume that player nine calls, but that players two and three fold. The pot is now $105 and we have two players left.

With the second round betting complete, the dealer now burns another card and then deals a fourth community card face up. This card is commonly called *the turn* or *fourth street*. Player five has the option to check or bet $20 (hence the game's $10-20 nomenclature: $10 bets for the first two rounds, $20 bets for the final two rounds).

Let's assume that player five checks, but player nine bets $20. Now player five (a tricky one) raises to $40. Player five is said to have *check-raised* player nine.

**Table Talk**

The **check-raise** is a perfectly legitimate (albeit tricky) play, although some very old poker books or very old poker players consider the check-raise unsporting. The idea is that you feign weakness by checking and trap your opponent into betting your hand for you, whereupon you fire back with a raise. The "unsporting" notion is about 40 years out of date and you will only find it in old, longstanding home games, or perhaps in a British Gentlemen's Club.

Let's assume that player nine calls the check-raise. Another $80 has gone into the pot, which now totals $185. The dealer burns one more card and deals a fifth and final community card face up. This card is commonly called *the river* or *fifth street*.

At this point, the players have received all the cards they are going to receive. As they ponder their final bets, they see what their best five-card hand is. They are allowed to use any combination of the two cards in their hand and the five on the board. This means they can choose to use zero, one, or two of their hole cards.

Why would a player choose not to use his hole cards? Suppose, for example, that a player started off with a very fine hand, K♥-K♦. Two kings, no matter what color, comprise the second-best starting hand in hold'em and are usually bet quite aggressively.

If the final community board is J♠-10♠-5♠-3♠-2♠, though, there is a spade flush on the board and neither of the two red kings is going to improve on that. If instead of two red kings, the player had owned the K♠-K♦, he would play one of his kings so that he would have a king-high flush instead of the jack-high flush that was owned by everyone in the game. If the final board was indeed a spade flush, and neither player had a spade, both players would be playing the community board as their hands, and the pot would be split.

Let's suppose that player five, who has already shown strength by check-raising, real-izes his chances of trapping player nine for a second check-raise aren't good. He goes ahead and bets out. If player nine doesn't call, player five never has to show his hand; he simply collects the pot. If player nine calls, each player turns his hand face up, and the best hand wins the pot.

### The Inside Straight

If your bet on the river goes uncalled, you should usually keep your hand a mystery. Why? You risk losing valuable "curiosity calls" if you routinely show uncalled hands. Most players *hate* the idea of being bluffed out of a pot and even if they think they're beaten, may call a bet on the end, just so they know for sure. If you get a reputation for showing your cards when you don't have to, players won't throw this practically hopeless money into your pots!

Why might player nine consider folding, and yielding his chance to collect $205 if his hand was best, after staying involved in the hand for so long? Suppose, for exam-ple, player nine had held 7-8 and had been encouraged by a flop of 5-6-K (giving him an open-ended straight draw), but failed to connect on his draw when the final two board cards were Q-J. In that situation, player nine would be silly to call another $20 with only eight-high as his hand—especially with three cards on board (the jack, queen, and king) that are frequently held in good starting hands.

# Starting Hand Values

It takes years to master hold'em and a full discussion of strategy could fill many books (and has done so; see *Appendix A* for a list of some of the better ones).

I can start you on your way, though, and one useful—but at the same time dangerous—tool is the following chart that groups starting hands into different value levels.

To use the rankings, consider that the hands within each group are noticeably better than the hands in the group immediately below it, and in turn significantly better than the hands two or more groups below. Within each group, the hands are roughly equal in value, although the hands are listed from strongest to weakest.

Do not start memorizing this chart until you have read what I have to say about it afterward!

### Texas Hold'em Starting Hand Chart

> **Group One**: A-A
>
> **Group Two**: K-K
>
> **Group Three**: Q-Q, A-K(s), A-K
>
> **Group Four**: J-J, A-Q(s), 10-10
>
> **Group Five**: A-Q, 9-9, 8-8, A-J(s), K-Q(s)
>
> **Group Six**: A-J, A-10(s), 7-7, K-J(s)
>
> **Group Seven**: A-10, K-J, A-9(s), K-10(s), Q-J(s), 6-6, Q-10(s), J-10(s), 5-5
>
> **Group Eight**: A-X(s), J-10, J-9(s), 10-9(s), 4-4, 3-3, 2-2, K-X(s)

(s) means the hand is suited, for example, A-K(s) means ace-king suited. The suit doesn't matter as long as both cards are the same suit.

X = any card nine or lower

All other starting hands should be considered speculative and not worth playing early in your poker career. This does not mean that the other hands are worthless; there will indeed be times when it is worth playing medium suited connectors such as 8-7(suited) or 7-6(suited), or just unsuited connectors. Given the right situation, even gapped medium connectors such as 9-7(suited) or 10-8 can be playable, but realistically, only an advanced player should be "fooling around" with hands like these.

This chart appears to be a valuable tool. Why, then, do I label this chart as "dangerous"? There are several reasons. First, although the values are approximately equal, each of the hands has unique properties and hands in the same group can play quite differently.

For example, 7-7 and A-10(s) are both Group Six hands, but most of the value from the two sevens comes in those rare (one time in eight) situations when a third seven hits the flop. Getting three of a kind this way is called *flopping a set*. Two sevens, unimproved, aren't going to win many pots and you flop a set only 12 percent of the time.

In contrast, when you hold A-10, you will flop an ace or a ten three times as often as you will flop a seven holding 7-7; this means you will make a playable hand more frequently, but it won't be as powerful. You also have more and better straight and flush possibilities holding A-10(s). This is what I mean when I say the two hands "play differently." They will win about the same amount of money, over the long run, but they will win it very differently. It's also much easier for a beginner to play the 7-7; if you flop a set, you play on, and if you don't, you can probably fold. With A-10, you can easily flop something hard to play and hard to know if it is winning. For example, what do you do with A-10 if the flop comes Q-10-4? You have a fairly good hand, middle pair, but figuring out whether you should play is difficult.

As a result, even though these two hands are "worth" about the same thing in terms of how much money you should make over the long run if you play them correctly, knowing this relative value doesn't teach you anything about how to play these hands. If you rush into a hold'em game convinced you know how to play simply because you understand the starting hand values, you know just enough to get yourself into trouble.

**Table Talk**

You **flop a set** when you start with a pair for your hole cards and a card that matches them is among the first three community cards. For example, you have flopped a set if you hold 7-7 and the board comes up as A-K-7.

**Perilous Play**

Distinguish flopping a set from flopping *trips*, which would happen if your hole cards were 10-J and the board came J-J-5. When you flop a set, you're the only person who can own that three of a kind. When you flop trips, someone else can be in with a hand like K-J, giving both of you trips but giving him a better *kicker*—and that figures to be very costly. A flopped set is also much better disguised than flopped trips.

**Table Talk**

A **kicker** is the extra card that accompanies your hand's primary value. If you hold A-10 and the flop comes A-J-4, you have a pair of aces with a ten kicker. A pair of aces is certainly a good hand, but because good players tend not to play ace-starting hands unless their kickers are at least ten or higher, there is a good chance that if you meet substantial resistance, you're up against A-J, A-Q, or A-K. Your "kicker trouble" will cost you money.

Another reason you should take the starting hand rank chart's advice with a grain of salt is that far too many players use the chart as a crutch. They rigidly adhere to the values presented in the chart and play by rote instead of with thought and in context. If they start with a high value hand such as A-A or K-K, they are often unwilling to release that hand after a dangerous flop comes.

What kind of flop could endanger A-A? Any flop with a pair of high cards, such as K-K-6 or Q-Q-7, because people tend to play starting hands that contain high cards. Similarly, a flop like 9♠-10♠-J♠ spells big trouble for A♥-A♦; there are so many straight possibilities, flush possibilities, and two-pair possibilities that your aces are probably worthless if either you face many opponents or get re-raised once or twice by a lone opponent. Someone is bound to hold a hand that fits together with this well-coordinated board.

When you are a complete hold'em rookie, you have to absorb a large amount of information before you play well. You're trying to learn about how your own starting hands fit together with different flops, how long to stay with a hand, what kinds of hands are likely to be in there against you, and much more. Free online games are a good place to get a feel for this.

It's difficult, to borrow a concept from mathematics, to solve an equation that contains so many simultaneous variables. It's for that reason that I present you with a starting hand chart. As long as you use it as a guide for getting started, and not as a master plan to control your every move, it will have served its cause.

Unlike a blackjack basic strategy chart, which should stay as your guide throughout your blackjack career (at least until or unless you become a card counter), the hold'em starting hand chart should be used only as an early training tool. The sooner you abandon it in favor of learning how to treat each hand separately, the better off you'll be.

# Evening Out the Odds

I've seen a lot of math professor-types try to make it in the poker world and more often than not, they fail pretty miserably at higher stakes because high stakes poker is much more of a people game than a card game. Math whizzes can perform fairly well at low stakes, because the games are relatively straightforward A-B-C affairs: Subtle trickery has no role. If you play good cards and know just a little math—relax, it's actually a *very* little math—you'll do fine.

Probably the single most important math or odds concept you need to learn in all forms of poker is the concept of *pot odds*.

Sometimes calculating pot odds is a very precise, straightforward matter; other times, you can be sure about some numbers in the equation but not about others and you simply have to make your best guess.

An example of the straightforward calculation occurs when there's one card to come and you only have to decide about calling one bet. For example, suppose there's $200 in the pot and you need to call $20 to see the last card. That's

10-1 pot odds. You are drawing to make a straight and know because there are 8 cards that will make it and 38 that won't (because of something you'll learn quite soon) that you have a 17 percent chance of making your straight. You also are positive that if you make your straight, you'll win the hand. A 17 percent chance is roughly 6-1, so this is an easy call.

If you're not comfortable converting percents to odds, you could do this math another way. What's 17 percent of $200? $34 (round it to 15 percent if you're looking for broad, ballpark numbers). That's the break-even figure on your call in this pot. If it were going to cost you $34 to call, you'd be indifferent about calling (although another subject called *implied odds* would induce you to call). At only $20, this pot is a bargain draw.

The next most important odds topic involves your ability to calculate how easy or difficult it will be for you to hit a draw of any kind on the flop. To do this, you first must figure out how many cards are in the deck that will win for you. A card that will win the pot for you is called an *out*.

**Table Talk**

**Outs** are cards that will win the hand for you. If you are drawing to a flush (with two hearts on board and two in your hand), there are nine hearts left in the deck and you have nine outs. It's important to be sure whether a card is truly an out. If you have two low hearts in your hand, you could be up against someone with two higher hearts. In that situation, hitting your flush would be very costly.

Fortunately, the math on calculating most of the common draws is easy to memorize. If you have a flush draw (either because there are two hearts on board and two in your hand, or three hearts on board and one in your hand—the odds are the same), you have exactly a 33 percent chance to make your draw, with two cards to come. If you have an open-ended straight draw, you have a 30 percent chance to make your hand with two cards to come.

What happens if there's only one card to come or if for some reason you can make adjustments because of exposed cards? Fortunately, there's a very simple formula for calculating winning chances. Just give yourself 2 percent winning chances for every out you have and multiply that times the number of cards to come. This formula is quite accurate when you only have a few outs; the more outs you have, the more you need to make a slight downward adjustment.

Let's take a look at this formula in action. Because there are 13 cards of any given suit in a deck, when you have a flush draw, there are nine cards remaining that can win for you. Nine times 2 percent is 18 percent. Because you're calculating your odds on the flop, you have two cards to come, so your 18 percent turns into 36 percent. You already know that a flush draw is 33 percent, so if you had used the 2 percent formula, you'd have been close—very close indeed if you had also made the slight downward adjustment required for a large number of outs (and nine outs twice—once on the turn and once on the river—is a large number).

Similarly, when trying to hit an open-ended straight draw, there are eight outs (four cards of each rank). Eight outs times 2 percent is 16 percent, and with two cards to come, 32 percent. You already know a straight draw is actually 30 percent. You can see that just by dropping from nine outs to eight, the formula is getting more accurate.

This formula will let you figure things like the advisability of trying the classic bad poker play—drawing to an inside straight. See if you can do it.

**Perilous Play** _____

Even complete duffers have heard that it's a bad idea to draw to an inside straight, but, if you get the right price—the right pot odds—it's fine. The reason people are told not to draw to inside straights is because you usually don't get the right price. With four outs winning for you and one card to come, you have an 8 percent chance via the 2 percent formula (the actual number is 8.7 percent).

# Strategies

Let's face it, most people are not playing low-stakes poker solely for the money. They may have aspirations about moving up to higher stakes games, or about making good money from their low-stakes games, but no matter what they say, they're also in the game because they enjoy the adrenaline rush, the excitement, and the camaraderie.

Folding hand after hand is no way to get an adrenaline rush, and therein lies your edge—if you're willing to play correctly.

### Poker Lore

This story has been told so many times that some consider it apocryphal, but even if it is, it's worth remembering. A player's mother accompanied him to a casino for a small hold'em tournament. She wanted to play, but had never played poker before. She had played blackjack, though, so the player told her, "Only play if you have blackjack (A-K, A-Q, A-J, or A-10), or a pair of tens or higher. Fold everything else, but raise whenever you get these hands." Mom allegedly won the tournament! Whether the tale is true or not, it demonstrates the value of playing only quality starting hands and of playing aggressively with them.

In the starting hand chart section, you see each starting hand that you should be willing to play. If a hand isn't on that chart, you shouldn't be playing it at this stage of your hold'em career.

The listed hands aren't all playable at all times; if they were, there wouldn't be many reasons to break then down into eight subgroups. The hands in groups one, two, and three are always playable in limit games from any position. All of the other hands are at least a little position-sensitive and sometimes very position-sensitive.

> **The Inside Straight** _____
>
> In real estate, the secret is location, location, location. In hold'em, the secret isn't too different: position, position, position. The first player to act after the blinds is said to be "under the gun," and his position is extremely unfavorable compared to the button. The button knows how many people have played and raised. The first player knows none of this. Except for the blinds on the first round, the button will get to act last on every betting round. As a result, the button can play weaker starting hands than an early position player.

The blinds can face difficult first betting round decisions. Because they have been forced to post bets before they ever see their cards, it sometimes makes economic sense to call raises in the blind (called "defending" your blind) with weak hands, because they are getting a good price on their participation—the big blind might, for example, only have to put $10 in to see the flop in a $125 pot.

If a blind hand connects with the flop strongly, the blind player can continue. If the hand misses the flop or only connects a little bit, the blind should get out because he is in the least favorable position of anyone at the table. He will be first to act for the final three betting rounds and that means three more times that he's going to have to act with less information than his opponents.

Generally, in a nine-player game, the nine spots are broken down into early position, middle position, and late position. As you might guess, the first three spots (the two blinds plus the under-the-gun player) are early position, the next three are middle position, and the last three, culminating with the button, are late position.

Of course, these labels are merely rough approximations. When you're the seventh of nine to act, you might technically be in late position, but your position is still significantly inferior to the player holding the button. This is why many players break the positions down still further, calling the fourth spot "early middle position" and the sixth spot "late middle position," and the like.

◆ **From the small blind, for half a bet.** You can play any hand from any of the eight groups and you can consider playing any connected cards (even 2-3). You can play one-gap connectors such as 10-8, 9-7, 8-6 or 7-5 (even better if they are suited). You get to look at a lot of hands from this position because it cost you so little to get into the pot. However, be prepared to get out immediately unless the flop hits you very well because you are going to be out of position for the next three betting rounds.

If someone raises and it will cost you 1.5 bets, you probably should play only category seven and above and it is better to play only category six and above. The more players who enter the pot, the easier it is to play hands in this position.

♦ **From the big blind.** Obviously you can play *any* hand if players *limp* in and you get to see the flop for free; even if you have 7-2 offsuit, the worst hand in hold'em, there's no law that prevents the flop from coming 7-7-2, so if you get a free ride, take it.

If you are faced with a raise in the big blind, you can defend with any of the eight categories of hands; if you have a Category One, Two, or Three, re-raise, and after you gain a little experience, you can re-raise with Category Four as well.

♦ **Under-the-gun.** Stick with Group Five and above, limping with Group Five and raising with Group Four or above.

♦ **Middle position.** Limp in with Group Six or Seven, depending on whether you're in early or late middle position. Bring the hand in for a raise with Group Five or above. If someone else has already raised, call with Group Six and Group Five, and re-raise with Group Four.

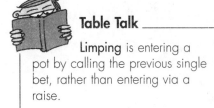

**Table Talk**

**Limping** is entering a pot by calling the previous single bet, rather than entering via a raise.

♦ **Late position.** If you are the first player to enter the pot, raise with Group Eight, and if you are on the button, you can consider raising with lesser hands, in an attempt to steal the blinds. If one or more players are already in, limp with Group Seven or Group Eight and raise with Group Six or better. If someone has already raised, call with Group Six and re-raise with Group Five.

Finally, although we have been examining hold'em mostly from the rather narrow viewpoint of starting hands and starting positions, you should remember that when you play your starting hand, you get to see three cards at once and often for the price of only one small bet. Contrast that with what happens on the turn, when it costs you a double-sized bet (also called a big bet) just to see one more card.

For that reason, the flop is said to truly "define your hand" in hold'em. If the flop connects with your hand well (also called hitting the flop well), you're probably in for the duration, unless some truly scary cards come off on the turn and/or the river.

Beginning hold'em players are well-advised to follow the "fit or fold" method of playing. That is, unless you start with a big pair and that pair either connects on the flop for a set or is higher than any cards on the flop (called, in that case, "an over-pair to the board"), you should throw your hand away unless the flop improves it. That means that you should strongly consider folding K-K if the flop comes A-X-X because, especially at the lower limits, players tend to play Ace-anything and once that ace hits the board, your two kings are usually no good any more.

Even the mighty A-K, such a wonderful hand when it hits because no matter which card hits, you always have top pair, top kicker, is practically useless if the flop comes something like J-8-6. Somebody out there is probably playing middle cards or middle pairs and even though your A-K is a very promising starting hand, if it misses the flop, you have only ace-high and only two cards yet to come in a situation when it's extremely likely that one or more opponents have some kind of pair.

## The Least You Need to Know

- Learn the starting hand chart, but don't adhere slavishly to it.

- Keep your position in mind at all times and don't play many hands in early position.

- Aggression is rewarded in poker. Most of the time, if your hand is worth a call, it's worth a raise.

- Fit or fold.

# Seven-Card Stud: An Oldie, But Still a Goodie

## In This Chapter

- ◆ Learning the rules
- ◆ Understanding starting hand values
- ◆ Calculating the odds
- ◆ Developing strategies
- ◆ A special look at Stud Eight-or-better

After hold'em, seven-card stud is probably the most important form of poker to understand. If you're a home game player, it's probably the most important, not just because it gets dealt in so many home games, but because so many other forms of poker are based on seven-card stud.

## Fundamental Rules for a Fundamental Game

Seven-card stud is a fairly straightforward game, but because ultimately three of your seven cards are dealt face down as hole cards, it's quite possible for someone who looks like he has a trash hand to own a powerhouse. Even four of a kind can be completely hidden.

The game can be played by two to eight players, even though if all eight stayed in to the river, the dealer would run out of cards (he'd need 56 cards, and the game is played with the standard 52-card deck). Normally, even in fairly loose games, a couple of players drop out early enough to allow everyone to complete his hand.

The game begins with everyone anteing a predetermined amount. The dealer gives everyone two cards face down and one card face up. This up card is often called the player's *doorcard*. A round of betting follows the deal with the player who shows the lowest card being forced to make what is called a *bring-in* bet.

> **Table Talk**
>
> A player's **doorcard** is his first upcard. Because players like to start out hands with pairs, there is a good chance that a player who enters a hand for a full bet has a paired doorcard: A doorcard pair is twice as likely as a buried (hidden in the hole) pair. Be *very* careful if a player later *pairs his doorcard*. There's a good chance he has trips.

Because seven-card stud is played for high, normally you would prefer not to face a forced bet when showing the worst card. The forced bring-in bet creates two different sums for the first raiser to attack: the antes and the bring-in. In some ways, this makes getting stuck with the bring-in worse than having the blinds in hold'em. At least in hold'em, your blind hand might be A-A. In seven stud, the forced bettor is starting with a card that is almost always bad. To compensate, the bring-in is smaller than a hold'em blind.

The bring-in is usually a fraction, perhaps one-fifth to one-half of a full bet. For example, in a $4-8 stud game, the lone bring-in would be either $1 or $2. In a $4-8 hold'em game, there would be two blinds, one $2 and one $4. Another difference: In hold'em, you post the blinds once each round. In stud, if you're unlucky enough to get dealt the low card nine times in a row, you have to make the forced bring-in nine times in a row. It does tend to even out over time, of course, but can still be annoying when it happens and extremely unlucky if it happens in the late stages of a tournament.

> **The Inside Straight**
>
> The size of the ante compared to the bet sizes is not standard in stud: You might find one $4-8 game where the ante is $0.25, another where it's $0.50, and another where it is $1. The ante size, relative to the bet size, plays a major role in starting hand strategy. If the antes are large, you must play more starting hands than if the antes are small. Any other approach would result in too much money lost to antes.

Let's assume you are playing $4-8 stud with a $1 bring-in. The lowest card visible is the 3♣. Its owner must bet at least $1, but he may, if he wishes, bring the hand in for the full $4 bet. It's far more common to bring the hand in for the minimum; indeed, many players make that minimum bet without even looking at their hole cards.

Let's say that Al owns the 3♣ and does indeed bet $1. The player to Al's left is next to act and the action proceeds in clockwise order. Bob is on Al's left. Bob can either call the $1, raise the bet to $4 (in stud, this raise of the bring-in is called *completing* the bet; all other bets and raises are called just that), or fold.

As soon as Bob, or anyone else, completes the bet to $4, there can be no more $1 bets. From that point on, all bets and raises are in $4 increments (except for Al, whose initial $1 is "live" and so can later choose to call for the remaining $3, or raise by betting $7).

After the first round betting is complete, the dealer gives each player a second upcard, called *fourth street*. On third street, the low card had to make a bring-in bet; on fourth street and thereafter the *high* hand has the option to bet or check and the action proceeds clockwise from there. Usually play is limited to a bet and three raises or a bet and four raises.

Fourth street betting is at the lower ($4) level, unless someone has made an open pair. If this happens, the bettor has the option to immediately move to the higher ($8) limit. If he bets $4, later players may call $4, raise to $8, or utilize the double bet option and raise his $4 to $12. As soon as anyone has utilized the double bet option, all bets and raises from that point forward are at the double bet size. For example, if the first bettor bets the full $8, it's not legal to raise to $12. A raiser must make it $16.

After fourth street betting is complete, the dealer gives everyone a third upcard, called *fifth street*. All bets and raises on this street are at the double bet level. There are no more $4 bets; all bets and raises are in $8 increments. The betting again commences with whomsoever owns the highest hand.

 **The Inside Straight** _____

Unlike button games such as hold'em, in stud games position can and often does change in the middle of a hand. The highest hand has the option to start the betting action on fourth, fifth, sixth, and seventh street, but because the turn of a card can change who has the highest visible hand, starting position can shift, making it riskier to play just because you have favorable betting position.

Play on sixth street is identical to play on fifth street. Play on seventh street (more commonly called the river) is identical to that on fifth and sixth street, except that the final card is dealt face down.

If too many players have stayed in and it becomes clear that the dealer is not going to have enough cards to give everyone a face down seventh street card, the dealer should give no one a face down hole card. Instead, he deals one card face up and everyone uses that card as a community card. (In some games, if someone has dropped out, the dealer instead shuffles the discards in with the undealt cards and give everyone a hole card. Stay alert: Some of the discards have been seen, giving alert players a better-than-average guess as to what they and their competitors might draw.

# Starting Hand Values

When discussing seven-card stud hands, I will use a common notation system, where-in known hole cards are shown in parentheses and unknown hole cards are shown as (?-?). For example the hand (K♠-K♦) 4♠-5♠-6♠-K♥ (2♠) started off nicely with a hidden pair of kings in the hole, and a two-flush (the 4♠ and the K♠). On sixth street, the hand became even stronger, trip kings with a flush draw and the flush draw hit when the hidden river card provided a fifth spade.

Unlike hold'em where the starting hands are relatively few in number and hence can be evaluated for strength for each position, seven-card stud starting hand values are much more approximate.

There are several reasons for this with the most important being your ability to look around the table and see how *live* your cards are. A starting hand that is worth playing or even raising if live can be a correct fold if the cards in it are *dead* (unavailable).

**Table Talk**

A **live** hand is one whose chances of improvement have not been hurt by needed cards appearing in other players' hands. For example, (J♠-J♦) 6♠ is a pretty reasonable starting hand, but if both the J♥ and the J♣ are visible in other players' hands, jacks are **dead** (unavailable) and this hand's value drops considerably. You probably should not play and you almost certainly shouldn't play if you see one or more hands behind you whose doorcards are a queen or higher.

Another reason why starting hands aren't easily ranked is how context-sensitive your hand is. (Q♠-Q♥) 10♣ is certainly a powerful hand, yet if someone showing (?-?) Ks raises, you face a very difficult decision. Playing with two queens against two kings, you are in deep, deep trouble. Yes, you can improve to queens-up or trip queens, but your opponent can improve to kings-up or trip kings.

Just because someone raises with an ace showing doesn't mean he has two aces. He might be trying to steal the antes, or he might have something like (9♠-9♣) A♠ and be hoping to improve to aces-up or trip nines. He might also have a strong drawing hand like (K♠-10♠) A♠. The problem is that you're unlikely to know just how strong this player's hand is for quite some time. You need to make hands to win in seven-card stud, but the hands you can represent also play a big part in your game.

Given the important proviso that virtually all starting hands are context sensitive (that is, their value depends on how live they are), the best starting hands are:

- ◆ **Rolled-up trips**, e.g., (J♠-J♣) J♥. This hand is so strong that it doesn't matter much if you see the fourth jack elsewhere; in fact, there's an argument you'd *like* to see it elsewhere because opponents will be less likely to believe you have a pair of jacks, or if you do, that you have little chance of improving. Larger trips such as (A-A) A are of course preferable to smaller ones, but there is an argument that you'd really like (10-10) 10 or even (5-5) 5, because you cannot make a straight without a ten or a five in your hand. By owning three of the key cards, your hand protects itself against one of its most likely rivals.

- ◆ **Large buried pairs**, e.g., (A-A) 5 or (Q-Q) 10. By having your pair buried, your opponents don't know when you've made trips. Your hand is a bit stronger if your third card coordinates somewhat with your pair, either by potentially making a straight or a flush.

- ◆ **Large split pairs**, e.g., (K-10) K or (J-9) J. You lose the element of disguise in case you pair your doorcard, but these are still premium hands.

- ◆ **Three large straight flush cards**, e.g., (K♠-Q♠) J♠. These hands are very strong drawing hands because they can make either a straight or a flush (don't count on making many straight flushes), and if you don't make those hands, you're off to a good start for one or two high pair. If you don't *catch good* on fourth street, you can usually take one more card, but if you don't improve on fifth street, get out.

**Table Talk**

It's obvious that to **catch good** means you received a good card. I mention it because for some unknown reason, virtually everyone in poker says or writes "catch good" rather than the correct "catch well." The same goes for "playing good" instead of "playing well."

◆ **Three large flush cards**, e.g., (A♠-9♠) J♠. These hands are strong drawing hands because they can make a flush, give you a small chance for a straight, and if you don't make those hands, you're off to a good start for one or two high pair. If you don't catch good on fourth street, you should usually get out.

◆ **Three large straight cards**, e.g., (K♥-Q♦) J♠. These hands are strong drawing hands because they can make a straight and if you don't make those hands, you're off to a good start for one or two high pair. If you don't catch good on fourth street, you should usually get out.

◆ **Three medium or small straight flush cards**, e.g., (4♠-5♠) 6♠. These hands are strong drawing hands because they can make either a straight or a flush. However, small pairs often lead to troubling second-place finishes in stud and if you don't quickly improve to a four-card draw to a straight or flush, you should probably get out. If you pair up on fourth street you can take another card, but you'll need to catch good on fifth street to continue. Two small pair are often a recipe for trouble.

---

### Poker Lore

When your opponent pairs his doorcard, you really must respect the possibility that he has trips, even if the game is shorthanded. At the 2004 Australasian Poker Championships $1,600 Seven-Card Stud Championship, I was heads-up with John Wylie for the title. I started with (J♥-Q♠) J♦ and on sixth street, caught another jack. Wylie showed (?-?) 10-6-7-4, and when I led out, Wylie raised. I re-raised and looked across the table in shock when Wylie made it four bets.

I visibly slumped (nice poker face, Andrew). I was almost sure he had a straight; I didn't see any other way he could have made it four bets when each bet was $12,000 and there was only $180,500 total in play. I called, hoping to fill up, but when I didn't improve, I checked and even more reluctantly called when Wylie bet the river. Paradoxically, aside from following a general principle of calling on the river once you've called on sixth street, I called mainly because I considered folding! If there was a chance I could fold, there was a chance he could be bluffing.

Wylie turned over trip sixes and I literally leapt from my seat at the unexpected triumph. I finished off Wylie's last $17,000 with a straight on the next hand to take the title. Had Wylie respected the paired doorcard, he could have saved at least $24,000, possibly more—certainly enough to have kept the contest going.

It's really a very nice trophy.

---

Most other hands should be considered speculative, even something that looks promising such as (6♥-5♦) 7♠ or (6-6) Q. Small three straights or flushes often win if you make the straight or flush, but if the more likely result happens—if you make a small pair or two—you'll probably just lose a lot of money. Small buried pairs can lead to similar trouble, although they can be playable if the third card is a king or an ace, giving you chances not just for trips but also for kings-up or aces-up.

# Calculating Odds in Seven-Card Stud

Unlike hold'em where if you flop a flush draw, you automatically know that you have a one-third chance of making it (with nine outs twice), in stud your chances of making a draw vary dramatically depending on what cards are out.

Suppose you start with a three-flush and catch a fourth suited card right away. This sounds like a promising situation in the abstract—but seven-card stud isn't played in the abstract! In an eight-handed game, if everyone else is still in after fourth street, you'll get a look at 14 other cards.

If seven of the nine spades you need are already in other players' hands, you should get out: Two outs aren't enough to warrant continued play and neither are three. Even four is a very marginal situation—you should probably let the hand go unless it has other equity, such as several high cards or straight potential.

### The Inside Straight

Most stud players don't have too much trouble remembering folded cards that directly impact their own hand's potential (if you do, you should find another game). Remembering folded cards is much more difficult when the cards don't seem relevant to anyone at the moment. If, for example, Opponent X catches clubs on fourth, fifth, and sixth street, it's awfully nice to be able to remember if it was the 4♠ or the 4♣ that Opponent Y folded on third street.

On the other hand, if you don't see a single spade anywhere, or just one, you're in excellent shape and should bet your hand quite aggressively. Note that your own cards haven't changed one bit: The decision about whether or not to continue was made based almost entirely on what cards were or weren't live.

Similarly, while you can't always be sure what your opponents are drawing to, you can make some educated guesses. Someone whose first two upcards are hearts probably isn't trying for a flush if you spot hearts all over the table. Someone who pairs his doorcard and who bets strongly into someone who owns a higher doorcard or an open pair probably does have the trips he's representing.

# Useful Strategies for Seven-Card Stud

What you can represent is almost as important as what you hold in stud. A player whose board (exposed cards) looks weak needs very good hidden strength, because his opponents are almost certainly going to attack. Similarly, a player whose board appears threatening can and should put his opponents to the test. It's entirely possible that by betting a visible king, you may be able to get an opponent to lay down a pair of queens—especially if no other kings are out.

There are few hard and fast rules about stud strategies, because the hands are so context-dependent. Still, there's one principle that has served stud players well for decades. If you decide to play on fifth street where the bet levels have doubled, you should probably play on through the river.

Even this rule isn't absolute. If your opponent pairs his doorcard and that pair is higher than the highest pair in your hand, you might consider giving up on sixth street. If you were drawing at a heart flush and on sixth street everyone catches a heart except you, it might not be worth continuing your draw. If an opponent who started (?-?) K♠-Q♠-10♠ catches the J♠, his board is just too scary to draw against unless you have at least three of a kind (giving you a chance for a full house).

---

### Poker Lore

The old rule that tells you "if you play on fifth street, you should stay through the river" has probably had fewer dramatic cases of reinforcement than were found at the final table of the $500 buy-in Seven-Card Stud Championship at the 2002 Tournament of Champions. I started with (4♠-2♠) 5♠, and by sixth street had a pair of twos, a flush draw, and a straight draw.

My opponent was Phil Ivey, the Atlantic City star who is considered the world's top seven-card stud player. I missed my draw on the river and had only his pair of twos. Ivey bet his last $3,000, and I decided to make a call that would have left me with only $2,000 if I lost.

"You win, Andy," Ivey said, after I called. I said nothing: Ivey could have been assuming that I had a pair of fives. "Queen-high," announced Ivey, who had been betting a high-card draw and missed.

"That I can beat," I said, showing the pair of twos and eliminating Ivey. When the pot is large and you're playing an aggressive player, you call on the river if you have almost any chance to win!

---

Even if Mr. (?-?) K♠-Q♠-10♠-J♠ is bluffing, having started (8♥-8♦) K♠, he has such a super draw that this is really only a semibluff. Any ace or nine gives him a straight, any spade gives him a king-high flush, the 8♣ gives him trips, any high card gives him two pair, and the A♠ or 9♠ gives him a straight flush. Whether or not you want to play against a draw that strong depends in part on your own hand and in part on how many of his cards are available.

Another important strategic concept involves changing your starting hand selection depending on how high the antes are. Poker rules are not at all standard for antes: a $5-10 stud game might have antes as low as $0.25, or as high as $2. In the former, you can afford to throw away hand after hand because it isn't costing you much to stay at the table. Just one good hand played even to fifth or sixth street can make up for four or five rounds of sitting out.

In the $2 ante game, though, you just cannot afford to sit back and be really picky about your starting hands. You definitely don't play just anything, but hands like small split pairs become playable, as do small three-straights or small three-flushes. Even a hand like (A♠-6♥) K♦ becomes worth playing if no one has an ace for a doorcard.

Most of the time, the ante in a $5-10 game will fall somewhere between those extremes and as you gain experience, you'll get a feel for what hands are playable at what ratio of antes-to-bets.

Finally, you should remain aware of your opponents' styles. Some players routinely play any ace or king doorcard as if they have a pair when the odds are certainly against that being the case on any given occasion. Against such aggressive players you can continue playing when you have a smaller pair, even though every once in a while you will get trapped when the aggressor really has the goods.

Against more conservative players, a raise from an ace or a king likely means you know just what you're up against and chasing is a bad idea unless you have a good drawing hand that can easily defeat kings-up or aces-up if you hit.

## Chasing Is More Worthwhile in Stud Than in Hold'em

In an ideal world, you would always have your money in with the best hand and have opponents trying to catch up from behind. However, the world isn't ideal. Especially once the pot is large, you will be faced with many difficult decisions about whether you should continue playing when you are fairly sure that you are behind at the moment.

In flop games like hold'em (less so for Omaha, but still true), chasing from behind is usually a poor idea because so many of the cards that arrive on the turn or river help both players equally. For example, suppose you start with (8♠-8♣) and your opponent starts with (J♠-J♣). The flop comes 9♥-Q♠-2♣. You make the dubious decision to call, even though you have failed to flop a set and are facing two overcards (single cards that if matched by something an opponent has in the hole would give him a bigger pair—in this case the nine or queen).

Now on the turn the 2♥ hits the board, which now reads 9♥-Q♠-2♣-2♥. Your hand has "improved" from a pair of eights to two pair, eights and twos, but it really hasn't improved at all because your opponent's hand has also improved, in this case to two pair, jacks and twos. The turn card helped you both equally, which is to say, not at all.

Some turn or river cards, naturally, do not help both players equally. If the turn card is the 8♦, it has helped you tremendously and has done nothing for your opponent. If the turn card is the J♥, it has helped your opponent, but curiously, not as much as it appears. You were already trailing and appeared to have only two outs. Now, with a board of 9♥-Q♠-2♣-J♥, you can win if any of the four tens hit the river. They give you a straight, although you will be hesitant to bet the *ignorant* (low) end of the straight, since anyone who has a king has a higher straight.

In stud, each player gets his own unique turn and river cards and the chance that you both get a card that helps you identically doesn't exist. It's possible that you'll each catch worthless cards or each catch very helpful cards, but it's more likely in stud that a turn or river card will help you catch up than it will in hold'em. For that reason, it is more "permissible" to try to come from behind in stud. You shouldn't make a habit of it, but if the pot is large enough, you're getting the right pot odds to continue playing.

# A Special Look at Stud Eight-or-Better

High-low seven-card stud is played with an eight-or-better *qualifier* in casinos and cardrooms. That means that at the showdown, the pot is split between the highest and lowest hands, if the lowest hand *qualifies*.

> **Table Talk**
>
> If a game is played with an **eight-or-better low qualifier**, the player with the best low hand must have at least an eight-low to claim the low share of the pot. If the "best" low hand is 9-5-4-3-2, the highest hand wins the whole pot.

In many home games, high-low stud is played with a declare option, instead of an eight-qualifier. See Chapter 13 for more information about playing stud with a declare. Declare options are not used in cardrooms or casinos.

Stud eight-or-better is dealt almost exactly the same as the high version with a few minor exceptions. Normally the low card still makes the bring-in (games that use a high-card bring-in are not unheard of, but are rare), but that's often not the burden that it is in high-only stud; low cards can be very valuable in stud eight-or-better. Also, there is no "double bet on an open pair" option in stud eight-or-better. The first two rounds are played at the single bet level and the final three at the double bet level, regardless of what cards are out.

Playable starting hands change dramatically when playing high-low poker. Most of the time in games featuring decent players only three (at the most four) players remain in the hand at the showdown. Because three-handed finishes are so common, it's quite normal to find yourself in a position where you own one of two apparently low hands facing one high or one of two obvious high hands going up against one apparent low. When you're putting in one third of the money, you don't make much profit when you only get to win half of the money … but you lose heavily when you don't escape with half the pot. Unless your hand has a chance to win both ways, you're risking a third of the pot to win a sixth of it.

### The Inside Straight

Aces are uniquely powerful starting cards in high-low poker because they can serve as the lowest card in a low hand, but can also make the highest pair. A starting hand like (2-3) 5 is a great start because it promises a powerful low and can make a straight, but a hand like (A-3) 5 is much better because a pair of aces is so much stronger than a pair of deuces. It's almost correct to think of an ace as being worth 1.5 cards.

For that reason, you should normally not get excited about hands that have only one-way potential. The really good stud eight-or-better starting hands consist of three connected low cards. These hands can turn into good lows, good highs (even a hand like (5-2) 3 can quickly turn into trips), or, better still, good two-way hands like low straights or flushes.

If your two-way start turns into A-2-3-4-5 (called a *wheel*), you are probably *freerolling*: You have the best possible low hand and your straight has an excellent chance to win the high. The only reason a wheel isn't absolutely a freeroll is you could run into a situation where two players have wheels and a third has a full house. The wheels split the low, getting one quarter of the pot each, and the full house gets the high half.

### Table Talk

A **freeroll** is a chance to win something at no risk. For example, if you and another player each own the same straight, but you also have a flush draw, you would raise forever, because you will either split or win the whole pot. Your bet has all upside and no downside.

The starting hands that drop the most in value in stud eight-or-better are the big pairs. A hand like (K-K) 10 (a premium hand in stud high) is virtually unplayable in eight-or-better, unless the game is shorthanded. In shorthanded games, it's less likely that someone will make a low, and high-only hands have a better chance to *scoop* (win both the high and the low).

Even a hand like (A-A) 5, which looks absolutely terrific (and which is far stronger than a pair of kings), isn't really much to write home about. You do have a pair of aces, but even if you improve to aces-up, you have to be worried about players who are drawing to make small straights or flushes. You do have two low cards, but that's a deceptively weak start. It's very difficult to make a qualifying low when you start with only two low cards out of three. You can play (A-A) 5, but if you catch a *brick* (bad card) on fourth street—in this case, any card from a nine through a king—you should probably get out if it looks like you're facing any kind of strength.

In stud eight-or-better if you consistently play with three good cards and one bad one against players who have four good cards, you will lose everything you bring to the table.

One of the more common eight-or-better mistakes is to play three unconnected low cards too strongly. Not all three low-card starts are created equal.

Suppose, for example, that you start (8-7) 2. This is a three low-card start, but it isn't playable. You're trying to make the worst of the lows, an eight-low, and not only that, you're trying to make a *rough* (weak) eight—an 8-7. Further, your three cards cannot work together to make a straight. This hand would be playable if it were higher: (8-7) 5 can at least make a straight, but you should dump the hand if it doesn't improve immediately.

Even (7-6) 2 is not a particularly good starting hand. It's much better to aim for a seven-low than an eight, but this too is a rough hand: 7-5 or 7-4 lows beat 7-6 lows more often than most players realize. While (7-6) 2 could theoretically turn into four of a kind, that's a statement you could make about any three starting cards. High potential comes not just from the chance to make trips, a full house, or quads, but much more from the chance to make straights and flushes. (7-6) 5 is a much stronger starting hand, even though as a low, it's pretty rough.

Naturally, if two or three of your low cards are suited, your hand is better. (7♠-6♠) 2♠ isn't merely playable: It's a premium starting hand.

Rolled up trips are still good starting hands in eight-or-better. Even a hand like (9-9) 9 has enough strength for high that it's worth playing (although you should get uneasy if you find yourself looking at a hand like (?-?) 3-2-4-6 and you haven't improved to a full house).

### The Inside Straight

The two best rolled up hands are (A-A) A and (5-5) 5. Trip aces are strong because they win so often unimproved. Trip fives get second place because of their defensive strength. You can't make a low straight without a five and not only are you denying your fellow players three of the low cards they need to make a qualifying low, you are also holding the card they need to make the most common strong two-way high-low hand, the low straight.

Be wary of playing hands like (4-5) 4. This looks like a great high-low hand, but it isn't low enough to be low and isn't high enough to be high (one low pair will rarely win anything and two low pair aren't much better). You can consider taking a card off with a hand like this, but if you don't immediately hit a third four, a five, a six, an ace, or a three, you should probably get out. You can keep playing on if you catch a deuce, so long as the other cards you need are still live.

If (4-5) 4 is a questionable starting hand, hopefully you see why (6-7) 6 is far worse. Your high possibilities are essentially unchanged, but your low possibilities are definitely much worse than a hand that starts with two wheel cards.

### Perilous Play

The stud guideline about playing to the finish if you play fifth street doesn't apply to eight-or-better. If your opponents are any good, they haven't started with junk, and an opposing board of (?-?) 3-6-5-4 is too scary. Get out unless your own hand is strong.

Stud eight-or-better is a wonderful game to play against weak opponents because weak players are almost always looking for excuses to get involved with hands and the game's high-low nature increases the number of excuses these players can find.

Naturally, you should avoid this approach. In some ways, you should consider that there are fewer good starting hands in eight-or-better than there are in stud high only. If you restrict your play to rolled up trips or three coordinated low cards, you will find yourself throwing a lot of hands away, but you'll also likely find yourself in the winner's circle!

## The Least You Need to Know

- Playable starting hands in stud are extremely context-dependent.
- The ante size plays a big role in determining how many starting hands you should play.

- Play cautiously any time an opponent pairs his doorcard.

- Your ability to keep track of cards folded by your opponents plays a huge role in your results.

- If you play on fifth street, most of the time you should keep on playing through the river.

- In stud eight-or-better, restrict your starting hands to rolled-up trips or three coordinated low cards until you have gained experience.

# 4

# Omaha: The Cruelest Game

## In This Chapter

- ◆ Learning Omaha's rules
- ◆ Developing principles for Omaha starting hand values
- ◆ Analyzing Omaha odds
- ◆ Useful Omaha strategies
- ◆ An overview of Omaha eight-or-better
- ◆ An overview of Pot-Limit Omaha

Omaha, or Omaha hold'em as it is sometimes called, came into its own in the 1980s and for a while people speculated that Omaha might supplant both hold'em and seven-card stud as the primary casino poker game. That failed to happen, but there's no question that Omaha is one of the three most important forms of poker in the twenty-first century.

## The Rules

Omaha is a tougher to learn than hold'em, although once you have already played hold'em, you only need to make a few simple adjustments to play a decent game of Omaha. Straight Omaha is played in high-only format. Because Omaha eight-or-better and pot-limit Omaha are both extremely popular variations, I'll spend almost as much time looking at those games as I will on limit Omaha high.

The rules about card distribution and betting rounds in hold'em are identical to Omaha, with one exception: In Omaha, each player is dealt four hole cards rather than two.

It might sound like an Omaha lesson only takes two minutes for a hold'em player, but there is one key difference that makes the game play out quite differently than hold'em.

In Omaha, you must use two, and exactly two, of your hole cards. This rule leads to confusion to players accustomed to hold'em. Suppose, for example, that the board is K-K-Q-Q-10, and your Omaha hand is A-K-9-9. You do not have a full house, even though your king would give you a full house in hold'em (K-K-K-Q-Q). When you must play two cards from your hand, the best five card hand you can assemble is A-K-K-K-Q: trip kings.

> **Perilous Play**
>
> Don't let pride get in your way when you're first learning Omaha. When in doubt, *table* your hand (turn it face up on the table in front of you; once you have tabled it, the dealer or anyone in the game is allowed to help you read it). It's extremely common for someone who has been focusing on his chances to make a flush to overlook that he has made a straight, or vice-versa.

Although you've just seen an example where the "must two" rule created a weaker final hand than would have existed in a hold'em game, make no mistake: The average winning hand in Omaha is substantially higher than it is in hold'em. Why? Even though players are occasionally constricted by the "must two" rule, ultimately they are trying to assemble their best five card hand out of nine cards, rather than assembling one from seven cards. A voyage from seven to nine is quite lengthy and all kinds of straight and flush possibilities arise.

In fact, a reasonable way to play Omaha when you are starting is to assume that someone holds the best possible hand (excluding four of a kind or a straight flush) available through the five community cards. This is especially likely in low-limit games where quite a few players are seeing the flop. That is, if you have a flop of K♠-9♣-10♥, you should consider the possibilities quite high that someone has a Q-J in his hand and has the king-high straight.

If that board winds up pairing and finishes K♠-9♣-10♥-9♠-4♣, you should assume it likely that someone has made a full house.

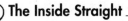

### The Inside Straight

Omaha, more than any form of casino poker, is a game where you often need the *nuts* to win. For this discussion, assume that with a paired board, the nuts is the top full house. Also assume that with an unpaired board, the nuts is the ace-high flush (if suited cards appear) or the top straight. Many hands will be won with something less, but when you're staying in on a draw, you'd be wise to be drawing to the nuts.

Similarly, if a board finishes with three cards of one suit, it's quite likely that someone has a flush. If the flush becomes possible because the turn and river fall in suit, it's slightly less likely that someone will have a *backdoor flush*, and if someone does have it, it's not as likely to be the nut flush.

### Table Talk

A **backdoor hand** is one that arrives in unlikely fashion because the two final cards had to be perfect for it to be possible. For example, if you get a *rainbow* flop of Q♠-8♥-6♣, and then the board finishes 2♠-3♠, it's now possible for someone to have made a backdoor spade flush. Similarly, if the flop comes K♣-7♠-2♦, but finishes 10♥-J♦, anyone who holds A-Q has made a backdoor straight. Q-9 would also make a backdoor straight, but it would not be the nut straight.

Because players tend to hold high connected cards if they stay in for the flop in Omaha, it's fairly common to see split pots.

# Omaha Starting Hand Values

It's a bit easier to rank Omaha starting hands than seven-card stud hands, but a bit tougher to rank them than hold'em hands. Because you don't see opponents' cards until the showdown, you don't have to adjust for visible or folded cards.

A number of players have suggested rather complex "point count" systems for determining whether an Omaha high (or high-low) starting hand is playable. I don't like that approach: It is difficult to memorize, and it favors rote memorization over thinking and understanding. Rote memorization can help you play a little better when you are starting, but it can impede your efforts to improve. Start thinking and comprehending as soon as possible.

Rather than listing the best starting Omaha hands for you, I'm going to give you a number of guidelines so you can make your own judgments about what qualifies as a playable, strong, or weak starting hand.

## Play Coordinated Cards

The "play cards that work together" guideline is the Golden Rule of Omaha strategy. Someone who follows this guideline religiously, but who doesn't play very well after the flop, actually rates to do better than someone who plays very well after the flop, but who regularly plays starting hands that contain only three (or, heaven forbid, two) good coordinated starting cards.

It is tempting to play a hand such as A♠-A♥-K♣-7♦, because you do have a pair of aces and your ace-king combination can make a nut straight. Yet, this hand is actually fairly weak unless you're playing shorthanded. Your aces are not suited, so you can't make any flushes. Worse still, the 7♦ doesn't coordinate with any of your other cards. It could still help, if the flop comes 7-7-K, but it's useless for straight or flush purposes and isn't a high card. The seven is a *dangler*.

> **Table Talk**
>
> A **dangler** is an Omaha card that doesn't coordinate well with your other three cards: It just sort of hangs there uselessly. A "never play danglers" strategy is sound for a beginner.

Why is the "no dangler" rule so important? In Omaha, the number of potential combinations increases exponentially with each additional card, rather than geometrically.

Omaha is a game of draws and *redraws* (additional ways to improve a made hand on later streets). When you look at an Omaha hand, you find a little equity here and a little equity there and it's the combination of all those pieces of equity that make a hand worthwhile. Let's break down a good Omaha starting hand to see how this works.

Suppose your hand is A♠-K♦-Q♠-10♦. This is a very strong Omaha hand even though it doesn't contain a single pair. How come? Let's see all the possible combinations:

- A♠-Q♠ can make the nut flush in spades. It can also make an ace-high straight and two very high pair, aces and queens. It can also make a royal flush.

- A♠-K♦ can make an ace-high straight and the two highest pair, aces and kings.

- A♠-10♦ can make an ace-high straight and two high pair, aces and tens.

- ◆ K◆-10◆ can make a king-high flush (only the second nuts, but possibly the nuts if the A◆ is on the board). It can also make either an ace-high or a king-high straight and it can make two fairly high pair, kings and tens. It can also make a royal flush.

- ◆ K◆-Q♠ can make an ace-high or king-high straight and can also make two fairly high pair, kings and queens.

- ◆ Q♠-10◆ can make an ace-, king-, or queen-high straight and can make two decent pair, queens and tens.

All of these hands can also make a full house and depending on what cards are on the community board, those full houses can be the nut full houses.

No single two-card combination here makes the A♠-K◆-Q♠-10◆ a playable hand. Instead, it is the combined value, or equity, that you get from the six overall combinations that makes this a premium Omaha hand.

If you assigned a dangler zero value (and while danglers should be avoided, that's too drastic an evaluation: They do help, occasionally), how many combinations would you have? Try the hand of A♠-K◆-Q♠:

A♠-K◆

A♠-Q♠

K◆-Q♠

That's a total of only three combinations. By adding a fourth usable card, you get *twice* as many usable two-card combinations, not one-third more.

 **The Inside Straight** _____

If a one-card dangler leads to trouble, just imagine how bad a two-card dangler is. If you get dealt A♠-A♥-9♠-6♣, you have "dry aces." They don't coordinate with either of your other cards. Play dry aces only in a big bet, heads-up situation, and even then, they are often an underdog if the hand is played to the river. Dry kings are far worse, so just say no!

## Play Big Cards

Big pairs beat small pairs. Two big pair beat two small pair. Big straights beat small straights. High flushes beat low flushes. Low-stakes Omaha games tend to feature lots of people seeing the flop. That makes this guideline particularly important when it comes to straights and flushes, because it's extremely common to see more than one straight or flush.

## Suited Aces Are More Valuable Than Suited Kings

Suited kings—or for that matter, suited queens, jacks, or tens—will certainly win you the occasional pot. Suited kings are definitely better than any of the smaller suited combinations because they can still give you a nut flush draw if a suited ace hits the board. Despite that, it's a long way down from a suited ace to a suited king. If you find yourself getting a lot of action when you have a suited king, the chances are good you have the second best hand, which is always a costly situation. Suited kings tend to win small pots and lose large pots, so play them carefully.

## Play Big Pairs

A-A, K-K, and Q-Q are definitely not as valuable in Omaha as they are in hold'em, but they still have considerable value if they are part of a coordinated hand. With aces, it's most important for the coordination to be in suit; with kings and queens, suits are nice, but it's probably more important that the cards coordinate for a straight, with starting hands like K-K-Q-J or Q-Q-K-10.

Small pairs are trouble in Omaha. They often lead to small sets that get beat by bigger sets, or more often still, small full houses that get beat by bigger full houses.

### The Inside Straight

Omaha is a game of draws and redraws. When you already have one hand made and can improve to something better, you have a redraw. Because the turn or river cards create new possibilities, it's vitally important to have redraws to something better than what you've flopped. For example, holding A♥-Q♥-J♣-10♦, you've flopped a straight with K♥-J♥-10♠. You have *terrific* redraw possibilities here because your two pair can become a full house and your heart draw can make the nut flush or even a straight flush.

## Avoid Double-Pair Hands Lacking Extra Strengths

If you get dealt two pairs, such as K♥-K♦-8♠-8♣, your hand is basically worthless unless you flop a set. Even then, you have to be careful that you aren't vulnerable to redraws for straights and flushes. If the hand were K♥-K♦-8♥-8♦, you'd be better off with two second-nut flush draws. Yet that hand is far worse than A♥-A♦-8♥-8♦, which in turn is worse than A♥-A♦-10♥-10♦ (two suited aces and some straight value).

A hand like Q♥-Q♦-J♠-J♣ is playable because of the straight possibilities (notice that by owning two each of these cards, you reduce the chance that someone else might make the same straight), but if you don't flop either a set or an open-ended straight, you should ditch the hand in a hurry.

Players differ on what starting hand they consider the best. I vote for A♠-A♥-J♠-10♥ (any double-suited aces with the jack-ten combination).

# The Odds

The most important odds calculations come on the flop when you need to check how well your coordinated starting hand has intermingled with the flop.

Although it's a comfortable feeling to flop the top full house, you're not going to be lucky enough to do that very often. If you're playing a hand with four different high cards—even one as low as Q-J-10-9—you have an excellent chance to flop one of the best Omaha drawing hands, a *wrap*.

**Table Talk**

A **wrap** is shorthand for a *wraparound straight draw*, a hand that offers far more outs than the open-ended straight draws we aim for in hold'em. Suppose you hold Q-J-10-9. If the flop comes an ungainly looking K-10-8, you make a straight if an ace, queen, jack, nine, or seven hits the board! That's 17 outs and you have two chances to hit. As long as the board doesn't pair or develop a flush possibility, your wrap draw is actually better than a flopped set.

When calculating Omaha odds, remember that it tends to be more difficult to be certain that a given card is an out. A card that is an out to the nuts on the turn can easily create possibilities for other, stronger hands on the river. Instead of trying to turn yourself into a human calculator, press advantages, be wary of drawing to hands that can easily be beaten, play conservatively without the nuts, and you'll soon enough develop a good feel for Omaha.

If the average winning hand is much higher in Omaha because you get to create your five-card hand from a selection of nine possible cards, it stands to reason that the ninth and final card changes the result much more often than the seventh and final card does in hold'em. That's why Omaha is "the cruelest game." It's the *infrequent* hand where the fifth community card does not make some kind of straight or flush possible.

**The Inside Straight** _____

Because the river card in Omaha so frequently creates new possibilities and turns a trailer into the leader/winner, it's more important for Omaha players to be "tilt-proof" than in almost any other form of poker. (It's more important in *no-limit* anything, because you can throw your entire stack away in one hand.)

Another important matter to remember is that when a fourth suited card hits the board, unlike the situation you face in hold'em, a flush is no more likely than it was with three suited cards on board (because of the "must two" rule). Indeed, the appearance of a fourth suited card actually makes it a bit less likely that someone else has a flush because one of the cards he needs is unavailable.

# Strategies

Probably the most important aspect of Omaha play to track is an easy one: How many people have looked at the flop? If only two or three players stay in, there's much less chance that someone holds the best possible hand (or draw) than if five or six players see the flop.

**The Inside Straight** _____

You've already read the phrase "fit or fold" in the hold'em section. If that advice was good in hold'em, in Omaha it's probably as close to an absolute concept as you're going to see in poker. In an Omaha game where plenty of players see the flop, either hit the flop strongly, or run away to live and play another day.

Low stakes Omaha games tend to be fairly passive before the flop with large numbers of players limping in trying to hit a magic flop. It's extremely unlikely that all of these players are playing quality hands. Your edge comes from not mimicking their too-loose play.

When you play in a game where pre-flop raises are uncommon, it is possible to play a few more hands than solid starting hand requirements dictate, especially from late position. This is a dangerous habit to begin because once you grow accustomed to loose play, you may find it difficult to shift back to proper play.

Exercise discipline when you're first learning the game and you won't have any bad habits that you have to unlearn.

Position is certainly relevant in Omaha, but it's far less important than it is in hold'em. *Hold'em is a game of position; Omaha is a game of card combinations.* If you have four good cards working together, you can play them from any position. If you only have three good cards, position isn't likely to help you overcome the card disadvantage you face.

**The Inside Straight** _____

Trying to chase down a probably better hand from behind in Omaha isn't necessarily wrong, but you have to chase the correct way. Chase probable straights with nut flush draws; chase probable flushes with top set. The keys are having enough draws that will win if they hit. There are few plays more unprofitable than spending money to draw at a hand that has a good chance of getting beat if you connect.

Where position can really help is if you find yourself with a strong hand in late position and a large number of limpers have already come in for one bet. Someone who has already called one bet is almost never going to fold for a second and you can create a large pot by putting in a raise. You're not going to play on if the flop misses you, but if it hits, the pot size may encourage players to try to chase you down.

You have to be a bit careful here. If the pot size gets truly huge, these players will actually be getting the right price to chase you. Two pre-flop bets, though, will often put your quality hand exactly where you want it: in the lead, with unduly optimistic players throwing away money trying to draw at the wrong end of straights, trying to make third- or fourth-best flush draws, or hoping that bottom full house might be good. This is where you really make your money in Omaha—punishing players who make "good" hands that aren't good enough, given the possibilities created by the community board.

# Omaha Eight-or-Better

Omaha eight-or-better is played exactly the same way as high-only Omaha, except that the hand that finishes with the best qualifying low gets half the pot. As the name implies, a low must be at least an eight-low to qualify.

Curiously, while many average skill Omaha-high players understand that they are really only average players, many eight-or-better players seem to think they are much more skilled than they really are. They believe that only they know it's far better to draw at an A-2 low than an A-3 or 2-3, and that only they know that hands containing an A-2 and two other wheel cards are extremely valuable.

This overconfidence can be intimidating to a new player. A truly good player keeps his mouth shut. He doesn't explain a weak player's mistakes to him, especially after that weak player has just "mistakenly" won a big pot.

Many of the principles that you learned in the previous chapter's discussion of stud eight-or-better apply to Omaha eight-or-better. Your goal is to scoop pots, not split them and hands that have potential in only one direction, such as K♠-Q♠-10♥-9♣ or A♥-2♣-7♠-8♦ (which, like all low hands, has at least a *little* high potential), drop significantly in value compared to hands that have two-way potential.

You are allowed to use either the same or different cards in assembling your low and high hands, but the "must two" rule applies in both directions.

The "must two" rule also limits the number of low hands that can be made. If the final community board doesn't contain at least three different low cards, there can be no qualifying low and the best high hand will take the entire pot.

It can be extremely frustrating to start with a promising low hand like A-2-3-4 and see the flop come K-J-10 (rendering your hand completely useless—remember, your singleton ace can't make that high straight), but in some ways, especially when you're first learning, this flop is better for your A-2-3-4 than something like K-J-3.

Many Omaha players just can't release such a promising starting hand, especially if they've shown a certain amount of restraint in waiting for it. One low card on the flop gives them false hope. "If a wheel card comes off on the turn," they rationalize, "I'll be drawing at a two-way hand that no one will expect me to have, and I can win a huge pot." While this logic is true enough on the surface, the reality is that you simply won't catch two perfect cards consecutively nearly enough to compensate for the losses you incur trying to pull off your *runner-runner* miracle.

**Table Talk**

When someone catches **runner-runner**, it means that he has caught two consecutive perfect cards. The term usually implies that the lucky recipient made a bad play.

Even if you have the perfect A-2-3-4, if only one low card flops, you don't even have a 25 percent chance to make a low. If you only have two low cards in your hand, the chance of getting *counterfeited* plunges your chances to just worse than one in six.

If the flop brings two different low cards, your low draw is playable but you had better be drawing to a very good low. The following table will show you the odds of making a low hand.

**Table Talk**

When your low gets **counterfeited**, you're not the victim of someone who printed cards in his basement. Instead, a low card from your hand has appeared on the board, giving someone else access to that rank. You certainly prefer to start with an A-2 instead of A-3, but if the flop comes 2-6-7, it is the player holding A-3 who has flopped the nut low. His own hand could be counterfeited if a trey hits the board later.

Your odds of making a wheel or other low straight aren't easily tabulated, but just because you have wheel cards in your hand doesn't mean you're going to have a good chance to make a wheel. The dealer has to cooperate by putting the other necessary wheel cards out onto the community board.

## Specific Odds and Odds Oddities

| Your Hand | Odds of Making a Low |
| --- | --- |
| **Two different low cards** | |
| Pre-flop | 24% |
| One unique low card in flop | 16%  (runner-runner) |
| Two unique low cards in flop | 59% |
| **Three different low cards** | |
| Pre-flop | 40% |
| One unique low card in flop | 26% (runner-runner) |
| Two unique low cards in flop | 72% |
| **Four different low cards** | |
| Pre-flop | 49% |
| One unique low card in flop | 24% (runner-runner) |
| Two unique low cards in flop | 70% |

If you study this table, you may notice some numbers "seem" wrong. Your chances of making a low certainly seem best if you hold four low cards in your hand, right? Then why, holding four low cards, do you only have a 70 percent chance of making a low when you have a *72 percent* chance holding three low cards? It's because you need another low card to hit the board, but you've got an extra one tied up in your hand.

Note that the table speaks of "different" low cards and "unique" low cards. That's because when your hand is 2-2-2-2, you don't have four low cards for Omaha purposes: You have one. Similarly, a flop of K-4-4 presents only one unique low card on the flop: You'll need two more and different low cards on the turn and river to make a low.

### Perilous Play

Do *not* freak out and assume Omaha can't be your game just because it's possible to prove certain possibilities with math. You don't have to be a mathematician to remember that three low cards in your hand plus two on the flop give you a good shot at making a low, or that with one on the flop, your low chances stink. If you can remember common situations and perform the minor math involved in figuring pot odds, you can play.

## The Amazing Rhythm Aces

Although starting hands that contain four wheel cards (especially if they contain the key card, an ace) are always playable, the ace's unique two-way nature makes hands like A-2-K-Q eminently playable, too. You have three cards aiming squarely at the high side, in case the flop contains only high cards, but you also have the best possible starting low draw.

Because you want your draws to be to the nuts, A-3-K-Q (or an A-3 with any other two high cards) isn't nearly as strong as the A-2-high-high hand; you'll need a deuce to hit the board to give you the nut low. Still, any hand with an ace, another wheel card, and two high cards should be considered playable, especially if the ace is suited.

### The Inside Straight

By now you're aware that a "naked" A-2 or other two low card hand is vulnerable to getting counterfeited. The good news is that if enough low cards hit the board, the counterfeit may not harm you, either because everyone has been counterfeited or because you can still form a terrific low with one of your cards on the board.

For example, you may be able to win just by having a "live ace." That is, suppose the final board is 2-6-7-3-4. You can play your A-2 to make an A-2-3-4-6 low, the second-best possible. An opponent who held A-3 and took the lead on the flop got counterfeited on the turn, and an A-4 player got counterfeited on the river. Only someone holding A-5 has a better low than you, although a number of holdings (A-3, A-4, and A-6) would tie you on the low side.

# Pot-Limit Omaha

Pot-Limit Omaha, a game that by unfortunate coincidence is also known by its initials (PLO), is probably *the* big money poker game, especially in side games at major tournaments. Pots can escalate exponentially. That can happen in any pot-limit or no-limit form of poker, of course, if someone makes a mistake or wants to gamble. PLO pots can grow huge *without* anyone making an error and that's why it's the game of choice for high stakes side games.

PLO pots escalate because Omaha is a game of draws and redraws. It's quite common for one player to flop the top set while another has a wrap; that situation will probably create a bet, a raise, and a re-raise. Because these raises are so often pot-sized, the pot grows quite large on the flop.

On the turn, the player who started with the wrap connects for his straight. He makes a large bet and the player who owns the top set faces a decision that would be easy in limit Omaha, but which isn't easy at all in pot-limit. If the bet is pot-sized, the top-set owner would probably lay the hand down if his set were all he had going for him (yet another reason why it is so important to have redraws). If the top set player also held the nut flush draw, he would have enough outs to continue playing in a pot that has now grown immense compared to the blinds.

On the river if the board pairs, the straight owner has to consider giving up if he didn't have some extra equity via a redraw of his own. The straight owner might have made a flush via the paired card and faces a tough decision. You don't want to be calling big bets with a flush when the board is paired. Often the decision to call is based more on one's perception of his opponent than on his hand: Would the opponent be willing to make a pot-sized bluff?

What can make PLO pots so huge with good players involved is that the availability of so many draws and redraws makes the raises and re-raises quite reasonable plays. You don't need two or three maniacs going at it for the pot to escalate. In other forms of pot-limit poker, there aren't enough reasonable raising hands to create lots of action among good players.

Because the possibility of big payoffs on late round bets exists, it is possible to play a wider range of starting hands in PLO than it is in either limit Omaha or Omaha eight-or-better. That doesn't mean you should go crazy, though. You still need to play quality hands or your chips will bleed off so fast that you won't have any money left when you finally do connect with a flop that appears to have helped no one.

---

### Poker Lore

My online readers often want to learn not just about tournament results, but also about big side games. At the 2002 World Series of Poker, I took a brief break from tournament coverage to visit a PLO game that used blinds of $200-400. I didn't have much time to watch, but didn't need it.

On the very first hand I observed, a player who flopped top set and the second nut flush draw bet his hand hard and heavy against a player who had flopped a straight draw and the nut flush draw. The river card brought a third heart, completing both flush draws and thanks to the exponential pot growth possible from two big hands, the player holding the ace-high flush was able to bet *less* than the full pot and still toss $40,000 into the middle. His opponent, who certainly would have preferred that his three queens hadn't "improved," finally decided there was too much money in the pot to throw the second-best possible hand (his king-high flush) away, and called. The first player dragged a $140,000 pot.

I returned to reporting tournament action, but visited the game the next day, and the action on the first hand he watched wasn't too bad then, either. The winner took down $190,000–in a game using $200-400 blinds. Timing can be everything, both when you're reporting, and when you make a king-high flush.

---

Another danger to playing a PLO hand like 6-7-8-9 is that when you do connect, you had better be connecting with small cards. If you get excited because you play 6-7-8-9 (playable in PLO and completely unplayable in both limit Omaha and Omaha eight-or-better) and get a flop of 10-J-Q, you will get your head handed to you. Yes, you've flopped a straight, but you've flopped the ignorant end of that straight and anyone who is in with an A-K will crush you.

If, on the other hand, you get what appears to be a dream flop of 3-4-5, while you have flopped the nut straight and also have cards that will let you make a higher straight if other middle cards come, you may have trouble getting paid off. Other players who have come in with four high cards will have no interest in this flop and players who started with big pairs probably won't (and certainly shouldn't) pay you off the way someone holding K-K might pay off someone who started with 6-7 in hold'em.

Develop good overall Omaha feel at the limit game first, and then try some tournaments in PLO. If you succeed at both of these ventures, you can try out the bigger PLO cash games … but remember, it isn't likely to be easy!

## The Least You Need to Know

♦ Omaha resembles hold'em in many superficial ways, but there are crucial differences.

♦ In low stakes games, assume that if a hand or draw is possible on the flop, someone has it.

♦ Play coordinated hands and avoid danglers.

♦ Omaha is a game of draws and redraws: have extra outs.

♦ In eight-or-better, favor all-low hands over all-high.

♦ Pot-Limit Omaha (PLO) is a very difficult game best left to more advanced players until you are ready.

# 5

# Games You Won't Find Everywhere

## In This Chapter

- ◆ An introduction to pineapple hold'em
- ◆ An introduction to razz
- ◆ An introduction to lowball
- ◆ An introduction to triple draw
- ◆ An introduction to five-card draw and five-card stud

You can pretty much be assured that you'll find hold'em, seven-card stud, and Omaha in all cardrooms (although in very small cardrooms, all three won't be offered at all hours). There are other forms of poker found in many cardrooms, but far more intermittently. You may chance upon the opportunity to play them, though, so it's good to know a little about them.

## Pineapples Aren't Just Hawaiian

*Pineapple* is a variant of hold'em in which players start with three cards instead of two. Pineapple is found in three variations, each with two sub-flavors, high and high-low. The high-low version always has an eight qualifier for low. The game is usually played limit with two blinds. Each player receives three starting cards instead of two. As in regular hold'em, there is a flop of three cards, a turn card, and a river card, each followed by a betting round.

The difference for each flavor of the game is what happens with those three starting cards in "regular," "crazy," and "lazy" pineapple.

## Regular Pineapple

In regular pineapple, after players receive their cards, there is a betting round. Active players then discard one of their three cards. When each active player has two cards, the game proceeds exactly as hold'em.

Big pairs are great starting cards in pineapple. An overpair, however, is not as strong as in hold'em and without improvement should be played somewhat cautiously. If you can get in cheap, suited connectors are also good. Pineapple is also played high-low, a game where you don't win much unless you *scoop* a pot. This makes small connectors much more desirable than they are in high-only pineapple.

> **The Inside Straight**
>
> Because each player can pick his two starting cards out of three dealt to him, players who stay in tend to have far stronger starting hands than one finds in regular hold'em. In turn, the average winning hand in pineapple is higher than for regular hold'em.

## Crazy Pineapple

Crazy pineapple is similar to pineapple, except players discard their third hole card *after* the flop (put another way, after the second round of betting).

Crazy pineapple is often played high-low, but there is also a high only version. In the high version, hands tend to be stronger than regular pineapple because you don't discard your third hole card until you've seen the flop. This means it's far more likely that you'll find a way to coordinate your hand with what appears on the flop.

> **The Inside Straight**
>
> In general, follow three principles on the flop in high-low crazy pineapple:
> - If your hand has a good chance of scooping, play.
> - If your hand has an extremely good chance of winning one way, play.
> - If your hand has only a moderate chance of winning one way, get out.

The same starting cards are good in crazy pineapple as in regular pineapple, although coordinated holdings are even more valuable.

## Lazy Pineapple

As in all versions of pineapple, players start with three hole cards. Unlike the other versions, players do not discard; instead, they keep the three cards throughout the hand. At the showdown, players may use zero, one, or two of their hole cards in combination with the board, but not all three.

In the high-low version, all three hole cards may end up being used, but no more than two hole cards may be used for the high hand and no more than two for the low hand.

The same starting cards are good in lazy pineapple as in crazy pineapple, with the exception that coordinated holdings are of even more value here and you pretty much must hit the flop well to continue. A couple of aces in your hand is a good start, but that pair of aces isn't likely to take the high without improving.

> **The Inside Straight**
>
> Because players have more cards from which to choose, winning hands tend to be higher than either of the preceding variations. Players needn't decide which of their three cards is least valuable and a card they might otherwise have been forced to discard can end up helping them win.

# All That Razz

Razz is seven-card stud played for low only. The hand rankings are identical to those used in ace-to-five lowball. There is no qualifier for low.

As in seven-card stud, each player antes prior to receiving cards. Each player starts with three cards, two dealt face-down and one up. The high card is forced to initiate the betting. The bring-in bet is generally a fourth to a third of the lower limit. Anyone can complete the bet (raise to the betting limit), or just call. In succeeding rounds, the lowest hand always gets the option to initiate the betting.

Razz has no equivalent of seven-card stud's optional higher betting limit when a pair appears on fourth street. The betting levels stay at the single bet level until fifth street, when they move to the double bet level.

> **Poker Lore**
>
> It's pretty easy to guess how razz started. Some seven-card stud players got tired of getting worthless cards and decided to try a game in which their low holdings were valuable. No doubt these players immediately started catching full houses.

**The Inside Straight**

A good razz player probably has a bigger edge over weak opponents than a good seven-card stud player does. Because it takes five low cards to make a good razz hand, you can often be certain that your hand is better than an opponent's. Unduly optimistic opponents may stay in with you and have no chance to catch you. However, all that information tends to reduce the action and that makes razz much less popular than seven-card stud.

If several low cards are out among the other upcards, you need three good cards to start. If an eight is among your cards, it should be in the hole. Having high cards showing puts you at a big strategic disadvantage.

# Lowball Is Not Just What a Hopeful Home Buyer Does

Lowball draw has two varieties, ace-to-five and deuce-to-seven.

## Ace-to-Five Lowball Draw

Ace-to-five lowball is a variant of five-card draw. The game is often called either *ace-to-five* or, simply lowball. Lowball is always played with the joker, which is wild. It becomes the lowest card that is not in your hand.

**The Inside Straight**

The joker must be the lowest card that does not pair one in the hand. It cannot be whatever you want it to be. This is because some clubs offer jackpots for a wheel beating a 6-4. If you have 4-3-2-A-joker, for example, and an opponent has A-2-3-4-5, your joker must be a five and you split the pot. You cannot call it a six and win the jackpot.

The game is usually played limit and generally with a two-tier structure. Very few clubs offer single-limit games, in which all betting increments, both before and after the draw, are multiples of the same limit. On rare occasions you'll encounter spread-limit and no-limit games.

Lowball is generally played with three blinds, as opposed to the two found in most community card games. The extra blind is put up by the button. Three blind structures exist: 1-1-2, 1-2-3, and 2-3-5. For example, a $10-$20 game has blinds of $5-$5-$10, while a $15-$30 game has blinds of $5-$10-$15.

Some lowball games have an added feature, the *kill* or *overblind*. In kill games, if a player wins two pots in a row, he must leave an amount equal to the upper limit, and the stakes double for the next hand.

**Perilous Play**

Everything else equal, you'd rather not have to post a kill pot blind. Why strive for a situation where you have to post money before you see your cards? In a *kill* game, when you've already won one pot and you face a very close decision with a mediocre hand, the kill "penalty" should be enough to convince you to throw your hand away. If you want to play for doubled stakes, go find a bigger game and play every hand at higher stakes.

Lowball is very position-dependent, primarily because knowing how many cards your opponent is drawing conveys a significant advantage. Good starting hands in early position are pat eights or better and one card to a seven or better. In later positions, you can draw to eights and play pat nines—and sometimes tens.

**The Inside Straight**

Except for tournaments, lowball games usually have no cap on the number of bets. Most tournaments also have no cap, but if they do, it would usually be more than five bets.

## Deuce-to-Seven

Deuce-to-seven lowball (sometimes just called Deuce, and sometimes called *Kansas City lowball*) is usually played no-limit and is one of the most exciting spectator games. Indeed, if any game other than no-limit hold'em is going to make it as a televised poker game, it will probably be Deuce.

The hand rankings are approximately opposite those of high poker and are detailed in Appendix F. Because the ace is treated as a high card and straights and flushes also count as high hands, the lowest possible hand is 7-5-4-3-2 offsuit (four cards in one suit are okay, but five, as a flush, are not). Deuce-to-seven is played in the World Series of Poker with a $5,000 entry and unlimited rebuys. The buy-in for side games during the WSOP is generally higher than that. Side games with over $1 million on the table aren't unheard of.

# To Double Your Pleasure, Triple Your Draw

Triple-draw lowball, or simply triple draw, is lowball with three draws and four betting rounds. Because players get so many tries to make their hands, the winning hands are necessarily much better than those of the single-draw varieties of lowball.

### The Inside Straight

Triple draw is a relatively new form of poker that has quickly become a high stakes favorite, in part because the game is so new that almost no literature is available on advanced tactics. With no "book learning" available, players who have naturally strong card sense and poker talent enjoy an even bigger advantage over their opponents than they do in games that have been analyzed extensively in print.

Triple draw has two varieties, ace-to-five and deuce-to-seven, with ace-to-five the more common. The games are usually played at limit stakes (albeit very high limits), although some cardrooms have pot-limit games. The game has two blinds. To ensure that there are enough cards available for three draws, generally six players are the maximum that can play this game.

Even limiting the game to six players, discards often must be shuffled and then used. As you can imagine, discarded cards tend to be high cards, but aren't always high because players must discard half of a small pair. Triple draw is sometimes played as one of the choices in a mixed game.

Players are dealt five cards, followed by a betting round. After the first betting round, players discard, and there is another betting round. Players discard a second time and a third, each followed by a betting round. After the last betting round, cards are shown down.

Position is arguably more important in triple draw than in any other form of poker. Not only does a player in last position see how the players before him bet, but he also sees how they draw and he sees this three times. This is a game of the nuts and you should rarely play if you can't draw to the nuts. One of the biggest mistakes beginners make is to play this game like single-draw lowball. Hand values here are completely different.

# Five-Card Draw

Five-card draw is the game that was played by the Mississippi river boat gamblers, in part because many modern forms of poker had not yet been invented, and probably in larger part because the game is so conducive to cheating. You don't see other players' cards until the showdown. In the old days, poker wasn't a "grind out a few dollars an hour" game. The idea was to separate the other fellow from his gold mining money as fast as possible and then move on. The deceptively simple and easy to learn draw poker game was ideal for this. The game now is usually called either draw poker or draw.

You also still see draw a lot in movies, because it is very easy for viewers to follow the action. The player holds all five cards up to the camera simultaneously, with no problems for the casual moviegoer having to learn about flops.

Modern draw often uses the *bug* (though in home games, it's more commonly dealt with just the standard 52-card deck). Draw has two varieties, jacks-or-better, and straight draw (where anyone can open on anything; occasionally this more common variety is called "guts to open").

### Table Talk

The **bug** is a not-completely-wild joker. It can serve as an ace or as a card used to complete straights and flushes. Thus the hand A♠-A♥-J♠-J♣-joker is a full house, aces full of jacks. The hand K♥-K♦-Q♥-Q♦-joker, however, is just two pair with an ace kicker. Any four cards to a straight or flush plus the bug makes that hand.

*Jacks-or-better* is usually played limit and with antes. The ante in a $5-$10 game might be $1 per player, so the pot starts with $8. The game has a qualifier: To initiate the betting, you must have at least a pair of jacks. In addition, you will have to prove at some point that what you started with (your openers) were at least jacks.

If you don't open, you can retain your cards to see if anyone behind you does open. You can then call that bet or raise. This kind of game is called pass-and-back in, as opposed to the bet-or-fold format of blind games. The difference is fairly straightforward. In a jacks-or-better game, you're passing on a chance to open a pot.

### The Inside Straight

You don't have to open if you have openers. A player in early position might pass (check) a very good hand in the hopes of being able to check-raise if someone opens behind. This is a risky play, because the pot might be *passed out* (checked all the way around and a new hand begun with carryover antes helping to build a big pot). If you're dealt four kings, pass in the hope of check-raising, and see the hand get passed out, you might pass out the old-fashioned way.

If no one opens, the button moves and everyone adds another ante to the pot. The betting remains at the $5-$10 limit, although the pot is now $16. If no one opens this time, everyone antes once more. At this point the limit doubles. Everyone has $3 in the pot and the limit is $10-$20. This is as big as an unopened pot gets. If no one opens the third time, the fourth (or fifth or sixth …) pot is played without any additional ante. This is called a triple-ante pot and the limit remains $10-$20 until someone finally has openers.

After someone has won a triple-ante pot, play reverts to $5-$10 with everyone anteing again.

After a pot has already been opened, any player can play any hand he wants. If the pot has not yet been opened, the first player to put any money voluntarily into the pot must have at least a pair of jacks.

The penalty for not being able to show openers at the appropriate time is loss of the pot. You can't just show any old hand. A straight, for example, certainly falls in the category of jacks or better. If the opener draws one card and ends up with a straight, he will lose the pot because you can't make a one-card draw, make a straight, and have started with at least a pair of jacks.

Sometimes you might wish to *split openers*. For example, you have J♣-J♦-9♦-6♦-4♦. You opened legitimately enough, but now you wish to draw to the flush. You must show the J♣ to the table and announce that you are splitting openers—and your hand had better have a jack in it at the showdown!

---

**CAUTION**

### Perilous Play _____

One of the biggest mistakes players make in jacks-or-better is playing *shorts* (pairs smaller than jacks). The very worst hand an opener can have is a pair of jacks, so if you enter behind him with a smaller pair, the best you can be is about a 3.25-to-1 underdog. Your chances are even worse against multiple players.

---

As it does in lowball, position offers a great advantage in draw. You can see how many cards opponents discard before your have to reveal your draw. The number of cards they draw helps define their hands.

# Five-Card Stud

Five-card stud is the other "pure" form of poker that survives from poker's early days. The game is commonly played either limit or no-limit, with antes. It's the other game you see in the movies. It was also played frequently on *Star Trek: The Next Generation*, but don't try to learn from this movie: They break almost every poker rule ever created, and as to the strategies employed, well, let's just say we should be glad, for the galaxy's sake, that the crew got most of their bad decisions out of their systems in their weekly poker game. The crew was, without question, the worst collection of poker players in the history of time, space, and fiction.

---

### Poker Lore

In Australia, they like to play draw with a stripped deck: All the cards deuce through six are removed. This changes the card-drawing odds considerably. It becomes more difficult to make a flush than a full house (think about that; if it makes sense, you're on your way to becoming a poker player), and so a flush beats a full house in that game.

A friend of mine once played in such a draw game for five hours without knowing the flush/full house dichotomy—and he was winning $300 in a $5-10 game! This might seem implausible, but both of these hands are so strong that in limit draw you'd play them just about the same. Disaster could strike if someone turned over a full house and you mucked a flush, but my friend never ran into that problem.

---

Each player antes prior to receiving two cards, one dealt face-down and one face-up. The low card is forced to initiate the betting. The bring-in bet is generally a fourth to a third of the minimum bet. Anyone can complete the bet (raise to the minimum), or just call. In succeeding rounds, the highest hand always gets the option to initiate the betting.

Because each player gets only five cards, with no replacements or extras, the average winning hand in five-card stud is quite low compared to almost any other form of poker. Straights and flushes are rare in this game. This is one of the many reasons experts scoff at the entertaining climactic scene in *The Cincinnati Kid*, when a straight flush beats a full house.

If all players play properly, most pots don't have more than one participant for long. It's just too obvious who's leading or trailing. This lack of action also explains why the game is almost dead. Unless you had a pair, why on earth would you continue playing when an opponent is showing an ace?

You should not play past the first round unless your hole card is higher than any exposed card or you have a pair. If you start with a pair and someone pairs on board higher than your pair, you should usually get out, unless the pot is by then so large that you are getting correct pot odds to try to chase your opponent down. If you start with a big hole card, and someone pairs, you should usually get out.

---

**Poker Lore**

In his wonderful book *The Biggest Game in Town,* A. Alvarez tells the story of the half-million-dollar pot that Johnny Moss, the first three-time winner of the main event of the World Series of Poker, lost to Nick "The Greek" Dandalos in 1949. In that game the Greek, as a huge underdog, paired the jack he'd started with in the hole—his only way to win. Luck like that doesn't hold forever. Moss had to get more ammunition from his backer, Benny Binion, but went on to win millions from the Greek. That heads-up game was the precursor to the World Series of Poker.

---

# Other Games

A few other games that you will on rare occasions find in casinos or cardrooms are discussed next. It's not worth your time to learn them until or unless you learn that a local cardroom offers the game.

## Reverse Hold'em

Reverse hold'em differs from regular hold'em in that the flop is one card, the turn is one card, and the river is three cards. The game is usually played limit.

Because a hand is not as well defined with the first two community cards as in regular hold'em at the same stage, players tend to speculate more. Additionally, because three cards hit at once at the end, the lead often changes at the finish. These characteristics attract action players who favor gambling over careful tactical play.

## Double-Flop Hold'em

Players start with two hole cards in double flop, as in regular hold'em. After the first betting round, the dealer puts out two flops simultaneously, each of three cards. After another betting round, the dealer puts out two turn cards, each on its respective board. After another betting round, the dealer puts out two river cards, again each on its respective board. Then there is a final betting round.

At the showdown, each player forms two hands, one consisting of the best five out seven of his cards in combination with the cards of one board, and the other consisting of the best five out seven of his cards in combination with the cards of other board. Because boards are rarely similar to each other, many pots are split, but scoops are common, too.

## Five-Card Omaha

In some cardrooms, when an Omaha table is not full, the players sometimes play five-card Omaha. In this form of the game, players start with five cards instead of four. Just as in regular Omaha, players must use exactly two of their hole cards in combination with three from among the community cards. The game is often played high-low.

Even six-card Omaha can be found, although it rears its ungainly head more commonly in home games than in cardrooms.

## Mississippi Stud

Mississippi stud is played either as a limit game, similar to regular seven-card stud, or pot-limit or no-limit. The game starts like seven-card stud. Each player receives two downcards and one upcard. After the first betting round, two upcards are dealt to each player. Each player now has two downcards and three up cards, which means there is no fourth street bet. After the second betting round, each active player receives another upcard and there is a third betting round. The last card is dealt face up, so each player ends up with two downcards and five upcards. Because of this, it's possible that your best five-card hand might be in full view. Following the seventh street bet is the usual showdown.

## Mexican Stud

Mexican stud is played like five-card stud. It uses a stripped deck, one from which the eights, nines, and tens have been removed. The deck thus contains 40 cards. Because those cards are out, the seven and the jack are treated as consecutive, so that, for example, 5-6-7-J-Q is a straight.

Each player starts with two cards, one face down and one face up. After the first two cards are dealt, betting begins with the high card to the left of the dealer button making a forced opening bet.

After the betting is complete, each player may expose, if he wishes, his downcard. This action must be completed prior to dealing the third card. The third card is dealt up or down depending on whether the player has a hidden card or all cards are exposed. There is a betting round. Players again make the same decision about exposing or not exposing their one downcard.

Upon completion of this action, a fourth card is dealt, followed by a betting round. The fifth card is similarly treated, followed by a final betting round, and a showdown. In this game, a flush beats a full house.

## The Least You Need to Know

◆ You may run into games other than hold'em, seven stud, and Omaha in card-rooms.

◆ Because these other poker variations aren't common, you're better off focusing on common games when first learning.

◆ Because infrequently dealt games often come in several variations, make sure you ask for a complete description of local rules before playing.

# Chapter 6

# Understanding How a Card Casino Operates

## In This Chapter

◆ How does the house make money?

◆ Who are the key casino employees?

◆ What should you tip?

Because cardrooms don't pit their own star players against the public, you may be wondering how they make money. Cardrooms provide many services and they charge for most of them, in essence renting you your seat. They do this by taking money from each pot, or by charging a fee based on the amount of time you play.

Cardrooms provide professional staff. You'll learn here what services floormen, chip runners, and dealers provide. You'll also find a few tips on tipping.

# The Rake: How the House Makes Its Money

Cardrooms provide you with a game in a convenient venue. Cardrooms and casinos are businesses, just as any other, and they need income. Generally they charge their fee, called the *rake*, in one of three ways:

- A percentage of the pot (small-limit games)

- A *button charge* (medium-limit games)

- A *time payment* (high-limit games).

A public cardroom provides all of the following:

- Cards and chips (try paying for your own and see how fast the bills mount)

- The facility (that is, a legally licensed place to play—no complaining spouses or neighbors, no clean-up duties)

- Parking (usually free, usually safe, and no need to worry about complaining neighbors who grow suspicious about the many cars taking their preferred spots)

- Dealers and other professional staff who can settle questions or disputes

- Other players (no need to make phone calls)

- Access to a wide variety of standardized games and limits (allowing you to play the game(s) you want without worrying about learning a bizarre new game and without fending off pleas of "one more round" or "let's double the stakes the last hour")

- Access to playing capital (in the form of check-cashing facilities and cash machines—sometimes a dubious "benefit")

- Guaranteed payment if you win (no need to worry about checks bouncing)

- Storage for playing capital (player banks and safety deposit boxes)

- Security

- Protection from most forms of cheating

- Quality tables and chairs

- Food and beverages (sometimes for a fee, although high-limit players often eat and drink free of charge)

- Almost always, multiple television screens showing sporting events that will distract your opponents (but not you, because you won't let that happen ... right?)

Sometimes the casino or cardroom also provides:

- ◆ Tournaments
- ◆ Jackpots
- ◆ Cash and merchandise drawings

When you start reviewing the lists, the rake starts to look like a pretty good deal and it usually is. It can be very difficult to overcome the rake in low-limit games because it represents a higher percentage of each pot. Typically low-limit players are not focused solely on monetary results.

## Percentage of the Pot

In low-limit games, the rake is frequently 10 percent up to a maximum of $3, although occasionally you will find lower percentages and occasionally you will find higher maximums. The house dealer withdraws the chips from the pot and at the end of the hand, drops the chips into a slot in the table, known, appropriately enough, as the *drop slot*.

### Perilous Play

Some casinos take a larger percentage than others and some have no cap on how much comes out of any one pot. Ask before you sit down. If the rake is too high, you may want to shop around for a better deal. If the cardroom is "the only game in town," you have to decide whether the games are worth it. Not surprisingly, high rakes tend to be found in low- or no-competition areas. Internet poker may help change that.

## Button Charges

Some cardrooms take a fixed amount from each pot, known as the *drop*, often varying depending on the size of the game and the number of players at the table. A $3 per hand (of a certain size) is common.

The drop comes from the player holding the button, who puts up the amount at the same time as the blinds put their chips in. In lower stakes games, the button charge is sometimes part rake, part posted blind.

In many cardrooms, especially at medium limits, the button charge goes entirely to the house and the player on the button must make an entirely separate decision about whether or not he wants to play. Many players feel this is the better rule, since the player who owns the button already has a significant advantage in most games.

### Chopping the Blinds

Many clubs have a policy in hold'em games known as "no flop, no drop." That is, if everyone folds to the opening raise or no one but the blinds play, nothing is taken from the pot for the house. This is a good rule that helps speed the game along and keeps the winner of a small pot from feeling even worse about his minimal victory.

The "no flop, no drop" rule has led to a practice in some states called *chopping the blinds*. If everyone, except the blinds, folds, the two blinds will often agree to chop. This means that each blind takes his money back. This practice deprives the house of a rake on this hand and because heads-up pots tend to be small, often the players would rather move on to the next hand and not incur a rake.

You're under no obligation to chop as long as you're consistent. No one will object if, when you first sit down, you announce "By the way, I just want everyone to know I don't chop." That way, there can be no question of wrongdoing if, the very first time the situation arises, you happen to find yourself holding pocket aces. If you agree to chop the blinds when you first sit down (and that's when you should ask or be asked—things can get a little dicey if you wait until the potential situation first arises), you should chop *every* time.

When you are a cardroom rookie, you might do well to avoid chopping the blinds until your face is a bit more familiar. Although no house rule prevents players from reneging on an agreement to chop, it is considered one of the lower, more disreputable plays in poker.

Chopping the blinds makes good economic sense if the house uses the "no flop no drop" policy or if the game uses a time charge. If you feel you are an excellent heads-up player, though, you're wise not to chop under any circumstances.

## Time Collection

Many cardrooms get their income by charging *time*, a rental fee for use of the facilities and providing of services. Most use time charges for the *top section* games and a rake or drop for the low and medium stakes games.

The *time collection* usually comes at half-hour intervals and depends on the size of the game. The time in a $20-$40 game might be $5 per half hour from each player, but the rate doesn't increase in a straight-line proportion: In an $80-$160 game it might be as little as $15, which would make the time charge an almost insignificant burden on a relative scale. Usually the house dealer halts the game momentarily every half hour to collect the time charge.

In most cardrooms, even though the dealer collects the money, the dealer usually does not physically drop it into the built-in "drop box" until a floorperson confirms the total.

If you have just entered a game when the time arises for time collection, you should remind the dealer (if he's been there all along) that you're a new player and as such don't need to pay time. If a new dealer has come *into the box* after you've sat down (they change every 20 minutes), the previous dealer should have told him something like "Seats two and seven are new players."

If the old dealer hasn't told the new dealer who's who, you need to speak up when it's time to pay time and your fellow players will usually back you up. Just how long you can play without being liable for that half hour's time charge varies from cardroom to cardroom, but you're usually safe if you've been there ten or fewer minutes. It never hurts to ask, even if you've been there a bit longer.

> **Table Talk**
>
> The high-stakes games in many cardrooms are in a special section, often separated from the rest by a barrier, on a raised platform, or in another room. This special area is often called the **top section**. Top section players often enjoy special privileges, such as free food.

> **Table Talk**
>
> When a dealer is working, he is said to be **in the box** once he sits down to do his job. His 20-minute stretch is called a "down," and when his replacement taps him lightly on the shoulder to announce his arrival, that is a "push" (which sends the dealer on to the next table in his shift rotation).

Although you may hate seeing a good dealer depart, there's good cause for the rotation system and it's not just to keep the weaker dealers from frustrating any particular table. In even a moderate-sized cardroom, the dealer rotation system ensures that people playing at one table will only see each dealer once a night (perhaps twice if it's a smaller room or a long night).

By keeping the dealers moving from table to table, cardrooms reduce the risk that any given dealer will wind up pitching cards to a confederate. Such cheating isn't allowed, of course, not even for 20 minutes. Constantly moving the dealers keeps potential trouble to a minimum. It's up to the players and the management to make sure that nothing untoward happens even in a relatively short *down*.

Sometimes in lower stakes games, an extra dollar is taken from each pot above a certain amount to go toward the *bad-beat jackpot*. The jackpot drop goes into a separate fund, often seeded by the club after being hit. Jackpots can run into the tens of thousands of dollars and higher.

> **Table Talk** _____
>
> Many cardrooms have **bad-beat jackpots**, awarded when a specified very strong hand or better gets beaten. A typical distribution is 50 percent to the player who lost the big hand (he gets the biggest share because he suffered the loss), 25 percent to the winning hand, and 25 percent divided among the remaining players at the table. Usually in hold'em, aces full or better must be beaten and both hole cards must play in both hands. The requirements are higher for stud and Omaha. In lowball, a 6-4 must be beaten.

Although the phrase "bad beat" is most often used to describe a particularly unlucky last card defeat, in the jackpot realm, it refers simply to the bad luck involved in losing with a very strong hand. For example, if Andy starts a hold'em hand with 6-6, and Bob starts with J-J, and the final board is 6-J-6-J-7, the betting will be quite spirited, because Andy has four sixes and Bob four jacks. Andy, in losing the hand, wins the lion's share of the bad-beat jackpot.

Normally, jackpot charges are only part of low-stakes games. In California, for example, it is fairly common to see jackpot charges (and hence eligibility) in games that are $9-18 and lower, while $10-20 games (and higher) do not employ the jackpot. This makes a certain amount of sense. It is tough to make a lot of money at low-stakes poker, so having the jackpot out there as a temptation keeps players coming back.

Because the jackpot is so large, relative to the amounts that can be won in low-stakes games, many low-stakes players go out of their way to try to win it. They will play any pocket pair, even making a bad play like calling three bets cold with 3-3, just because of the chance that a pocket pair could lead to four of a kind that get beaten. Smart low-stakes players recognize when someone is putting too much money and energy into trying to win the jackpot, and adopt a style that makes him pay heavily for his greed.

## Tools of the Trade

High-quality casino plastic cards come into the game as a "setup" featuring two differently colored decks to a box. Normally when a new setup is brought in, the plastic seal and jokers have been removed from each deck to save time (unless it's a draw or lowball game, in which case one joker may stay).

Most of the time, when players ask for a new deck or setup, the cards aren't really new. Plastic cards are fairly durable and most requests for deck changes are made for silly, superstitious reasons. Cardrooms take the old cards out of play, but take them into the back and rearrange them so they look like a new deck. Unless a deck is inadvertently or intentionally compromised (say, by a crimp in a card), there's no reason to throw it away.

Do yourself a favor and don't become a slave to mindless superstition. Don't request a deck change just because you lose a pot or two. This generally just annoys the others and slows the game down (a bigger sin in a time charge game). A new deck stands as much chance of worsening your luck as it does of improving it and you'll lose the respect of the game's better players.

# Who's Running This Show, Anyway?

A well-run cardroom usually has a large staff to help make the play pleasant for customers.

## The Floorman

A large cardroom usually has one shift manager and several floormen. Each floorman is in charge of several tables. The floorman seats arriving players, brings deck and setup changes, answers questions, settles disputes, arranges table changes, and ensures the decorum of his section. Sometimes he sells chips and keeps a seat change list, although those functions are handled by other employees in some casinos. If a situation arises that the dealer can't or shouldn't handle, the dealer calls the floorman to the table. A good floorman is often already present when such a situation comes up.

## The Chip Runner

A chip runner sells chips to players as they arrive at a table. Depending on the casino, chip runners may have a locked cabinet where they keep all the chips necessary to meet player needs, carry the chips in a special apron that has multiple deep pockets, or just go to the cashier's cage to handle transactions as needed.

If you run out of chips or want to add to your stack, you can signal a chip runner or ask the dealer to call one for you. Players who have accumulated lots of chips may sell those chips to you, but because of a universal rule that forbids players to take money

**The Inside Straight**

A *chip runner* does not cash checks or handle credit cards. You must go to the cashier's cage for those transactions.

off the table (unless changing tables or leaving), they must keep your cash on the table. If you buy chips from another player, count the stacks in plain sight before you commingle them. Normally players don't intentionally sell short stacks, but mistakes do happen.

## The Dealer

Your most important employee interactions are with dealers. The dealer shuffles and distributes the cards, makes sure that the betting and pots are correct, reminds distracted players that it is their turn to act, handles side pots and split pots, reads and announces winning hands, sometimes sells chips, makes time collections or takes the rake or drop out of each pot, interprets some of the rules, handles minor disputes, brings in new decks as needed, and answers questions. A good dealer keeps the game running smoothly and a poor dealer does not.

Even though a good dealer does his best to read hands properly, anyone can make a mistake. It is each player's responsibility to make sure every pot is awarded and/or split correctly. Whether you should speak up if you see a mistake depends on what kind of mistake it is, and to discuss and categorize all potential errors into "keep quiet, this is a 'one player to a hand' situation" vs. "speak up, this is an 'everyone is supposed to help' situation" would take a full chapter. When you're new, you're better off keeping quiet and leaning toward the "one player to a hand" rule until you're sure that etiquette calls for you to speak up.

A good dealer does not chatter unnecessarily (especially with just one player in the game), watch the game on that huge TV across the room, chew gum, need a shave, or look ungroomed.

A good dealer manages the game but does not micromanage. He gives the players leeway without letting them get out of control. As soon as one player acts, a good dealer does not a fraction of a second later jab his finger at the next player while saying testily, "It's up to you, *sir*; what do you do?" He especially does not do this to someone who clearly knows it's his turn. But if the player is daydreaming or a newcomer, he does gently let the player know it's time to do something.

A good dealer does not attempt to solve disputes that should clearly be left to a floorman, nor does he attempt to discipline unruly drunks. If he's diplomatic and proactive, though, he can head off clashes before they happen.

A good dealer pays attention to the game and is proud of doing his best. He does not accidentally put out a flop before everyone is done with the first round of betting.

Neither does he deal out a flop in a seven-card stud game simply because he wasn't paying attention to what game is being played at his new table.

---

**Poker Lore**

In 2000, I had just finished play for the night at San Jose, California's Bay 101 card-room and I approached a floorperson (Donna) and asked her if she had a moment.

"Of course," she said, taking a deep breath.

"I just want to tell you," I said, "that I think Chuck Agnew is the best I have ever seen at walking that fine line that's needed to manage a game properly. Most dealers seem to think their job begins and ends with pitching cards and, of those who do more, most turn into dictators. Chuck doesn't just show up. He pays attention."

Donna was taken aback. "I know Chuck's good," she said, "but I have to tell you, you really caught me off guard. Ninety-nine percent of the time when someone asks to speak to me, it's because they have a complaint."

Remember to speak up at times when you have something other than a complaint to offer and when you do have a constructive criticism, you're much more likely to be taken seriously.

---

## Tips on Tipping

Do your part to reward and encourage good service from a good dealer and discourage bad service from a poor dealer. Many players automatically *toke* whenever they win a pot, but the dealer deserves no more special credit for a win than he deserves a rebuke when you lose.

That the word "tips" comes from an acronym, "to ensure proper service" is actually an urban legend. It predates acronyms and I'm including this tidbit here just so you can make some money with a bar bet. The concept is still correct, though.

Tips should go to those who earn them. Bad dealers deserve no tips. Average dealers deserve average tips. Good dealers deserve good tips. What makes a dealer good is proper execution of all the little (and sometimes not so little) things described in the preceding section. Consider toking (tipping) $1 on each pot you win when the dealer is average, $2 (or more) when he is exceptional, and—so long as you do tip more to those dealers who are clearly working hard—don't worry too much about tipping dealers who take no pride in their work.

If everyone took this approach to dealer toking, players would soon find the average dealer doing a much better job. Unfortunately, many players are afraid not to tip, even when a dealer is weak. They worry that the dealer might give them bad cards or bad rulings. While you shouldn't tempt fate by trying to make enemies out of dealers, because an enemy can make life difficult for you, a dealer isn't going to risk his job by cheating just because you didn't tip. If you don't like a ruling, you can always take it up with the floorman.

If somehow you wind up with a certain dealer as an enemy or if you can't work past a superstitious belief that one dealer is unlucky for you, you can always choose that down for a meal break or a walk.

Good dealers may understand if you don't toke when losing heavily, even though your tipping shouldn't be confined to winning nights; they will not understand if you never toke.

A good dealer can only help you in the long run by putting out more hands per hour, keeping your table happy and running smoothly, reading hands properly, and splitting pots correctly. If a dispute comes up when you have treated a dealer fairly and professionally, he will treat you fairly in describing the pertinent events to the floorman who gets called over.

If a floorman helps you or simply does a good job in general of keeping his section running smoothly, you might give him $5 or $10 at the end of your session. If you know that the floorman generally does a good job, you can tip up front when the floorman puts you on the game list or gets you your chips. A properly motivated floorman might keep a closer eye on the table change list for a player who has toked, or who regularly tokes. It's not quite a bribe; it's just human nature to provide better service for regular tippers.

## The Least You Need to Know

♦ Cardrooms provide a service and get paid for that service via the rake.

♦ The rake can be charged as a percentage of the pot, a button charge, or a time fee.

♦ Cardrooms in some states offer bad-beat jackpots if you lose with a very powerful hand, but only in low stakes games.

♦ Cardroom staff help make your playing experience pleasant and profitable; know how to encourage excellence.

# Chapter 7

# Finding Your Way to the People Who Play

## In This Chapter

- ◆ To find opponents, first understand them
- ◆ The people who play poker
- ◆ Selecting your games
- ◆ Deciding when to play
- ◆ Choosing where to play

Your ability to win or lose at poker is defined almost as much by your opponents' skill as it is by your own; indeed, once you reach a certain minimum level of competence, you can make a rational argument that your winning chances depend *more* on your opponents' skill than on your own.

At an even more basic level, you can't even play poker unless you can find some opponents. Unlike a casino blackjack game, which will commence anytime you are ready to play, a casino poker game can't start unless at least two people are willing to play. The ability to find opponents who are less skilled than you lies at the very heart of your poker hopes. Let's take a look at how you can and should find the right opponents.

# To Find The Right Opponents, Understand Their Motivations

People play poker for two main reasons: social and financial. Sometimes people play for both reasons; however, for most players, one reason is of primary importance. Before you decide that a highly developed sense of ethics and poker cannot go together, think again. Some highly ethical people *love* poker because they get to indulge sneaky desires within a framework where such conduct is not merely ethical but praiseworthy (within certain limits). With their less "evolved" traits safely exercised, they can engage in completely honorable personal and professional relationships.

## It's a Social Thing

The thrills and excitement of poker are often part and parcel of the social reasons to play poker. Making a big bet on a good hand and getting called generates an adrenaline rush. This rush is equaled for some by making a big bet as a bluff and getting away with it. For many players that rush is more important to them than winning.

For some players, the social aspect of poker includes the camaraderie. For people who do not have very exciting social lives, sitting at a friendly game takes the place of the social life they lack. For others, poker games supplement their social lives.

## It's the Money, Honey

For some people, the main reason to play poker is to win money. They approach poker like a job. Many find out that the game is not as easy or as glamorous as they first envisioned, because their images were formed through dramatic movie or television scenes; just as the hour-to-hour life of a lawyer or policeman isn't as exciting as television would have us believe, so too goes life at the poker tables. As the old card-room saying goes, "It's a tough way to make an easy living."

# Who Plays Poker?

We are in the Golden Age of Poker. You have much more access to all kinds of poker games than you did even a few years ago. As recently as the 60s, most areas did not even have poker. Thirty years ago, poker existed only in a few western states and in Europe—primarily in England. Those who wanted to play elsewhere had to find private games and they were a lot harder to find then than now.

Now more than half the states have public cardrooms and casinos. Many European countries have poker and it is growing more popular there all the time. Poker flourishes in Canada and Costa Rica. It is expanding in Australia, New Zealand, and Russia, and many other countries are joining in.

## Find It Online

Perhaps the greatest innovation for poker is the online version of the game, which has the potential to dwarf other variations. As of this writing, one popular site sometimes has 25,000 players testing their luck simultaneously (albeit at different tables!), and by the time this book reaches you, that number might be twice as high. Even the biggest brick-and-mortar cardrooms, the 200-table "poker factories" of Southern California, can only accommodate 2,000 simultaneous players, and they usually have fewer.

## The Great Melting Pot

The players in private games include literally anyone. Whether a group of dentists or Supreme Court justices, players often tend to come from the same social stratum. Women play (currently they comprise about 10 percent of players; we generally use male pronouns in the book simply for stylistic ease), as do people of all ethnicities and ages. Cardrooms and casinos are even more of a melting pot. I've played in the same game with movie stars and gas station attendants, renowned professors and the CEOs of Fortune 500 companies, motorcycle gang members and former Mob members (as of this writing, I've never played in a game that had one each of those groups ... but it could happen!).

Everyone is equal in a poker game. The high school dropout might win all the money from the world-renowned professor of psychology, and the homemaker with *card sense* might bust them both!

**Table Talk**

**Card sense** is an acute awareness of everything that happens. Its owner doesn't narrow his focus to only his own hand. Card sense implies the ability to act on observations and think on-the-fly. You must have imagination in playing your own hand and a strong memory for reconstructing opponents' hands and betting patterns. Card sense lets you play the same cards differently in different situations. Someone without card sense usually plays the same cards the same in all situations. There's a word for such players: losers (at least financially).

Given all that, the answer to "Who plays poker?" is ... everyone! Poker is probably the most widely played game in the world.

# How Many Varieties of Poker Should You Play?

Beginners and those who have been playing for awhile often ask how many varieties of poker they should play. Some pros specialize in one particular form of poker, while others play a wide variety and are experts in them all.

> **Poker Lore**
>
> Although well-heeled gamblers play stunning stakes, even the world's richest man—Bill Gates—sometimes plays poker. He usually plays no higher than $3-6. There's no rule that says you have to risk a significant percentage of your income to enjoy poker.

Before you can answer the question, you may need to ask and answer another: Do you want to play socially or seriously—that is, for the companionship or for the money?

If you play exclusively in social games, then you should be familiar with a wide variety of games, some of which are very strange. To hold your own, you should be able to jump into any weird variant your friends can devise. But if you've played Southern Cross, for example, you should have no trouble with twin beds.

However, if you play in serious games—both private games and in cardrooms—the best path to success is specialization: Learn one game and learn it well before trying to learn another.

> **The Inside Straight**
>
> Sometimes the best game in the house is not the one in which you specialize, and that's an argument for learning to play more than one game well. A hold'em specialist may look across the room, and there in the $15-$30 seven-stud game is the live one that last week sat down in his hold'em game and lost $5,000 in one session. If that specialist played seven stud a little better, he could "follow the money" and enjoy another profitable opportunity.

## Mix It Up

Some cardroom players have an idea that they need to be expert in all games, because the very highest stakes games are almost always *mixed games*.

**Table Talk**

Poker games at the highest limits are often **mixed games**. This is a format in which several forms of poker are played in rotation, usually either a half hour of each or a round of each. A mixed game usually consists of between two and five games from a list that includes limit hold'em, Omaha, Omaha eight-or-better, razz, seven-card stud (high), seven-card stud high-low, triple-draw, and/or lowball. Mixed games are also called *rotation games*.

These very high limit games usually are $200-$400 and up, so they aren't something you'll encounter anytime soon. Such a game requires a bankroll in excess of $50,000. Participants play rotation games to keep specialists from dominating. For example, a world champion hold'em player might want to sit in, but if the players know that his triple-draw game is not very good, they will be sure to throw that into the mix.

Because a beginner is not going to play at such high levels for quite a while, you can choose to specialize without fear; add other games after you are comfortable with one.

**Perilous Play**

Prove to yourself you can regularly beat middle-limit games before looking higher. Good players aspire to winning one to two *big bets* per hour (a big bet is $20 in a $10-20 game). If you're barely scraping by at less than half a bet per hour, you're probably not ready to test higher limits. Don't start playing several games just because you think you might one day play the highest-stakes games in the world. There will be time enough for that later.

# Cross-Training

When you play only one form of poker, you may start playing on autopilot and that won't help your learning process.

A good poker player tries to learn something every time he plays. Playing an unfamiliar form of poker may help you focus. If you're primarily a hold'em player, when you sit in on a seven stud game, you will be forced to concentrate on everything that is going on—at least partly because the game is not so familiar. If you later bring that concentration back to your hold'em game, you will probably enjoy the results.

# When to Play Poker

You can play poker whenever you like. Casinos in Nevada and New Jersey are open 24 hours, as are most cardrooms in California. Many Indian casinos are open all the time, as well as some riverboats with cardrooms. In some cases, you are limited by operating hours, because some close for a few hours at night. Some casinos in Europe close for eight hours or so. But with the explosion of Internet poker, you truly can play 24 hours a day, 7 days a week, 365 days a year.

A better question is when *should* you play? If you're playing for the social aspect of the game, evenings and weekends are best. If you want to keep those hours available for other kinds of social activities, you can play during the daytime; however, you can expect to run into more serious players then.

By the same token, if you're focused on financial return and you don't have obligations that restrict you to specific times, evenings and weekends are better times to play because the social players are there to have a good time. They're happy to give you their money, as long as you're willing to socialize in return.

## Something in Return

Many people play poker for social reasons and although it's going too far to say they don't care if they lose, it's probably reasonable to say they don't worry about it excessively. They figure that they're paying for entertainment. They may rationalize that it costs them no more to indulge in an evening of poker than it would to go to a movie or have some other night out on the town (and if all they lose is the price of a movie ticket, they aren't rationalizing).

If you regale them with a string of insults like "How could you play that hand … Didn't you know I had a big hand … You were way behind all the way … You're an idiot," you may feel better for getting all that off your chest, but all you've done is prove to the real professionals that you're a rank amateur. If you were really a good player, you'd know to keep your mouth shut and you'd know that sooner or later, the same bad play would cost the social player dearly.

You will win a lot from these people if you treat them kindly and with dignity. Just because someone loses at poker doesn't mean he is an idiot. He may make 10 times as much as you and not mind dropping a few hundred—or a few thousand—as long as he has a good time. Don't teach lessons at the table. Don't berate those who beat you, no matter how poorly they played and how little justification they had for being in the pot.

When you lose a pot to a bad beat, don't complain about your poor luck. Say "Nice hand," and say it sincerely—or say nothing at all (an insincere "nice hand" can be more insulting than a direct attack). After all, the hand itself is nice. You're not lying about that. It just happens to have beaten you.

You may not like the circumstances that brought about your loss, but realize that if you berate the winner of the pot, he may not try to defy the odds against you the next time—if indeed you're lucky enough to have a shot at a "next time" against him. After all, he doesn't want to hear you complaining and he doesn't want a lecture. Do you really want all your opponents to play well against you?

### The Inside Straight

Giving lessons that no one has asked for is one of the worst things a player can do. The "teacher" is usually stinging from a perceived bad beat and lashes out by sarcastically questioning the winner's abilities. The lecturer is often wrong in his assessment; but even if he is correct, why would he want to teach his opponent to play correctly? Does he think that if the opponent plays better he will start making more money from the opponent? Does he want to improve the play of everyone at the table? There's a nice saying that covers the situation: "Don't tap on the aquarium."

Find out something about your neighbors and engage them in conversation if they seem interested. Many players are there for companionship that they couldn't find elsewhere and they don't mind paying for it in the form of losing a little.

Don't pry, but be pleasant. If you discover something that interests the player to your right and you know something about that topic, talk about it. Of course, don't disrupt the game and don't talk to your neighbor when she is involved in a hand.

Because your "new friend" probably likes the sound of his own voice more than he likes the sound of yours, ask questions and listen to his answers. Popular attendees of cocktail parties and therapists know that, by being good listeners, they can appear to be the best conversationalists in the world. Most people don't mind losing to someone they see as kind and respectful.

## Where Can and Should You Play Poker?

You should play poker where you feel comfortable and in a place that suits your temperament.

If your main reason for playing is social, a friendly home game is probably your ideal venue. A small cardroom also fits the bill, particularly if you're a little more serious

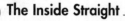

**The Inside Straight**

Some say that the best game in a cardroom is not the biggest game in the house, but the second biggest. People with ego problems feel they always have to be seen in the biggest game and that it would be demeaning to step down. However, because that game might be too serious, the wild gamblers sometimes feel more comfortable one level down.

**Table Talk**

A **railbird** is someone who hangs on the rail (sometimes literally a rope or a wall) watching the action, often too broke to get into a game. Someone who just busted out of a game is said to "be on the rail," and often looks for a loan or stake.

about the play, but still are interested in the social aspect. In a large cardroom, you're probably best off in the smaller limits. You might not want to play in the very smallest games, which are sometimes full of desperate players grimly hanging on to the dregs of their bankrolls.

Such a game might be filled with *railbirds* who manage to scrape together only enough to get into such a small game, those with gambling problems who can afford only small stakes and very tight players who don't want to risk much. For these reasons, it is generally the tightest game in the house. Such a game might also have so prohibitively high a rake in relation to the size of the game that it is virtually impossible for anyone to win. You're better off moving a level or two.

If your main reason for playing is the money, then you want to be in a serious private game, a cardroom, or online.

A serious private game may have the advantage of a stable of resident contributors (live ones), but it might not always be accessible. Also, your style of play may not be compatible with those of the regulars and you may not feel welcome there.

You also have to be more concerned about being cheated in a private game than in a cardroom, because private games do not have the elaborate protections for players that cardrooms and casinos have. Many cardrooms have cameras trained on every game, with a tape constantly being made and all tapes archived for at least a day. The tape can be examined if ever there is a question of impropriety.

Usually the camera is concealed behind an overhead one-way mirror, or positioned unobtrusively behind a smoky plastic hemisphere extending from the ceiling. Cardrooms also have experienced personnel who know what to look out for and are always on the watch. The best dealers are trained to handle suspicious circumstances, but you cannot depend on them to intervene; dealers depend on player tips and cheaters are often excellent tippers. Their tips aren't quite bribes, but they do earn them the benefit of the doubt from casino personnel who appreciate their money.

In a regular cardroom (not an online one), you can play in any game and no one can bar you because you play well. If players don't like your play, they can always leave, but new players are always waiting to take the empty seats. Many cardrooms are sensitive to and do not permit abusive behavior, although the levels of abuse that are tolerated vary dramatically from room to room and state to state.

Online cardrooms are perfect for players who want to drop in anytime, without waiting or having to go anywhere. Portable computers and ubiquitous wireless connections (Wi-Fi) now allow play from almost anywhere.

You can probably find a larger selection of games on the Internet than anywhere else. You can play everything from hold'em to draw poker (rarely found in brick-and-mortar cardrooms) to triple-draw lowball (never found in brick-and-mortar cardrooms at small stakes). You can find limit, pot-limit, and no-limit games. You can find stakes from 1¢-2¢ to $100-$200; you can get in for under $1 to more than $1,000.

Poker is anywhere and everywhere. The revolution is now. Thanks to the popularity of television shows depicting ongoing and famous tournaments and to the successes of online players in brick-and-mortar tournaments, the Golden Age is just beginning. This is one Golden Age that is likely to keep on growing for quite awhile, creating opportunities for players everywhere.

## The Least You Need to Know

- ◆ Understand why you play poker.
- ◆ Know what games to play and why.
- ◆ Know when and where to play.

# Chapter 8

# Before You Bet, Don't Forget

## In This Chapter

- ◆ Identifying common poker myths and misunderstandings
- ◆ Understanding tilt
- ◆ Avoiding classic dangers

Before you begin learning specific poker strategies, it's important for you to learn some basic poker safety concepts, classic errors, myths, and math.

In a sense, you will unlearn much of what may have filtered down to you through playing in or observing poker games in your youth or information you may have picked up from an even more unreliable source: television and the movies. Let's examine some conventional—and some unconventional—poker wisdom.

## Advice That Applies to All Forms of Poker

Because poker plays such an intricate role in many American myths, legends, and stories, there are few people who don't have at least a passing familiarity with the game. Unfortunately, the elements that make for a good story don't always conform to reality and the lessons we learn from legends and movies don't always serve us well when it comes time to risk our own money playing. Probably the most famous poker scene in movie history is the climactic showdown hand in *The Cincinnati Kid*, but while it makes for great theatre, the characters make so many mistakes in the hand that good players have a hard time avoiding convulsing with laughter when they watch the scene.

## Luck Versus Skill: Is Poker Gambling?

In one sense, it would be absurd to claim that playing poker for money is anything other than gambling. Unlike chess or even checkers, which can be played at the highest levels without a single dollar being risked, poker without money is an empty pursuit. If your opponent isn't risking something by remaining in a hand, he has very little incentive to play correctly and throw away a hand whose chances of improving enough to win are slight. Although it is possible to learn a few extremely basic poker lessons in free games, you're more likely to pick up bad habits in such games.

### The Inside Straight

If a game truly involves skill, someone somewhere is making a living at it. You may see books written by alleged roulette or craps experts, but there is no such thing as a "professional roulette player" or a "professional craps player"—at least not unless that player is a cheat. You can reduce the house advantage in some games by playing well, but that's not the same as winning long-term. If a pro can make a living, a skilled amateur can win consistently.

Because money must be involved and because who gets to take the money home can change on the turn of a single card, you'll have a hard time claiming that poker isn't gambling. At the same time, you'll hear some poker professionals dryly respond to the "Is poker gambling?" question by saying, "Not the way I play it," over the long run, they'll be right.

## The Long Run Is Longer Than You Think

One of the biggest problems new players have in assessing their progress and the likelihood that good results will continue is that "the long run" is far longer than most people think. As startling as this may seem, it's difficult to draw accurate long-term conclusions based on anything less than several hundred hours of play. If your typical evening's poker session is 5 hours long, it will be difficult for you to accumulate reliable data until you have played 50 or more sessions.

This may seem like an unreasonably long time, but the reality is that one big hand can skew your results for one 5-hour session. One outrageously lucky or unlucky card can turn a winning session into a losing one, and vice-versa. A few lucky hands might convince you your *hourly rate* for $20-40 hold'em is $20/hour, while your actual *hourly rate* might be $5 or even minus $10/hour. Only after you have played so many hands that your luck has evened out can you possibly gauge your *established hourly rate*.

This doesn't mean that if you get your head handed to you five times in a row, you shouldn't suspect that you're in over your head. If you start right off with five big losing sessions, there's a very good chance that you are indeed in over your head, especially if you're new to the game and don't have other empirical evidence to the contrary.

> **Table Talk**
>
> A player calculates his **hourly rate** by adding up his total net win or loss and dividing that by his total number of hours played.

You should not go out and play for a total of 20 or 30 hours, take your net result, and assume you now have a reliable "established hourly rate" figure. Yet you will find many new players who win $1,000 in 20 hours of play in a $10-20 hold'em game and who make the assumption that this short term result of winning $50 an hour ($20 X 50 = $1,000) will hold true for the long run.

These players get a rude awakening when they lose $500 in their next session. Now they've played 25 total hours, but have won only $500. Their "hourly rate" has dropped to $20 per hour ($500 divided by 25 hours = $20/hour). Three losing sessions later, they find that their hourly rate is a $15 loss. Do they stop and try to learn? Usually not; they "know" that their "real" hourly rate is a $50 win and they've just been unlucky lately.

Even for a more advanced player, the ability to separate the luck and skill elements in short-term results is quite difficult. However, those players who are capable of honest self-assessment in other areas of their lives stand a much better chance of performing accurate assessments in poker.

> **The Inside Straight**
>
> One of the most famous "wise" answers in mythology came from the Oracle at Delphi, who gave advice that also serves as probably the single most important thing any poker player can do toward improving: "Know thyself." By honestly assessing your weaknesses and strengths, you'll not only continue to learn, but you'll find yourself sitting in games where you have a chance to win.

## Assessing Your Play

One of poker's most golden rules is quite straightforward: "If something keeps happening, it's probably happening for a reason, even if you aren't able to identify the reason." If you keep losing in a game where you believe yourself more skilled than the opposition, one or more of the following three things is happening:

◆ You are the victim of a bad run of luck (something that becomes less and less likely the longer your losing streak continues).

◆ You are less skillful than you believe (or your opponents are more skillful than you believe).

◆ You are being cheated.

It's human nature to look to the first explanation for the answer, because we don't like to admit the possibility that we're in over our heads. Yet it is the player who is willing to consider the possibility that he is being outplayed who has the best chance of eventually coming out on top. That player will do everything possible to try to improve. To improve, he'll read more poker books and remain more alert when he plays. He'll not only try to take in more information about his opponents, but he'll also be willing to try analyzing it in different ways. He'll consider the possibility that he is inadvertently revealing too much information about his own game/cards, and will look for ways to stop the bleeding.

If, on the other hand, you look for the easy way out and blame your losses exclusively on bad luck, you may not have to swallow the bitter short-term pill of inadequacy, but you will likely have to remain on a long-term diet of losses; only those players who work at it make big and steady gains.

---

### Poker Lore

Poker players are famous for their love of sports betting; any casino in the world that has both a sports book and a poker room has the two next to each other. One of the most important poker lessons comes from the world of baseball. Branch Rickey, the General Manager of the then Brooklyn Dodgers, is famous for saying that "Luck is the residue of design." You will find that the harder you study, the luckier you'll appear, because you will be putting yourself into positions where luck can complement your skill.

---

A player who blames luck for his losses will probably improve a little over time, simply through osmosis and experience, but it's possible to practice one's mistakes for years. If you want to improve, keep your ego in your pocket; eventually you won't have to blame your losses on bad luck, because you won't lose very often.

# How Poker Differs from Other Casino Games

Casinos offer a few other games where skill plays a role large enough for the expert player to reasonably expect to win long term. Those games include video poker, blackjack, and sports betting. Nonetheless, there is a fundamental difference between poker and those games: In poker, players compete against each other. In video poker, blackjack, and sports betting, players compete against the casino.

Casinos are not social service organizations; they have no interest in distributing their wealth to their customers. They offer games that allow the average customer to win occasionally, and the expert customer to win more frequently, solely because those wins are the carrots that lure losing players back time after time.

If you are truly expert in video poker, blackjack, or sports betting, though, you will quickly find that casinos will either cut you off entirely (most people have heard stories of blackjack players getting barred), or reduce the amount you are allowed to bet (the most common approach taken with winning sports bettors).

---

### Poker Lore

One of the most famous series of sessions in modern poker history took place in 2002 and 2003 at the Bellagio in Las Vegas, when a Dallas banker, Andy Beal, (playing with his own money) asked to play against the world's best players at stakes that started at $3,000-$6,000, and that wound up at $30,000-$60,000. The banker lost almost $10,000,000 in a single week (and millions more in other visits during this stretch), to players whose reputations earned them the financial opportunity of a lifetime—precisely the opposite of what would have happened if they had been known to be the world's best blackjack players, because the best-known blackjack experts get barred from play. In 2004, Beal returned and played for stakes as high as $100,000-$200,000!

---

In poker, the casino has no such fear of a top player. Casinos make their money in poker by taking a small percentage of each pot (the rake), or by charging players an hourly fee for time played. In essence, the casino is merely providing a service—a table, chips, players, a dealer, and a guarantee of getting paid if you win—and rents you your chair to collect for that service.

Therefore, while top players might occasionally wear out their welcomes in private games, they are always welcome in casinos. Indeed, average players often spot a famous player in a casino poker game and decide to buy in, merely so they can tell their friends back home that they "played against Doyle Brunson" or "won a hand against Phil Hellmuth." So what if the *session* turns out to be a losing one? There are always more ways to get money ... but to these amateurs, the story they get is priceless.

**Table Talk**

A **session** is the amount of time you spend sitting in one poker game, from the time you buy in until the time you cash out. Many players get themselves into trouble by focusing on session results rather than long-term results. Players often make risky plays near the end of a session, hoping to get lucky and come out on top; the more likely result is a bad session instead of a moderately weak one.

**The Inside Straight**

What would you rather do: win $50 in each of four sessions and lose $300 in the fifth, or lose $50 in each of four sessions, but win $300 in the fifth? If you make the second choice, you've won $100 instead of losing $100. Players who treat life as "one long session" don't need to take big risks just to avoid a losing session. They play their best game all the time and let the results take care of themselves. There's a word for players who treat life as one long session: winners.

For most players, it's far wiser to enter a large tournament, such as one of the events at the *World Series of Poker*, and get their stories out of tournament play instead of money play. See Chapter 19 to learn how such opportunities can arise; for now, it's enough to know that in a tournament, your downside risk is limited strictly to your entry fee and buy-in; in a money game, you can lose as much as you have with you.

# Tilt Is Doom in Pinball and Poker

You can lose still more if you use ATM cards, credit card cash advance machines, or cash checks. If you get on a bad losing streak in a cash game, you are vulnerable to *going on tilt* and your plans for how much you are willing to lose for a good story can go right out the window.

**Table Talk**

When a player **goes on tilt,** he has suffered an all-too-common loss of emotional control. Players typically go on tilt as a result of one hugely unlucky moment or a series of mildly unlucky results.

It's entirely possible for a highly skilled player to have long-term results that are far worse than someone whose technical skills are inferior, if the technically skilled player is vulnerable to tilt. One bad session can wipe out results from dozens of good ones. It's difficult to learn emotional control from a book, but if you ever find yourself at a poker table and hear the words "I don't care" echoing in your head, you're probably on tilt; the smartest thing you can do is take your loss and get out of the game as quickly as possible.

You won't make as many stirring comebacks this way, but players who are on tilt almost invariably start making bad decisions. They are easy targets for those who recognize the tell-tale signs of tilt: visible anger, a sudden departure from a usual style, and playing far more hands than is advisable.

> **Perilous Play** _____
>
> There are few poker stories with more predictable endings than those that begin, "He was on tilt, and ..." The "and ..." invariably finishes with, "he lost everything he had." Players who are on tilt often become self-destructive and can be heard making comments like, "Playing good starting cards hasn't worked, so I'll try playing bad starting cards." Unfortunately, a player on tilt lacks, by definition, the good judgment to stop. Sometimes taking a short walk is enough to cool you down. If that doesn't work, it might at least give you enough judgment to leave.

It is certainly possible to make comebacks in poker; just because you lose for the first hour or two of a session doesn't mean you won't come out on top. Players who have retained their emotional control and who continue to play their regular game make the vast majority of such comebacks. When you're on tilt, you lack the skills necessary to win and only an extraordinary run of cards can bring you back.

## Winning and Losing Streaks

While a player on tilt is going to suffer a losing session, he doesn't necessarily have to go on a losing streak. If you lose several sessions in a row, you need to start asking yourself some tough questions. Are you playing against players who are too strong for you? Are you playing less than your best?

The answers to these questions aren't necessarily "yes" just because you're on a losing streak. Even the best players run into streaks where the cards don't favor them. The key is to avoid letting your inevitable run of bad cards cost you more than it should.

Knowing that even great players can lose for weeks should help you avoid tilt, and understanding that the cards have no memory will also help. By that I mean that a bad run of cards can stop at any time, and if you haven't changed the way you play, you'll be able to take advantage of the good cards when they come.

If, on the other hand, you start to believe that the run of bad cards won't stop, you're likely to start playing scared and a scared player is usually a losing player.

Just as it's a mathematical certainty that you'll encounter a run of bad cards sooner or later in your poker career, it's equally likely that you will encounter a run of good cards. The key to taking advantage of this is similar to what you must do when you run into a streak of bad cards: Don't change the way you play, other than making adjustments based on your *table image*.

### The Inside Straight

Image often becomes the reality in poker. Someone who is perceived as being on a run of bad luck becomes a target; he can't bluff anyone. Similarly, someone who has been hot becomes feared and avoided and his run of good cards enables him to win even more pots than the cards entitle him to. It is important to understand what your current table image is when betting. Even though you don't want to make fundamental changes in your style because of a run of cards, you can and should make minor adjustments to take advantage of, or reduce the damage from, your current image.

Here is another of those pesky situations for which the correct way to proceed isn't clear. Paradoxically, while perhaps one of the most important choices you can make is to not alter your game because the cards have or have not been coming in, you must consider making minor and temporary adjustments because of your *table image*.

### Table Talk

**Table image** doesn't win or lose many pots by itself, but it can come close. You earn your image over a period of time: Are you a strong player or a weak player? Are you a bluffer or a tight player? Are you lucky or unlucky? Your image can change over the course of just a few minutes, if table events draw enough attention to you. Your image is a factor of how you should be perceived and how you actually are perceived ... if you are perceived at all! Many weaker players pay no attention to their opponents and focus exclusively on their own hands.

You must be able to judge not only what your image should be, but whether your opponents are paying enough attention to what is happening to consider your image. Someone who has a *tight* image is usually viewed as playing only when he has strong cards, so that person is in a good position to steal a pot here and there with a bluff. However, if your opponents aren't paying attention, your image can't help.

> **Table Talk**
>
> **Tight players** play only premium starting hands. They understand that the player who leads at the start tends to stay that way and don't like to get involved in a hand without proper ammunition. Tight players tend to win a good percentage of those few hands they get involved in, partly because they start with good cards and partly because their infrequent bluffs get more respect. Usually the pots they win are small because opponents respect their bets and don't chase after them.

The pattern of playing tight for the first 20 minutes or so to establish a tight image and then trying to take advantage of that image is so common that it's almost comical. The problem with this approach is that many players aren't paying attention to your early tight play, and if they are savvy enough to be paying attention, they are probably experienced enough to know exactly why you're doing it. You can't develop a subtle image in 20 minutes.

Sometimes you can develop a hot or cold image in that much time, though. If you turn over a series of hugely strong hands, people will notice, just as they will notice a series of spectacularly unsuccessful bluffs. In general, an image is something you develop over a series of months or years and it only changes if people are paying attention or something calls their attention to it in dramatic fashion.

# How Long Should You Play?

If you play in a regular weekly home game, you don't have many decisions to make about how long you should play. The starting time is set and, within certain limits (discussed more fully in Chapter 15), the quitting time is also set.

Players who win early and then leave quickly (sometimes called "hit and run artists") are generally not invited back to regular home games, although players who have lost a tidy sum over a period of time are usually not breaching any protocols if they want to leave before the traditional quitting time.

Outside of such a structured weekly home environment, decisions about when to keep playing and when to quit are much more difficult.

# When to Quit and When to Stay

Hopefully you've already accepted the principles of poker inertia and momentum: A player who has started off winning has a better chance of winning from that point forward than a player who has started off losing, primarily because he has a good table image and has no reason to go on tilt.

The converse principle also applies: A player who has started off losing for the first hour or two is usually more likely to continue losing for the remainder of the session than he is at the start of a fresh session. His table image isn't ideal, and even if he isn't on tilt, he may not be playing with complete confidence.

Does it make sense, then, to play only for an hour or two, and then leave if you're losing? If you're on tilt, the answer is yes, but there's a wide gulf between being down a few dollars and being on tilt. There's even a significant gulf between being down *a lot* of dollars and being on tilt. In the first instance, you've had nonideal results, but unless you've allowed yourself to crumble, the only uphill battle you're fighting is your table image—and we've already seen that many people won't be paying much attention to your "current" table image.

Quite a few players actually find that they play better after losing a little bit because the losses force them to bring more focus to the table. They may have fallen behind because unfocused early *loose* play caused them to play a few too many hands and when Lady Luck fails to bail them out from this less than optimal playing style, they tighten up their play.

**Table Talk**

**Loose players** employ a style that is quite different than that of tight players. They are willing to gamble more—not necessarily playing bad cards, but at least hands that fall into the speculative category. Their chip stacks tend to fluctuate up and down much more than those of tight players, and when they win a pot, it is often large because other players give them action. They suffer more beats at the end of hands, though, because those players giving them action will often catch up with them. Their bluffs tend not to work well.

Most players have to drive a significant distance to get into a poker game and often have to wait a while to get a seat, so quitting the moment they get off to a slow start isn't a practical option. As long as you let early losses sharpen your focus rather than put you on tilt, there's nothing wrong with continuing to play after a few setbacks.

There are few aspects of poker where the advice "know thyself" is more important than when it comes to deciding whether you should stay in a poker game or leave. Only you can gauge whether you are playing well and have simply been the victim of some rough luck. Only you can judge whether you can play well after you've fallen behind.

If, for example, you know yourself well enough to know that once you've fallen behind by 30 big bets or more ($180 in a $3-6 game, $900 in a $15-30 game), you're not capable of playing your best poker, you can use that level as your leave/stay benchmark. Even though you may not be on full tilt when you are down 30 big bets, you may know that you're just depressed enough to lose a certain sharpness, and that sharpness is the edge you need to win.

Only experience will tell you whether you tend to lose it at a certain loss level. Some players never encounter this problem and are capable of playing their best game all the time. If you find that description fits you, great—you can continue to play until some other reason sends you home.

Watch out for the converse danger: Many players find themselves unable to keep from playing almost every hand if they get ahead, and end up giving much of their winnings back.

The ideal poker player's game doesn't deteriorate because he's down or up; however, we aren't all ideal players and if you know you have such a weakness, it's probably better to respect it. Over time, you can work on correcting it, but that process can be expensive unless you remain focused.

Why else might you leave a game? Your own common sense can tell you when job or family responsibilities should send you home for the night. Outside of those important considerations, most of the leave or stay factors come not from you, but from those around you.

A financially motivated player whose own game doesn't deteriorate makes his leave-or-stay decision based on how good the game is. If the opposition (or at least some significant percentage of it) is weak, or if one player is on tilt enough to be *throwing a party* for everyone else, you stay because the prospects for winning more are good.

If, on the other hand, the likely sources of chips (big winners who might get careless with their winnings, and losers who have given up) have left the game and the only remaining players are both talented and playing well, there is little financial incentive to keep playing. The true pro uses this distinction. He plays on when the prospects for winning more are good and he moves on when the prospects for winning more are bad.

**Table Talk**

Someone who **throws a party** isn't out buying hats and party favors, although his opponents might be tempted to do so after the session ends. A party thrower is single-handedly losing so much money that he makes the game a winning proposition for everyone else there. Every opponent may not win, but with the big loser donating far more than the rake is taking out of the game, everyone else finds himself in a positive equity situation.

## Do You Have a Gambling Problem?

Although a complete analysis of problem gambling is beyond the scope of this book, it's easy to identify warning signs of a potential gambling problem. If you find that any of the following statements apply to you, you may have a problem; the more that apply, the more likely it is that you should be avoiding gambling in general, and poker in particular:

- You go on tilt easily and remain in the game when tilted.

- You frequently utilize ATM or credit card cash advance machines, ask people for loans, or take other steps to borrow money to play.

- You play with money you cannot afford to lose.

- When you win, you disrespect your winnings and blow the money on foolish expenditures.

- If something comes up that prevents you from playing on your usual night, you experience severe discomfort.

- You argue strongly with those who are close to you about the frequency and/or impact of your gambling.

- You lie to those close to you about what you are going out to do or about your results.

Poker can be a wonderful hobby, but if you find that more than one of these applies to you, seek help.

## The Least You Need to Know

- Poker involves both luck and skill.

- It is difficult to draw absolute conclusions with short-term results data.

- The best players are honest with themselves about their strengths and weaknesses.

- If you can't stop when you go on tilt, you risk losing everything.

# Chapter 9

# Important Strategic Considerations in Poker

## In This Chapter

◆ Problems involved with coming from behind

◆ The importance of position

◆ Bluffing is both an art and a science

◆ Playing cards, people, or both

Some concepts are universal to poker. For example, playing catch-up is generally a losing proposition. Position is all-important. Bluffing is both a science and an art. You should fold a lot, you should raise a little, and you should rarely call. Poker is both a card game and a people game.

## Strategic Concepts

Although strategies and tactics for many forms of poker vary considerably from game to game—plays that work well in draw can be useless in hold'em, and vice-versa—certain concepts are universal to all forms of poker. This chapter examines some new ideas and reviews some previously discussed important general strategic concepts.

# Coming From Behind Is More Difficult Than You Think

When players start with a hand that is likely to be substandard, they hope to improve by catching good cards later in the hand and win a big pot. What they tend to forget is that they can improve and still lose. No matter what form of poker you play, when you start a hand with cards that are worse than your opponent's, four things can happen, and three of them are bad:

- Your opponent improves, you don't: opponent wins

- Your opponent improves, you improve: opponent wins

- Your opponent doesn't improve, you don't improve: opponent wins

- Your opponent doesn't improve, you do: you win

That is, you lose three times out of four. Although these four scenarios oversimplify the situation somewhat, the picture is actually worse than it seems, because one of those times—when both your opponent and you improve—you lose a *lot*. You lose much more than when you win the one time in four that you do win. When you both improve, you both make a good hand. When a good hand loses to a better hand, more money is involved than when a hand that did improve beats a hand that didn't. For example, suppose you have a pair of fours and your opponent has a pair of aces. If you both improve to three of a kind, both hands are strong, and you will likely lose a lot of money in the justifiably enthusiastic later betting.

Now suppose that you again improve to three fours, but your opponent fails to improve and is stuck with his pair of aces. He probably won't call a large bet and certainly won't raise you. You won't win as much here as you lost in the trips vs. trips hand.

This is not to say that it is always wrong to play when you do not have the best hand. Sometimes the pot odds can make a play with the inferior hand very profitable.

For example, if the pot is very large, and you can call with a hand that is probably losing at the moment, but which has good potential to improve to a hand that will almost certainly win (a description that applies most of the time when you are trying to draw to a flush), the large pot you can win if your hand improves makes the call correct.

Let's look at a no-limit hold'em example. The flop is 4♠-6♠-A♣. You have 9♠-10♠. Your opponent accidentally exposes his hand (this rarely happens, but it makes the teaching example simpler), and you see he holds A♦-9♦, so he has a pair of aces, and cannot make a flush or a straight.

If you ignore the *extremely* unlikely possibilities that you might make three tens or he might make a full house, basically the outcome is very simple: You win if you make a flush, and lose if you don't. The pot currently contains $1,000, and your opponent has bet all his remaining chips, which happen to be $300. Because your opponent is going all-in, there won't be any additional betting. You have to make a one-time decision. You have enough chips to call. Should you call?

You are currently behind. You know that the only way to win is for another spade to come. The odds against this happening are approximately 2-1 (expressed another way, one-in-three). The pot odds are better than that, though: For a $300 call, you can win $1,300 (the $1,000 that was already in the pot plus the $300 your opponent just added to it).

To see why this is favorable, imagine this hand came up three times. You are supposed to win one time in three, so that one time, you'd win $1,300. On the two losses, you'd lose $300 each time, so you would come out ahead a net $700. That makes this a very easy and favorable pot odds call.

If the pot had contained only $600, you'd be indifferent about making the call: You'd be risking a $300 call to win $600, exactly the 2-1 odds against you making the hand. Again supposing the situation occurred three times, you'd have two $300 losses, and one $600 win. You'd break exactly even. As long as the pot is greater than $600, you are making a bet you would love to make all day long.

If you want to look at the problem a different way, suppose some odd person made you the following offer: You can put two white marbles and one black marble into an opaque bag. If you pull out the black marble, you win. You have to bet $300, but if you can pull out the black marble, he'll pay you $1,300. As you'll quickly see if you try your own version of this experiment, you win a lot of money if you can make this bet often.

If he'd offered to pay you $600, it would be just like offering to flip a fair coin for money: There's no reason to do it, but no reason not to, either, as long as you can afford to do a little straight gambling. If he'd offered to pay you $500, you'd lose money.

Because in the actual example you win $700 every three times this scenario plays out, your *EV* is +$233.33 on the call.

> **Table Talk**
>
> EV, or **Expected Value**, is the mathematical way to express what your average result would be for a given play if you got to make it enough times for the "law of averages," or the long run, to take effect. A winning play has a positive EV; a losing play has a negative EV.

Don't be intimidated by math terms like *EV/expected value*. As long as you can calculate pot odds—and that calculation is usually just a little addition with some multiplication or division of pretty small numbers, and even *that* can be approximate or rough—you know enough math to play poker. Former world champion Puggy Pearson's formal education ended in the second grade.

Unless you enjoy math, let other people worry about developing the formulae to make calculations. You can almost always just follow predetermined instructions. If I have to pick someone to bet on to become a winner in poker, give me someone who understands people over a math professor, any day of the week. I don't know how to program a computer, but my word processor works just fine. I don't know how they developed the recipe for baking a cake, but I can follow it and bake one. The math you need for poker is much the same.

Returning to the general problem of what to do when you're behind at the beginning of a hand, often the wisest thing to do is fold. This is particularly true when you are playing against only one opponent, because you don't get paid off as much when you win. If you're going to try to pull off an unlikely win, at least make sure you get paid handsomely when you connect.

The situation you want to avoid most is finding yourself *drawing dead*.

If you are trying to improve a hand that cannot win if you make it, you've stumbled into a "heads I lose, tails you win" situation.

### Table Talk

When you are **drawing dead**, you are putting money into the pot for the right to draw cards to a hand that cannot win, even if you make your draw. For example, if it appears obvious (or at least very likely) that an opponent already has a flush, it makes little sense to invest money trying to make a weaker hand like a straight.

Another potential time you might be drawing dead is if you are drawing to a flush when a pair is on the board. For example, the board in hold'em is 10♠-6♠-6♦. Your hole cards are the K♠-J♠, and (unbeknownst to you) your opponent has A♥-6♥. You might be delighted when the A♠ is dealt as the Turn card, because it gives you your flush, but this very same card has given your opponent a full house (three sixes and two aces). Ouch.

This does not mean that straight or flush draws become unplayable if there is a pair visible, but you must proceed with caution: If a pair is visible, the possibility of a full house or even four of a kind must now be considered.

In draw and lowball, playing the worst hand generally is also very bad. Because there are only two betting rounds and only one chance to improve a starting hand, it's much harder to come from behind.

One of the biggest mistakes in draw poker is playing shorts (small pairs). What constitutes "small" depends on position, but, if you're playing a pair of nines against a pair of kings, you are almost always taking too much the worst of it. Pair against pair is usually worse than 3-to-1 for the smaller pair in draw. Rarely does the smaller pair get pot odds to play.

## Position, Position, Position

Position involves two concepts: where you sit with respect to the dealer button and where you sit with respect to a particular player.

Position relating to the dealer button has already been discussed in the hold'em and Omaha chapters (2 and 4).

Position also refers to where you sit in relation to a particular player.

In general, you want wild gamblers and those who bet with abandon to your right. Then you have position on them. You want to have position on *calling stations* ( players who call bets with questionable holdings and who rarely raise). Money generally flows in a clockwise direction around a poker table, due to the dynamics of position.

Everyone has an edge on players to their right because they get to see what those players do before having to act. This edge promotes this flow of money in the same direction, from the player on your right, to you, to the player on your left: clockwise.

In general, you want weak, conservative players to your left. You can afford to give them position on you because they won't take full advantage of it. Ideally, you'd want position on *everyone*, but that's physically impossible! Some players have to be on your right, and some on your left. You just try to get position on the more dangerous foes.

> **The Inside Straight**
>
> Position has an added advantage in draw games because you can see how many cards players' opponents discard before you have to reveal your draw. The number of cards drawn helps define the hand in both draw and lowball and it also usually helps determine the opponent's chances of winning.

## The Art and Science of Bluffing

Bluffing, a term that has certainly worked its way into everyday English, can in poker be defined as trying to win a hand with your bet rather than with your cards. It is as much an art as it is a science.

Although a successful bluff can win you pots outright, your unsuccessful bluffs (bets where you get called and hence "got caught running without the ball," as former world champion Amarillo Slim Preston liked to say) can also help you out. Your opponents' belief in the possibility that you might be bluffing increases after you've been caught in the act. This allows you to win much more money on your strong and even just medium strong hands, because your opponents will call you thinking you might be bluffing. If you have a reputation as a very tight, conservative player who doesn't bluff, players won't call when you bet.

Naturally, if you find that your reputation is so conservative that when you bet, players fold faster than Superman on laundry day (think about it), you can take advantage of that reputation by betting when you don't have a good hand: bluffing. You will probably be allowed to get away with this for a while, but sooner or later, someone will suspect that perhaps you have altered your style, and call you. You'll lose that pot, but now if you catch good cards, people will pay you off. Indeed, you may have heard players say, "You have to advertise to get called on your good hands. Expect to lose on your bluffs so you can make money the rest of the time." This is one of the most widely misunderstood concepts in poker and has cost more players more money than almost any other "conventional poker wisdom," because actually it is not wise at all.

The reality is that in the course of making bluffs that you hope will succeed (win the pot), you will get caught/called often enough to do all the "advertising" you need. People will remember these unsuccessful bluffs, and because they are looking for excuses to play, and hate the idea of getting bluffed out of a pot, will later call you when you actually have a real hand. This means you certainly don't need to make bluffs you know will fail.

Bluffing because you "have a hunch you might get away with it" is not a good reason for bluffing. You should have a plan, just as you do for playing any hand. The plan might be that your intended victim has been playing very tight or scared poker; it might stem from a scary board that creates the impression you have a strong hand, or rely on the fact that you haven't played a hand for 45 minutes and therefore currently have a tight image (don't rely on this last one too much, because you'd be amazed how little attention other people pay to you when you're not actively involved in hands).

These are just a few good reasons to bluff. Your plan should involve bluffing more when you are not likely to be called and bluffing less when you are. That kind of decision is based on observation and playing of situations, not whim.

## When to Play Cards, People, or Both

Poker is a game of both cards and people—sometimes more of one and sometimes more of the other. It tends to become more of a people game as the stakes escalate.

Poker tends to be more of a game of cards when you're contemplating whether to get involved with a hand to begin with. Mathematically sound starting hand strategies have been worked out for all common forms of poker and beginners are well advised not to deviate from that too much. You may sometimes stray from a strategy to vary your game and so you don't become too predictable, but make sure that you don't use "making your play unpredictable" an excuse for playing too many hands.

### The Inside Straight

Poker is much more a game of cards in limit games than in big bet games (pot-limit and no-limit). In those games, one or two key decisions can make or break your night, or your tournament. Long-term probabilities aren't nearly as important in those situations as are your assessment of how a particular opponent is playing at that particular moment.

### Poker Lore

Playing too predictably can be dangerous. After all the cards have been dealt, if you have a completely useless hand (as can happen if you fail to connect on a draw) and an opponent bets, you have only two options. You can (and usually should) fold. If you think a bluff has a reasonable chance to succeed, you can bet or raise. Calling with a worthless hand is a pure waste of money … usually.

In one $15-30 game in the San Jose, California Bay 101 cardroom, I played regularly with a player who liked to bluff at pots on the end. If he got called, this opponent (whom I'll call Predictable) would invariably muck his hand quickly, knowing that a caller had to have some kind of hand.

One night, I had 2-3 in the big blind, and got to look at the flop for free when no one raised. The flop came 10-4-5, and suddenly I was interested because he had an open-ended straight draw, and better still, if an ace hit to complete the straight, there was a good chance someone holding an ace would pay the hand off.

Everyone checked the flop and I bet out on the turn in an effort to steal the pot. Only Predictable called. When the river card also failed to give me a straight, I was struck by a sudden inspiration (which should probably be placed in the category of "don't try this at home, folks"). I checked and, sure enough, Predictable bet. I did the unthinkable: I just called the bet, holding the worst possible hand, and Predictable immediately threw his hand away!

## The Least You Need to Know

- ◆ Avoid trying to come from behind, unless you are getting good pot odds.

- ◆ Position is one of the most important aspects of poker.

- ◆ Usually fold, raise when you have the best, and hardly ever simply call.

- ◆ Play cards or play people—sometimes play both.

# Chapter 10

# Show Me the Money

## In This Chapter

- ◆ Keeping good records
- ◆ Deciding how much of a bankroll to start with and maintain
- ◆ Paying taxes on your poker winnings

You can't be a winner unless you know how you're doing, and you can't know that without keeping good records. Keeping records will help improve your play and will also keep you from getting in trouble with the taxman. The starting point in your records should be your starting bankroll.

## Keep the Record Straight

Any poker player who doesn't keep records is fooling himself. Most good winning players keep records. If you're going to play poker with any sort of regularity, you need to keep good records. Do this for two reasons: to realistically assess your play and to keep accurate records for tax purposes.

## Improve Your Play

You bought this book because you want to be a better poker player and probably a winning player. It's difficult to be sure you're a winning player without knowing how you're doing. The only way to know how you are doing is to keep good records.

Your records should contain details such as where you played, when (including time of day), what you played (including stakes), how long you played, and how you did. The more detailed your records are, the more conclusions you can draw, and the more likely the IRS is to accept them.

**Perilous Play**

Lying is part of poker, at least at the table, but lying to the IRS about your winnings is asking for big trouble. The IRS will hit you with penalties and interest if your deductions are too aggressive, but their penalties get really serious when you don't report income. That's when they start talking about things like jail time. Omitting the twenty bucks you won at your uncle's house probably won't land you in the slammer, but think twice before you fail to report serious earnings.

For many players, not keeping records is a way of denying to themselves how they're doing. The player who tells others (and convinces himself) that he's breaking even may well be losing hundreds or thousands of dollars over the course of a year. Someone who plays weekly and has huge fluctuations—ahead $500 one week, down $1,000 the next—could easily average losing $100 a week and never realize it or face it. That's over $5,000 a year.

Similarly, the player who claims to "lose just a little" might well be losing tens of thousands of dollars.

Having it recorded forces a player to confront the situation and it may also cause him to attempt to do something about it. Doing something could involve playing for smaller stakes, playing different games, playing elsewhere, or other adjustments.

If you keep your records contemporaneously with your playing, you might consider also keeping a log assessing how you think you played. Write down plays that did and didn't work, mistakes you might have made, and patterns and *tells* you picked up about other players.

You can keep your log in a small spiral-bound notepad that fits in your pocket. Or you might maintain a database of players on a PDA. You might keep track of how they play when winning versus losing, in what situations they're most likely to have the goods or bluffing, whether they get looser or tighter right after winning or losing one or more pots, any mannerisms or other *tells* you might have picked up. Maybe T. J. Cloutier and Phil Hellmuth, Jr. can keep all that information on every opponent they've ever had in their heads for years; I know *I* can't.

**Table Talk**

**Tells** is an umbrella term for a large group of physical gestures or comments that give away more information than you intend. Someone who invariably holds his breath when bluffing has a tell, as does someone who gently slides his chips into a pot when he has a big hand. A truly reliable tell is worth its weight in gold; it's so valuable, in fact, that you probably should not expect your friends to inform you if they have one on you.

If you play in more than one game, keep separate track of that. For example, if you start in a $3-$6 hold'em game, move to $4-$8 Omaha, and then end up in $5-$10 seven-stud high-low, make separate entries for each with complete statistics. That way you'll know how you do in each variety of poker. You don't necessarily have to keep track of table changes if you go from one game to the same game at the same limit, but if you do very well at one table and poorly at the other, you may want to log those results separately to help track the factors that make the difference.

You don't have to be as precise in your records about a home game, particularly a small-stakes social game, but you still ought to keep track of hours played and how you did. You might want to keep separate track of the games played and how you did in each for later analysis.

Do you, for example, generally lose in the games with many community cards, but do well in the various flavors of draw? You can attack this problem in a couple of different ways. First, try to improve your play in the community card games. You might fold earlier and more often, or perhaps play more aggressively when you have the best of it. Alternatively, you can avoid the troublesome game by calling some other form of poker when it's your turn to deal.

## Poker Winnings and the Taxman

> Let me tell you how it will be
> There's one for you, nineteen for me
> 'Cause I'm the taxman, yeah I'm the taxman

*Should five per cent appear too small*
*Be thankful I don't take it all*
*'Cause I'm the taxman, yeah I'm the taxman*

*"I'm the Taxman," The Beatles (George Harrison)*

Before you decide the U.S. laws about gambling winnings are too onerous, remember, it could be worse. Our British cousins, fortunately, no longer pay at a 95% top rate either.

The other good reason to keep good records is for tax purposes. If you get lucky—or skillful—and win a large amount of money in a tournament, you don't have to pay taxes on the entire win if you can show losses in other gambling enterprises, so long as you either file as a professional gambler or itemize deductions.

A lot of people, probably exercising their wishful thinking muscles, assume that if a casino (or any other income provider) doesn't report the income to the IRS, it isn't taxable. Sorry. Income is income. If you choose not to report it and get audited, get a lawyer, because the failure to report income gets the IRS more upset than just about anything else. Money won in cash games is income that should be reported too. If you win a substantial amount, the taxman will find you.

If you are not a professional, the IRS does not permit you to simply subtract your losses from your winnings and claim the result as your gambling income. Your gambling winnings must be declared as ordinary income, while your losses, if allowed, go in as a deduction. That might sound no different from the "subtract your losses from your winnings" approach, but if you don't itemize deductions, it's a problem, likely enough of one to require a shift to itemizing if you had a big win and a lot of legitimate offsetting losses. If you are a professional, then you subtract gambling losses from your gambling winnings to compute your Schedule C income. For reasons that should be obvious, consult an accountant who is well-versed in how gambling relates to tax law when dealing with gambling wins and losses of any substantial size.

If you are audited, the IRS requires detailed records, including many things you might not think of, such as who played at your table and how much you bought in for and cashed out.

Unfortunately, the way tax law currently works, you pay in a winning year but in a losing year you can't offset winnings against other income; you can't income average from one year to the next, either, so if you win $100,000 gambling in Year One and lose $100,000 gambling in Year Two, you might have broken even at the tables, but your net worth has dropped by the amount of the Year One taxes. This goes for both those who declare themselves professionals and those who don't play for a living.

# Establishing and Managing Your Bankroll

If you're not playing poker for a living, and you probably won't do that for a long time, you don't want to live from your poker money. That may seem obvious, but it's something many don't understand. Keep your poker bankroll separate from your other money. Start with a certain amount of seed money, enough for the games you plan to play in, and then let that bankroll build up.

Examine your overall financial picture and pick an amount that you are willing to put at risk. Many authorities suggest a bankroll equal to 400 times the size of the big bet in the game you regularly play. If you can comfortably put aside $1,600, then you can play $2-$4 without fear of ever going broke.

That's the key to bankroll size: having enough money to know even a horribly bad streak of luck won't wipe out your bankroll. Naturally, you don't need anything like that much for one session's play. Going to the cardroom with 50 or 60 big bets should be plenty (a 50-big bet loss is a very bad night; the only reason you might bring more is if there's a chance you might want or need to play a little higher than usual). If you play to your established potential, you will most likely not lose a sufficiently large amount of your bankroll even if you run badly for an extended period.

## The Inside Straight

A poker bankroll of 100 big bets should easily allow a winning player to withstand one session's swings, although you really need more like 300-400 big bets to be safe against a bad run. Naturally, if you're a long-term losing player, no bankroll is sufficient; eventually, you'll lose all the money you're willing to lose. It's still a good idea to segregate your bankroll; if you run out, you're more likely to start over in an easier game.

If you build your bankroll up, you can then see if you want to play higher. Just don't expect to start playing $10-$20 if all you can comfortably start your playing bankroll with is $500. Doing so could easily lead to disaster, if the $500 is really all you can afford to devote to poker. If your bankroll is truly $500, you need to start out playing no higher than $3-6, and you'd be well-advised to start lower than that. It might be better to wait until you've done more reading and have saved up a bigger bankroll. Even a world-class player can easily lose 25 big bets in one session. This is because of two factors: variance (expected plausible fluctuations) and short-term luck.

Variance can be measured mathematically in terms of standard deviation. If you don't know what that means, forget it for now. You don't really *ever* need to learn it, and for goodness sake, you certainly don't need to halt your poker education to start learning math principles that have zero impact on your ability to win or lose poker hands. Anyone who tells you differently is either trying to intimidate or impress you with his vast intelligence and education, or has no idea what he's talking about.

### The Inside Straight

Poker is Everyman's game. Only in poker can rank amateurs compete against world-class poker players and sometimes get lucky and win. This is not true in any other form of competition. You cannot expect to get lucky playing golf against the likes of Tiger Woods or survive in the ring against Riddick Bowe or Lennox Lewis. In fact, you wouldn't even be allowed on the course or in the ring! But anyone with the money can sit down with Chris Ferguson, Annie Duke, or Andy Glazer—and maybe get lucky and win.

Do not start out playing with more money than you can comfortably afford to lose and be realistic. If you lose your bankroll, you'll be out of action. This is sometimes called "Gambler's Ruin." That won't allow you to put in the hours necessary to improve your play and you won't be able to build up a sufficient bankroll to play higher. You're on the sidelines.

Unfortunately, beginning players have no good way to figure out what their expected winning rate is (and indeed because they are beginners, will probably at least start out losing). Writer Mason Malmuth has developed many excellent formulae that allow you to figure out a necessary bankroll size for your skill level, but these aren't particularly helpful until you have acquired enough statistical data to plug in your expected win rate. As a practical matter, when you're starting out, you just need to segregate some poker capital, learn, play, and let the chips fall where they may.

### Perilous Play

Until you put in a lot of hours, you don't know if you're winning because you're good or because you're lucky. Maybe it's some of both, but short-term luck can cause you to think you're a better player than you really are.

If you don't have a lot of discretionary capital to devote to poker, start low and stay low until you start winning so you're not just throwing money away. Play at the lowest level that gets your attention. If you enjoy winning at $3-$6, there is no need to play $10-$20 just because you're rich. Succeed at one level before moving up, because even most wealthy people prefer winning moderate amounts at small stakes to losing large amounts at high stakes.

## The Least You Need to Know

- ◆ Keep good records.
- ◆ Establish a bankroll large enough to avoid losing all of it (Gambler's Ruin).
- ◆ Pay your taxes.

# Chapter 11

# Poker Etiquette and Protocol

## In This Chapter

- ◆ Employing standards of ethics
- ◆ Learning what filmmakers don't know—how to play poker
- ◆ Signing up for a game
- ◆ Choosing a seat
- ◆ Playing poker publicly
- ◆ Understanding the betting structures of games

There is a lot to poker ethics and protocol that isn't intuitively obvious. You're going to learn about many of those items here. I'm going to discuss the difference between deception in your play and dishonorable or unacceptable actions; how to sign up for a game; how to choose the best seat; and how to change to another seat or game.

## Telling Lies and Getting Paid

Poker is a language and it's a language of deceit and lying. The vocabulary of this language consists mainly of bets, although there are verbal and nonverbal deceptions, too.

Using this language, players try to get their opponents to pay them off when they have good hands and to fold when they have bad hands. This is when the deceit and lying come into play. If a bet truly meant, "I have a strong hand," then that would be the end of it unless the opponent had a very good hand of his own. Poker is a game of incomplete information with a lot of built-in deception, though, so confrontations are frequent. Good hands get paid off and bluffs succeed.

Of course, because most players are aware that everyone is trying to deceive everyone else, good hands often *don't* get paid off and bluffs frequently *do* get called.

Perhaps because of this underlying acceptance of deception, questionable ethics can creep into other areas of poker. These are situations for which there are rules and these rules and ethical guidelines need to be enforced for the good of the game.

## Ethics

You will likely see people display questionable ethical qualities in poker games. For example, someone might lean back a bit in his chair to see if he can get a glimpse of his neighbor's hole cards (perhaps bothering to rationalize that it's his neighbor's duty to hide his hand and therefore his own fault). If you do this, I'm happy to inform you and your wonderful self-image that you've been cheating. If your neighbor accidentally flashes his cards, you should try to look away, but if you see the cards, the rules say you're allowed to use the information. The player who comports himself above the bare rules minimum would inform the table that he'd seen his neighbor's cards.

> **CAUTION**
>
> **Perilous Play**
>
> Almost unbelievably, while lying about your hand is acceptable, you can get in trouble for telling the truth! Casinos have rules against collusion and if you tell the truth about your hand, you can run afoul of casino rules designed to protect players from those who exchange information. Until you're sure what's okay, you're better off saying nothing.

Announcing to the table that you have seen a neighbor's cards when you actually haven't is not an acceptable decision, by the way. Oh what a tangled web we weave.

The kind of lie that is implied in a bet or raise on a bluff is communicated with the "words" of poker. Outright lying about a hand is permitted in some instances and not others. You need to know the difference.

You can lie about your hand verbally in most pre-showdown situations. For example, your opponent in a no-limit hold'em game bets when the high card on the flop is a king, "alleging" with his bet that he likely has a king in the hole. You call. An ace comes on the turn. Your opponent makes a moderate-size bet and you raise all your chips. Your opponent, trying to get some information, asks, "Do you have an ace?" You can say "yes" if you're bluffing and he has to decide whether to believe you. It's usually okay to lie this way.

The same rules apply to tournaments, but tournament officials have more weapons at their disposal to penalize someone for a rules violation. Your hand can be declared *dead* (ineligible to win any part of the pot) if you disclose the specific cards in your hand in either a ring or tournament game. In a tournament you can also be given a penalty, such as having to sit out for 20 minutes.

### Perilous Play

Tournament officials have a broad range of penalties available to them. The lightest is a warning that puts you on notice of the intended penalty for a repeat infraction. In some situations, your hand may be declared dead. Time penalties are also possible: You must physically leave the table for a stated number of minutes, during which time blinds and/or antes are coming off your stack (possibly devastating late in an event). Repeat offenses usually call for greater penalties; a first time penalty might be 20 minutes, while a second might be 40, a third 60, and a fourth disqualification. A tournament director need not take all intermediate penalty steps. For something unforgivable, like hitting a dealer, the first penalty would probably be disqualification. Normally no money is refunded.

You might simply be given a warning for a first offense; tournament directors have (and need) a fair amount of discretion to interpret the rules, if for no other reason that sometimes an unusual situation will arise where two different rules apply and each calls for a different result.

An important part of proper play is acting on your hand in turn. This means you should not bet or fold until the player on your right has acted on his hand. Even if you know you are going to fold and a call of nature summons you, you are supposed to wait until your turn to fold. Any other action can affect the hand, because players who know someone behind them is going to fold can bet more aggressively. Usually a cardroom's rules include specific mention of this.

Betting too early is also a violation. You must wait before playing. If the player two positions to your right has just made a bet and the player to your right is still looking at his cards, don't bet. Wait until your neighbor acts on his hand and then make your move. If you act out of turn, you may cause the players on your left to fold or bet thinking that you have acted properly. Then an argument necessitating a floorman's decision can arise when the player on your right now decides he either wants to raise or do something that negates the action to your left.

**The Inside Straight** _____

It's easier to call a bluff on the final betting round if the person to your left has improperly "pre-folded" and no one else remains; you don't need to worry about a raise behind you or an *overcall*. This is unfair to the player who made the bluff. At the same time, if the player is not bluffing, then it has put you in an unfortunate position because you are now more likely to call.

**Table Talk** _____

If one player has bet on the end (final betting round) and has already been called when a third player decides to call also, that third player is said to be **overcalling**. Someone who overcalls almost always has a fairly strong hand, because he is not trying to force anyone out with a raise; his bet announces, in effect, "I believe my hand is better than either of yours."

Acting in turn means more than just waiting until the player on your right does "something" before you act on your hand. This is especially true in a big bet game. Wait until the player to your right has *completed* his action, not simply started it. For example, if a no-limit hold'em player says "I raise," and you immediately dump your cards before waiting to find out how much the raise is, he can make that raise larger because he has one less player to worry about.

## Slow-Rolling

**Table Talk** _____

If a player at the showdown knows he has a sure winner, but waits an unreasonable period of time until showing that hand, this player has **slow-rolled his opponent(s)**. This is usually done to annoy or anger one or more of the active players, by creating false hope of victory.

*Slow-rolling* is one of the rudest things someone can do in a poker game.

If you are entitled to show your hand after another player (for example, if you called his bet) it is not slow-rolling to wait to see his hand, because the rules do entitle you to a look. Some players will still get irritated by this, but if someone complains, just say "I wanted to see what he bet with."

This is a far smaller etiquette breach. Usually, players who know they have the winning hand will just reveal it and not force the other player(s) to show their hands, and they will usually fold their hands quickly without showing (called *mucking*).

However, just because the rules allow you to see a player's hand doesn't mean that you always want to stand on your rights. It is considered a courtesy to allow a player who mucks unseen to do so. People who have played very weak hands are usually eager to muck because they are a bit embarrassed at having to show the weak hand.

Especially in a money game, you are probably smart to avoid irritating someone who plays weak cards. He might leave the game, or (perhaps as bad or worse) he might start playing better starting hands, because he doesn't want to be embarrassed by another demand to see his cards again. In a tournament, where the player can't leave, and where it might be important to quickly get a feel for how he plays, standing on your right to see an opponent's cards can make more sense.

A new player may slowroll inadvertently. The first player exposes his cards and he looks at the hand for several seconds trying to figure out what the other player has. Then, when he realizes he has the winner, he spreads his own cards. If this happens to you, apologize immediately by saying something like "I'm sorry, I wasn't trying to slow-roll you, I was having a problem reading my hand."

Different games and cardrooms have different rules about what order to expose hands on the showdown. Usually the last player to bet or raise must show first. If there was no bet on the last round, usually hands are exposed in order starting from the left of the button.

Table or fold your cards promptly and in turn, so players get the information to which they are entitled; the exception, as mentioned, is that it's considered particularly sporting to table the winner right away if you know you have it. If you're not sure if you have the winner, when you table your hand the dealer or other players will say whose hand wins. If you're sure you have a loser, don't hold onto your cards. This makes everyone wonder if you're finally going to turn over a winner.

## When You Expose Cards

In some games (most commonly tournaments), exposing a card to induce a reaction can lead to trouble. Depending on the circumstances and the house rules, your hand may be declared dead; you'll also encounter situations where the hand isn't declared dead but you receive a time penalty.

In some tournaments, exposing a card, even accidentally, means an automatic penalty. Sometimes the first instance brings only a warning.

How this situation is handled in a ring game depends on the club, but this is why you need to know the rules. Some clubs have a zero-tolerance policy for certain infractions; the Bicycle Casino in Bell Gardens, California is well known for its automatic penalties for "use of the f-word" and for a thrown card landing on the floor (the pre-tournament announcement usually brings a chuckle: "If you accidentally toss a card on the floor, you will accidentally be given a 10-minute penalty"). Others do not even consider certain director discretion tournament infractions to be infractions in ring games.

> **The Inside Straight** _____
>
> When the betting action is complete except for one player's decision, or when a hand is heads-up, it used to be perfectly acceptable to show a card or cards to see if you could get a reaction out of an opposing player. If you watch old WSOP videos, you'll see players exposing their hands at the final table and studying their opponents to see if the sight frightened or calmed them. About a decade ago, though, the rule changed, and in most tournaments, you can no longer show even one card, much less two.

The issues involved with exposing cards during a hand to induce action are quite different from those involved in a player's decision to voluntarily show his winning uncalled hand to others in the game. Experienced players sometimes show cards when not forced to after the hand is over because they want to establish something in an opponent's mind. I usually advise beginners to avoid giving any information away for free.

## When Someone Else Exposes Cards

How should you react when your opponent shows you his cards after the hand is over just to let you know that he really had the goods? Some players feel obligated to do the same in return. That may be just why the player does it. He wants an unspoken agreement between the two of you that you will always show your cards and that will prove you weren't bluffing. But then he won't call when you have a good hand and anything that saves him money costs you money. So don't feel as though you must do the same for him.

> **The Inside Straight** _____
>
> Don't assume that just because an opponent shows you a good hand or two, he always has good cards when he bets or raises. Realize that often your opponent is trying to confuse you. Generally you are better off taking this information for what it's worth, which isn't much. If your opponent shows *every* hand and always "has the goods," you might start to believe he's a conservative player. If he only shows intermittently, he's probably trying to create a false image.

When a player inadvertently but regularly flashes his cards during play, opinion is divided on how to handle the situation. Many say you have a moral obligation to warn that player. Others say that you don't. I strongly advocate taking the high road. Integrity is it's own reward. Even if you don't feel that way, recognize that if you develop a reputation as an ethical player, it might help you out from time to time in ways that can't easily be predicted or projected.

There are practical issues involved as well as ethical ones. What happens when someday it's your opponent who is getting too many unfair looks at a neighbor's cards? If you've established a precedent of trying to put a stop to it, you can try to milk that when you own the wrong seat.

# The "Western Rules" Myth

Poker players know that until recently, Hollywood didn't know how to play poker. We've all seen the movie situation in which the bad guy bets more than the cowboy hero has and the hero rides off to get the deed to the ranch so he can call that bet. This never happened in a real card game. The other players would not stop a game to wait for someone to come up with enough money to call a bet. What would they do? Set the deck down and play on from another deck? Would the cowboy ride off with his cards clutched in his hand?

## Raise Him Out

If the player with the most money could win any pot by betting more than any opponent had, you wouldn't have much of a poker game. The player with the most money would win every hand. He'd be foolish not to do so and his opponents could never win, no matter what their cards. That silliness is carried to its extreme in the otherwise entertaining film *"Big Hand for the Little Lady."*

## Table Stakes and Side Pots

Poker is normally played for *table stakes*. You can't be pushed out of a pot because you don't have enough chips to call. If one player runs out of chips (goes all-in), and other players still have chips, a *side pot* (auxiliary or secondary pot) is created among the remaining players. The player who goes all-in can win from any one player only as much as he put into the pot.

An example makes this clear. Let's play a no-limit hold'em pot with Tom, Dick, Harry, and Jane. Tom has only $20 left from his original buy-in. Dick isn't doing well either and has $100 in chips. Harry has $1,000. Jane has been doing extremely well and has $5,000. The blinds are $5-10.

Tom starts with pocket kings (K-K), and Dick pocket fives (5-5). Harry has A♠-K♠, and Jane pocket aces (A-A). The community board ends up 4♠-4♥-K♦-4♦-5♥. Neither the big blind nor the small blind puts any additional chips into the pot.

On the first round of betting (pre-flop), the first bet puts Tom in and a raise ensures that Harry, too, has all his chips in the pot. On the turn, Jane puts Harry all-in and he calls happily with his fours full of kings.

When we sort out the carnage, it's easy to see how everyone got involved. Let's figure out the hands and who wins what from whom:

- ◆ Tom has the best hand, kings full of fours.

- ◆ Dick is next, with fives full of fours.

- ◆ Jane comes in third, with fours full of aces.

- ◆ Harry's fours full of kings comes in last.

Tom started with $20, so that's the most he can win from any one player. He wins that from Dick, Jane, and Harry, and also wins the $15 in blind money. He now has a total of $95 (a profit of $75).

Dick started with $100. He loses $20 to Tom, but wins $80 from both Jane and Harry. He wins the first side pot, which contains a total of $240 (a profit of $140).

Jane started with $5,000, so she could have won all her opponents' chips. She came in third in the hand, though, and wins "only" the second side pot.

Harry had $1,000 when the hand started, but lost $20 to Tom and $80 to Dick. He had $900 left for his battle with Jane, and loses that: Jane comes away from the hand having won $900 from Harry, but losing $20 to Harry and $80 to Dick, so she makes a profit of $800 and now has $5,800. The person to win the most in the pot came in third in this four-horse race, but because she had more chips at risk when the hand started, and because she won the only really important battle—the clash against the other big stack—she was entitled to win more.

**Perilous Play** _____

If you want to make sure you can always win the maximum, don't play short-stacked. There are few lost poker opportunities as easily avoided as the player who loses all but a few chips on one hand and says to himself, "I'll buy more chips as soon as I lose these." He immediately catches terrific cards and beats a good hand, but he doesn't win very much because he didn't start with many chips. The only real advantage to playing short-stacked is that you can't lose a lot in one hand, but that's a flawed approach. If you have a lot of chips in front of you, you can choose to keep them safe by folding, but you can't choose to win a lot when you own a short stack.

# Sign-Up Boards and Waiting Lists

When you first arrive in a cardroom, you will see an area for game sign-ups. This might be a raised platform in front of a large whiteboard. You tell the employee (usually called a *boardman*, although a floorman might be fulfilling the role) in charge of the lists what game or games you'd like to play. If a seat in one of your preferred games is currently open, a different employee directs you to the seat and sometimes arranges for your purchase of chips.

**The Inside Straight** _____

If you like your privacy, you'll be glad to know you don't have to use your full name or even your real name when you sign up for a game. A first name plus an initial is sufficient. Many players just give a nickname. In some casinos, they just want initials.

In smaller cardrooms, the board might be a list maintained on a pad of paper at a lectern near the entrance.

If no seat is open, the boardman adds your name or initials to the bottom of the list for each game that you are interested in. A separate list is maintained for each limit of each game. When you get seated in one game, your name remains on the other lists for which you signed up. If your name comes up on another list, the boardman calls your name and you can choose to move to that game or to stay where you are.

When you are in one game and wish to play at another table at the same limit, you can ask a floorperson to put your name on a waiting list. You will be told when a seat becomes available in the other game.

# Selecting and Changing Your Seat

When you first sit down at a game, if more than one seat is open you have your choice. Usually seated players are allowed to move to any open seat before you take it. You can change seats later if you don't like the seat.

The process of changing seats differs widely among cardrooms. In some, particularly smaller clubs, if a seat opens up, whoever gets there first gets the seat. Sometimes players claim seats by tossing chips to the empty seat. In such case, the player first to throw a chip gets the seat.

In most clubs, though, a verbal signup list for seat changes is maintained. The first person to request a seat change (by asking the dealer), gets first shot at any seat that opens. In some clubs, seat change opportunities are awarded by seniority: Whoever has been at the table the longest gets first crack at an open seat.

## The Best Seat in the House

If you've had an opportunity to observe the game you're preparing to enter, you may have been able to see the various players' styles. Given a choice, you would prefer to have wild, aggressive players and those who play many pots on your right, and passive, conservative players on your left.

If you can't tell who's who, you can still make a choice based on chip stacks. In general, you would prefer to have players who own large stacks on your right and those with the small stacks on your left, because you'd rather get to act after the richer players. This is especially true in no-limit and pot-limit, but still holds true in limit poker.

If the chip stacks are relatively equal, you should opt for the jumbled, disarranged stacks on your right and the neat stacks (particularly if the chips are all arranged in some geometric pattern) on your left.

In general, how a player stacks (or doesn't stack) his chips tells you a bit about his style. Orderly stacks signal orderly, conservative players, and jumbled stacks tend to be owned by unpredictable players. You want to see what wild and unpredictable players do before you have to make your decision, because you have a fairly good idea what the predictable players will do.

You want the predictable players, those with insufficient chips to threaten you, and those who don't play many pots to act after you do.

## Good Reasons to Change Your Seat

Change your seat if you think you can improve your position relative to other players. For example, if the player on your left apparently has a good read on you and seems to raise whenever you have a weak hand and a seat to his left opens up, you probably want it so that he'll act before you. If the dynamics of the game change and you see a better strategic position is or will be available, you may want to change. If the player on either side of you insists on carrying on a conversation to the point that you cannot concentrate, you may want another seat.

It might seem obvious, but you're unlikely to play your best poker if you're physically uncomfortable. If you're stuck between two large people, or smokers, or are having trouble seeing the board, try to change your seat.

## Bad Reasons to Change Your Seat

Unless you are trying to convince the other players that you're a superstitious weak player, the worst reason to change your seat is because you think an abandoned seat is "hot." Cards are not drawn to seats like metal to magnets.

Similarly, losing several hands in a row is not reason enough to change seats, especially if you're positioned properly against weak and strong players. If someone tells you "You're sitting in the death seat, no one has won a hand there all day," that's not by itself reason to change. It may be that the existing players are trying to intimidate you. Such a warning should, though, alert you to table dynamics that might be making a seat a tough one.

**The Inside Straight**

If you're warned that a particular seat has been "the death seat" or "the ejector seat," don't totally dismiss that as superstitious nonsense. Although the cards don't know who's sitting in any given seat, it may be that table dynamics have been conspiring to give whoever is sitting in a particular seat a tough time. For example, if the two toughest and most aggressive players are sitting to the left of a seat, it wouldn't be that surprising for various seat occupants to have struggled there.

Not having been dealt playable hands for the last hour is not a good reason to change. The distribution of the cards is random and you'll have the same chances for good and bad hands in any other seat. One hour is nothing compared with the long run during which everything is supposed to even out. Having had several bad beats recently is not a good reason. You'll experience bad beats wherever you sit.

# Casinos, Cardrooms, Riverboats, and Cruises

You have many choices of where to play poker in a public venue. Many casinos, large and small, have cardrooms, but usually the cardroom is only a small part of the casino.

Nevada and New Jersey have big casinos, many of which have large cardrooms that are supported by the casino management. That is also the case in many casinos outside of the United States. Native American casinos also frequently have cardrooms.

Several western states have casinos devoted almost solely to poker. California is the largest of these, with the best variety and selection of games. Riverboats, whether those rare ones that actually cruise or the more common permanently docked variety, focus primarily on the more lucrative casino-type games. Some have cardrooms which don't even operate full-time, having to yield space on high-attendance days to the other games.

The phenomenon of the "poker cruise" is becoming increasingly popular. Usually a block of rooms is reserved on a large cruise ship for a group of poker players, with a poker room open for the duration of the cruise. Sometimes the poker room has such a low profile that many of the regular passengers are not even aware of its existence, although they are welcome to play. For some passengers the poker activities may be the prime reason for the cruise. Several major tournaments are now held on cruise ships.

In a cardroom, you will likely see the same regular players over and over. In a casino in one of the gambling destinations, you still find the same regulars, but you also see a lot of drop-in trade from the other gaming patrons. In the smaller games in casinos, you are likely never to see your opponents again.

Reservation cardrooms lie somewhere in between, but tend to have more regulars. On a cruise, players are probably the most relaxed, even though you'll see the same players for the entire cruise. On a riverboat, where there's no real scenery, people go specifically to play poker and they're serious. In general, you will do best in the venues that have weak, unfocused opponents.

# Limit, Spread-Limit, Pot-Limit, and No-Limit Play

Every poker game has a structure related to the betting. There are four such structures: limit, spread-limit, pot-limit, and no-limit.

# Limit

In limit games, all bets proceed in increments, or multiples, of the limit. More than one structure exists in limit games, but one thing is always true: Bets always proceed in equal increments on each round. The most common structure is two-tier.

For example, in a $2-4 hold'em game, bets proceed in the first two rounds in multiples of $2 and in the second two rounds in multiples of $4. The first player to enter a pot has two choices: open for $2 (*limp*) or $4 (raise). If the first player opens for $2, the next player has three choices: fold, call $2, or raise to $4. If the first player opens for a raise to $4, the next player still has three choices: fold, call $4, or raise to $6. Each player in turn has those three choices: fold, call the preceding bet, or raise by $2.

> **The Inside Straight**
>
> If you're heads-up and the limit on the number of raises has been lifted, you should keep re-raising with the best possible hand, as long as someone else can't have the same hand with a better draw. For example, if you hold K♥-J♥, and the flop comes A♥-Q♠-10♥, you've flopped the nut straight, as has an opponent who holds K♠-J♣. He can't improve to a flush like you, though. You are "freerolling" on this opponent and should keep re-raising until you run out of chips or until he realizes he's putting more money into a pot that he'll split at best, but might lose.

When the betting reaches a certain level, called the *cap*, no further raises are permitted. Some clubs permit one bet and three raises, while others permit an initial bet and four raises. Most clubs remove the cap when only two players remain heads-up in the pot. That is, with two players, unlimited raises are permitted. (That is usually not the case in tournaments, however.)

In the second two rounds, bets proceed in multiples of $4. Because the blind bet no longer starts the action, the first player may now choose to not bet (check). The betting is exactly the same as at the first two levels; the only difference is the bet size.

The situation is exactly the same at any other limit. In a $20-40 game, bets proceed in the first two rounds in multiples of $20 and in the second two rounds in multiples of $40.

Some limit games have more than one tier; nonetheless, bets in any one round always proceed in increments. Hold'em games exist with varying structures. Although the aforementioned two-tiered structure is most common, you will occasionally encounter three-tier structures, like $2-2-4-8. Here the betting is $2 on the first two rounds, $4 on the third, and $8 on the last.

Once in a blue moon, you'll run into a four-tiered structure, like $1-2-4-8. In four-tier structure games, you can afford to look at a lot more flops because the initial bets are so small compared to the bets you can make later if you connect with a flop.

## Spread-Limit

Spread-limit permits bets over a range. For example, in a $1-$5 game (common in seven-card stud), a player may, at any point, bet either $1, $2, $3, $4, or $5. A raise may also be any of those amounts, with the proviso that a raise must always equal or exceed the previous bet or raise. Thus, if Jim bets $1, Sue can raise $1, $2, $3, $4, or $5. If Jim bets $3, however, Sue can raise only $3, $4, or $5. If Jim bets $1, and Sue raises $3, Jim can re-raise only $3, $4, or $5. (Obviously, Jim can also just call or even fold.)

> ### The Inside Straight
>
> Although you'll encounter spread-limit structure most often in low stakes seven-card stud, you occasionally see it in bigger hold'em games. Such spreads are usually within a multiple of ten; that is, $20-200 or $30-300. The high stakes involved aside, you should avoid these games while you're new. The possibility of one big bet breaking you is something you should postpone until you're a bit more seasoned.

On each round of betting, no matter the previous betting, the limit again is $1-$5. Thus, if Jim and Sue had capped the betting on the first round and all in $5 increments, either could initiate the betting in the next round at $1.

## Pot-Limit

Pot-limit also involves a range of permitted betting, but in a different way. The upper limit is always equal to the current size of the pot. A raise is always calculated such that the cost to call is included in the size of the pot.

Here's how it works. In a $1-$2 pot-limit game, the first player in the pot has several choices. He can, of course, fold. He can call for the minimum, $2. He can raise. If he raises, he can choose from a range of bets. The minimum raise is $2. The maximum is the size of the pot after he puts in the $2 (which is considered a call), or $5. Thus the opener can make any of the following bets: $2, $4, $5, $6, or $7.

Most pot-limit games feature a 1-2 ratio blind structure (although occasionally you'll encounter 1-1 or 1-1-2). That could be $1-$2, $5-$10, or $100-$200. In all such structures, a simple formula to figure the maximum amount that an opener who comes in for a raise can bet is to multiply the little blind by seven. So, in the $1-$2 game, the maximum raise-open would be $7, and in the $5-$10 game, $35.

Subsequent players have the same choices as in the spread-limit game: Fold, call the preceding bet, or raise by any amount between the call and the size of the pot. From the previous example, if Jim opens for the minimum, $2,
Sue can call the $2, or raise any amount from $2 to $7 (the size of the pot after she puts in the $2 call). That is, she can bet anywhere from $2 to $9. If Jim opens for the maximum, $7, Sue can call the $7, or raise any amount from $5 (Jim's raise) to $17 (the size of the pot after she puts in the $7 call). That is, she can bet anywhere from $7 to $24.

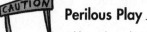

**Perilous Play**

Although individual bets in pot-limit games are not generally as large as those in no-limit games, pot-limit games can be much bigger than they initially appear. Bets in a game with $1-$2 blinds, for example, could quickly grow large enough to necessitate a player's entire stack to call. Pot-limit, like spread-limit and no-limit, is a tough game for the beginner.

## No-Limit

No-limit betting is easier to figure out than pot-limit. On your turn you can always bet any amount up to the size of your stack. The minimum bet is always the size of the big blind; the maximum is the size of your stack.

**The Inside Straight**

The actual practical limit on the maximum amount that can be bet is an amount equal to the size of the second-largest stack at the table. That is, if three players at a nine-handed no-limit table have $100, four players have $500, one player has $1,000, and one player has $5,000. The practical maximum bet that can be made is $1,000. The player with $5,000 may push his entire stack forward, but that's just a convenient shortcut that says "I bet as much as the second-biggest stack has."

For example, in a $1-$2 no-limit game, the first player in the pot has several choices. He can fold. He can open for the minimum, $2. He can raise. If he raises, he can

**The Inside Straight**

Theoretically, a player could open for his entire $1,000 stack. This is not a very good play. Most of the time, he'll win the $3 in blinds. Once in awhile, someone behind the "bully" will wake up with a great hand and call this *overbet into a dry pot* (bet a large amount at a small pot). You will sometimes see this happen, however, particularly in online tournaments.

choose from a range of bets. The minimum raise is $2. The maximum is the size of his stack. The next player can fold, call that bet, or raise any amount ranging from the size of the previous bet or raise to the size of his own stack.

As in all games, a raise must always equal or exceed the previous bet or raise.

Cardrooms interpret differently how an all-in raise affects reopening the betting for other players. Suppose, for example, that Andy opens the betting for $100. Bob raises to $500, and Carl and Dave call. Now Andy moves all-in for his entire remaining $404. Even though Andy has technically re-raised, because that all-in raise is only an insignificant $4, most cardrooms don't permit Bob, Carl, or Dave to now put in another re-raise. Most cardrooms require in this situation that Andy's re-raise must be at least half the previous bet or raise before Bob, Carl, or Dave can then re-raise.

Still others permit a re-raise only if the all-in raise is at least equal to the previous bet or raise.

## The Least You Need to Know

- Even though poker is a game of deception, it still has ethical standards.

- Most of the poker you see in the movies is technically inaccurate and/or outdated.

- Understand the betting structure before you sit down in a game.

# Chapter 12

# Obtaining Funds to Play Poker

## In This Chapter

- ◆ The dangers of borrowing and lending money
- ◆ The perils of misery indifference
- ◆ Considerations involved in investing in another player or becoming the investment yourself

Smart poker players separate their poker money from their expense money and savings and keep it separated. It's extremely difficult to win playing with money you can't afford to lose. Nonetheless, some players try to play with borrowed money or find an investor to back their play. Some of these arrangements make sense. Many do not.

## Other Ways to Gather Ammunition

Normally you will be playing with your own money. This makes sense. For almost everyone, poker is a hobby, even though it can be a profitable hobby. You don't borrow money to go to the movies or collect coins, so why should you borrow money to play poker? There are many good reasons why both borrowing and lending money for poker are usually bad ideas. Let's examine them.

# Neither a Borrower Nor a Lender Be

Cardrooms are full of people who are down on their luck and who want to borrow a few dollars. These *railbirds* inevitably claim that whatever game they are trying to get into is their best game. "Just one buy-in and I'll be back on my feet again," they claim, "I play ten times as good as anyone in that game."

**Table Talk**

Because the playing section of a poker room is often divided from the non-playing section by a rail or rope, people who loiter near the playing section are frequently called **railbirds** (a term also used in horseracing to describe similar nonplayers). Sometimes **railbirds** just want to watch; often they are seeking a way to get into a game.

That explains, of course, why they don't have enough money to buy in. How could anyone ten times better than anyone in the game possibly ever get lucky enough to win?

You will also encounter railbirds who don't claim to want a loan. They just want someone to cash a check, because, after all, it's after hours and their bank is closed, etc., etc. Occasionally you'll find one who tries the "honest creativity" approach.

**Perilous Play**

Whether you lend poker money to a friend, an acquaintance, or a stranger, there are almost no possible scenarios wherein you wind up better off long term. Even in those rare cases when nothing bad happens immediately, there are unpleasant long-term side effects. Be anti-Nike and "Just don't do it."

"This check isn't good right now," they'll say, "but it'll be good as gold on Friday, I get paid on Friday."

Examine the situation. If the fellow is a local, surely he has friends, or at least people who know him better than you do. If these people aren't cashing the check, why should you? If the fellow isn't a local, how did he wind up in a strange cardroom without money? Where is the job that is paying him on Friday, if he isn't local?

You shouldn't ask these questions: that leads to more trouble. Just say sorry, you don't lend and you don't borrow and if he keeps bothering you, ask the management to clear him out.

**The Inside Straight** _____

You probably never realized how many friends you had until you win a tournament or hit a bad beat jackpot. "I was rooting for you, I hate that other punk" works better with a tournament win than a bad beat jackpot. For those, the old "Man, I wish I could win a jackpot. I just lose with flushes to full houses" works better. Railbirds aren't your friends. If you want to help the human race, donate money (or time) to a *real* charity.

## Lending Money in Home Games

When you play in a home game, a fellow player who gets *tapped out* (broke) will often ask for a loan. It can be tempting to lend money in these situations, for the following reasons:

♦ The borrower may be a friend.

♦ The borrower is often a regular loser whom you want to keep in the game; he might not lose the money back to you immediately, but he will eventually, as long as he keeps coming back.

♦ A player who is losing tends to keep losing and it may be easy to win the loaned money back immediately.

♦ It can feel awkward to say no to someone whose money you've just won, especially if you're a big winner.

♦ You think you might later be in a situation when you want to borrow money and your own chances will be improved if you have a reputation as a lender.

Despite these reasons, lending money in such situations is fraught with peril. You don't have to be a poker player to know how many friendships break up over the stresses that loaned money can create. Regular losers may appreciate a loan in the moment, but if it helps them lose far more in an evening than they originally were prepared to lose, they may be unhappy the next day ("Why did you lend me money when I was throwing it away so foolishly?!?"). Someone who loses a truly huge sum may decide he can't pay it back and quit the game owing it all. Watching someone use money you lent him to come back and beat you is almost as bad.

It might feel awkward to say no, but once you say yes, it feels doubly awkward to say no the next time, and if you say yes to someone you know to be trustworthy, it's practically impossible to say no to someone else in the game, because your actions are tantamount to saying "I trust Joe, but not you."

Finally, if you lend money because you think you'll want to borrow it later, you might be surprised to find that your former grateful borrowers have no interest in becoming lenders. After all, they might need the money to play in another poker game somewhere else. Even if you can successfully apply "moral" pressure to get a loan, I've already mentioned that playing on borrowed money isn't a good idea. Let's see why.

## And Don't Forget, Stay Out of Debt

Occasionally you will use someone else's money to play poker. Whether this is a good idea or a bad one depends on whose money it is and how you get it.

Borrowing money to play poker is not a good idea. It's hard enough to play well when you are on *tough money*, that is, money you already have, but need for another purpose, like rent or food. As I noted in my book *Casino Gambling the Smart Way*, "If you play with money you can't afford to lose, you will lose." Playing perfect poker often requires you to bet or raise with small advantages: This practice makes money in the long run but creates unacceptable fluctuations for the inadequately capitalized player.

If you are determined to borrow from someone other than a casual poker acquaintance, you basically have three possible sources. Only people with a death wish borrow from loan sharks. Your best possible result from that scenario is that you get to pay the money back at an exorbitant interest rate. In the worst possible scenario, your loan shark may introduce to you a real shark, and I don't mean a lawyer.

Another source, better than a loan shark in some ways but worse in others, is your friends and/or family. These folks may not kill you if you fail to repay them, but loans have a funny way of destroying relationships. If the loans aren't repaid, you're afraid to talk to the lender again and you lose a relationship, even if the lender is willing to let you off the hook. If the loan is repaid, the lender often wants some kind of *quid pro quo* that you wind up resenting.

Alternatively, once you have borrowed money and paid it back, you may feel that with your "established credit record" you are entitled to another loan anytime you need it. Your private lender may not be in a position to grant the loan the next time and may be embarrassed to admit it. Even if he is in a position to help out, he may not like the trend. A friend will often loan money once, figuring a friend really needs a helping hand. When the friend returns a second time for more money, the lender starts to feel less like a friend and more like a bank.

**The Inside Straight**

Although no trick will substitute for self-discipline, here's a good one for people who know they have a weakness for credit card cash advance machines (and who have more than one credit card). It's risky to travel without a credit card, because you never know when you might really need one. If you know you lack discipline, though, take a spare credit card and sand off the magnetic stripe. You can still use it for goods and services, but ATM machines won't take it.

Probably the best person to borrow money from is yourself, and that's no bargain either. The credit card cash advance machines in casinos charge *outrageous* fees, even if you pay the money back instantly. If you don't pay it back instantly, the interest charges, although tiny by loan shark standards, will grow and multiply faster than you believe possible.

A good way to learn how to stay away from credit card cash advance machines is to wander over to one sometime when you *don't* need money. Just pretend you're exploring the idea of walking around with $1,200 in your pocket, instead of $200, and take a look at the fees you'll incur. Then, take whatever the fee would be, remove that money from your wallet, borrow a cigarette lighter, and burn the fee money.

*"What?!?"* you exclaim. *"Are you out of your ever-loving mind?!?"*

No, I'm not … but when you borrow money from one of those machines, you might as well be burning the fee money, because it's gone forever and it hasn't done you one bit of good, other than getting you cash that, upon later cooler reflection, you probably will have wished you didn't use for gambling. Put another way, the money you just burned paves the way for you to burn more money.

Doesn't seem like a very good idea, does it?

Yes, there's a *chance* that by borrowing money, you'll win and be able to repay it quickly. Let's face reality, though: If you were tapped out enough to need a credit card cash advance, you're either not playing well or not running well, and the pressure presented by a need to repay a loan isn't likely to help.

Possibly the single greatest danger to any poker player involves reaching his *point of misery indifference*. Almost everyone has a number at which his spirit breaks. For some people, it might be $300, for others, $3,000 or $30,000, but most of us have such a point. When you reach your point of misery indifference, more losing doesn't hurt any worse, because you're already so upset, you can't feel worse just then. Lose $3,000, lose $5,000, what's the difference? You feel absolutely awful in both cases.

---

**Poker Lore**

One of the more common (and sad) sights you'll see in any casino is a line forming at the ATM starting about 11:55 P.M. Can you guess why?

Virtually all ATM cards have bank-imposed daily withdrawal limits. When the clock strikes midnight, it's a new day, and ATM users can then get into their bank accounts for another day's limit.

Using ATM cards makes far more sense than credit card cash advance machines. At least with an ATM card, you do have the money; you're not borrowing it. While you might incur a $2 fee for using another bank's ATM, that's far better than a $50 charge for tapping your credit card (and starting the interest charge clock running at what is likely 20 percent or more). Still, unless you come to the casino *planning* on using your ATM card (so you don't have to carry a lot of cash), using it means you have probably lost the maximum you were willing to lose before you arrived. You may now be a little on tilt, and if you're not careful, the credit card machine might be next.

---

The difference, as you have probably guessed, is $2,000. If losing $3,000 is enough to seriously upset you, it's a pretty good bet that when you get out of bed the next day, you will feel a good deal worse about losing $5,000 than you would about losing $3,000. It's no different than losing another $2,000 on your next trip to the poker room.

The moment you sense you've reached your point of misery indifference, you should quickly get out of the card room. If you can do this, you might have a future in poker. If you can't—if once you start losing heavily, you're going to go off for every dollar you can get your hands on—you should probably consider another hobby. This one is too dangerous for you.

# If You're Good Enough, Getting Staked Is Gravy

The best way to play poker with other peoples' money is only available to the very best players, so don't expect access to it anytime soon. A great player with a proven track record can often find investors, called *backers*, who are willing to front money to the star player in return for a significant percentage of his winnings (and often other fringe benefits like lessons from the star, or simply being seen with or associated with the star). To get a player into action in this manner is called *staking* him.

There are a great many variations on the staking game, and the best ones offer value both to the player and the backer.

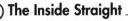

**The Inside Straight** _____

Why would a truly great player want/need to be staked? A *tournament* player may just not have the bankroll to handle the swings (bankroll fluctuations) inevitable to tournament life, where a player might lose 20 events in a row before a big score. A *money* player's bankroll could be vulnerable for non-poker reasons, or he might have an opportunity in a high stakes game where he isn't willing to risk his whole bankroll, even if he believes he's a favorite to win.

*Single stake arrangements* involve putting someone into action for one game or, more commonly, one tournament. The backer pays the entire entry fee and buy-in, and gets a percentage of the player's winnings.

World champions can sometimes negotiate deals that allow them to keep 60 percent or even 70 percent of their own winnings, but such deals are rare. Most great players are quite content to play for a 50 percent *freeroll*, and many great players are content with deals that let them keep 40 percent, 30 percent, or even as little as 20 percent of any profits. (Remember, profits are monies that come back over and above the buy-in. A player who enters a $500 tournament on his backer's money and "wins" $650 has only netted $150, and "playing for 50 percent," would get $75, with the other $575 going to the backer.)

*Long-term staking arrangements* require a great deal more trust between player and backer, because the backer is typically not present for every tournament and/or money game, and has to accept the player's word for the results (receipts help a lot with tournaments; if the staking includes money play, there is little a backer can do but trust).

There are many kinds of long-term staking arrangements. Sometimes the deal is simple: The backer provides all buy-ins to both tournaments and money games for a year. The player keeps good records and updates the backer regularly and at year's end, the two settle up. In a losing year, the backer pays all losses. In a winning year, the duo split winnings according to a predetermined percentage, such as 50 percent. The backer often advances money to the player under such arrangements. At year's end, the slate is cleaned and the duo decide if they wish to continue for another year.

Sometimes long-term staking deals aren't quite so long term, or at least are not created for a term certain. The backer agrees to put the player into action for a period of time, but can withdraw at will. As long as the player keeps playing, there are either profits to be divided, or a *make-up* number that the player must win back before he can collect any share of winnings.

Although a complete tax analysis is beyond this book's scope, profits are generally treated just like ordinary gambling winnings. That means different things in different jurisdictions.

> **CAUTION**
>
> ## Perilous Play _____
>
> Fans of the movie/play *The Producers* can probably guess one big staking risk. You don't have to put on the show "Springtime for Hitler" to try to lose money. Poker players, even some extremely famous poker players, have been known to sell 200 percent, 300 percent, and even 500 percent of themselves for big tournaments, 10 percent here and 20 percent there. After accepting backing of $50,000 for a $10,000 buy-in tournament, the famous (and unscrupulous) player makes sure that he busts out in unspectacular fashion long before he's a threat to win.

Backers should monitor players to ensure that the make-up number doesn't become so huge that the player has little chance to win it back without taking huge risks with the backer's money (such as entering very high stakes games during the last week or two of a fiscal year). An ethical player won't do this, but at last count, not every player in poker was ethical.

Players should make sure that backers aren't making unreasonable demands. A few poker lessons are certainly a reasonable request. If the player is famous enough, a motivational speech for the backer's employees wouldn't be out of the question.

At some point, though, a backer's demands can become too onerous. Any backing scheme should have a fair exit strategy for both player and backer. A player who has been in debt for years and who has suddenly gotten ahead owes the backer—at least morally—the opportunity to continue backing for a while, should the backer wish to.

At the same time, a backer who has finally gotten out from under a significant debt burden should have the right to break the arrangement off. Only creativity limits the bounds of player-backer arrangements. If both parties are fair and honest, they can be mutually beneficial. Historically, though, players tend to benefit from backing arrangements more than backers do. It's harder to make a living playing poker than most people realize.

## The Least You Need to Know

- Don't lend or borrow money.

- If you reach your point of misery indifference, get out of the poker room as quickly as possible.

- Staking players can be a good and profitable business arrangement for both backer and player, but there are risks.

# Part 2

## Home Game Poker

With occasional exceptions, most of us first encounter poker in a home environment. That means the material you encounter in Part 2 may feel more familiar to you than much of what you find elsewhere in the text. Home poker games vary in size and shape even more than actual kitchen tables do, though. Part 2 walks you through potential opportunities and classic errors in joining or starting your own game. It also offers its share of strategic tips, money management considerations, and solutions for practical problems that plague poorly planned home games.

Don't make the mistake of thinking "I've played poker at home and done well; I can skip Part 2 and focus on the rest of the book." Even those readers who have played in dozens of different kinds of home games will find important tips here. A few of the home game (and home game management) tips will help you with your casino and/or Internet poker, too.

# Chapter 13

# Home Game Etiquette and Protocols Vary

## In This Chapter

- Know the specific rules for the game, including what games are played
- Is the game social or serious?
- Be aware of local customs
- Know what beats what, what is wild, and how split pots are handled

Home games are different from those played in public cardrooms and casinos.

*Private games* (which include home games) fall into two categories, *social* and *serious*. You should be aware of the conventions and expectations in each. It's important to know the rules and how they're interpreted.

# Local Rules: Wheels, Deals, and Kangaroo Straights

You need to know all the rules that apply to the private game you're in or you might end up losing your shirt. Chapters 2 through 5 have already examined rules of traditional games. Some home games feature unusual games or traditional games with unusual rules. Before you risk your money, you'll want to be clear about unusual local rules or games.

> **Table Talk** _____
>
> A **private** game is one not played in a public cardroom or casino. It can be played at someone's house (curiously, private games are often called home games even if they aren't played in a home), in a fraternal organization, a company's meeting room, or even a hotel room. Private games usually meet regularly (once a week is common) but can also be one-shot affairs.

## Special Hands

You may think, "Well it's poker, isn't it? The hands are *always* the same." Assumptions can be dangerous throughout poker, but particularly in private games. For example, many private games feature split-pot games with half the pot going to the high hand and half to the low hand. What constitutes a low hand or the lowest hand often varies, though.

Some groups consider low hands to be the same as those in *ace-to-five lowball* where the lowest hand is 5-4-3-2-A (the *wheel*), with suits having no bearing. Others go the other extreme, ranking low hands using the *deuce-to-seven lowball* method—exactly opposite of high hands. Aces are high only and straights and flushes count against you, so the lowest hand is 7-5-4-3-2 of mixed suits. Appendix F will help you, but you'll still need to know which low rules are employed.

Other private games count straights and flushes as high hands, but rank the ace low so the lowest hand is 6-4-3-2-A. It can be a pretty sick feeling to bet ferociously with an "unbeatable" 5-4-3-2-A low, only to discover at the end that you've been betting with a straight that can't even beat someone who paired up on his low draw. Know what's low.

*Five of a kind* is the best hand in high draw poker played with the 53-card deck, the regular deck plus the joker (sometimes called the *bug*, a special wild card that can be used to complete a straight or flush, or as an ace, but not for any other purpose). It beats any straight flush. In any wild-card game, five of a kind is some combination of cards all of the same rank plus one or more wild cards. For example, in a *deuces wild* game three sevens and two deuces would be five sevens. Similarly, four deuces plus an eight would constitute five eights.

For example, in the hand 2♠-3♥-4♦-5♣-bug, the bug is a six and it makes a six-high straight. (This assumes you want the highest possible hand; if you're playing high-low draw, the bug can represent an ace for the low side and a six for the high side.) In the hand A♠-A♥-K♠-K♦-joker, the bug is another ace and the hand is aces full of kings; because the bug can be an ace, it can complete this full house. But in the hand K♠-K♥-J♠-J♦-bug, the bug is just an ace kicker.

With four cards of the same suit, the bug usually becomes the highest card that makes a flush. For example, in the hand 9♠-7♠-4♠-3♠-bug, the bug is the same as the A♠; this hand would beat K♦-Q♦-J♦-9♦-7♦. In the hand A♥-9♥-7♥-4♥-bug, the bug would play the same role as the K♥, and the hand would lose to A♦-K♦-10♦-4♦-2♦, since its third card (the 9♥) is lower than the third card of the second hand (the 10♥).

## It's a Lollapalooza

An old story illustrates why you better be certain you know all the hands recognized in a particular game. Jim is playing draw poker in a home game with a bunch of strangers and he's losing. Finally he gets the hand he's been waiting for, a royal flush, and he and Tex get all their chips in the pot. Jim proudly shows his cards and starts to pull in the chips.

"Hold it," says Tex, "I got me a lollapalooza." Tex spreads 10♠-9♦-7♣-4♥-3♠. "What are you trying to pull?" demands Jim. "I never heard of a lollapalooza." Tex goes over to a cabinet, rummages around, and comes back with a typed sheet on which is a table of hand rankings, where Jim sees, "Lollapalooza: 10♠-9♦-7♣-4♥-3♠; beats any other hand." Jim fumes but realizes it's his own fault for not asking for a detailed explanation of local rules. He buys more chips.

Much later, Jim gets dealt his own 10♠-9♦-7♣-4♥-3♠. The betting is spirited and again he and Tex put all their chips in the pot. At the showdown, Jim spreads his lollapalooza and reaches for the pot. "Sorry," says Tex, and goes back to the cabinet, returning with another typed sheet. On it, among other rules, he shows Jim where it says, "Lollapalooza: Good only once per night."

(If you were sharp enough to wonder if a new night began at 12:01 A.M., you probably won't fall into many home game traps!)

## Special Hand Rankings

In three-card poker (not the casino game, but a home game called *guts* in some parts of the country), three of a kind ranks higher than a straight or flush and a straight may rank higher than a flush. Straights also almost always rank higher than flushes in stripped deck games (like the Australian game Manila, where all the cards deuce through six—20 cards—are removed from play before the deal). Find out before you play!

# Social or Serious

People play private games for many reasons, but two predominate ones. The emphasis is usually either on the social aspect of the game (that is, to have fun, be with their friends, drink some beer, and eat some food), or on the money. The stakes and how strictly players adhere to the rules will be good indicators of the answer to an important question: whether you're in a *social* or *serious* game.

## It's Social

In *social games* (also called *friendly games*), frequently almost anything goes. No one is a great stickler for the rules. Disputes are handled inconsistently. Most people don't care too much how much they win or lose. In such games, players who seem to be more interested in winning big at the expense of the others are often not invited back. Players are there to have fun. Social games often go for years and involve many of the same players.

Games like these might take place in a college fraternity or dorm, in a faculty club, or among a group of professional colleagues who meet weekly or monthly. They also often rotate among the participants' homes. There have been well-known games among literary celebrities that endured literally for decades. These games are often played for relatively small stakes. The smallest games are called *penny-ante games.* Social games are sometimes called *kitchen table poker* (even though they are as likely to meet in a basement or den as in a kitchen).

Social games are often played dealer's choice. The dealers choose games with lots of wild cards, games in which cards are passed to left and right, and games with many community cards (often arranged in complicated formations). "If you can tell us the rules, we'll play" might be heard at a typical session. It's not uncommon for games to be made up on the spot: "I like that game we just played. Let's play it again, except this time we'll add another card at the end."

## We're Serious About This

In *serious games*, the rules are important and may even be written down after agreement among the regulars. If the rules aren't written, players generally agree to abide by rules presented in a given book. Players comport themselves in a manner similar to that of a public cardroom or casino. Rule infractions are treated seriously and anyone who seems to deliberately break the rules may be requested to leave immediately. The stakes are usually higher than those in social games.

The game selection is usually limited to the same games as found in cardrooms and casinos, although you will occasionally run into a serious game that features a few slightly nonstandard games.

# Local Customs

Often, the previous dealer gathers the cards from the hand he just dealt and shuffles them in preparation for the deal after the current one. While he is doing this, the current dealer uses a second deck to deal out this hand. Keeping two decks in play speeds up the game.

In *social games*, the players often don't care whether the cards are cut, and, if they're cut, they don't care what method is used to cut the cards. In *serious games*, the cards should be cut by the player to the right of the shuffler or dealer. If this player declines to cut, anyone else can request to cut. The cards must be cut only by lifting some portion of the cards from the top of the deck (leaving no fewer than four cards in either portion) and set down next to the remaining cards.

In social games, there are as many shuffling and cutting practices as there are players.

In some very informal social games, you might see a player out of a hand run across to the other side of the table to peek at his buddy's hole cards. That would be inappropriate in a serious game. In a social game, a player with a difficult decision might consult with a neighbor who is out of the hand on how best to play the hand. That would be even more strictly forbidden in serious games.

# Rules of the Game

We have seen how important it is to know if the game has any special hands, what beats what, and what is wild. It's equally as important is to know how split pots are handled.

## Split the Pot

Many home games, particularly those in the social category, feature a lot of split-pot games. In serious games, the rules are often spelled out and modeled on cardroom rules.

In *high-low split* games that have no *declaration*, the pot is split at the end among active contenders with half the pot going to the holder of the highest hand and half the pot going to the holder of the lowest hand. This is called *cards speak*. If a tie exists for either half, that half is also split. Sometimes the entire pot can be won by the same player because that player holds both the highest and the lowest hand. Sometimes that player may get three-fourths of the pot if another player ties for the low or high half.

> **Table Talk**
>
> **High-low split** is a form of poker in which the pot is split between the highest and lowest active qualifying hands. To **qualify** for the low side of a split pot game, a low must be an eight-low in standard or casino-style games. Home games that use a qualifier also normally use an eight-low as the minimum, but because "anything goes" in some home games, you should make sure.

If there are *qualifiers*, the best low hand might not be eligible for a share of the pot. In such case, the best high hand takes the entire pot. If there are ties, the affected pots are also split appropriately.

*Qualifiers* are much more common on the low side (for example, an eight-low can qualify for the low side of a pot, while a nine-low can't), but occasionally you run into high qualifiers like "jacks or better to open, trips to win." If there are qualifying requirements and no one meets them on one side (for example, no one has a qualifying low), the best hand of the other kind (in this example the best high) wins the whole pot. Sometimes both the highest and lowest hand are held by the same player, in which case that player wins the whole pot (often called *scooping* or *hogging*).

## When Cards Speak

This example shows how the cards speak concept works in a high-low split game. Here are the hands of the four remaining players at the showdown in a seven-card stud high-low split game with *no* qualifier:

Andy: (K♠-K♥) 4♠-2♦-3♣-4♦ (4♣)

Bill: (Q♣–K♣) A♣-9♣-T♣-T♥ (7♠)

Chloe: (A♠-2♦) 3♥-4♥-3♦-K♦ (9♠)

Dave: (9♦-8♦) 7♦-6♣-5♣-Q♦ (9♥)

Andy gets half the pot with his full house. Bill (a flush) and Dave (a straight) get no share of the pot with their flush and straight, and probably lose a lot by getting those hands beat because with no obviously strong hands showing, the betting would have gotten spirited on the end. Chloe gets half the pot with her 9-4 low, which is better than Dave's 9-8 low.

If the game were being played with the standard eight *qualifier* for low, Andy would win the entire pot. Chloe, who had been drawing at an A-2-3-4 low after four cards, would be justifiably frustrated … although if she lets her frustration spill over onto the next hand, she will probably lose money there unnecessarily.

## "I Declare!"

Home games sometimes use a *declaration* in high-low split games, that is, the use of chips or voice to indicate whether players wish to contend for high, low, or both. Declaration is practically nonexistent in public cardrooms, where high-low split games are usually played in *cards speak* style.

In games with a declaration, the pot is split between the holder of the highest hand who declares high and the holder of the lowest hand who declares low. This makes it theoretically possible for the highest hand to win low and the lowest hand to win high; if only one player declares in a single direction, he wins that half of the pot, regardless of his cards. I have seen players win low with a full house because they had declared low in the presence of an apparently stronger high.

High-low split is often called simply *high-low*, or simply a *split game*.

**Table Talk**

In a **cards speak** game, the hands are turned face up at the conclusion of the betting, and the best hand wins. This may seem obvious, but the phrase exists to distinguish the game from a **declaration game**, where a player can only win in a given direction (or directions, such as "high" or "high and low") if he has declared himself in contention for that direction.

In high-low split games with a *declaration*, after all the cards are out, players use chips or a sequential verbal announcement to indicate whether they wish to contend for ("go for") high, low, or both. If one player declares both ways, that player loses the entire pot if he is clearly beaten in either direction (this penalty is necessary, or else everyone would always declare both ways). If a "both" declarer wins in one direction and ties in the other, in some games he loses everything, while in others he receives varying shares, depending on local rules.

For example, here are the hands of the four remaining players at the showdown in a seven-card stud high-low split game:

Hal: (Q♠-Q♥) 6♠-2♦-3♠-6♦ (6♣) (a full house, sixes full of queens)

Lois: (A♠-2♠) 3♥-4♥-3♥-7♦ (Q♥) (a 7-4 low)

Betty: (2♥-3♣) 4♠-5♦-9♠-9♥ (6♥) (a 6-5 low and a straight for high)

Lance: (7♦-A♥) 4♣-5♣-2♣-K♠ (K♥) (a 7-5 low)

After the betting is over, the players declare. The mechanics of this process works as follows. Players put their hands behind their backs or (more commonly) beneath the table, each with two chips in one hand. Each transfers (or pretends to transfer; the acting is sometimes rather comical) a number of chips that will indicate the portion of the pot he or she is contending for into the other hand.

On a signal, each player puts one hand forward and all simultaneously open up to disclose their declarations. Hal has one chip in his hand, which is a standard way to declare high. Lois shows no chips, indicating she is declaring low. Betty has two chips, declaring she is *going both ways* (that is, contending for both high and low). Lance indicates a declaration for low with no chips.

> ![CAUTION] **Perilous Play** _____
>
> When opponents come forward with chips, make sure they bring only one hand forward. If they bring two hands up, they can wait a split second, see how people have declared, and try to get half the pot by declaring the other way. They just open their left hand instead of their right, to go low instead of high (or vice versa). Also, be wary of players who slap their chips onto the table rather than simply opening their hands. They might be concealing a chip.

Betty declared both ways, but because her straight is beaten for high by Hal's full house, she loses everything, despite owning the best low. Who gets the rest of the pot is a matter of local interpretation.

In some games, the pot is split between Hal (the best remaining high, with a full house) and Lois (the best remaining low, with her 7-4). This method allows Lois to win half the pot even though she did not win the direction she declared for, an approach called "allowing players to back in." In other games, the entire pot goes to Hal, who won his direction and beat the both ways declarer for that half. Lance, whose 7-5 low is inferior to Lois's 7-4, gets no part of the pot in any interpretation.

The rules get even trickier when there is a tie in either direction (ties are much more common on the low side, but can happen either way). In some games, tying either way eliminates the two-way hand from contention. In other games, a tie earns the declarer a share of the pot.

The number of different permutations possible with ties and multiple both-ways de-clarers is truly astonishing, and is something better experienced than read. This is one reason why an absolute rule like "no backing in allowed" will sometimes make these complex situations easier to decide.

If you know before you play that a tie can cost you the entire pot, you'll declare both ways less often. If you don't know the rule before you play, you'll find out the hard way when the situation comes up. The zero, one, or two chip method also varies; some games use one, two, or three chips. Ask!

If you play in more than one private game and each uses a different method, it's easy to mistakenly use one game's method in the other game, thereby costing yourself a pot. Don't be ashamed to ask more than once a night.

Declaring can be a true art form. Suppose, for example, you are playing seven-stud high-low with a declare. Your hand is (4-5) 2-2-2-2 (7): Your four exposed cards are all deuces, so you are showing quads. Your opponent shows (?-?) K-K-K-Q (?).

How should you declare? There are many good arguments in favor of declaring low! If your opponent only has a full house, why would he declare high when he's staring at four of a kind? If he declares high, he can beat your four deuces. If he goes low, thinking he must do so to avoid losing to your quads, you win if he had a full house, but lose the whole pot if he just had three kings (his K-Q-x-x-x low will beat your 2-2-3-4-7 low). You'll also lose the whole pot if he gets fancy and goes both ways with just three kings because the fact that your high beats his doesn't matter. Because you declared low only, your high hand is irrelevant. Obvious decisions are not always so obvious in declare-form poker!

Less common (fortunately!) is verbal *consecutive declaration*. Each player states in order whether he or she is contending for low, high, or the whole pot. This gives such a big advantage to the last player to declare that it is almost unfair, because it forces you to call a similar game when it is your turn to deal, just to obtain a similar advantage.

**Perilous Play**

Be careful about trying any kind of fancy play or tricky bluff against an inexperienced player. Players new to the game tend to focus exclusively on their own hands and ignore oppo-nents' cards or subtle moves. Inexperienced players will give you enough money by calling on hands they don't belong in; don't hope to get more with finesse plays they'll never see coming.

How is the declaration order determined in consecutive declaration games? Some games just start to the dealer's left. Just as late position can turn a moderate holding into a playable hand in hold'em, so too can late declaration position encourage you to play more starting hands in a split game. (Its converse is also true: If you know your declaration position will be early, you should play fewer hands.)

In most games, though, you can't know before the hand starts who will declare last because in most games the first declarer is the last player to bet or raise. This is a better rule than always starting to the left of the dealer, but as long as the rule stays consistent, everyone knows it, and everyone has a chance to call such a game when it is his turn to deal, any rule is fair.

Many players consider consecutive declaration to be less skillful than simultaneous declaration. I am one of those and always strongly lobby for simultaneous declaration if a new game is starting. Be wary of doing any lobbying as a new player in an established game, though. As a newcomer, part of the etiquette of home games is to not disturb tradition and you may find yourself having to go with the flow.

You may encounter the *bet after the declare* variation (sometimes called *bet-declare-bet*) on the declaration concept. After everyone has declared, a further round of betting takes place before the hands are revealed. This adds one more element of skill for the skillful players.

## Call Dealer-Advantage Games

Most home games are *dealer's choice*. A winning strategy is to choose *dealer-advantage games* when it's your turn to choose. Games dependent on position have built-in dealer advantage because the dealer gets to act last.

Forms of draw poker top the list because you get to see how many cards the others will draw before having to make your own decision. You also get to act last on each of the betting rounds.

The best dealer advantage games:

- ◆ High draw poker
- ◆ Lowball (both single- and triple-draw)
- ◆ High-low draw
- ◆ Hold'em

To address the dealer advantage problem, many private games use one of two methods.

One method has each player in turn call a game and then that game is played for a full round. When the deal returns in rotation to the player who called the last game, that player skips his next deal and the deal—and the right to select a new game— passes one position to the left.

The other method is a form of rotation. Each time a button game (any version of draw or hold'em or Omaha) is called, the button, wherever it is, moves one spot to the left. If someone calls a stud game, the button just stays where it is. In most games, players call a mix of button games and stud or draw games, so ten-handed, it might take 20 to 25 hands for the button to make its way all the way around the table. This eliminates the "I'll call hold'em to get the positional advantage" problem.

---

### Poker Lore

Some of my poker foes got an early sample of my creativity before I became famous. As a youngster playing in a $10-20 six-card stud high-low bet-declare-bet game, I was drawing at both a straight and a six-low going to the final card. I caught a useless king, leaving me with (6) 5-6-3-2 (K) (a pair of sixes for high, and a king for low). This hand had no chance to win a showdown, so desperation led to inspiration.

With three opponents still live, I declared both ways and tossed $20 into the pot. My first opponent "smelled something fishy" but only had a pair of aces and was worried about a later competitor having a better high, and folded. My next opponent had an eight-low, but felt I "obviously" had a six-straight and folded. My final opponent was showing a lot of high cards, but had been drawing at a high straight and couldn't even beat a pair of sixes! I won a $1,000 pot with the third-worst hand at the table.

I wouldn't have shown the move, because it was too profitable, but a player who had been sitting behind me saw my last card, and said (showing poor poker etiquette) "What did you just *do*?!?"

As compensation for this exposed move, for the next six months I got paid off every time I made a low straight because no one wanted to "fall for that one" again. Finally, I decided to try a similar bluff, and sure enough, my opponent said "I'm tired of paying you an extra $20 every time just because you used that move once," and folded. Bet-declare-bet poker offers some interesting possibilities!

---

## The Least You Need to Know

- Know the particular rules for your game.
- Know if the game is social or serious.

- Know what is expected and accepted behavior.

- Know about dealer-advantage games.

- Know how split pots are handled.

# Chapter 14

# Handling Money in Home Games

## In This Chapter

- ◆ Cash or credit?
- ◆ Selecting stakes
- ◆ Don't get hijacked

People participating in private games face some different money concerns from those playing in public cardrooms and casinos. Let's examine those concerns and issues.

## To Your Credit

Unless players choose to play with cash—which can be cumbersome and also tends to create smaller pots because players treat cash with more respect than chips—someone must be responsible for the chips. In both friendly and serious games, that someone is designated as the *banker*. The banker is responsible for collecting player buy-ins and distributing chips.

In serious games, you may see a player put a wad of bills behind his chips. This would be the case in an extremely large game (where $100 bills are usually the only currency allowed on the table so that opposing players can estimate how much money their opponents have). It's usually good practice to convert all cash to chips. This way, when someone wants to know how _deep_ an opponent is in a pot-limit or no-limit hand, he doesn't have to slow the game by asking for a count. It's much easier to eyeball a stack of chips than a stack of bills, even if you know the bills' denomination.

When the player's chips are all in the pot and betting still continues, can a player still continue to bet or be forced to call?

In social games, a player may put his wallet behind his chips, signifying that he guarantees never to run out of chips during the play of a particular hand. This also can cause problems and is a practice that should be discouraged. There's no guarantee that the wallet contains sufficient cash to cover any pot that might arise.

Some games permit _going light_, but this causes more problems than it's worth. Just as is the practice in serious games, it's better to insist on table stakes. If a player wants to have sufficient chips to play the next hand, he should buy more chips before the start of that hand.

In social games, particularly where the players have been playing together for a long time, credit is common. Some players may buy in for cash, but others get marked down on a sheet or "on the books" for their buy-ins, with the understanding that they will pay off at the end of the session. In a very informal game, that paying off might involve players trading debts with each other.

**CAUTION**  **Perilous Play** _____

In serious games, the banker is well advised to buy unique chips. If you play with cheap plastic universally available chips, it's too easy for someone to buy matching chips before arriving and slip some into the game. Because the banker has promised to redeem all chips for cash at settle-up time, he can get stuck paying out more than he took in.

Sometimes a particular player might not pay up at the end of the session, promising to do so at the start of the next session. There usually is an understanding that the player will not be allowed to participate in the next session until he makes good on his debts of the previous session.

In serious games, strictly cash is usually the rule, although a well-known player's check may be accepted, as well as any checks he guarantees. In some games, the players may all know each other well enough to accept each other's checks. Checks become more desirable if the stakes are high enough for the players to fear a robbery (called a *hijacking*).

**CAUTION**  **Perilous Play** _____

If you're playing in a private game with stakes higher than a few dollars per betting round, you may need to take precautions against being hijacked. Stakes of $20-$40, for example, can easily mean the players are carrying a combined $10,000 to $20,000 in their pockets, an inviting target for one or more thieves to forcibly enter and hold up the players. Door security is a good precaution. Using checks is another.

At the end of a session, the banker buys back each player's chips. If the game is strictly on a cash basis, the banker pays each player out of the cash bank. If players are on credit, how much they owe is subtracted from their chips. In friendly games if anyone remains on the books, usually the big winner for the night accepts that player's debt. If the banker plays and has a net loss for the evening, he must pay some of the winners out of his own pocket, or, in some social games, go on the books himself.

If a player left a blank check (if you do this, do not sign the check until you are ready to fill in an amount; otherwise, you leave yourself open to all kinds of legal difficulties), he retrieves and tears up the check if he won. If he loses, he fills it out for the proper amount and signs it.

A player who lacks sufficient funds in his account to cover the check will often ask if he can post-date his check. Although it is better for the person who is being paid via the check to learn this news at the game than through his bank when the check bounces, it is poor etiquette to play for a sum that you know you cannot cover immediately. A player in that situation should announce this before play by saying something like "If I lose, I will have to write a check and that check won't be good until I get paid on Friday."

## Your Own Private Banker

In many serious games, the banker does not play. Rather, he deals and often hosts the game with food and drink. Such bankers usually charge players for their services. A set fee is more desirable than a situation in which the banker *cuts the pot* (somewhat randomly taking money from the pot) regularly. You would be amazed how much $5 here and $5 there ends up taking out of a game by an evening's end. If you play eight hours at 40 hands per hour, that's 320 hands. The banker won't cut every one of them (some of the pots are too small), but if he takes a $5 chip out of three-fourths of the hands, he's removed $1,200 from the game!

A game may also employ a professional dealer. This situation is more common for a private tournament. The players agree that everyone will contribute toward his pay with toking (tipping) optional. Usually a banker-host and a professional dealer are entirely different people. Sometimes a game has just a banker-host. He may deal all of the time or the deal may just rotate among the players. Often the banker-host plays if there is an open seat but gives his seat up if one of his "cash" players arrives wanting a seat.

### The Inside Straight

Anytime a game's rake comes out of the pot (as opposed to coming as a button charge or an hourly rate), players who play a lot of hands pay a disproportionate share of the rake. You shouldn't change a winning style just to avoid rake; that would be silly. Most players play too many hands anyway. By trying to avoid rake responsibility, most loose players would improve their overall results.

With a set fee, the banker might cut each pot at an agreed-upon rate until that fee is reached. At that point the banker no longer takes anything from the pots.

In social games, the player might agree to cut the pots until a certain amount is reached to repay the host for the cost of refreshments—or maybe for a present to mollify the host's spouse for putting up with the disruption!

---

**Poker Lore**

In one noted private game, players take $1 out of each pot and put it in a special fund until $12,000 is reached. This usually takes most of the year. They then have a *freeze-out* tournament among all the regulars and send the winner to compete in the main event of the World Series of Poker. The prize includes the $10,000 buy-in, airfare, and money for hotel and expenses. Their representative agrees to split 25 percent of any winnings with the other members of the regular game. They have been doing this for years.

If you consider doing something like this yourself, note that you will need very clear definitions of just what constitutes a "regular." Because those $1 chips add up over time, this is not a good game to "drop in on." You should probably be a regular or not play at all.

---

If you have ever hosted a poker game, you understand why players are willing to pay someone something to run it. You face issues involving smoke, noise, damage, late hours, neighbors, food, drinks, and clean-up, to say nothing of the labor involved in making sure neither too many nor too few players show up to play. Paying someone a fee to take on all these responsibilities is reasonable, as long as you understand how much you are paying.

Such a raked private game might take place at the home of the nonplaying host or in a rented meeting room or hotel room.

Rotating the game among the players' homes is a decent alternative, but what do you do if one player has a spouse who just won't allow the game? It can also be confusing trying to find a different location each week. These hurdles are among the many reasons why players are willing to play in cut-pot games, and of course in cardrooms or on the Internet where the host casino takes a rake.

## Enforce Your Money Rules Strictly

It seems easier and friendlier to let players go "on the books" at the start of each session rather than buy in for cash. However, in the long run this can prove harmful to the game. If a strictly cash (or check) policy is firmly enforced from the beginning, then the following scenario can never happen:

> Joe goes on the books for $100. At the end of the night, he says, "I forgot my checkbook," and promises to pay next session. Next week he arrives *sans* checkbook, but professes always to have paid up before. He either talks someone into lending him money for that night or convinces the regulars to allow him to stay on the books one more week. This night Joe has a particularly bad session and loses $300. That is the last anyone ever sees Joe.

It turns out that no one really knew Joe all that well and no one knows where he lives or works. Indeed, even if the players do know where to find him, what are they going to do—hire a leg breaker? Even if Joe has written a hot check, gambling debts are not legally collectible. The players—or the unfortunate good Samaritan who lent him all the cash—get stuck for the $400. If the players don't agree to split the loss equally, something like this can break up a regular weekly game. Even if they do share it, no one is very happy about it.

> **The Inside Straight**
>
> Insisting that everyone either pay cash at the start or show that they have brought a blank check eliminates most problems. Even checks have been known to bounce among friends. There's no one ideal solution, but if the stakes aren't high enough to encourage hijacking, cash upfront is the best way to go.

It might even be that Joe would have remained as a long-term losing player if no one had allowed him to get heavily enough in debt to make it worth his emotional while to skip out on the debt burden. The Joes of the world are often willing to lose $50 a week forever (as long as they win occasionally), but when faced with a single large payoff, the temptation to avoid responsibility becomes too much to handle.

# Selecting the Stakes

Whatever stakes you play should be comfortable for the players. When trying to figure out the stakes, it's usually easier for players to think about how much downside risk they will be taking. A good rule of thumb is that on a typical night in a typically loose game, the big winner will win (and the big loser will lose) 30 to 50 big bets. If your stakes are nickel-dime-quarter, no one is likely to win or lose more than $12.50. If your stakes are $5-10, the big loser is unlikely to drop more than $500.

It's certainly possible that the number could be higher (and on most nights, it will be lower), but the 30-50 big bet rule of thumb will allow you to set stakes your players will be comfortable with.

## Considerations Involved in Changing the Stakes

Sometimes players want or need to change stakes. Usually the players want to play higher, but sometimes the stakes need to be reduced.

There are two different times when the stake-changing issue arises.

The first comes up when the players decide the overall game dynamic isn't what they want: It's either too rough or too meaningless. Before changing stakes, make sure that everyone in the group is comfortable with the change and doesn't feel trapped by peer pressure. If Fred is already losing enough each week to jeopardize his home situation and the game changes from $5-10 to $10-20, Fred may need to drop out even if he doesn't want to say so in front of everyone. But if the game just seems no fun because the stakes are too low for everyone but Fred, talk it over as a group and, if appropriate, take a vote.

It doesn't have to be unanimous, but seriously consider how much the lone objector contributes to the ambience and dynamic of the game. If everyone really likes Fred, or if Fred is the game's biggest regular loser and doubling the stakes will mean Fred will drop out, raising the stakes could prove much costlier to the remaining players than it initially appears. Instead of winning twice as much, good players may actually win less.

Discussions about permanent stake changes don't happen too often in a poker game: Once a year is a lot. The second kind of stake-changing happens quite often in private games, though.

## Just One Round

Some private games modify the stakes for the last hour or maybe only the last one or more rounds. Often the losers request a "chance to get even."

Players might double the limit completely or increase the limit on the last round of betting. Everyone should be comfortable with such a change. If any player is not, the best rule is that the stakes do not change. If your group wants to use a majority-rules approach, any dissenters should be permitted to leave early without embarrassment. Players should be consistent, though. A player who pleads for doubled stakes one week while losing should not object on another occasion when he is winning.

Usually, the player who has pleaded for the increased stakes to get even loses even more during that last period. If this regularly happens, particularly to someone who cannot afford the loss, you need to decide just how serious you are. Whether or not you have a moral duty to look out for another player's best interests really depends on whether the game truly is a "friendly" game, or whether, as is often the case in poker, everyone is trying to maximize his own winning chances.

If your game is truly friendly, even though for serious stakes, it makes sense to help a player protect himself from his short-term bad judgment. Most of the time, even when the players like one another, everyone is presumed to be "a grown-up" and must protect himself. In such situations, you may still want to protect a player from himself, figuring that you can shear a sheep many times, but only kill him once. It is often better to ensure the longevity of the game than worry about temporary unhappiness of one player.

**Perilous Play** _____

Don't feel that just because you're the big winner you're obligated to play at increased stakes to give the losers a chance at getting "their" money back. After they lose that money, it's not theirs anymore. You don't have to jeopardize your win out of a feeling of guilt. Most private games have rules, either written or unwritten, governing when a player may leave; as long as you comply with these, you won't lose your regular seat.

Playing the last hour or the last round at increased stakes usually works out more to the advantage of the winners than the losers. If you're winning and leaving would be socially imprudent, then just play *supertight* for those last rounds. You'll win more money as the losers play even more recklessly in a desperate effort to get even for the night.

**Table Talk** _____

A tight player chooses his starting hands selectively. A **supertight** player is even more selective and usually proceeds with great care through the later betting rounds, too. Supertight play is usually not the best way to win over the course of a game, but it's not a bad way to preserve a lead if your friends are insisting you play longer than you'd prefer.

# Don't Get Hijacked

The best way to avoid being hijacked or minimize the risk is to take precautions in advance. Deal with a reputable host only, someone known to you and the other players. Don't play in a game with a bunch of fellows you run into in a cardroom. Such a game is called an *after-hours game* if the cardroom from which you came closes at a certain time (such as 2 A.M.). It might also be called a *steer game* because someone in a cardroom steers you to a private game. The steerer might even get paid for what he does. Such a game is often crooked or in danger of being hijacked.

In theory it might seem right to decide that you won't play with people you don't know very well, but in practice, that doesn't work well in most games. Unless a game has been around for a long time and is very stable, friends of friends (and acquaintances of acquaintances) are always coming and going.

Don't tell the world about your game. It may seem obvious to someone not to talk publicly about his game in a public place, but that same person may freely talk about the game on a portable phone (which is not very different from a radio) or a cell phone (which is not much harder to tap). It may be harder to resist talking about the game than you think, especially after a big win. A spouse who talks about the game can also put it at risk.

## The Least You Need to Know

- ◆ Play for cash up front rather than playing for credit.
- ◆ In a serious game, consider using checks rather than cash.
- ◆ Consider hiring a professional banker/dealer.
- ◆ Take precautions to avoid getting hijacked.

# Chapter 15

# The Perfect Home Poker Game

## In This Chapter

◆ How to find a game or start your own

◆ Setting a starting and ending time

◆ Protecting yourself from cheaters

If you want to play in a private game, you can look for one or you can start your own. Whichever you play in, you'll find it best to have established starting and ending times.

When you're in a game, even a friendly game with people you've known for years, there is the possibility that cheating exists. A little vigilance, coupled with the knowledge of what to look for, will go a long way toward protecting both you and the game.

Dealer's choice is what you'll find in most private games, where you will probably see poker variations not played in public cardrooms.

# Finding a Home Game

Whether you want to find an existing game or start your own depends on what you're looking for from your home poker game. How much control do you want to have over it? How much effort are you willing to put not just into the search for players and/or a game, but also into the long-term maintenance, care, and development of your home game?

## Joining an Existing Game

In this modern age, perhaps the fastest way to find an existing game is on the Internet, but as is so often the case in life, the fastest route to success can be fraught with peril. Let's look at how the Internet can work for you and examine reasons why you might want to be cautious in using it.

There are many online poker discussion groups and mailing lists and all have frequent postings either from participants in existing games soliciting more players or from those looking for games.

The granddaddy of all online poker discussion groups is rec.gambling.poker (this is a newsgroup, not a website), widely known among participants simply as *RGP*. And those participants are frequently called *RGPers*.

You'll see regular RGP postings such as, "I'm looking for a small-stakes home game in the Chicago area." The poster will likely get many responses, usually private, because home games are usually illegal (at least technically), and the players have no desire to advertise their activities to the world. Recognize, though, that the players you find while searching advanced poker resources, such as RGP, are likely to be more highly skilled than the typical random home game player.

**CAUTION**   **Perilous Play** _____

RGP is an unmoderated newsgroup, which has both good and bad aspects. On the plus side, there's no censorship, so if you want a forum to express yourself, you can make yourself heard. The flip side of that freedom means that you have to be willing to accept exposure to irresponsible people who frequently post their opinions and claim them to be facts. RGP debates often turn into cruel, vicious, *ad hominem* flame wars, which often cause better poker players to abandon the forum.

RGP isn't just a spot where you can find a home poker game. You can get good poker advice there, but you can also get bad advice. It's probably better to "lurk" (read, but do not post) for awhile until you get a feel for what flies and what doesn't. Some wags refer to it as rec.gossip.poker because of the highly personal nature of many posts.

It's a certainty I will get flamed on RGP for mentioning the negative aspects here, because some RGP denizens get highly defensive about the group. Saying something bad about their discussion group is, to these Internet-focused souls, no different from saying something bad about them, even though the difference should seem obvious. The newsgroup has quite literally become their life's focus.

Because individuals can post anonymously on RGP, the posters are safely hidden behind their screen names and keyboards. A vocal minority act both brave and tough when the reality is that by posting anonymously and irresponsibly, they are proving that they are precisely the opposite. Once you realize this, you can develop a thick skin and accept the forum for what it is, taking the bad along with the good.

If you attend a college or university, you can easily find a game. Many dormitories and fraternities have regular games, usually at stakes that students can afford. Ask around or post a notice on a community bulletin board at the student union or similar location.

Many country clubs and fraternal and service organizations have regular member games. Sometimes people join these groups just to get into the poker games! Sports bars offer another good hunting ground, because avid sports bettors are often poker players.

Your co-workers are good sources of information about private games. Sometimes these consist entirely of fellow workers, while sometimes your co-workers are just part of the networking process. Employees sometimes have regular after-hours games in company meeting rooms, although you're well-advised to make sure management doesn't frown on this practice. The lunch hour is not a promising time to play: An hour is usually not time enough for much of a game.

Another good place to find a "one shot" private game is at a professional convention. Among a group of bored conventioneers you will surely find some who have arranged a "friendly" game. Usually such games are either pure candy

**CAUTION   Perilous Play**

Anytime you enter a new poker game "cold," you should be a little wary and the higher the stakes, the warier you should grow. If you know no one in the game, you're probably a bit more at risk of being cheated or stiffed (unpaid) than if you enter knowing at least one person well.

or traps for the unwary (that is, either great or terrible). Bored, rich professionals make easy poker targets, but anytime something looks too good to be true, it usually is.

You can also find out about private games in cardrooms that cater primarily to local traffic. Ask the players at your table the next time you play. Just be careful of getting *steered* to a crooked game.

Finally, although casino junkets or charter tours are far less common than they used to be, any group traveling to a casino destination usually contains more than a few folks who play poker regularly. These privately chartered jets or buses usually feature more social interaction than public transportation and you'll probably be able to find either a game to play in or some new players for your own game.

## Starting Your Own Game

If you can't find the perfect preexisting private game, you may want to tailor one to your desires. Your own home game can be a lot of fun and it doesn't need to be yours exclusively. The game can rotate among the homes of those participants willing to host a regular session. If you want the game to be successful and last for months or years, do things right from the start.

Probably most important is to establish a nucleus of regulars who share your desire for a long-term successful game. Depending on their enthusiasm, this should be 10 to 12 players. Eight to ten players make a nice game, but on any given night, one or two players are likely not to show up, so you need a few more.

Before you select your ideal number of starting players, you should decide what games will be played. Ten or even 11 can work nicely for community card games (assuming your table is big enough), but if you play stud games, you may not want more than eight (lest you risk running out of cards).

### The Inside Straight

Running a home game can take a tremendous amount of time and energy, especially if you don't have dependable regulars. Someone has to worry about food, clean-up, noise, parking, banking the game, ending the game, making rulings, and ensuring that enough players show up. Make sure you know what you're in for before you volunteer to take all this on. It's quite reasonable to require the players to pay for food and a post-game maid service (usually preferred over bringing food and assisting with clean-up).

If you have more players show up than you need, you can have a player or players sit out each round and then rotate back in.

If all 12 show up, you can, if the room will accommodate it, have two tables running simultaneously, although many players dislike playing shorthanded. If you're worried about too many players, develop procedures that ensure neither too many nor too few players will show. A signup list and a waiting list for the next game can help.

It's fairly common to have a core of regular players who can always have a seat if they request it by a certain date (for understandable reasons, truly bad players who lose cheerfully often achieve core regular status without complaint from others). Once the regulars have indicated whether or not they can attend, the alternates get invited.

There are an almost infinite number of ways to regulate who gets to play when, but one rule is usually common to all of them: If you say you're going to show up and you don't, you fall to the bottom of the pecking order when it comes to priority seating for the next game.

If the game is at the home of one player, that player should own a poker table or tables, or at least be willing to store them. This doesn't have to be expensive. You can buy portable poker table tops that fit an ordinary card table and can accommodate eight or more players.

Good cards are also important. Four to eight plastic decks are not very expensive and replacing decks regularly keeps cards that get marked (intentionally or inadvertently) out of play.

Quality uniquely imprinted clay chips are fun at low stakes and imperative at high stakes, because it's too easy—and maybe too much of a temptation—for a losing player to slip his own cheap red, white, and blue plastic chips into a game.

You can buy a nice set of distinctive clay or composite chips from any of several online gaming supply houses. These have a feel similar to cardroom chips and are hard to counterfeit.

Because private games face their own unique challenges and situations, make sure to address those before they come up. To head off problems, you may want to hold a group discussion about etiquette, such as how buy-ins and credit will be handled. If you establish a rule right from the start that there will be no credit and that every player must settle up immediately, you can avoid a potentially awkward moment or problem situation from ever arising.

# The Best of Times

Reliable starting and ending times are important elements of a good private game. Your game should have a specific starting time and always start promptly. If the game is supposed to start at 7:00 P.M. and the latecomers aren't somehow penalized, they'll get the mistaken impression that they can show up late every time. This problem gets worse over time, rather than better, as players try to outwait each other.

Among the more useful penalties for late arrival:

♦ You have to rotate out if too many players show up, while prompt arrivals do not (or perhaps have to rotate out less frequently)

♦ Loss of a guaranteed seat for the next game (shifting their status from "regular" to "alternate")

♦ Paying a disproportionate share of food and/or cleaning fees

♦ Loss of the right to call dealer's choice games

Ending on time is equally important. Establish a quitting time, probably by majority vote, and *stick to it*. At the end of a session, there will often be plaintive, dramatic and sometimes desperate-sounding requests from those losing for "just one more round" or hour.

Acceding to a request for one round usually leads to several extra rounds, one extra hour becomes two, and soon people who have to be at work the next morning or have family obligations find themselves playing all night and then not returning the following week—sometimes as a result of instructions from a disturbed significant other. If everyone wants to play till 4 A.M., fine, but the winners shouldn't feel bullied or obligated by the losers.

# Cheats and Cheating

Whether you run a private game or play in one regularly, you have to be able to protect yourself by identifying the cheaters and knowing what to do when you find them.

You might think your game invulnerable to this problem. You've been playing with the same bunch of friends for years. None of them would ever cheat. I'm sorry to disillusion you. Even in the smallest and friendliest of games, you find cheats.

Lou doesn't conceal his cards very well. Charlie always arrives early enough to grab the chair to Lou's right. Before Charlie acts, he glances out of the corner of his eye to see what Lou has. Bob riffle shuffles with the deck facing him and observes in what portion of the deck certain cards land. When Bill deals, he briefly tilts the deck forward to glimpse the bottom card.

Small matters like these happen all the time and these are just the smaller offenses. In games that allow players to go light (a practice we discourage), players will often remove them from the pot rather than repay their lights—a double theft.

**The Inside Straight** _____

If the dealer properly uses a *cut card* in your game, no one can see the bottom card.

## To Catch a Thief

Whole books have been written on cheats and cheating methods. Some of these are listed in Appendix A.

*Holdout artists* remove cards from play for reintroduction later into the game. This is harder to do in a game that uses two decks of cards, but if the players don't count down the deck at the end of each deal (something that not even professional dealers do as often as they should), the holdout artist can get away with it.

This *move* used to be more common in draw games, but it can still happen in hold'em and seven-card stud. A held-out card is more likely to be hidden in the cheat's lap or under the table. Have you stared at your opponent's lap lately? Didn't think so.

Wherever he hides the card (or cards), though, the cheat needs to do three things: remove the card from play, introduce it back again at the opportune moment, and *clean up* (get rid of the extra cards) at the end.

**Table Talk** _____

A **move** is any cheating manipulation of the deck. You'll also hear the phrase *to make a move*.

You can detect this move because the player doesn't toss his discards out, but slides them, often pressed under his hand, into the discard pile. This is more easily done in a game in which the discards all sit sloppily in the center of the table awaiting the next shuffle, a description that fits the cards in most private games.

A cheat might also just draw too many cards in draw games. He might, for example, discard two cards but ask for three (it's amazing what you can get away with when everyone trusts you). This allows him to choose the best five of the six cards he has, a monstrously huge advantage.

**The Inside Straight** _____

You're well-advised to encourage those eating to sit out a hand or two. It's better for their digestion and it keeps greasy hands off the cards. Even someone who doesn't intend to mark a card may do so for someone else who notices the stain and takes advantage. If food is part of your game, have plenty of extra decks on hand.

*Marked cards* are another ruse. These range from what to those in the know would call blatantly obvious to very sophisticated markings that even experts have trouble identifying. Magic supply houses, both online and in specialty shops, sell marked decks for magicians.

You don't need to visit a magic supply house to mark a card, of course. At the low tech end of the spectrum, a sharp fingernail or a little ketchup from that delicious burger can work wonders.

Sophisticated cheats sometimes create a composite deck, called *sorts*, by taking portions from several decks whose patterns don't seem markable, such as the uniform red and white diamonds common on paper decks. This takes advantage of slight differences in patterns in different runs of cards. The diamonds on one deck may meet at the edges slightly differently from one deck to another, but, to the untrained eye, the patterns look the same on the backs of all the cards.

More sophisticated markings include *white on white*, a white paint that can be seen only at a certain angle. Thieves sometimes wear red contacts that can detect infrared markings on the backs of cards. There has also been talk in the poker world lately about cobalt blue sunglasses used to pick up markings on cards in very high stakes games.

**The Inside Straight** _____

One way to identify a marked deck is with a reverse riffle, flipping through the deck from the rear and observing how the markings seem to dance, similar to those animated flip books made for kids. Even if you can't see the markings on individual cards, such as with sorts, you can see the differences from card to card by this kind of flipping motion.

Many cheats mark cards on-the-fly. A thief might put a slight nick along the edge of each ace as he gets it. Just knowing the locations of one of the four aces gives a thief a huge edge.

Unsophisticated players don't notice the markings because they're usually small. If confronted, a thief can claim the markings just got there naturally, and, even if they're noticed, who's to say who put them there? A cheat can conceal a tack in his hand and put a small indentation in key cards (called *nailing*), so he can tell by feel what the rank of a card is—quite an advantage when dealing.

Keep your eyes open. Glance at the cards from unusual light angles and run your fingers over your cards to see if you detect any bumps, cuts, paint, or food markings.

Card manipulation can avoid many marked cards problems; if you have the dexterity to manipulate cards, you don't have to run the risk of leaving physical card evidence sitting around. Eliminating such cheating edges from games is one of the best reasons to pay a cardroom's rake. The dealers change games every 20 minutes, and in a big cardroom, you might seen a given dealer only once a night. If you play much high stakes poker in games where the players handle the cards, invest in some of the many books that have been written about cheating. It's too big a topic to, if you'll pardon the expression, even scratch the surface here.

### The Inside Straight

Although it's difficult to catch a good card manipulator dealer, you should probably suspect trouble if you see that the dealer holds the cards using the so-called "mechanic's grip." Most people hold the deck with four fingers on the long side of the cards. Most card mechanics move their index finger and middle finger from the long side of the deck to the short side of the deck away from them. It's no accident that more of the deck is now concealed by your hand.

The hardest cheating plays to detect are those not involving marked cards or manipulation. These involve partners (sometimes called colluders). Colluders often play in teams of two or more. If they're not good, they're easy to detect. If they are good, it might be almost impossible, especially if they don't get greedy and work together too often.

Thieves in partnership work off a communal bankroll, and they might raise for each other to build a pot when one of them has a very strong hand. One quietly folds before the showdown. If they're clever enough, they might raise in situations where it is clear that an opponent has a substandard holding, but might call if the cost of calling doesn't get too expensive. Identifying this practice is easier in online poker, where hand histories are available, than it is in live poker games.

This is done to steal pots by driving out a marginal hand because it looks less suspicious. It's risky, though, because the player or players from whom they're trying to steal the pot might just get stubborn and call. Thieves prefer to build pots when they have powerhouse hands.

One scam almost impossible to detect is called *best hand*. The partners play only the best hand among them, thus avoiding both of them losing money in the same pot. That way only one team member loses, saving the team money. Such a scheme works best in draw games, but can also be of use in hold'em, when, for example, one holds a pair and the other a higher pair, or one has A-K and the other A-Q or K-Q.

In all such partnership arrangements, the players have to signal each other their holdings. It isn't hard, especially given all the nervous habits that even honest players have.

### The Inside Straight

You aren't necessarily doomed if you're up against a cheat or a partnership. Although there are certainly exceptions, players usually turn to cheating because they aren't able to win playing straight poker. A cheat might have extra information available to him, but if he doesn't know how best to use it, he can still be a losing player. Indeed, many private games have regulars who are known to be cheats and who are tolerated, because they are among the game's most regular losers.

### Poker Lore

Another probably apocryphal tale involves a grizzled old man who walked into a saloon in the old west. He approached a poker table and pulled a big Bowie knife from his belt. "If anybody in this here game cheats me, they get this!" he roared, and plunged the knife into the table. No one cheated the old man, but he cheated quite handily by using his knife blade as a *shiner*—a mirrored surface object on which he could see the cards' reflections as he dealt them.

Few modern games will be played with a knife stuck in the table, but beware any unusually shiny objects placed on the table – even smooth and shiny rings. If you experiment with them and see that you can pick up some kind of reflection (perhaps just enough to see if a card is red or black, or a face card), there's a pretty good chance that someone else is using the shiner the same way.

# An Ounce of Prevention Is Worth a Pound of Cure

You can prevent a lot of the potential for problems by establishing procedures that obviate the likelihood of cheating.

Using plastic decks instead of paper forestalls many of the impromptu markings. Using fresh (unopened!) decks each session heads off the possibility of cards being marked in advance (but not of purchased magic cards, which are often resealed by the seller).

Insist on using the same shuffling techniques as in cardrooms and casinos. The deck must remain flat on the table, with each half of the deck lifted to interlace with the other half, leaving no large, unshuffled clumps. Several shuffles, intermingled with cuts, should be performed. No overhand shuffles, or perfunctory hand-to-hand shuffles (techniques used by many honest players who lack dexterity) should be allowed.

The deck should be cut also flat on the table and into just two halves. The deck should always be cut. Your rules can perhaps allow an additional shuffle by another player if so requested, and a cut by the player to his right.

Discards should not be scattered all over the table, but placed in a neat pile to the left of the current dealer. No one should be permitted to "play around" with the discards prior to the next dealer gathering and shuffling the cards. If two decks are in play, the second deck should be shuffled by the *previous* dealer, rather than the next dealer.

If two or three players always seem to take the same positions relative to each other, you might consider taking action to randomize the seating.

Educate your players how to protect their hands (conceal their cards from their neighbor's glance). If you know that someone regularly exposes his cards, tell him about it. You'll be doing him a favor, and in the long run, helping the integrity of your game.

# You've Got to Know When to Scold 'Em

Whether it's a social game or serious, you don't want cheaters in the game.

If you're just a player and you spot a cheating problem, you might want to have a private word with the host, rather than trying to correct the problem yourself. Tell him you know that Bill always sits to the right of Johnny because Bill always exposes his cards and Bill knows what Johnny will do almost before Johnny knows. This gives Bill an unfair advantage.

**The Inside Straight**

Peeking at the bottom card or looking at a neighbor's hand is cheating, whether the perpetrator understands that or not.

If the host won't do anything about it, refuses to believe you, or says that everyone knows but they just tolerate that behavior, you have to decide how important playing in the game is.

## The Least You Need to Know

♦ Know how to find or start a game.

♦ Establish firm starting and ending times.

♦ Realize that cheating exists and learn how to protect yourself and the game.

# Chapter 16

# Unusual Home Game Variations

## In This Chapter

- ◆ Popular home games
- ◆ Basic strategies that can be applied to most forms of poker
- ◆ How to adjust to other variations

Now that you've learned how to find a social home game or start your own, you'll want to know what games are played and how to beat them. You'll find some strange poker variations in social games. These poker variations are played only in home games and generally only in games with relatively small stakes.

What makes these games different from cardroom games are wild cards, additional cards, and card replacement. You need to know how to adjust to these changes.

# An Introduction to Dealer's Choice Poker

Most private games feature more than one form of poker, usually by agreement of all the participants. There are two ways of deciding what gets played. Both fall under the category of *dealer's choice*.

In dealer's choice, each dealer gets to decide in turn what game is played. The choice can be either hand-by-hand or round-by-round. (Round-by-round is better: It eliminates the built-in dealer edge in some games.)

Dealers usually do not and should not choose games that require too many cards for the number of players. For example, if there are 10 players, a dealer probably would not be permitted to choose any form of draw, and seven-card stud also would be out.

If there were nine players, draw could theoretically be played with the discards being shuffled if not enough cards remain on the draw, but that's not an ideal situation. The rules should include what to do when the cards run out on the draw. For example, players might be permitted to hold their discards aside, so they couldn't get back any of the same cards they had discarded. The draw cards would come from the folded hands and the discards of earlier drawers.

### The Inside Straight

Although some players feel that wild card games or bizarre poker variations are strictly for amateurs and offer no hope to the skilled player, actually the opposite is true. There are usually no books available on optimal strategy for newly invented games and with no educational tools available, the more talented players will be the ones who can discern what kinds of hands are playable and what aren't.

A social game usually has a larger mix of permitted games than a serious game. Social games have lots of wild card games, like baseball, night baseball, deuces wild, and community card games that feature many shared cards, like Twin Beds, Southern Cross, and the like.

Social games also feature *twists* (the replacing of a card on the end in stud games, sometimes by having to pay something extra for the replacement card), passing cards to left and right, passing cards along in turn, *rolling* cards (exposing them one at a time from already completed hands), and sometimes games that are like poker but are not quite poker, such as 7-27, Bourre, three-card guts, and the like. Some allow the dealer to choose anything he likes or can invent; others have a large, but not infinite choice of possibilities.

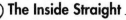

**The Inside Straight** _____

For every extra card that a player gets to access in a home game variation, the playability requirements grow exponentially. To see why, play a little five-card stud and then play seven-card stud. You'll see the winning hands in seven-card stud are invariably far stronger. Imagine, then, how strong the average winning hand would be in a game that allows players to see a dozen cards! If you don't have a straight flush in such a game, your hand is probably quite vulnerable.

# It Takes Guts to Pass the Trash in Wrigley Field

Among the more popular home games are Baseball, Chicago, Pass the Trash, Big Cross, Guts, and five-card stud high-low with a twist.

## And That's #70 for Mark McGwire!

In a stadium, baseball is often a wild game, figuratively. At the poker tables, Baseball is a wild game, literally. The numbers three (strikes), four (balls), and nine (innings) are important on the diamond and they also have special significance in this poker game.

Baseball, like many home games, is a variant of seven-card stud. Threes and nines are wild. A nine is always "free," as is a three in the hole, but a player dealt a three face up is, "hit" with a penalty. The penalty differs from game to game.

In most variations, a player dealt a three face up must either immediately match the pot or fold. Although poker novices frequently pay the pot-matching penalty, figuring their wild card will give them a great chance to win the pot, this is almost always wrong. There are too many other wild and extra cards in the game. Unless the three gives you an almost certain winner (like a high five of a kind), fold.

In some games, the player is not even offered a chance to fold; he _must_ match the pot. Usually, rules are neither good nor bad, as long as everyone knows them in advance. This rule is an exception. Avoid games where you have no control over the decision to make a large bet.

A player dealt a four face up immediately receives another card face down to be used as an extra hole card. It would be theoretically possible for one player to end up with seven hole cards. Someone who holds eight or nine cards has a significant advantage over someone holding seven.

Proper strategy is to play fairly tight and go for straight flushes and five of a kind. (If you play in a game where your opponents proudly bet *regular* straights or flushes, please contact me; I'll be there momentarily.)

Your minimum starting hand should include at least one wild card and preferably two. Let your opponents start with (J-J) J and commit a lot of chips. You shouldn't. You stand a good chance of improving to four jacks, but not five, and four of a kind won't win often enough.

The game is sometimes played high-low and then it becomes even wilder. Be sure it's clear what the lowest hand is. If it's 6-4, then you probably don't want to play with anything less than that hand. The next-best, 6-5-3-2-A will just cost you money. If the lowest hand is a wheel, you want to play a 6-4 extremely cautiously, if at all.

### Perilous Play

It is very easy for an opponent to have a *lock* (unbeatable hand) in Chicago. A player who holds the A♠ in the hole (or the K♠, if the A♠ is visible) can know on the first three cards that he is *guaranteed* at least half the pot. Without a high spade, you're fighting for only half the pot, which is usually a losing proposition.

### Poker Lore

Tracking the upcards is important in all forms of seven-card stud, but particularly so in Chicago. I once played a game starting with (9♠-9♥) 9♣, and by the time fifth street had been dealt, my 9♠ was locked in as the high spade in the hole (meaning that the A♠, K♠, Q♠, J♠ and 10♠ were all visible). It was a good thing, too, because my nines full got beaten by a bigger full house!

If the game has a declare and you end up with a five-high straight flush (a *steel wheel*), it would often be a mistake to declare both ways. You can't get beat for low, of course, but your high hand can be quite vulnerable. If you're facing an opponent who shows two or more wild cards, it would probably be a big mistake to declare your steel wheel both ways. Remember, someone who owns three wild cards must, by definition, have at least four of a kind and an open-ended straight flush draw!

## The Windy City's Game: Chicago

Chicago is a variant of seven-card stud. The pot is split between the high hand and the holder of the highest spade in the hole.

The tight strategy for this game is simple. Don't play on the first three cards without at least rolled up trips for the high half, or the A♠ or K♠ in the hole. Unless the ante is prohibitively high, it is hard to lose playing this way. However, it can also be hard to win much because you won't get those hands very often, and if you play that tightly, even weak opponents may learn to run and hide when you enter a pot.

When you crank the social element into the equation—and any gathering in which you're playing games like Chicago has a social element—you should probably relax your starting hand requirements a bit. Your opponents will play with far lesser hands.

To show you how big a difference there is between even good looking high spades, know that against seven opponents, your K♠ wins over half the time (57.1 percent), while the Q♠ wins less than a third of the time (32.1 percent)!

| Poker Lore |
| --- |
| A group of sailors was playing poker on deck and the pot had grown fairly large. A breeze sprung up and one player's hole card blew overboard. Although the deck was 50 feet from the water surface, the sailor dove in after the card, retrieved it, and then screamed for help because he couldn't swim. |
| His fellow players threw him a life preserver and hauled him and his card back on deck. Bringing the soggy card back to the table, the sailor refused medical assistance, coughed up a lot of seawater, and bet all his chips. Obviously the card had filled some huge hand, like a straight flush, and everyone folded. The sailor collected his money and left the game. The other players took a look at his hand. The sailor had a pair of twos ... and one whopping talent for sensing the right moment to bluff in a home game! |

## Talking Trash

Pass the Trash, sometimes also called *Pass the Garbage* or *Anaconda*, has a few variations. All of them involve passing cards to your neighbors and exposing your final five-card hand one card at a time.

Players start with seven cards and the game is played high-low. There is a betting round when players have their first seven cards.

Each player then passes two cards to the player to his left and one to the player to his right. Players discard two of the cards from their seven-card hand, arrange the cards in the order they want them seen, and then "roll them" (players may not change the order once they have set their hands). To "roll them," players turn their face-down cards up, one at a time, with a betting round following each exposure.

After the fourth card has been exposed, players declare which half of the pot they're competing for. Sometimes the game is played with a bet after the declare.

One strategic key is to remember what you passed and to whom. If, for example, one of the cards you passed to the left is the key to that player's hand and it does not show up during the rolling phase, you can be sure he has the card in the hole. If you passed two face cards (often called "paints" or "pictures") to the left and the player appears to be going low, it is less likely that he has a strong low hand.

### The Inside Straight

A player who starts with 2♠-5♠ and then turns over the 2♦ almost certainly has a full house and it's probably fives full and not deuces full. He wanted opponents to think after two cards that he was either going low or had a flush—maybe both. However, unless the player is both wild and bad, that

Pass the Trash has other names, such as the colorful *Screw Your Neighbor*.

The other important part of the strategy—and this applies to all roll'em games—is to be aware of the patterns your opponents employ in exposing their cards. You can count on some players always to have the opposite of what they appear to be exposing.

Following this reasoning, an ace exposed as the first card usually indicates a low hand. Be aware of a *double fake*, also known as *double reverse*. That is, a good player may expose his hand straightforwardly to make people think that he has something other than what he is apparently showing.

Another indication of the direction an opponent is going is the cards he passed you. Someone who passes you an ace and a deuce is not likely going low.

Pass the Trash is a game of the nuts. With so many cards to choose from, players usually come up with monster hands. Be very wary of declaring both ways with a wheel.

Several variations of this game exist. One passes three cards to the left before assembling the final hand. Another variation passes three cards to the left, then two, then one. Each pass is followed by a round of betting. Winning hands are better than the other version because players see more cards and get more draws to make their hands.

In the last version, try for low or four of a kind. Straights and flushes have little value.

## Let's Do the Twist

Five-card high-low stud with a twist is a form of five-card stud. After each player has been dealt one hole card and four upcards (each followed by a round of betting), each player has the option of replacing one of those cards. Replacing a card in this fashion is called the *twist*. An upcard is replaced with an upcard and a hole card with a hole card. After the twist, there is one more round of betting and then a declaration.

In most games, the high hand starts the betting, including the first round.

In most high-low split games, going for low is the optimal strategy for two main reasons. First, even little cards can turn into full houses. Second, you can also end up with a hand that can declare both ways, such as a low straight or flush. In this game, though, starting out going for high is a more viable plan: A great high start can't be busted, while a great low start can. A pair or face card midway through can easily ruin a good start. You do have two chances to repair the damage, given the twist, but it still is hard to end up with five good low cards out of six.

If you go for low, both your starting cards should be lower than anything showing or your upcard an ace through five and your hole card no higher than a seven. For high, you should start with a pair or an ace together with a card higher than any showing.

**The Inside Straight** _____

If you are going for low and you catch a card higher than other likely lows, you should probably get out. You would have to catch perfect cards for the rest of the hand, including not busting out on the twist. In addition, you will have to keep calling when other hands are in the lead. This advice is fairly good for almost any high-low game, unless you have many other strong cards.

If you have a made seven-low on the end, do not replace a card, even if it looks like lower hands are out. If you end up with a low straight after the twist, you should almost always declare both ways. If you have a hand on the end that is not a lock for one way, do not bet into a hand that might be.

## Big Cross Isn't Always a Burden

Big Cross, sometimes called *Southern Cross*, is one representative of a large group of multicommunity card games. In Big Cross, the players are dealt (depending on where you are) two, three, four, or even five hole cards. At the same time, the dealer places nine cards on the board face down, five in a vertical column and four in a horizontal row that shares the center card from the vertical column.

Players first bet after they receive their hole cards. The dealer then exposes the four outermost cards simultaneously, which makes two cards visible horizontally and two vertically. There is a second betting round. The dealer then exposes one more vertical card and one more horizontal card, followed by a third betting round. Then he exposes the remaining vertical and horizontal cards (leaving the center card face down). A fourth betting round ensues and the center card gets turned over, followed by the fifth and final betting round.

Players form their best five-card hand by combining any number of their hole cards with any number of the cards in either the vertical or horizontal role, but not both.

A Big Cross board might look like this:

*In this Big Cross board, players can choose to combine some of their hole cards either with the horizontal row: (2♥-2♣-K♥-4♣-7♦), or with the vertical column: (4♦-Q♦-K♥-8♦-J♠).*

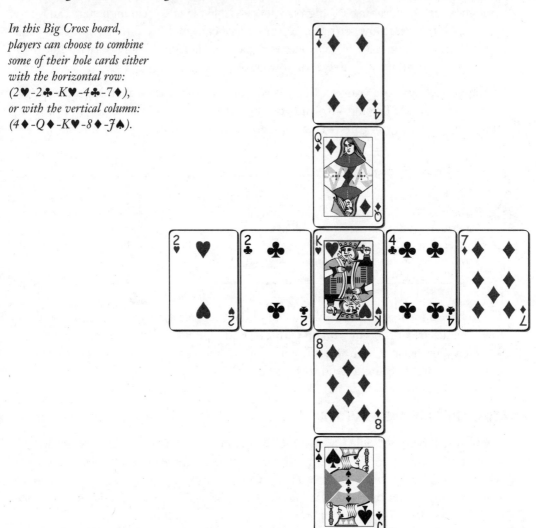

Let's suppose these Big Cross players are engaging in one of the more sane versions of the game and get only two hole cards. What hands are possible and what should someone be "proud" of?

The best possible hand here is quad deuces, formed using the horizontal row. Indeed, anyone forced to use the vertical column is probably in trouble, because any of the following hands make a full house horizontally: K-2, 4-2, 7-2, K-K, 4-4, 7-7. Using the vertical column, a flush is possible because there are three diamonds. A straight is possible too, but in a game where both flushes and full houses are possible, players shouldn't get unduly excited about a straight.

The number of Big Cross variations is almost limitless. You can play it high-low, you can give players additional hole cards, and you can impose limitations on how many board or hole cards a player can use. About the only universal rule is that you cannot use cards from both the column and the row, except for the center card (here, the K♥).

Among the more popular other multiboard card games played are a collection of games that have about a dozen names, most commonly called *Tic-Tac-Toe*, although lately it has been encountered as *Death Square* (possibly in homage to the orbital weapons platform in *Star Wars*, the Death Star). In Tic-Tac-Toe, nine cards are placed in three horizontal rows, like this:

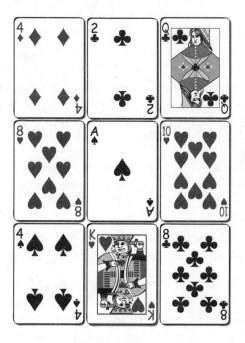

*In this grid, players can chose to combine their hole cards with any of the following eight 3-card combinations: Vertical (4♦-8♥-4♠; 2♣-A♠-K♥; Q♣-10♥-8♣), Horizontal (4♦-2♣-Q♣; 8♥-A♠-10♥; 4♠-K♥-8♣), or Diagonal (4♦-A♠-8♣; Q♣-A♠-4♠). Note how important the center A♠ is; it plays a role in four of the eight possible combinations.*

Although the number of hole cards dealt varies, usually players are required to use exactly two of their hole cards in combination with any of the three rows or columns, as well as either of the two diagonals (here, 4♠-A♠-Q♣ or 4♦-A♠-8♣). Typically the players bet after getting their hole cards and then the cards are turned as in Big Cross: first the four corners, then two outside center cards (such as the 2♣-8♥ or K♥-10♥; you don't turn two cards in a row or column, such as 8♠-10♠ or 2♣-K♥), then two more outside center cards, and finally, the middle card. A betting round follows each turn of the cards.

Although you can have a very strong hand before the middle card is turned, the middle card affects four of the eight possible three-card combinations. It often turns a trailer into a winner. Because there have already been four betting rounds before the middle card gets turned, huge pots often swing and missed draws often curse. Someone holding 7♥-9♥ would have his heart(s) broken by that ace of spades: His open-ended straight flush draw, a likely winner with any heart, six, or jack (14 outs: one of the hearts, the K♥, isn't available), is now worthless.

> ### The Inside Straight _____
>
> If you want your game to resemble poker, try to hold the line when players suggest games that offer players access to 15 or 20 cards. Someone might see Tic-Tac-Toe and get the bright idea to allow 25 cards in five rows or suggest that all cards from deuces to sixes are wild. You should absolutely draw the line if someone wants to create a game that requires two decks; that's not only silly, but it also makes cheating too easy.

Another popular variation is called Elevator. Two vertical columns of five cards each are dealt face down and they are separated by a single face down card which can be slid up or down "the elevator" to be used to form any of five different rows. See the following figure.

The 5♥ can be used in the first row to make a straight, in the second row to make very little of consequence, in the third row to make a wheel, in the fourth row to make quad fives, tens full of fives, fives full of tens, or trip fives, and in the fifth row to make a six-high straight (with 6-3) or a wheel (with A-3). You cannot use the vertical columns, so the owner of 4♠-3♠ does not have a straight flush. The best hand that can be made here with 4♠-3♠ is a straight, using the top row.

Typically, there is a bet after receiving the hole cards and one card is turned from each column (but not two cards from the same row; you can't turn a second card over in a row until there is at least one card showing in every row). The elevator card is turned over last and there is a final betting round.

Like most multicard home games, these geometric games can be fun, but the pots tend to get very large. The last card changes so much that these games bear more resemblance to gambling than to poker. If only two hole cards are dealt, pocket pairs go way up in value because they stand an excellent chance of turning into a set. If more hole cards are dealt, straight and flush possibilities become more playable, but are still quite risky because they can't connect for sure until the final card.

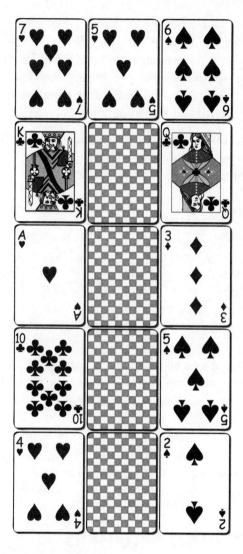

*By sliding the center 5♥ up or down the "elevator shaft," players gain access to five different three-card combinations: 7♥-5♥-6♠; K♣-5♥-Q♣; A♥-5♥-3♦; 10♣-5♥-5♠; or 4♥-5♥-2♠. (A sample completed board in Elevator.)*

## Do You Have the Stomach for Guts?

More than a few players have been introduced to poker as youths playing *Guts* (sometimes called *Balls* for reasons I need not discuss). There are two main variations, two-card Guts and three-card Guts. In both games, the rules are simple. Everyone antes and the dealer gives everyone the requisite number of cards. The players sequentially state whether they are "in" or "out." This gives the late position players such a huge advantage that the game should only be played in full rounds, where everyone has a turn dealing. Curiously, the very early position players can have an advantage as well if the other players are at all conservative. In some variations, the declaration is simultaneous with chips (one for in, none for out).

After everyone has finished declaring, the hands are opened. The owner of the highest hand who has opted "in" wins, but anyone who loses must match the pot! Once someone has declared "in," it takes a gutsy opponent to follow with another "in" because he knows that someone is going to get whacked for a big number. When a third player also declares "in," you know that two players are going to get burned (the third—or fourth or fifth—player in only has to match the original pot).

Usually, the money from these pot-matching bets goes directly to the player who has the best hand. In some games, it carries over to the next hand, creating extra incentive to stay in—and also a larger penalty for losing.

### The Inside Straight

*Guts* is even less of a real poker game than *Elevator*, but it can be a place to first learn whether you have people-reading skills, a *poker face*, or a knack for bluffing. Just make sure—as with all home games—that everyone agrees on the rules *before* you start. It's an awful feeling to bet three diamonds and then find out flushes don't count.

In two-card Guts, pairs are excellent hands, as are aces with good kickers. In three-card Guts, some games allow straights and flushes and some don't. If straights and flushes count, otherwise good-looking hands like A-A-Q drop severely in value. Some games pay "royalties" for trips (remember, there's no draw); everyone must give the lucky owner an extra ante. You may also encounter games with a bad beat feature. If someone has trips beaten by other trips, he gets a double ante from everyone else. Usually, if a game allows straights and flushes, straights beat pairs, flushes beat straights, straight flushes beat flushes, and trips beat straight flushes.

# How to Adjust to Other Variations

Many of the following wild poker variants involve things you don't see in cardroom games. Wild cards, additional cards, and replacement cards change hand values. The net effect of these is to raise the average values of winning hands, often considerably.

## That's Wild!

As more wild cards become available to the players, the average winning hand gets better. This may seem self-evident, but you need to be able to make new estimates of what a good hand is on-the-fly in many home games because players invent new games as the hour grows late (and particularly if the beer is flowing).

# A Few Concluding Split Pot, Wild Card, New Game Remarks

In many split-pot games, a final betting round occurs after the declaration. This is a subtle way of increasing the stakes because it puts more money into the pot.

You should be more reluctant to play marginal hands in this variation because you will have to call twice as many bets on the end. A player with a *lock* is sure to bet or raise the maximum on that last round of betting.

If someone appears to have invented a new game variation right at the table, don't discount the possibility that the inventor has actually played the game before elsewhere and is reasonably familiar with the odds. Because it may not be immediately obvious that a new game offers a strong dealer advantage, it is a good idea to employ a rule that requires all new games to be dealt for an entire round.

While this rule may give a false inventor the chance to play his game more often, he won't enjoy any dealer advantage and other players will learn the game much more quickly if they play several hands in a row.

 **The Inside Straight**

One good way to slow the introduction of new games is to enforce a waiting period. A player can suggest a new game, but it can't be played until the following week. This gives you a chance to see if other friends might be familiar with it. It also gives you time to deal out some practice hands and perhaps catch up a little to someone who might have learned the unusual game elsewhere.

Don't hesitate to argue against inclusion of any truly bizarre-sounding game. Although a dealer should be able to call any reasonable game in dealer's choice, it's no fun spending fifteen minutes discussing all the rules and permutations of a new game.

Another good practice is to keep rules about hand values consistent. By keeping the hand values consistent from odd game to odd game, you greatly reduce the chances that someone will get confused and play the wrong low. If that doesn't bother you, perhaps the other associated problem will: If the best possible low changes from hand to hand, players will invariably slow the game down by asking "What's the best low in Omaha Soweto?" Keeping the number of games limited and consistent will greatly reduce the amount of time needed to review rules.

## The Least You Need to Know

◆ The number of potential home games is limited only by imagination.

◆ Although a few wild cards actually help the best players, try to keep their number relatively small.

◆ Adding wild or extra cards greatly increases the average winning hand's strength.

◆ Try to keep the number of dealer's choice games somewhat limited and employ universal hand rankings.

# Part 3

## Internet Poker

Part 3 will open your eyes to the fastest-growing segment of what is overall a fast-growing industry—real money Internet poker played in realtime against players from around the globe. You'll learn online etiquette, hugely important material about how first to pick a good site, and how to pick a good game within that site. You'll also learn how to take advantage of industry competition and how to use Internet poker to improve not just your Internet results, but your home and/or casino and/or tournament results, too.

Many competent players have avoided Internet poker, fearful of tainted software and/or collusion. Part 3 will show you why these fears shouldn't be dismissed entirely, why they are far less significant issues than most nonplayers think, and how it is relatively easy to avoid the difficulties when they do exist.

# Chapter 17

# These Days, You Don't Need to Play Strip Poker to Play in Your Underwear

## In This Chapter

- The Internet poker phenomenon
- Legal considerations
- Internet poker basics, etiquette, and ethics
- Handling money on the Internet

It seems hard to believe that as recently as early 1998, there wasn't a site where one could play poker on the Internet for money. Over the past six years, the number of Internet sites that allow money play and the number of people who play there has grown explosively. Over the next four chapters, I examine this phenomenon, help you decide if you want to play Internet poker, and if you do, teach you how to succeed.

# Internet Poker: No Longer a Mere Curiosity

When PlanetPoker.com, the first Internet poker room where you could play for real money, opened for business in 1998, no one quite knew what to make of it. People worried about everything. Was it legal? Was the software honest? How could you stop players from colluding? What would poker be like without being able to stare a potential bluffer in the eye? Was the site honest? Could you be sure of collecting if you won? What if you were up against a table full of professionals? What would happen if your modem lost its connection? What would happen if the site malfunctioned?

Gosh, what a bunch of worrywarts we all were.

Today, thanks to the concatenation of a few fortunate circumstances, Internet poker is a huge business with dozens of cardrooms operating 24 hours a day, 7 days a week, 365 days a year. Almost all of the worrisome questions have been answered to most players' satisfaction and you'll soon learn the answers to those questions, as well as many more.

## What Caused the Boom?

Every once in a while, the planets and stars align perfectly for a business segment. The Internet poker boom owes its success to several events happening, or being in place, all in one year's time. In no particular order, those events were:

◆ The Internet itself was ready. You don't need a high speed connection to play Internet poker, but it doesn't hurt.

◆ The software grew more and more sophisticated, reliable, and user friendly.

◆ Technology improved to the point where multitable tournaments were possible.

◆ As true stories emerged about large sums being won online, players started relaxing their fears about collusion and software engineers who left backdoors in their programs. If flaws did exist, they weren't stopping people from winning.

◆ Poker entered what is clearly "The Golden Age of Poker" with big money tournaments proliferating, thanks in no small part to technology that allowed television viewers to see player hole cards. This turned what was previously a boring spectator experience into a tense, edge-of-your-seat drama that people wanted to experience themselves.

♦ The 2003 World Series of Poker was won by the implausibly named Chris Moneymaker, a relative tournament novice who won his seat in the $10,000 World Championship event by paying $40 to enter an online satellite tournament. Moneymaker turned that seat into a $2,500,000 payday that the television public got to see over and over, thanks to a seven-part ESPN special.

The result was an Internet poker boom that has shocked the gaming world and drawn considerable attention outside it. As of this writing, PartyPoker.com is the world's largest Internet poker room. It typically has 10,000 or more (sometimes a *lot* more) players playing for real money *at any given moment*—which means a large multiple of that number of people play there for money occasionally. Roughly three times those numbers play on the site in free games.

A mere 18 months earlier, a site's owners would have been doing cartwheels to have 1,000 simultaneous players. At that point, ParadisePoker.com was the industry leader and had such a huge market share that overcoming its lead seemed inconceivable. The other contenders looked like they would be happy fighting over Paradise's leftovers. In that 18 months, Paradise has more than doubled its player base and has fallen from the top spot to third or fourth place.

> **The Inside Straight**
>
> Welcome to Wonderland. "A slow sort of country," said the Queen, "Now, here, you see, it takes all the running you can do, to keep in the same place. If you want to get somewhere else, you must run at least twice as fast as that!" It was good advice for Alice, and in the current Internet poker boom, good advice for an Internet poker room.

In a growth industry like this, it's entirely possible that by the time you read this, some other cardroom could own the lion's share of the market. The leader's role has already shifted from Planet to Paradise to Party; it could shift again.

Size matters because you want a stable organization that offers plenty of game variety and enough players (this gives you options at the stake level you choose, and if you're a tournament fan, lets you find new tournaments starting much more quickly), but you don't necessarily have to play at the *largest* room to find those qualities.

# Can the Farmer and the Rancher Still Be Friends?

Many owners of land-based poker rooms (usually called brick & mortar, or B&M, cardrooms) have viewed Internet poker as an enemy that might steal away their customers by providing similar games without the need for a drive to the cardroom.

Although there's no question that occasionally you will ask yourself, "Why the heck do I want to drive forty minutes in the rain when I can just log on," Internet poker is not the enemy of B&M poker. Even as Internet poker was in the middle of its huge growth spurt, the world's largest B&M poker casino, The Commerce Casino in Los Angeles, California, was building a huge addition and hotel, and it doesn't appear to be suffering one whit.

What the industry will eventually realize is that home game players frequently play different kinds of poker than are played in cardrooms. If B&M cardrooms could get every home game player into their tables, every one of them would grow, at a casual estimate, by a good 3,000 percent.

Internet poker rooms are creating a transitional ground for many home game players who will then move to B&M cardrooms. Internet cardrooms aren't as intimidating because it's harder to make a mistake or to breach etiquette, and if you do, no one knows who you are.

### The Inside Straight

Should you play B&M poker or Internet poker? Not everyone has a choice, but if you do, you'll probably find that if you're good at the "people" side of poker—picking up on tells, talking your opponents into giving away information, and owning a good poker face—you'll probably excel in cardrooms. If you're more of a technical player and/or blush whenever you pick up a pair, you and the Internet are a match made in poker heaven.

Furthermore, you can't play Baseball or Pass the Trash on the Internet. For the most part, Internet cardrooms spread exactly the same games that B&M rooms do. This will allow you to learn hold'em, Omaha, seven-card stud, and the other B&M staples. After you've grown comfortable with these games, you're far more likely to risk a visit to a live casino poker game.

As great as Internet poker is, it will never be able to replace the live game. Rather, it will supplement it and develop an entire Next Generation of B&M poker players.

# Is Internet Poker Legal?

Yes. No. Maybe. Yes in some countries, no in others. Yes in some states, no in others. Yes today, no tomorrow. No today, yes tomorrow.

Who knows? Only The Shadow knows and he's not talking.

Although you can run into quite intelligent people who will take absolutely contrary positions on this issue, a more reasonable person would probably acknowledge that the United States Constitution, and indeed most of the law passed since, was not written with the Internet in mind. Therefore, before anyone can be absolutely certain about much of anything, an entirely new body of law will have to develop.

Nothing I write in this book has a chance of being legally current by the time the book reaches the bookstores, and I wouldn't try to give you legal advice anyway.

Reading what lawyers have to say can help, but many lawyers have agendas, either being on retainer to members of the gambling industry, or working for a prosecutor's office. It's a fine mess and is likely to stay that way for awhile.

I can cite some practical legal traditions. In most gambling prosecutions, the illegal casino owner or the bookie is the target. During Prohibition, the speakeasy owner was targeted far more than the drinker.

It is the rare case indeed where the mere player gets targeted. When a player is prosecuted, it is almost always in conjunction with some other activity where the gaming prosecution comes along for the ride.

> **Perilous Play**
>
> Just because playing Internet poker may be safe in your jurisdiction doesn't mean you should call attention to your activities. The more you leave lawmen alone, the more likely it is that they'll leave you alone.

In other words, don't go play Internet poker because I told you it was legal and safe. I make no such promise. The race is not always to the swift—but that is the way to bet.

# An Introduction to Online Play

Although the process may vary a bit from site to site, if you decide to play online poker, you usually have to (or in some cases, should) take a few preliminary steps:

- ◆ Select a site (see Chapter 19).

- ◆ Download the site's proprietary software. This is free, usually takes only a few minutes, and is extremely simple. Some sites don't require a download.

- ◆ Play for a while in the "play money" games that virtually all sites offer. This isn't a required step, but it's smart. It makes sense to learn where all the buttons are without risking any money.

- ◆ Set up an account. This involves selecting a screen name and a password. Depositing some money is necessary only if you've decided not just to play, but to play for money. You can't play on credit as you can with some B&M pit games like craps; it's cash in advance, and many credit card companies are refusing to allow customers to buy chips with their cards. Unless you're dealing with a large, well-established cardroom, you should probably make your initial deposit small.

◆ Visit the site's "lobby" to select a game and stake limit you want to play. Often you will have to join a waiting list to get a virtual "seat," but usually the wait is quite short if you indicate you are willing to play at any table that offers the size game you want.

◆ Use the buttons to fold, call, bet, or raise, just like you would in a regular game … and play poker!

# Establishing Your Account

Most Internet poker rooms make establishing your account trivially simple. It is important to give your correct name and address because the cardroom will mail/wire your winnings to the person and address listed when you establish your account.

You don't have to (and probably shouldn't) *play* under your real name. The overwhelming majority of players select a screen name. Popular trends in screen names include:

◆ Men selecting female names (they think it will cause other players to underestimate them).

◆ Selecting names that sound tough, like "Pokersuperstar" or "DrDeath."

◆ Selecting names that sound like pushovers, like "Helpless123" or "Dumbo." (Personally, I'm more concerned about a player who uses a name like "Dumbo" than one whose name implies greatness.)

◆ Selecting names that sound like famous players (usually spelled wrong), like "JChan" or "Hellmouth"

> **Poker Lore**
>
> What's in a name? Although it's a good bet that someone using a screen name like "JohnnyChan" isn't really the two-time world champion, these names aren't *always* wrong: Phil Hellmuth used to play as "PhilHell," but many opponents refused to believe it was actually him. A number of true stars play under their real names.

The shrinking number of credit card companies that allow players to buy chips with their cards frequently impose onerous conditions, such as treating chip purchases like cash advances (with the attendant fees and high interest rates).

At most cardrooms, it is possible to buy chips by mailing a check to the cardroom's home base (and waiting for it to clear, if it isn't a cashier's check), but most players want instant gratification (or something close thereto), which has created an entirely new business for gaming e-cash providers.

For awhile, the popular e-cash system PayPal became the leading easy method to buy chips. PayPal eventually decided it didn't want to be involved in this business (there are certain headaches involved with chargebacks) and got out.

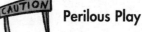

**Perilous Play**

When you review the various chip purchase options available to you, make sure you read the fine print about associated fees. Many e-cash services charge you nothing and even pay you interest on your balance, but some methods do involve fees.

As of this writing, another e-cash vendor, Neteller, has become a leader in easy chip purchase, but things can change quickly in the Internet world. One thing you can be sure of: Whatever Internet cardroom you select will present you with a list of options for buying chips because if you can't buy chips, the cardroom is out of business.

**The Inside Straight**

Because Internet poker rooms frequently offer short-term deposit bonuses, it can be a good idea to keep a little money stored in whatever e-cash system you settle on. That way, you can take advantage of the deposit bonuses whenever they are offered. Even if you already have sufficient chips to play in your account, why not take advantage of a deal where you're offered $600 in chips for a $500 deposit?

# Cashing Out

The best-looking bet in the world is a bad bet if you can't collect when you win. As of this writing, only one Internet poker room has closed its doors owing players money (another was in trouble, but a famous player who endorsed the room made good on its debts from his own pocket). Even one collapse is enough to create proper cause for concern, though.

For this reason, in an era of huge online cardrooms that have a multi-year history of tremendous profitability, there is little incentive to patronize a small, new cardroom, unless you have certain guarantees or assurances. Among the more comforting assurances are:

- Ownership by a known (ideally, publicly traded) corporation (or individual) that has substantial assets.

◆ Endorsement by one or more well-known individuals who have a reputation for integrity *and* who have substantial assets of their own. Not all endorsers are created equal.

◆ Licensing and bonding by a governing body that actually cares and regulates. Australia is a difficult place to get an Internet gaming license. The regulators there actually care about client safety. Some jurisdictions care "a little." Many others view their "regulatory" process as nothing more than an excuse to collect nice fees from the gaming operator and wouldn't investigate, much less revoke a license, in the face of multiple complaints. That a license comes from an "open door" market proves nothing bad: Actually some of the best cardrooms are licensed by such entities. You just need more before you can be comfortable with a new cardroom.

Although a cardroom's size, profitability, history, and regulatory backdrop can all provide excellent indicators of likely safety, the Internet still hasn't quite left its Wild, Wild West days behind. Good old-fashioned word of mouth is still an excellent aid in determining where your money is likely safest.

Test out the waters and then put the cardroom to the test. Ask for a cash-out and see how promptly and courteously your request is handled. You can always buy more chips later. In fact, there's an excellent chance you will be offered a deposit bonus because cardrooms frequently offer them to customers who haven't played for a little while.

# Interacting with Your Fellow Players

Just because you're playing on the Internet, you don't have to give up the entire interactive bonding experience that draws many players to poker. Every Internet poker room offers what is known as a "chat" feature. Whether you want to use it is quite another matter. Sometimes chatting is great fun. Other times, angry or foolish players make it very unpleasant.

**The Inside Straight**

It can at first be frustrating to listen to someone spout noxious anonymous verbiage, but consider the source. What kind of person acts like a bully while hiding in the basement? If you want to keep the chat window on, try to laugh (inwardly—there's no need to give the bully what he wants, which is attention) and recognize the words for what they are: proof positive that the speaker is an easy target. Good players don't try to run off weak players.

When this happens, you have a few options. The simplest is turning off your chat feature. All cardrooms give you this option. You won't see a single word they type.

Unfortunately, taking this approach also robs you of your right to interact with your fellow players in a friendly way. That can be a big loss because the number of nice people playing on the Internet is far greater than the number of nasty ones.

You might try one neutral conversational foray and if someone picks up on the chat, fine. If you receive a stony silence, it's time to visit the lobby and get yourself on the waiting list for one or more other games because this one isn't off to a promising start: Silent opponents tend to be serious opponents.

If you get a nice response, don't hesitate to engage in a little chat—but remember that word "little." If you chat too much, you're probably not paying enough attention to what's going on in the game.

# Online Etiquette

You don't have to worry about blowing smoke in someone's face online or about spilling your drink on the table. There are still a few points of etiquette that online players should observe. Failure to observe some of them is merely boorish, while failure to observe certain others can result in penalties as severe as a loss of playing privileges.

The first rule is to play reasonably quickly. Even though almost all Internet cardrooms give you at least 20 seconds to act on your hand, you don't need that long for most decisions. If you consistently slow the game down, you may find that the players you most want at the table—the action gamblers—get up and leave.

The next rule is: Don't abuse the all-in function. Because players sometimes must rush away from their computers in mid-hand (a baby might start crying, someone could come to the door, a child could injure himself), most cardrooms allow players who are still connected one or two "all-ins" when they fail to act on their hand. Rather than folding the hand of someone who has chips in the pot, the system treats the player as if he is all-in. He is eligible to win only the part of the pot he has contested and a side pot develops for the remaining bets.

Occasionally, an unscrupulous player will take unfair advantage of this. For example, if someone has a weak drawing hand like an inside straight draw, he might just sit there and fail to call a bet on the turn. The system treats him as all-in. If he makes his straight, he collects the pot, but if he doesn't, he hasn't had to invest a big bet to draw to it. Similarly, someone who has a fairly weak hand like middle pair might want to know if his hand is good, but not want to pay a bet on the end. He fails to make a move and collects the pot if his opponent was bluffing, but doesn't have to pay the bet to see his opponent's hand.

This isn't just unethical. It's cheating. If someone does it to you, you should report them to support. A good cardroom will keep track of such incidents and even if a player is allowed one or two all-ins during any given 24-hour period, they are allowed for emergencies and accidents, not for tactics. If this happens often enough, a player will be warned and then barred.

### The Inside Straight _____

Most of us were brought up instructed to handle our own battles. "Tattling" or "ratting someone out" isn't supposed to be done. Because you have no way to handle your own problems with a faceless nameless Internet opponent, you need to ignore this conditioning and feel comfortable reporting violators to the only people in a position to enforce proper etiquette and halt cheating: customer support.

A variation of this situation occurs when a player doesn't want to call a bet, but doesn't want to sit there while obviously still connected. The player literally pulls the plug on his own connection and claims he had computer trouble.

Players do indeed lose their connections for valid reasons. However, it becomes quite suspicious when these accidents occur just as someone who owns a modest hand is faced with a tough decision. You should report the player and if he makes a habit out of this unethical stunt, he won't be playing at the site for long.

If you happen to lose your connection for valid reasons at a suspicious time, it's a good idea to get back online, apologize to the opponent, and tell him that you are writing to Support to have them check the hand. If you were indeed trailing, offer to have the value of a bet (or whatever is fair) transferred from your account to the winning player's account. This can be a cheap way to protect your reputation. I did it myself once when I was babysitting for a friend.

Usually players are impressed enough by this offer that they won't even take you up on it and your record stays sterling—a good thing, in the event you run into another accident later, as players who have unreliable Internet connections often do. If someone offers to go to a one-on-one table to default a bet to you, ask them to have the site transfer funds. It's quicker and easier.

Another important etiquette guideline: Don't fold unless you face a bet you don't want to call. Some software won't even allow you to do this, but some will. It's wrong to fold in a situation where you can check because your presence in a hand affects other players. It's easier for someone behind you to bet when he doesn't have to worry about you coming back with a check-raise.

> ### The Inside Straight
>
> Sometimes a hand appears to be so far behind that victory is impossible and its owner wants to fold it out of turn to make sure he doesn't get sucked in by a free card. If you have that big a problem with self-control, this practice won't save you. Just don't fold until someone bets, or if the site has one, select the "fold to any bet" option. It keeps the game fair and occasionally you'll catch consecutive free cards and win a hand that looked hopeless.

Virtually all software offers you buttons you can preselect that say "check/fold," which means the computer will automatically check if no one has bet and automatically fold if someone does. By selecting this button, you can leave your computer to grab something from the refrigerator with a clean conscience. The "fold to any bet" option is a bit different because it carries over from one round to the next (although, as with all pre-select buttons, you can always unselect it if you change your mind before the action reaches you).

More etiquette that comes from the B&M world: Don't discuss your hand, especially when you're no longer involved in the pot. It's fine to make an obvious (albeit weak) joke like "Why did I fold my pocket aces before the flop?" when the board comes A-A-7. When the flop comes 9-6-6, though, it's horrible etiquette to type in a comment like "ARGH! Why did I fold my 7-6!" The all-caps "ARGH" makes your statement fairly believable and you've just made it much easier for someone who holds an overpair like J-J to bet aggressively because the chances are now only half as likely that someone might hold a six for trips.

If you are still involved in the hand, you're allowed more leeway because a certain amount of lying is acceptable gamesmanship. If you're not involved in a hand you should keep completely silent, not just about what cards you held, but about any theories you have about what the other players might have or any strategic suggestions. Even though you may be very curious about what a bettor holds, and so would love to see a call, do not type "Call him!" in the chat box.

As in the B&M world, most etiquette issues don't arise if you use a little common sense and apply the Golden Rule ("Do unto others as you would have them do unto you," not "He who has the gold makes the rules").

# Who Plays Online Poker?

World Series *bracelet owners* play online and so do rank amateurs. Online players tend to play a bit more loosely than B&M players, but they aren't innately worse or better. You can't even be sure who you're up against just by looking at the stakes. Sometimes a champion will be fooling around at low stakes and sometimes a relative novice will be playing for high stakes simply because he has the money.

**Table Talk**

Whenever someone wins a tournament at the World Series of Poker, he wins a lot of money, but no trophy. Instead, he wins a highly coveted gold **bracelet**. When you hear that Phil Hellmuth has won nine bracelets (his total as of this writing, tied for the all-time lead with Johnny Chan and Doyle Brunson), that means he has won nine WSOP tournaments (in his case "only" one of those was the $10,000 buy-in World Championship).

Normally, you can expect to encounter stronger players as you move up the stakes ladder, but that's a generalization that has almost enough exceptions to invalidate it.

Hidden behind those screen names are the young and the old, men and women, boys and girls (players affirm that they are of legal age, but it's practically impossible for a site to verify this, especially if a child plays on his parent's account—another good reason for parents not to keep their passwords stored), experts and novices, solid players and inconsistent players, Americans and foreigners. Who plays Internet poker? Just about anyone.

**The Inside Straight**

Although normally you'd rather not face an expert, sometimes he's an easy target. When someone plays for stakes far lower than his usual, he rarely plays well. It's hard for someone who regularly plays $200-400 to focus on a $10-20 game. He'll play too many hands, fool around with silly "creative" plays, and not worry much about losing 20 bets because that's one bet in his regular game. Online and in person, an expert playing far below his typical stake is usually a desired opponent.

## The Least You Need to Know

- Internet poker has grown explosively over the last few years.

- The legal climate for Internet poker is uncertain.

- Select an Internet poker room that is (relatively) old and large, or which has the endorsement of wealthy, highly credible individuals.

- Learn and follow Internet poker etiquette.

- People of all ages and ability levels play Internet poker.

# Chapter **18**

# You Want Action? How About Two Games at Once!

## In This Chapter

- ◆ Advantages and disadvantages of playing multiple games simultaneously
- ◆ How poker speeds up online
- ◆ How Internet poker helps you face the truth about your results and abilities

Most Internet poker rooms allow their players to participate in more than one game simultaneously; even if your favorite cardroom doesn't, there's nothing stopping you from playing on two different sites simultaneously. Whether or not you should take advantage of this option isn't clear and the correct answer varies depending on your goals and abilities.

## Simultaneous Games

Sometimes playing two or more games at once can be highly profitable. There are some potential problems, though, so let's examine the arguments for and against this approach. For simplicity's sake, I will examine only the benefits and drawbacks of playing two simultaneous games, but you can apply all reasoning and arguments about two games to situations where you are playing three or more. One player I know likes to play six games simultaneously!

## Reasons to Play More Than One Game Simultaneously

There are four primary arguments in favor of playing multiple games. First, if you are a winning player, you get to play twice as many hands per hour. Most capable players tend to track their results in terms of how many big bets (the uppermost betting limit) they average winning per hour. (In a $10-20 game, a "big bet" is $20.) Usually good players are happy winning one big bet per hour and are overjoyed to win two big bets per hour long-term. If you can win one big bet per hour playing 50 hands per hour (one game), all else equal you should be able to win two big bets per hour playing 100 hands per hour (two games). As you'll soon learn, "all else" is not always equal, though.

> **The Inside Straight** _____
>
> Record-keeping is important for both winners and losers, but it's astounding how many players decide to start keeping records only after they have a three-or four-session win streak, so they can gleefully talk about their "four big bets per hour" average. A couple of big losses follow and not only does the player stop talking about his average, he often stops keeping records. Players *want* positive reinforcement, but they *need* reality.

Before you decide that you should play two games at once because you have an established track record of winning one big bet an hour or more, you should log enough hours at your level of choice to have reliable statistical data, not short-term "of course this rate will keep up" data.

A second "pro-multiplicity" argument arises if you're impatient and tend to play too many hands because you can't stand sitting out. A second game lets you be choosier in your starting hand selection because you have twice as many chances to pick up something playable. Because playing too many starting hands is one of the most common (and most serious) flaws in the average player's game, this is one of the better reasons to play multiple games.

For example, it's easier to throw that 8♣-7♣ away in early position if you see that over in your other game you have A♦-J♦ in late position. Even if you don't see a good starting hand over in the other game, you know lots more starting hands will be coming your way and the odds are you won't have to sit idly by for very long.

Another reason to play multiple hands is to spread out your risk. It's less likely that you'll get pummeled for the night. If you play at just one table, you run the risk that you will sit down with an extremely strong group of players, or that you'll just run into a bad run of cards. It's far less likely that the opposition will be unusually strong at two different tables and it's also far less likely that your luck will be horrible at two different tables. Put another way, if the long-term favors you, you will reach the long-term more quickly by playing multiple games. It's a statistical oddity that even though you are actually putting more money into play, if you are a relatively average player for the level of competition, you won't experience as many high highs or low lows. The increased number of hands and opponents brings your result closer to the mean.

The fourth reason isn't a reason so much as a clearer way of examining your goals. Although your average win rate per hour may drop playing two tables, your total win may increase. Let's suppose you're a terrific player who through long experience knows he should win about 1.5 big bets per hour in a single game ($30 an hour in a $10-20 game).

For most terrific players, a considerable amount of success comes from an ability to analyze your opponents' styles—not merely their long-term tendencies or reputation, but how they are playing at any given moment. Still more of that success comes from the ability to project an opponent's likely hand based on his betting pattern in that hand.

When you play two games at once, you don't have as much time to make these kinds of evaluations.

**Perilous Play** _____

In the text, you saw a 1.5 big bet win rate drop to 0.9. You can't assume that your drop-off will be that mild. Your win rate might drop to 0.3 per game, which makes playing two games wrong, but it can get worse. Many players who win playing one table *lose* playing two. The more you depend on accurate reads of your opponents for success, the more dangerous it becomes to play simultaneous games.

As a result, it's quite possible that your expected win rate from each table isn't 1.5 big bets per hour; it might drop to 0.9. Nonetheless, if those are the correct figures, playing two tables is an easily correct decision. You will win a total of 1.8 big bets per hour, instead of 1.5 (in the $10-20 game I was using as an example, you win $36 per hour instead of $30). When it comes time to deposit 100 hours worth of wins into your bank account, the teller doesn't care what your bet-per-hour rate is. He cares only that you are depositing $3,600, not $3,000 and so should you.

# Reasons to Play Only One Game at a Time

As I mentioned above, you can't follow and learn about your opponents' style as well when playing at more than one table. You may be able to make good "snapshot" decisions rushing from table to table, but you can't film a movie with much continuity. The best time to study opponents is when you're not in a hand, but you have to be at the table to be able to study them. If you're somewhere else, you miss the opportunity to collect that information.

**The Inside Straight** _____

Roughly half of online players like to play two or more games simultaneously. This creates an opportunity for those who can content themselves with one game, because they will have more information at their fingertips than the multitable players.

You might also lose track of the betting sequence at a table when playing more than one table. When you're trying to "put a player on a hand" (estimate his likely holding), it can be hugely important to know who bet what when. Although it's often possible to reconstruct betting sequences, you won't always be able to do it. In a game where success is measured by one or two bets an hour, just one mistake per hour can completely destroy your edge—or turn a modest loser into a big loser.

A subset of this problem occurs in stud games where it becomes much more difficult to remember what cards were folded in which games. It's far more difficult to play two games at once when stud games are involved.

This may be one of the reasons why stud, a popular game in many B&M cardrooms, occupies a far smaller percentage of online tables. There has to be *some* explanation because by playing online you have one huge advantage in stud that you can't employ in a B&M cardroom: You can literally write down all exposed/folded cards and never have to guess how many diamonds were folded or whether there are two sevens left, or three.

The following illustration shows a PartyPoker.com "Play Money" table. Note the box in the lower right for typing in player chat, the button option to join the game's waiting list, the bar that connects the player to live chat with a floorperson who can answer questions or resolve abusive chat issues, the player chip counts immediately next to their screen names, and the easy graphic representation of chips, allowing the next player to act to know exactly how much money he must bet to call or raise.

Another problem with playing two games at once is that you might accidentally push the wrong button. Assume that you are playing at Table One and you set to press the "Fold" button, when suddenly the game software yanks you back to Table Two. You continue with the motion and accidentally hit "fold" when you have four kings. You don't have to be horribly uncoordinated for this to happen. Probably every online player in the world has had this happen to him. Folding a big winner is your worst result, but it isn't much fun to accidentally re-raise a hand you planned to fold, either (although I confess I did this once and everyone else folded, giving me a quite accidental pot and proving yet again the power of a raise).

*A PartyPoker.com Play Money table.*

---

### Poker Lore

One of the oldest gambling axioms—so old that it's impossible to know for sure to whom it should be attributed—is "The secret to winning is to do the wrong thing at the right time." This isn't exactly a strategy you should plan your game around because doing the wrong thing usually leads to losing.

Nonetheless, the axiom does hold up more than logicians care to admit. I've related my accidental raise story in the main text. A player who accidentally folds when he flops a set of kings will occasionally see that he would have eventually lost to a flush. Don't try to make mistakes, but don't assume that every mistake you make will cost you dearly. Similarly, don't assume that every brilliant play you make will win you money.

---

One of the strongest arguments against multitasking is that if you *do* go on tilt, your money will evaporate just that much faster. You'll have twice as many opportunities to throw your money away.

Finally, you can also tire more rapidly, because you have to make both more decisions and more rapid decisions. The old Romans had it right: a sound mind in a sound body. Poker players aren't famous for their physical stamina or exercise regimens (eating poorly and all that sitting doesn't help, either), and the odd, irregular hours that frequent players endure often lead to sleep disorders. The more you can do to keep your body in good shape, the sharper your mind should be.

# You Can Run, but You Can't Hide

Online poker tends to accentuate all aspects of poker play except the all-important people skills. Many players become convinced that they are being cheated online, but while collusion (discussed more in Chapter 20) does occasionally happen, what really happens to most unhappy players is that their weaknesses are exposed, accelerated, and almost impossible to ignore. This becomes doubly true for players who play two games simultaneously.

## You Double Your Pleasure, but Do You Double Your Fun?

Online poker tends to play at about twice the speed of B&M poker. There are several reasons for this:

- Computer software deals cards and awards pots (and when necessary, splits pots) far faster than any human dealer can.

- Because players can use pre-selected action buttons, many hands move along quickly. If five consecutive players preselect "fold in turn," good software folds their hands so quickly, it appears that all five have folded simultaneously.

- B&M players occasionally take a minute or two to decide what they want to do with their hands. Online players rarely get more than 20 seconds. (There is a nice trend for tournament software to allow people a "time bank," a period of perhaps a minute *total* that people can use a little here and a little there for the occasional very difficult decision.)

- Players can't waste time asking for deck changes, "an extra good *scramble*," or cause a need for a new deck by accidentally or intentionally marking or crimping a card.

**Table Talk**

To **scramble** the cards, the dealer spreads them out haphazardly face-down on the table and mixes them with two hands, much as a child who lacks the hand-eye coordination to shuffle might mix cards.

- Clicking a mouse button to bet, call, raise, or fold takes far less time than a human needs to count out the requisite number of chips and no time is wasted on dramatic style or flair in moving chips.

- Rulings debates don't arise (although occasionally a problem leads to an offline e-mail to technical support) and players don't slow the game down to berate a dealer.

- Players concerned with pot odds or the number of chips an opponent has don't have to try to count or ask for a count. One move of their mouse answers any questions with answers that aren't already obvious (like how many chips an opponent has).

Because the game moves along at such a rapid pace, results are intensified. Big winners become bigger winners. Small losers become big losers. If you lose $10 an hour playing 30 hands an hour, it makes sense that you'd lose $20 an hour playing 60 hands an hour.

## Can You Handle the Truth?

Paradoxically, one of the biggest differences between multigame online play and B&M play really isn't a difference at all. It's merely a forced exposure to reality.

**The Inside Straight**

Although weak players often believe it is harder to win online because they are faced with hard proof of losses that they can ignore in B&M play, the reality is that as massive numbers of new players come into poker, many of them are taking their first poker steps in online cardrooms. I know quite a few people who have made small and large fortunes playing online poker.

Online poker often forces players to face reality. The process by its very nature creates correct records that many players can't or won't keep in the B&M world. Because losing players usually don't want to face reality, they search for excuses: "I'm being cheated by colluders, the software is fixed, the players are so bad that no one can figure out how to play against them, the dog ate my homework ...." Sadly, many players will not only believe, but shout to the world anything except reality. Why go through the painful process of accepting responsibility, when you can try to blame someone else for your troubles?

---

**Poker Lore**

Actor Jeff Goldblum in the movie *The Big Chill* established that rationalizations are more important than sex when he asked rhetorically, "Ever go a week without a good rationalization?"

I've heard many gambling rationalizations over the years, but my favorite is from an old poker acquaintance (let's call him Worf) who had been a heavy loser the previous year but who had been doing better recently. I mentioned this to him and the following ensued:

"Oh, yeah, I am doing much better this year," Worf agreed. "If you don't count those two games where I dropped three dimes each (a "dime" is $1,000 in gambling parlance), I'm up $500 for the year."

"Um, er, um," I managed to stammer. "Why aren't you counting the six thousand you lost?"

"Those were weird nights," Worf said. "One time I was drunk and the other time I'd just had a big fight with my wife and I was in a crazy mood."

I pressed on. "But ... you still had to pay the $6,000, right?"

"Sure," he admitted. "I just don't count it in my records."

I decided to drop the matter there.

---

In a way, this aspect of online poker does players a tremendous service. Some players are able to recognize that their problems lie with their own approach to the game, rather than a Luck God who hates them or a software program that is "fixed" for no rational reason (a B&M casino doesn't need to rig its roulette wheel; it will win anyway; an online poker room gets its rake no matter who wins). The players who are able to accept reality are the players who can and will improve through study and practice, and may turn into big winners even if their early results aren't impressive.

The players who choose to deny responsibility are, for the most part, doomed to repeating their errors. They may return to the B&M rooms and start losing more slowly again, but lose they will. Only someone who is willing to admit to himself that he has something to learn has a good chance of learning it. Confidence is important in poker, but it should be based on reality, not fantasy.

## The Least You Need to Know

- Playing two online games at once has advantages and disadvantages: Make sure you understand them.

- Focus not on your average win or loss rate per hour for each game, but your total hourly win or loss.

♦ When playing two simultaneous games, you have access to less information in each.

♦ Many poker players are reluctant to face the truth about their results, but online poker's nature forces them to examine it.

# Chapter 19

# Picking the Right Site and Game

## In This Chapter

◆ Selecting an Internet poker site

◆ Choosing the right games on that site

◆ Selecting a screen name

◆ Handling money on the Internet

There are now dozens of Internet poker sites a player can choose from and the selection process isn't always easy. Sometimes the difficulty springs from how similar the sites are and sometimes it springs from performing the poker equivalent of comparing apples to oranges. Rather than getting one recommendation in a fast-changing world, here you'll find factors to consider in selecting a site, a game, a screen name, and ways to handle your money.

## 2001: A Cyberspace Oddity

Eons ago, in 2001, online poker players didn't have many options, and of course you had to worry that a dinosaur might eat or step on your computer (they were usually drawn to the smells that those ancient coal-burning computers produced).

There were a few Internet poker rooms that had enough players to offer games 24 hours a day, seven days a week, 365 days a year. If you were lucky, they even offered one table of the exact game and stake level you were looking for. Online tournaments were a gleam in programmers' eyes and software wasn't too buggy. You could find lots of games and players everywhere, as long as you were playing at ParadisePoker.com.

Now, as we enter The Golden Age of Poker, the only dinosaurs players have to worry about are 56k modem connections and even those work beautifully. Software works well, the Internet community is so large that many sites offer a wide variety of populated games at all stake levels and companies now realize that if they don't offer their players incentives and good customer service, they might take their business elsewhere.

You have many excellent choices and there's no reason why you must give all your business to one site, although you should probably limit yourself to a few for reasons you'll soon learn.

# Factors to Consider in Selecting Your Internet Poker Room(s)

The following sections take a look at the factors you should consider when choosing a site.

## Reliability of the Owners

The first thing to consider in selecting a site is the reliability of the site, which starts with an analysis of how reliable the site owners are. No matter what deposit incentives a site offers, if you can't get your money out once you've put it in, you're playing at the wrong site.

Fortunately, fears on this account are almost gone. As of this writing, only one site has failed while taking customer deposits with it, Pokerspot.com. It was a small, undercapitalized operation whose owners used customer deposits to try to keep the business going (an Internet poker room can't lose money to overly successful customers, but if it spends too much on advertising and other business expenses and doesn't take in enough revenue, it can fail like any other business). Other sites have failed, but customers haven't lost money, either because the business owners properly segregated client funds, or (in one case) a wealthy site endorser made good on the site's debts.

Well-run Internet poker rooms are highly profitable ventures for their owners, and any large, well-established room should be perfectly safe. As of this writing, the fastest way to see which rooms are the largest is to visit PokerPulse.com, which tracks the number of games and players at leading sites.

This doesn't mean you should necessarily rule out a newer or smaller Internet poker room from consideration, but unless it is owned by people of substantial means, and/or has people of high established integrity and fame committing their names and assets to it, you're probably better off waiting a little while to see how the new room performs.

## Games and Limits

The next consideration is whether or not your favorite games and limits regularly *spread*. If you love playing Omaha, the fact that a site offers a hundred different hold'em games doesn't do you much good. If you like playing $2-4 limits, there's no need to play at a site that regularly gets only $1-2 and $4-8 games.

Almost all large sites "offer" just about every game and every possible betting limit, but offering those games and actually having those games regularly populated with players are entirely different matters. Downloading software from a number of different big sites is quick, easy, and it enables you to look not just at what games are *theoretically* available, but what games actually run at the times of day you like to play.

Theoretically you could open accounts at a dozen or more different cardrooms, giving you the maximum chance to find an open seat in your game of choice at any given moment. As a practical matter, you don't even need to have a very large poker bankroll to take this approach, so long as all of your rooms are quick to accept deposits from your credit card or a service like Neteller.

**Table Talk**

To say that a site **spreads** a particular game is exactly the same thing as saying it offers or deals that game to or for its customers.

**Perilous Play**

Before you experiment with making small deposits at numerous sites to see how quickly you can get money in and out, make sure none of your target sites has a rule insisting that cashouts be larger than the small minimum with which you are experimenting.

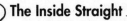

### The Inside Straight

In today's highly competitive market, many sites offer deposit bonuses (usually limited to 20 percent of a maximum dollar figure, often $500). All else equal, play where you can get a bonus, but all else is rarely equal, though!) There is invariably a substantial raked-hand play requirement before you can cash out and a limited time in which to play those hands. Reaching the target is easy if you stick to one site, but if you spread out your play, you could fail to qualify for your bonus.

## Tournaments: Software and How Long They Run

If you are going to play tournaments, you also need to know how good the tournament software is and how frequently tournaments run. Not everyone likes to play tournaments, but they are becoming more and more popular and some B&M tournament players (myself included) have credited extensive online tournament experience with helping them "finish" (win, rather than just making a final table) events.

### Table Talk

A **sit and go** event derives its name from how it is played: You park your buy-in ("sit") at a desired seat, and the tournament begins ("goes") as soon as the table is full.

There are two basic kinds of Internet tournaments: single table *sit and go* events, which are continually starting throughout the day and night, commencing as soon as a starting table is full, and multitable events that commence at predetermined times.

At large sites, sit and go tournaments start literally every few minutes. The larger the site, the less waiting time you'll experience.

## The User Interface

Although most Internet poker rooms utilize certain conventions that make it easy to learn to play at one room once you've learned how to play at another, there are still minor differences. The cards are easier to read at some sites, and at others, the cards are occasionally partially obscured by your chip total or screen name.

Some sites use avatars (graphic representations of people sitting in chairs). Some people find these "silicon avatars" annoying, while others love them. Other sites allow you to upload any (presentable) image you want to symbolize yourself and players there upload anything from baby photos to school insignia. Still others dispense with such graphics and simply present your screen name and home town, state, or country (although many allow you to choose not to display your geographical data). All sites indicate your chip total.

**The Inside Straight** _____

Sites that use preset avatars have only ten images; you can't, at the moment, select an avatar from hundreds of options. While most players ignore the avatar and take either the available empty seat or (if more than one seat is open) their favorite location, some people actually prefer "the guy in the hat" or "the well-endowed woman." Keep an eye peeled for avatar-related play trends. Certain avatars are selected more frequently by people who have certain styles!

Liking a user interface involves more than enjoying the view. Some interfaces feature pull-down menus that are more useful than others. Many now have a note-taking feature. This can be hugely helpful: You merely click on a player to note something like "Cannot be pushed off a modest hand like second pair. Do not bluff him, but with a decent hand, *bet him for value* on the end."

**Table Talk** _____

A **value bet** is made when you believe you are likely to be called, but you have a better than 50 percent chance of winning the pot. Normally when you bet, you prefer (unless you have an unbeatable hand, or something very close thereto) for your bet to win the pot for you immediately. In a value bet situation, you know that won't happen, but you do expect the bet to be profitable.

## Customer Service

If you have friends who play, their word of mouth can be useful in assessing customer service, but there's no substitute for your own experience.

In the ideal cardroom, both the "front line" customer service personnel and the supervisory "appeals process" personnel will be knowledgeable, efficient, and courteous, but as cardrooms grow larger and larger, it becomes more difficult for each and every front line person to know how to handle every situation. (Also remember that front line personnel continually interact with players who lie or exaggerate about their experiences, either to defend their own actions or to try to get something for nothing.)

If you have to choose, pick the cardroom where the supervisory personnel are consistently excellent, but you shouldn't have to choose.

Another part of customer service you need to consider is collusion. Good sites have extensive anticollusion programs, some aspects of which are triggered automatically (such as when players from the same area code often play at the same table), and some aspects of which are triggered in response to customer complaints and/or inquiries.

If you complain about apparently collusive conduct, you have a right to expect a detailed analysis and explanation of why the site has decided that the alleged colluders are or are not guilty. Collusion is discussed in more detail in Chapter 20.

**Table Talk**

Freeroll tournaments offer prizes but charge no entry fee or buy-in, and aren't just online phenomena: B&M card-rooms frequently offer them as well. Loyal customers (those who play a requisite number of raked money hands, or perhaps fee-based tournaments) are given free entry to these events, which sometimes offer quite substantial prizes to the winners.

## Special Offers

As competition increases, sites choose to offer special incentives to their players. Some offer frequent deposit bonuses. Others offer their loyal players *freeroll tournaments*. Still others offer merchandise or education in programs that resemble embryonic "frequent flier" programs. It seems logical to project that "frequent player" programs will grow more creative and player-friendly as sites compete not merely to attract new players, but to hold on to the business of existing players.

## Wins and Losses

Although there is little reason to expect that your results should be better at one site than at another, don't ignore the classic gambling wisdom "If something keeps happening, it's probably happening for a reason, even if you can't figure out what the reason is."

Most of the time, that advice is meant to tell people who are losing to quit playing, but it can be interpreted in a positive fashion, too. It's possible, for example, that one site gets the bulk of its players from a certain time zone, and at the time you like playing, those other players are at the end of their day and tired. If you consistently achieve better results at one site, stay there. It could be nothing more than a self-fulfilling prophecy—filled with more confidence, you play better—or there could be an actual reason.

Similarly, if you just keep getting your head handed to you on one site, there's no reason to stick around. If you believe a site is unlucky for you, sooner or later that belief will damage your play.

# Screen Names: Now Clark Kent Isn't the Only One with a Secret Identity

Although sites welcome you to play under your real name, there are a number of good reasons why you should select a screen name to play under:

- ◆ If you get into a nasty chat debate with an offensive player, it's probably better that he can't locate you.

- ◆ It might seem sophomoric, but screen names can be fun.

- ◆ If you make a weak play and someone who happens to know you is in the game, your reputation is safe.

- ◆ Although more sophisticated players don't get sucked into the trap, weaker players—your best source of chips—can sometimes be fooled into thinking your style is something other than it is via the right screen name. Of course, calling yourself "BlitheringIdiot" will probably make someone suspect you've won at least three WSOP titles.

- ◆ By playing under different screen names at different sites, you make it more difficult for players who move around to collect information about you. They don't know that player "Wolverine" on Site A is player "MarysLamb" at Site B. (You can use the same screen name on two or more sites, if it is available, but don't have to.)

- ◆ If your name is well-known outside the poker world, you might not want people to know how much time you spend playing poker.

- ◆ If you have a position of responsibility, or a job where poker playing would be frowned upon, a screen name is helpful. For example, a banker, police officer, or clergyman might prefer not to have his fondness for poker known.

## Reasons Not to Play Under a Screen Name

Probably the single best reason to play under your own name comes up when you know your own weaknesses and that you have a hard time controlling them. If you're reasonably sure that when playing under a screen name, you'd be vulnerable to going on tilt or making crazy plays, using your real name might force you to play more responsibly.

If you are a talented player who is trying to build a reputation (possibly to attract endorsement money or a backer), you might want to play under your real name for the same reasons you might want to enter high profile B&M tournaments.

Most sites don't let you switch screen names without a very good reason, so make sure you pick one you think you can be comfortable with for a long time.

## The Least You Need to Know

◆ Although many Internet poker sites share similar features, there are important differences that you need to consider when choosing a site to play on.

◆ Try to take advantage of promotions like deposit bonuses.

◆ Select a site with a user interface that you find comfortable.

◆ Unless you have a good reason to play under your own name, play Internet poker under a screen name.

# 20

# Unique Aspects of Internet Play

## In This Chapter

- ◆ Key differences between B&M and Internet play
- ◆ How and when to use certain pre-select buttons
- ◆ Selecting and changing seats
- ◆ Cheating and collusion on the Internet

The single most important difference between Internet poker and B&M poker is also the most obvious difference: the inability to see, hear, (and occasionally smell) your opponents and their inability to do the same in reverse.

This changes the game in a number of ways and you'll learn whether one form of the game might be better for you than the other. You'll also learn certain technical aspects of Internet play and which aspects of Internet cheating and/or collusion are myth, which are reality, and what you can do about them.

# All the Comforts of Home

It's hard to hold a discussion about the relative merits of Internet poker and casino poker without someone raising the comfort issue.

"I can eat what I want when I want," the Internet advocate begins. " I can do other computer work when I'm not in a game. I don't have to tip the dealer, and I don't have to listen to other players yap—I can even turn of the chat feature if I want. I'm king of my castle."

## Is the Comfort Worth It?

Although one might debate the merits of questionable grooming habits, it's certainly clear that in many ways one can be more comfortable playing Internet poker than B&M poker. Leaving the companionship issues aside, there's a threshold question you should examine before you decide one of the strong arguments in favor of Internet poker is that extra comfort.

Is feeling so very comfortable really in your best interest when playing poker, especially if (as would seem when playing on the Internet, where the social aspect is greatly diminished) your goal is to win money?

A strong case can be made that you *don't* want to be quite so comfortable when you play to win. A winning poker player is focused. He's looking for every clue he can find, pushing every small edge he can find.

> **Perilous Play** _____
>
> Playing in your bathrobe probably won't hurt your Internet poker results, but many of the other acts you can indulge in while safely ensconced in the privacy of your own home can. Beer and poker might go together, but beer (and/or other drugs) and winning poker don't go together.

Just as playing multiple games can lower your expected bets-per-hour winning rate, so, too, can distractions such as television, food, drink, and other work. These other distractions can't add to your bottom line the way playing in a second or third game can.

Playing in a completely relaxed state might be fine if you're looking to Internet poker as a way to relax. If you want to win, you might want to turn the TV off and stay focused on the task at hand.

# "Who Was That Masked Man? I Wanted to Thank Him."

It's often said that at low stakes, poker is a card game played by people and at high stakes, poker is a people game that happens to be played with cards. This is certainly true in the B&M world, but it's only partially true on the Internet. Many of the clues that good players depend on in live games simply aren't available on the Internet. On the Internet you are playing against unknown opponents whom you can't see, hear, or smell, and that makes a difference.

## The Unseen Opponent

Visual clues are hugely important in poker. When you see your opponent's hand tremble as he releases his chips, you know, absent specific observations to the contrary, that there's roughly a 90 percent chance that he has a strong hand. The tremble doesn't come from the fear associated from a bluff, but from a release of tension. Good players learn to mask this and great players learn how to produce it on demand, but it's still a useful tell. You'll never see that on the Internet.

Similarly, you can't see your opponent licking his lips from a dry mouth, can't see the veins in his neck pulsing, can't see his chest heaving, and can't see that his eye pupils are dilated (from looking at something he likes seeing, such as a good hand).

### The Inside Straight

When poker players first learn the game, they believe they are being hugely deceptive by acting strong when they are weak and weak when they are strong. Good players see past this in a few seconds. The reality is that very few of us are the great actors we believe ourselves to be and being able to play in an environment where our opponents can't see our attempts at a poker face is helpful to all but the best players.

It sounds like you're giving up a lot of valuable information and you are, but remember—your opponents have no way to pick up any of these tells on you, either. If you've been having a problem playing live, for example if your opponents seem to fold when you have a strong hand but call you when you're bluffing, there's a decent chance that you have some sort of tell that's giving your hand's strength away. That problem vanishes online.

## The Inaudible Opponent

Fans of the classic television show *M.A.S.H.* may remember an episode wherein rookie poker player Major Charles Emerson Winchester III starts cleaning out everyone in camp in a large poker game. He takes a short break and his fellow players complain bitterly about his luck and his insufferable attitude. "And that whistling! It never stops! He just whistles even louder when he's bluffing!"

Pause.

*"He just whistles louder when he's bluffing!!!"* came the unanimous reply. When Major Winchester returned, he soon got cleaned out.

Few of us have auditory tells as bad as Major Winchester's, but sound—or the lack of it—can tell a very loud story. A nervous player's voice has a different timbre and if someone who has been silent suddenly starts yapping (or vice-versa), opponents have information. They may not know what the information means the first time they encounter it, but they'll know what to do the second time around.

## "Just When You Thought It Was Safe to Get Back in the Water ..."

Don't abandon your search for tells online because they do exist!

Probably the most important tells stem from the speed with which one bets, checks, or calls. You should keep your own betting speed patterns random and pay close attention to your opponents. Someone who checks like lightning has probably pre-selected the "check-fold" button, a sure sign of weakness that can be exploited on the next betting round. Similarly, if someone re-re-raises in an instant, he has probably selected the "raise any" button, a reasonably sure sign of a strong hand rather than a bluff.

For this reason, even though the pre-select buttons do speed up on the online game, you are better off avoiding their use except when you are planning to fold. Even then, you should not use the buttons if you are in the last three positions because if everyone has folded to you, it's possible that you may want to try a steal raise with a hand you weren't planning on playing. Such efforts are usually wasted in low stakes "no fold'em" games, but when the stakes get a bit higher, it is possible to steal the blinds every once in a while.

For similar reasons, you shouldn't always bet with blinding speed when you have the nuts. Occasionally you will want to pause a bit. This will allow you to pause on occasions when you have a good but not great hand and need a moment or two to decide if you want to raise or not. If you always raise quickly with a strong hand, any delay invites your more aware opponents to call or re-raise when you raise after a delay.

**Perilous Play**

There's an old saying: "When I was in my twenties, I was worried about what people thought about me. When I reached my thirties, I stopped caring what people thought about me. When I reached my forties, I realized no one was thinking about me." Don't assume that because you have been sending out some clever false signals, everyone has noticed, especially at lower stakes. Many of your opponents are doing well if they notice their own hands, let alone your subtle signals.

# Internet Waiting Lists

In PartyPoker.com's lobby, you can see how many different games are currently running at each stake level, how many players are seated in each game, how long each waiting list is, the average pot size, and the average number of hands played per hour. By analyzing this information, you may decide that one particular table at a given stake level is much more promising than another.

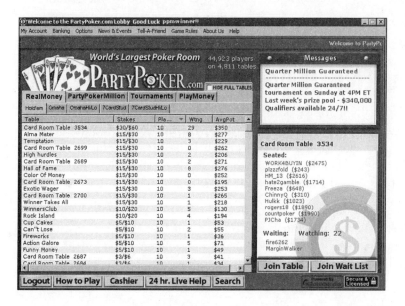

*An Internet poker "lobby" from PartyPoker.com.*

Waiting lists work a bit differently on the Internet than they do in casinos. When you visit an Internet "lobby," you can go directly to any table that has an open seat, but if there are no seats currently open at the stake level you wish to play, you can join waiting lists in one of two ways:

◆ You can join a "global" waiting list where you agree to take the first open seat in any game at your desired stake level, as long as that game has a certain minimum number of players at the table (the minimum to be decided by you).

◆ You can join several individual waiting lists. Although this process is more time-consuming, it is the better way to go. If you join a global wait list, as soon as you get taken to a table with an open seat, your name comes off the waiting list for all the other tables at that stake level.

**The Inside Straight** _____

Some cardrooms make it very easy to locate a particular player; in others, you may need to scan the open tables one by one. If you keep good notes about weak players, you'll want to follow them around. Most of your profit in poker comes not from your own brilliant plays, but from your opponents' mistakes.

If it turns out you're not all that fond of the table where you're first seated, you need to start the waiting list process all over again if you used the global method. If you joined all the individual waiting lists, you will be notified each time a seat opens in any of those other games. This may let you escape a table that has too many good players (or not enough bad ones), and it also may let you "follow" one or more of your favorite pigeons to wherever he is currently playing.

# Don't Put All Your Chips in One Basket

It can be tempting, especially if you've been winning and want to show off you big chip total (it can intimidate others), to bring every chip in your account to the first table where you get a seat. Most of the time, this is a bad idea. If you want to change tables and get the opportunity because you joined waiting lists individually rather than globally, you will be offered a new seat when it opens.

When you try to sit down, though, you will be asked how many chips you want to bring to the new table. If all of your chips are sitting at your first table, your account balance will be zero and you won't be allowed to take a seat. Even if you hurriedly leave your seat in the first game, it usually takes most software systems a while to move your chips from your first table back to the *virtual cashier*.

When your new seat opens up in a game featuring your favorite fish, you only have a limited amount of time to take the seat before you lose your claim to it. It's entirely possible that your time could run out before the system gets your chips back from your first table to the cashier.

**Table Talk**

The **virtual cashier** plays a role similar to the B&M cashier. This is where money remains in your account from one session to the next and where you go to buy more chips if you find yourself running short. It's also normally where you go to instruct the system to cash you out, sending money either back into your e-cash service account or your credit card, or to request a check be sent to you.

As a result, unless you need every chip in your account to play at your first table, you should leave enough chips in your account to give yourself a legal buy-in (normally just five big bets, but in some cardrooms ten) at a second table. After you settle in, you can click on the dealer's chip tray (a nearly universal signal that you want to bring more chips to the table) and arrange to bring some additional chips to your new table.

Naturally, you'll want to leave a full buy-in behind in case your second table doesn't turn out to be much of a bargain, either!

# Seat Change, Please

In a B&M casino, changing seats (not tables: seats) is relatively simple. You tell the dealer you want a seat change and (assuming you're first on the seat change list) as soon as a seat opens up, you're given the option to take it. If you pass on the open seat because you only want to move to one of a few special seats, you normally don't lose your place in line on the seat change list as long as you tell the dealer you want to keep it.

Online, changing seats is a bit more problematic. You cannot change seats unless a seat opens *and* there is no waiting list. This lets you leave the game and then return, buying in as if you were a new player. This has its risks; others could jump in and claim the empty seats in the few seconds you're away.

If there is no waiting list and there are a couple of open seats, you can probably get out and then back in again quickly enough to not risk losing your seat entirely. You can't always change, though. Some sites put you right back in the seat you left if you try this.

**The Inside Straight**

A quick reminder: Don't change seats for superstitious reasons (as Obi-Wan Kenobi would say, "That leads to the Dark Side"). You try for a change because you want to get certain types of players on your right where you can know what they're going to do before you. Remember, money tends to flow around a table in a clockwise fashion.

The potential of losing your seat entirely aside, there's one other reason why you might not put as much effort into getting a seat change online as you would in a B&M room: Players hop in and out of seats online far more quickly than they do in the B&M world.

Sometimes this happens because people play more short sessions online. Few players visit a B&M room planning on such a short session. Sometimes it happens because the player is playing two games until he can decide which is more promising. Perhaps most commonly, a player may be sitting in your game only until the seat he really wants (at a different stake, or even a different kind of poker) becomes available.

Unless the players in your game appear to have settled in for awhile and there are a couple of open seats and no waiting list, plan on staying wherever you first land. It's more important to keep an eye open for promising table changes than promising seat changes.

# Cheating and Collusion on the Internet

When Internet poker first got rolling, many players smugly declared it wouldn't last, couldn't last, at least for any kind of substantial stakes. You might be able to run games up to the $5-10 level, they proclaimed, but once you got higher than that, it wouldn't be possible.

"What's to stop some computer geek," began the argument, "from setting up a room somewhere with five computers and five telephone lines, opening five different accounts, and putting the squeeze on everyone in his game? Not only would he know the whereabouts or availability of eight more cards than everyone else (in hold'em— 16 more in Omaha!), but he could easily trap someone else. He wouldn't even need a hand. Someone could open, his first account could raise, his second could re-raise, and his third could re-re-raise. The opener would just have to fold unless he had two aces or two kings and he'll almost never have that hand."

## The Inside Straight

Did you spot the first fatal flaw in the "five computers" argument? Just because someone has information doesn't mean he knows how to use it well. A true "computer geek" isn't going to be much of a poker player. He'll have spent his time learning computers. If the argument began "Suppose a *poker genius* set up five computers ..." you'd have a better case—but as you'll soon learn, there are flaws in that line of thinking, too.

"The cheater," the naysayers continued, "could also wait until at least one of his hands was great and perhaps another was good. He could trap someone else in the middle, making sure that whenever the cheater had a good hand, he could force the opposition to play a capped (maximum number of bets) pot."

Of course, it doesn't have to be one computer geek in one room. You could have several friends who have unlimited long distance telephone plans hooked up and they could discuss their hands and what best to do. The prophets of doom were certain that this would halt online poker in its tracks.

Although it would be silly to claim that no collusion happens online, the prophets of online poker doom can go get in line with the stock pickers who told their clients to remain heavily invested in the dot.com boom. Not all predictions come to pass. Let's see why the "collusion will kill online poker" predictions didn't.

## Collusion Happens in B&M Rooms, Too

Gifted colluders don't have to stare at each other's cards to know what they have. It's remarkably simple to work out a set of hand signals to notify one's friends of just about anything ("head scratch means hearts, turning around to watch the TV means a big pocket pair, shuffling chips means low cards …"). If the colluders are gifted, they can ply their trade anywhere.

Note the key phrase, "If the colluders are gifted."

The great majority of cheaters became cheaters because they couldn't beat the games honestly. They just weren't very good. Armed with more knowledge, they are more dangerous, but they still don't know how to use that information.

**Perilous Play** _____

You certainly need to stay aware of possible cheating and/or collusion in any poker game, be it Internet, casino, or home. If your fear of cheating becomes obsessive, though, you should quit playing poker. Poker is challenging under any circumstances, but if you routinely assume that a loss means you were cheated, your chances of becoming a winning player are miniscule. You need to take responsibility and consider the possibility that you lost because you were outplayed.

Curiously, the fact that it seems easier to collude on the Internet means even less talented players will try it. It's trivially easy to imagine some frat boys thinking they'll be able to pay for spring break by trying this. However, if the frat boys are still drawing to inside straights, their "information edge" will only serve to keep them playing long after their losses should have told them to quit.

It only *seems* easier to collude online. Determined colluders can do it in live games, too, but in those games, there are no *hand histories* available for reviewing betting patterns.

> **Table Talk**
>
> All Internet poker rooms make **hand histories** available to their players via speedy automated e-mail requests. Usually it takes less than 10 seconds to request that these detailed lists of every single bet, card, and chat comment for as many as your last 100 hands be e-mailed to you and they arrive within minutes. If two or more players appear to be up to something funny, the hand history will usually show it.

## Information Makes Prolonged Collusion Almost Impossible

You've already seen how hand histories can provide you with data you never could assemble in a B&M room, but Internet poker rooms collect many other types of information that makes a colluder's life appropriately miserable:

♦ If two people have ever accessed the poker room from the same computer at different times (a common way for one colluder to show a would-be partner how it all works), most rooms can track that.

♦ Players must typically provide a real name and a valid mailing address to collect winnings. A lone player with five accounts may find it easy enough to find friends who will accept mail for him, but will they accept Internet poker checks in their names, cash them, and hand over the money?

♦ Identical area codes and/or zip codes increase collusion likelihood and get flagged automatically. It can be difficult to get multiple different telephone number exchanges (the first three numbers) at the same address, so even if a player finds four friends to accept checks for him, a red flag appears when multiple players have not merely the same area code but also the same exchange.

♦ Most rooms can track how often two players play at the same table. In large cardrooms, there are often ten or more tables going that feature the same game at the same limit. If two players routinely play at the same table in these situations, they'd better come up smelling like roses in their betting patterns.

> ◆ If someone complains or requests an investigation, better rooms assign live personnel to watch suspected colluders. Once that happens, it's easy to spot questionable betting practices or timing lags that make it likely two or more players are conferring before acting.

There are many more automatic computer-driven ways that colluder accounts get flagged, but the best defense lies with the players themselves. They are the ones who alert the cardrooms to watch players and often use hand histories to supply cardroom employees with evidence, rather than just saying, "Please investigate so and so."

It's not as profitable to try to cheat at low stakes for the same reason it's hard to profit playing straight at low stakes: The rake takes a bigger proportion of the pot. At higher stakes, the players are better at spotting "funny business."

Also remember that if you play five accounts, you're posting five times as many blinds. Colluding online is not the simple practice the early Doubting Thomases thought it would be.

## They Still Have to Play Good Poker

If a colluder is a weak player, his collusion is probably only going to slow his bleeding.

If a would-be colluder runs into a player or players who see what's going on, his cheating efforts can blow up in his face. If you suspect collusion, you should probably get out of the game. If you don't leave, you can fight back by playing better starting hands (almost always good advice to beginners anyway).

Instead of getting squeezed for extra bets when you're in there with marginal holdings you shouldn't have been playing in the first place, when colluders try to apply pressure with raises and re-raises to your good hands, you're happy to play along because they're doing your betting work for you.

## Poker Has Changed

In the old days (the *real* old days, not the Internet old days), many players felt they had to try to cheat just to maintain a level playing field with the other cheaters.

Today, an entirely new generation has entered poker while never experiencing road games filled with characters carrying guns and marked cards. The sleight of hand skills that were so useful in fleecing a visiting *mark* still exist, but far fewer players are capable of practicing them. Many cheating techniques are, thankfully, becoming a lost "art." Naturally, even where that art still exists, it's useless on the Internet.

Faced with casinos full of security cameras and Internet cardrooms that keep records about every bet, the bright and talented have in the main decided their best play involves developing a real talent for playing honestly.

If you're good enough to beat the games straight up, why risk being ostracized, barred, and/or beaten up? If you cheat with a partner, you have to forever fear that he might decide to threaten you with exposure (or cheat you or steal from you himself). Even if you're confident of your cheating partner's morals—think about that one for a minute—he might expose you to save his own skin.

Although you've just seen most of the collusion arguments crumbled, you probably should remain a bit careful about mid-limit Omaha. Because Omaha is a game of draws and redraws more than of made hands, knowledge of what cards are or aren't available is far more helpful in Omaha. If a player holds the A♥ in one of his hands, he knows that a king-high heart flush draw in another is a nut draw.

Curiously, you probably don't have much to worry about at the lower and higher Omaha limits. There isn't enough money available at low limits and in high-limit games (not just in Omaha) Internet poker rooms usually have someone actively policing the game. High-limit Omaha players are pretty good at spotting something amiss themselves, too.

## The Least You Need to Know

- A style or skill set that wins in B&M cardrooms may not work on the Internet, and vice versa.

- B&M poker requires more people skills, while Internet poker is a more technical game.

- Although table changes are easier, seat changes are a bit more problematical on the Internet.

- You shouldn't ignore the possibility of collusion online, but it's far less likely than early prognosticators believed.

- In many ways it is more difficult to cheat on the Internet than it is in B&M games.

# Part 4

# Tournament Poker

Part 4 walks you through the ins and outs of the most exciting and fame-attracting form of poker. You'll learn about how a wide variety of tournaments are run and how proper tournament selection and play can allow you to turn a relatively small investment into fame and fortune. Tournaments allow you to take a legitimate shot at winning big money without risking big money, something not possible in money poker, but tournament success requires its own unique brand of strategy.

You'll also learn how to ask the threshold question, "Does the combination of my personality, skill set, and emotional nature make it likely that I will enjoy being a tournament player?" If the answer to the threshold question is "Yes," you'll learn how to find the best path to success.

# Chapter 21

# Tournament Poker Basics

## In This Chapter

- ◆ Elements common to all forms of poker tournaments
- ◆ Nonmonetary reasons to play poker tournaments
- ◆ What kind of personality type succeeds in tournaments?
- ◆ What sort of tipping is appropriate in tournaments?

Despite what you might have seen in the Mel Gibson/Jodie Foster movie *Maverick*, poker tournaments do not share money poker's rich century and a half of folklore and tradition. The tournament phenomenon is much more recent, but has been enjoying a period of explosive growth in the twenty-first century.

There are many different kinds of poker tournaments, but certain elements are common to all. I'll discuss the common elements before you start learning the differences.

# Matters Common to Virtually All Poker Tournaments

With the exception of freeroll tournaments, all tournaments require players to pay both an *entry fee* (a relatively small number that goes to the house) and a *buy-in* (a relatively much larger number that creates, or helps create, the tournament prize pool).

Entry fees alone usually cannot justify a B&M cardroom's expense in advertising and running a tournament. Normally, whenever a cardroom runs a series of major tournaments, its side action (money games) increases substantially in both size and number, and that's where the casino makes its real money.

## Before It Can End with Money, It Must Start with Money

An entry fee can be as much as 30 percent of the buy-in for very small tournaments (for example, a $10 buy-in event might use a $3 entry fee). Usually the entry fee falls somewhere between 5 percent and 10 percent of the buy-in. A $500 buy-in tournament would commonly require an entry fee of $40 (8 percent).

With rare exceptions (such as the Shooting Stars tournament at San Jose, California's Bay 101), tournament directors don't know how many entrants they will get to any given tournament until the moment the tournament begins (which is usually when registration closes). Occasionally in large events, anyone who is in line when registration closes will still be allowed to enter.

For this reason, entrants usually don't know how large the prize pool will be in any given tournament. For events with several years of history behind them, it is usually possible to create an educated guess.

In some very large tournaments, the promoters guarantee a big number for first place. The World Series of Poker drew headlines for a number of years with its $1,000,000 first prize guarantee for the $10,000 buy-in Championship Event, until the number of entrants grew so large that the 2000 guarantee jumped to $1,500,000, and hit $2,500,000 in 2003.

The WSOP numbers have been growing so rapidly that now the promoters simply promise a first prize of a certain round and impressive size based on a given number of entrants. Barring some kind of economic upheaval, first place in 2004 will certainly be at least $3,000,000; I wouldn't be surprised if the number of entrants more than doubles in 2004, which will mean either a $5,000,000+ first prize or (more likely) much better payoffs to other high finishers.

A million bucks just doesn't buy what it used to.

### The Inside Straight

Although there has been a steadily increasing call for flatter payout percentages, a quick look at the numbers shows that today's really big payoffs go to the top three finishers. Because of this, if a *deal* (discussed in Chapter 24) is to be made, it is usually negotiated by the top three finalists. This can make the climb from third to fourth almost as fiscally important as the climb from second to first!

All finishes other than first in a tournament that guarantees a special first-place payout, and all finishes period in most tournaments, are paid out based on a percentage of the prize pool. The percentages are not standardized, but common rules of thumb call for one table (nine players in flop games and eight in stud games) to get paid for each 100 entrants.

A hold'em tournament entered by 115 players would probably pay nine places, and one entered by 145 or more would probably pay 18 spots. (I use "probably" because these rules are not standardized, although the break points are announced either before an event or the instant registration is closed.)

A tournament that paid nine spots would pay out percentages fairly close to these:

First:            40%

Second:          20%

Third:           12%

Fourth:           8%

Fifth:            6%

Sixth:            5%

Seventh:          4%

Eighth:           3%

Ninth:            2%

If another nine places are paid, usually the tenth–twelfth place finishers each get the same amount, as do the thirteenth–fifteenth place finishers and the sixteenth–eighteenth place finishers. When third or fourth tables are paid (five used to be quite rare, but with 839 entrants in the 2003 WSOP, *seven* tables—63 places—were paid!), all the finishers at those tables are paid equally.

### Poker Lore

The twenty-eighth through thirty-sixth place finishers at the 2003 WSOP each received about 0.58 percent of the prize pool, which might not sound like much until you realize that the prize pool approached $8,000,000. Therefore, that paltry-sounding 0.58 percent was worth $45,000. That's not bad money for five day's work. As one wag noted, "Some people have to work a whole month to make that much."

The money for these extra finishers has to come from somewhere. Usually it is the winner who takes the biggest "hit," seeing his percentage reduced down into the low 30s. While final tablists lose a little in percentage when multiple tables are paid, they don't necessarily make less money, because the prize pool is larger.

## Your Loss Is Limited in Poker Tournaments

Money distribution is hardly the only element common to all types of tournaments. Unlike certain other types of gambling tournaments (most commonly blackjack), poker tournaments employ special "no cash value" *tournament chips*.

With the exception of rebuy tournaments, you know when you first sit down to play a tournament that the most you can lose is your buy-in and entry fee. That's comforting to gamblers who lack certain kinds of self-control. If you lose your tournament chips, you're out only that entry money.

> **Table Talk**
>
> The **cage** is a high-stakes casino or cardroom cashier, so named because of the bars or thick glass that make breaking and entering a bit more difficult than it is at you local Kwik-E Mart (or, in towns outside Springfield, a Seven-Eleven).

Unfortunately, if you get hot, you can't take these tournament chips to the *cage* and ask for their face value. You must play them in the tournament until either you've eliminated everyone else, have gotten knocked out yourself, or (in the case of *supersatellite* tournaments discussed in Chapter 22) play is halted because everyone remaining has won an equal share of prize money.

## "Okay, Podner, We'll Draw on the Count of Three"

Another element common to all poker tournaments is the random draw. A given number of players choose to enter (for continuity's sake, we'll assume that number to be 105 for all following examples). The random draw determines each player's table and seat number.

Poker tournament tables are prenumbered one through some maximum estimated number. For example, you might draw Table 4, Seat 6 (seats are numbered clockwise starting with #1 on the dealer's immediate left). In an event that happened to draw 105 players, the tournament director (TD) would probably have been prepared to handle as many as 200 entrants. With nine players usually assigned to hold'em event tables (some tournaments start with ten, to preserve precious table space, and then drop the number to nine as players get knocked out), you would need 12 tables to start.

The TD couldn't be sure about the 105 entrants until the last minute. Therefore, rather than an arrangement of 11 full tables and one table with only six players, he'd probably set up 15 tables with chips and then have dealers pass out starting chips to nine seats at 12 of those tables. That means 108 chip stacks would be out as play commenced. No table would have more than one empty seat.

If someone had been in line to register at the starting time, he would get one of those empty seats. To encourage on-time arrivals, chips start getting *blinded off* stacks from non-present players as soon as the event begins.

Sometimes players who do not wish to get caught in a line just before a tournament begins buy in the day before. This also can be a wise practice if you think there is a chance you might be a few minutes late. Normally you won't be allowed to join the buy-in line after the event's nominal starting time.

**Table Talk**

If a player is not in his seat when it is his turn to post an ante or blind, the dealer **blinds off** that player by removing the appropriate number of chips from his stack. The same thing happens to a chip stack passed out to a seat that has not yet been sold.

It's quite possible that a player who arrives very late could have lost 10 percent, 20 percent, or even more of his starting stack to blind-offs. Normally being just a few minutes late costs you only one set of blinds and it's rare for that to represent more than 2.5 percent of a player's stack—an essentially irrelevant amount.

**Poker Lore**

Youngest-ever World Series of Poker Champion Phil Hellmuth is famous for his late tournament arrivals. He buys in the day before and has sometimes arrived as much as three hours late, finding his starting stack has shrunk to 65 percent of its starting size.

Hellmuth insists the late arrivals are due to his desire to get enough sleep. "The chips I lose are much less important than being well-rested," he says. His practice is *so* consistent, though, that most opponents believe he could arrive on time if he really wanted to and that the late arrivals are a psychological ploy designed to intimidate opponents. By arriving so late, Hellmuth is, in effect, announcing, "I don't need as many starting chips as you do to beat you." Once a wag criticized a late-starting tournament by saying "This tournament started so late, Phil Hellmuth was on time."

The rest isn't worthless, of course, but it's hard to put a price on psychological dominance. Beginners are well-advised not to try this one.

# Registration Ends and Musical Chairs Begins

After the final starting number is known, the stacks for nonstarters are removed. This explains why sometimes a tournament with 105 starters who are each given $1,000 in tournament chips finds itself with something like $105,895 in play. The extra chips come from stacks that got blinded off and then removed.

In some events, the draw resembles a raffle with seat cards that say "Table 4, Seat 6" and "Table 9, Seat 1" actually drawn one at a time from a rotating drum. It's more common in the technological age for a computer to spit out assignments randomly and for a Tournament Assistant (TA) to have a large stack of preprinted random seat slips waiting for players as they check in.

Players get the next seat in the stack when they buy in. The player just behind the fellow who draws Table 3, Seat 7 does not get Table 3, Seat 8 (barring an unusual coincidence). He gets a random seat and is not allowed to ask for a different one.

> **The Inside Straight** _____
>
> If you want to avoid a super-tough starting table, don't buy in at the last possible moment. The very last players to buy in are often the strongest. They may not wish to commit to a tournament in case an attractive side game starts and are less worried about missing blinds than average players. If a TD hasn't set up enough tables, late-comers may be placed together at a hurriedly-added new table—and they won't be happy about it.

With extremely rare exceptions, players are not "seeded" in poker tournaments as they are in tennis. Table 8 might feature the six strongest players in the field, while Table 9 might feature nine rookies. Random means exactly that.

Another feature you will encounter in larger tournaments of most varieties is the redraw. For reasons discussed at many different points in the text, it can be advantageous to have certain kinds of players on your right and certain kinds on your left.

In an effort to minimize the purely lucky advantage some player might get from having a frequent bluffer on his right, most tournaments redraw for new seating positions once players have reached the money and many redraw each time a moneyed table is eliminated. (For example, in a 300 player-tournament that pays 27 places, there might be a redraw for new seats when 27, 18, and 9 players remain). In multi-day tournaments, there is usually a redraw each night.

## Don't Worry: The Tournament Will Only *Seem* Endless

To make sure that tournaments finish within a reasonable period of time, all tournaments utilize an increasing blind structure. The blinds remain the same size for the length of one tournament round. Tournament rounds might be as short as twenty minutes or as long as two hours; most medium-sized tournaments use thirty- to forty-minute rounds.

At the end of the round, the blinds increase according to a prearranged published schedule. As the blinds increase, so too do the betting limits (when the blinds are $15-30, the bets in a limit tournament are $30-60; when the blinds move to $25-50, the betting limits concurrently move up to $50-100).

Because the blinds increase at regular intervals, players cannot sit back and wait forever for a premium hand. If they play *too tight*, they will lose too many chips in blinds. By the time a tournament has reached its sixth or seventh level, the blinds are usually high enough that a player who has not increased his starting stack will find that one trip through the blinds might cost him half of his chips.

### Table Talk

Poker has its own unique terminology and grammatical forms. Someone who plays a conservative game is a **tight player**. Even though it would appear grammatically correct to extend that to "he plays too tightly," players almost universally say "too tight." They also say that someone is "playing good" and not "playing well." If you say someone "plays pretty good," your listeners are more likely to believe your evaluation because the usage would mean you hang around poker rooms!

What happens as players start to get knocked out depends on the event format, as discussed in Chapter 22.

# Personalities and Styles Suited to Tournament Poker

Succeeding at tournament poker requires a different skill set than does succeeding at money poker. It also requires a different kind of emotional stability. The amount of luck needed to win a tournament varies dramatically depending on how the tournament is structured.

Possibly the best metaphor anyone has ever used to explain why the notion "poker is poker" is dead wrong when it comes to tournament poker and money poker comes from the world of tennis. Top-ranked hard-court players often find themselves almost helpless against relatively unknown clay-court specialists and the world's finest clay-court players often don't even bother to enter hard-court tournaments. The two games look the same, but they aren't, an evaluation that applies even more forcefully to poker.

Just as a few truly great tennis players have skills that transcend the clay-hard court differences, so too can a few poker superstars excel equally in money and tournament play. The key word is "few."

## Should You Become a Tournament Specialist?

There's no reason why a player must choose between money poker and tournament poker. Most tournament players also play in money games and many money specialists occasionally dip their toes into tournament waters.

Still, the cold, hard reality is that very few players find themselves equally talented in both arenas. Different technical and emotional skills are required and while many players are good enough to win reasonably consistently at each kind of game, the overwhelming majority find their results tend to be much better at one or the other.

Before you try to decide whether you're likely better suited to tournament or money play, examine some of the unique aspects of tournament play presented in the following sections.

## Suggestions for Those Vulnerable to Tilt

Probably the best suggestion available to people who have volatile personalities susceptible to tilt is not to play poker. If you let bad beats throw you off your game, you're not going to be a successful poker player.

If an unfortunate result turns your normally solid game into jelly, you won't merely lose one hand, you'll probably lose everything you have with you. In a money game, that's disastrous, especially when you have ways you can go get more money and return to the game. Someone vulnerable to tilt needs either to solidify his psyche or avoid money poker.

Going on tilt isn't ideal in a tournament, either, but at least there your losses are limited to your entry fee and buy-in.

**The Inside Straight**

If you go on tilt when you have a huge tournament payday in your sights, tilt can be even more damaging than in money play. If you have a shot at $70,000 but win only $3,000 because you went on tilt, that's one mighty expensive tilt.

Although tournaments are definitely a better arena for the tilt-prone than money games, there's another area where you need to be careful.

There are few worse poker feelings than that moment when your last chips get pushed by the dealer over to another player and you have to stand up from the table and leave. It hurts badly, even if the moment occurs at a final table where you've finished fifth and are taking home a big paycheck. It doesn't feel much better when you bust out one-hundred-and-fiftieth out of 200 starters.

If you remember the climatic moment in the Eddie Murphy/Dan Aykroyd film *Trading Places* when Mortimer Duke (Don Ameche) screams "*Turn those* (stock trading) *machines back on! Turn those machines back on!*" you know what it feels like to be told your day is over and there won't be any way to get more money out of this poker tournament this day.

---

**Poker Lore**

Author James McManus (*Going to the Sun, Positively Fifth Street*) had just finished achieving an absolute poker miracle by finishing fifth in the 2000 World Series of Poker, winning a quarter of a million dollars in the process. It had been a miracle because McManus was a writer, not a poker pro, and over the course of four improbable days, he became part of the story that *Harpers Magazine* had sent him to cover.

As soon as the TV folks were through with McManus, I approached this new friend as reporter and informal coach and asked, "So, do you feel like a rock star now?"

"If ace-queen had held up against ace-four (the key and unlikely final card defeat that had effectively ended McManus' chances to win), I might," McManus said glumly. "Right now, I feel like a back-up band."

Unless you've won the event, it's never easy to stand up at the end of your poker tournament day—no matter how much money you've won, or how unlikely it was that you got as far as you did in the first place.

---

Unfortunately, there is a poker equivalent of "turning those machines back on." It's a short walk from the tournament area to the money game area in almost any cardroom or casino. Players who are "hot" about their defeat sometimes choose to turn the machines back on by jumping into a money game.

Top money players travel to major tournaments without ever intending to play a single hand of tournament poker for this very reason. They lie in wait for the tournament players, who at best are specialists playing their second-best form of poker, and who at worst are on tilt from their tournament defeat.

If you want to hang around and play money poker after your tournament day is done, make sure you take a break—a *long* break—before you resume.

## Ever Wanted to Be an Auto Racer?

Good money poker players tend to be rock steady (they don't have to play like ultra-tight rocks, but they do need to be rock *steady*). When they sit down in a game, they know the blinds won't be changing throughout the night and they know there's a fairly decent chance they will be playing with many of the same people throughout the night.

That's not true in tournament poker. The steadily increasing blind structure means that tournament players must be good at *changing gears*. They need to be able to alternate playing fast (aggressively) with playing slow (conservatively). They must be good at adapting to a table full of new opponents when their table breaks or redraws, or to changing table dynamics caused when a weak short-stacked player busts out and is replaced by a chip-laden star.

If you adapt to new circumstances better than most, you may have the makings of a tournament player. If you can analyze extensive and subtle data better than most, you may perform better as a money player.

**The Inside Straight** _____

Although the "auto racer" heading was mostly a play on gear-shifting's importance, the endorsement opportunities now becoming available to tournament players solidify the auto racing metaphor. Poker hasn't yet reached the point where player clothing exists mainly to hold together a collection of sponsor labels, but there's no question that success brings fame and fame offers opportunities that won't ever be available to money specialists.

## Do Win-Lose Scenarios Bother You?

Many poker players understand from practical experience that most of their big winning nights in money games happen when one or more opponents are getting crushed. Even though they may feel for the guy who is getting walloped, they stick around for the kill, knowing that if they abandon their seat, some other player will win the money that the doomed player seems determined to lose.

> **CAUTION**
>
> **Perilous Play** _____
>
> A conscience and love for one's fellow man are traits to be admired. Nonetheless, poker, even tournament poker, is competitive. If you don't burn with desire to defeat your opponents, you probably won't. A fiercely competitive spirit can be the difference between a winning player and a losing player. If you're only happy when everyone wins, you may be a worthy human being, but poker isn't your game.

Players whose conscience bothers them a bit in these situations shouldn't really feel too bad because we're all adults (or should be) and nobody takes mercy on *them* during *their* off nights. Nonetheless, there is an alternative: tournament poker. No one loses more than his buy-in and entry fee, and if your success does deprive an opponent of a big win, at least you're not forcing him to buy cat food for the family that week.

## Tournament Tipping

In money games, it is common practice for the person who wins the hand to tip the dealer a small sum. This sum is usually closely tied to the game or pot size. In small games, players often tip fifty cents after a win. In medium games, it's a dollar, and in larger games, two dollars or more.

In tournaments, players not only should not try to tip after winning individual hands, they *may not*. Instead, players who make the money do all the tipping. If the casino has not withheld anything from the prize pool for tips, a gratuity in the 3–4 percent range is considered fair. (Note tips should come not merely from the winner, but from *all players who cash*, although many players who cash for relatively small amounts wrongly feel it's okay to stiff the staff).

Tipping less than 3 percent is considered rather chintzy, while tipping more than 4 percent is rather generous. If in the wake of your long day you have trouble figuring out what 1 percent of your win is and then multiplying that number by three, the tournament staff will be glad to provide a calculator.

All tip money is held by the TD or TA and it is divided among the dealers and the floor staff.

Recently, in order to ensure that reasonably qualified dealers are willing to work major tournaments, some casinos have taken to withholding some percentage of the prize pool to be distributed to tournament staff. Make sure you learn what the with-held percentage is. If the casino is already holding out 3 percent for the dealers, you shouldn't feel an obligation to tip more.

### The Inside Straight

Don't object if a local casino decides to start withholding money for tips. Many qualified dealers won't work tournaments knowing that their jobs are secure and that they will earn more tips dealing money games because so many players stiff the dealers. It will only take you one experience playing an event full of inexperienced dealers to decide that required tips are well worth it. If a casino wants to withhold an unreasonably high amount for the dealers, that's a different story.

## The Least You Need to Know

◆ Poker tournament prize pools are created by player buy-ins, while the house makes its money from entry fees and side games.

◆ You don't have to win to make money. Many high finishers take home substantial paydays.

◆ You can't select your seat. Tournament seats are assigned by random draw.

◆ Because blinds and/or antes increase steadily throughout a tournament, players eventually must get involved in the action.

◆ Certain styles and personality types are better suited to tournament poker than money poker, and vice versa.

# 22

# Specific Kinds of Poker Tournaments

## In This Chapter

- ◆ Common kinds of poker tournaments
- ◆ How strategies change as poker tournaments do
- ◆ Common misconceptions about satellites and supersatellites
- ◆ How tournament structure determines the luck to skill ratio

There are many different kinds of poker tournaments. Features common to all were discussed in Chapter 21. Here we're going to examine some of the differences and some basic strategic concepts.

## Kinds of Poker Tournaments

The main kinds of poker tournaments are:

- ◆ Elimination tournaments
- ◆ Single-table and Satellite tournaments
- ◆ Shootout tournaments

- Rebuy tournaments

- Heads-up tournaments

- Supersatellite tournaments

- Multistage tournaments

- Freeroll tournaments

- Internet tournaments

- Nonmutinous Bounty tournaments

For most examples, I continue to use the 105 entrant, one-table paid model from the previous chapter.

## The Elimination Tournament

The *elimination tournament* is by far the single most important kind of event.

In an elimination tournament, the 105 hypothetical starters are assigned seats at tables 1-12. The 108 total seats mean players at three lucky tables will be able to attack one defenseless stack until one of three things happens:

- One or more late arrivals are permitted to pay the entry fee and buy-in and take a seat with a slightly depleted chip stack.

**Table Talk**

A player who gets knocked out of a tournament is said to have **busted out**.

- Tournament officials determine that registration is closed and they remove the stacks from play, leaving those tables temporarily eight-handed.

- Six players *bust out*, allowing officials to *break a table* and now have 11 full tables going.

Let's assume the chip stacks do get taken out of play. Sooner or later, players are going to start busting out. Normally, play continues at a table even if it is two players short (that is, seven of nine seats are occupied).

If a table loses a third player, a TA (normally; in a small tournament, there may be no TA and the TD fulfills all functions) finds the full table next set to break and has the dealer *high card a player* out. He does this in between hands by dealing each player one card face up. The player receiving the highest card takes his chips and moves over to the table that had been down to six players.

**Table Talk** _____

When a TA **breaks a table**, he isn't punishing the furniture. He sends the players from that table all across the tournament area to fill empty seats in other tables. Before a tournament begins, a predetermined table breaking order is established and posted.

In some tournaments, instead of high carding a player to fill a gap, the TA moves the player sitting in the same position relative to the blinds. Don't worry if this seems confusing in the abstract. Tournament personnel handle it for you and it will soon become second nature.

The process of high-carding players and breaking tables continues as the tournament moves forward and the blinds increase each level. Players bust out and a table breaks each time there are nine open slots. The players continue to consolidate until they finally reach the point where everyone left will win at least *some* money except for the next person out.

In our 105-person tournament example, nine players are to be paid and finisher #10 will be the player who has worked the longest and hardest for the least. When he gets knocked out, he is said to have finished "on the bubble" and everyone else is in the money.

When ten players remain in this tournament, there are two tables going, with five players at each. Normally in any situation when the payoff for remaining players will increase when someone gets knocked out, play shifts to *hand-for-hand* mode.

**Table Talk** _____

Players like to move up the pay ladder without taking risk, which would happen if someone busted out at the other table while nothing was happening at their own. To avoid stalling, play shifts to **hand-for-hand** mode. A hand is dealt at each table. A second hand does not start at either table until both hands finish. With no incentive to stall, players contest pots at regular speed.

If two players happen to bust out on the same hand, the player who began the hand owning more chips is awarded the higher finish.

After everyone has reached the final table, there is no reason to stall. Players move up the pay ladder as others move out. Going into a defensive shell in the hope that others will bust out is a viable strategy if you're content with a middle-of-the-pack payday, but if you want to win, you must take some risks.

## The Single-Table Tournament

Normally, single-table events are played as *satellite* tournaments for larger events, although they needn't necessarily lead to a larger event.

A single-table event begins with between eight and ten players, depending on whether the game is a stud or flop variety. Usually there is only one prize. If the event is a satellite, the prize is a seat in a bigger event.

For example, suppose a $1,060 seven-card stud tournament ($1,000 of which is the buy-in, and $60 the entry fee). Eight players enter each such tournament. As soon as eight players pay up, a TA starts accepting entries for the next satellite. The event costs $145 to enter; with eight players starting, the casino collects $1,160. The satellite winner receives a fully paid $1,060 seat into the day's main event. No one else receives anything (except the casino, which has made a $100 profit ... actually $160 when you count the money it will collect from the main event entry fee).

Tournament rounds in one-table events are often quite short, greatly increasing the luck factor. Because of this, when two or three players are left, they will often decide to *chop* the tournament (split the prize money either evenly or in accord with some negotiation).

Some B&M casinos do offer single table events that aren't satellites, but these are fairly uncommon (they are common on the Internet, where they are called "sit and go" tournaments). In most casinos, even when a single table event is a satellite, the winner need not use the money (or tournament buy-in chips called *lammers*) to enter that day's event.

**Table Talk**

To make life easy on assistants who handle tournament buy-ins, many tournaments insist that players first visit the cage to buy special tournament buy-in chips (often with a face value of $500) called **lammers**. Unlike tournament chips, lammers do have cash value but at least theoretically are not supposed to be sold from player to player. As a practical matter, players sell lammers to one another all the time.

Probably the least understood element of satellite tournaments is their relationship (or rather, lack thereof) to the tournament they are offering entry into.

Playing in one-table satellites makes a great deal of sense if you want to gain short-handed tournament play practice or if you are already skillful at shorthanded play and view these events as profitable opportunities in and of their own right.

Unfortunately, many players seem to miss these points entirely. They play in satellites because they believe the satellites are smart ways to gain cheap entry into more expensive tournaments.

In reality, playing satellites is a profitable practice if you are good at playing satellites—they are an art form unto themselves. There are quite a few players who play satellites for hours every day, never intending to play a single main tournament because they know their abilities in playing main tournaments are marginal.

These players know how to play correctly in ultra-fast satellite action and tend to be excellent deal negotiators, too, knowing how to play on opponent fears of coming a long way for no return.

There are reasons to consider avoiding single-table satellites on tournament day. To play satellites properly, you need an extremely fast, aggressive style. Toward the end, it becomes correct to shove your chips in with all kinds of weak hands. When you are first growing accustomed to tournament play, the speed and style you see and then emulate in satellites won't work well at all in main events that use much slower structures.

Further, if you plan to play the day's main tournament, you're doing so, one would hope, with the intention of getting to the final table and winning. That makes for a very long day and often the winner is the player who makes the fewest mistakes when tired. If you start out your day playing several hours worth of satellite events, you'll be that much more tired when the play in the main event is most important.

## The Shootout Tournament

A *shootout tournament* is in many ways the opposite of an elimination tournament. Tables are not broken down and recombined. When you meet your starting table, take a look around because only one of you can advance to the money.

Unless a shootout tournament is unusually large, normally anyone who wins a table is guaranteed at least some money. Once all the individual table winners are decided, the first-round winners become part of a relatively small elimination tournament.

For example, if 180 hold'em players enter a shootout event, there will be 20 table winners if the event is played nine to a table or 18 if played ten to a table. If we assume we have 18 first-round winners, all 18 are in the money and they play in conventional elimination format to see who gets the really big prize money.

## Table Talk

An **add-on** is the final opportunity to buy additional chips in a rebuy tournament. Often add-ons are offered at bargain prices (more tournament chips for real dollars than previously offered) in one final attempt to swell the tournament's prize pool.

## The Inside Straight

The real value in rebuy tournaments comes from getting through the rebuy period less expensively than your opponents. If you own an average stack but have spent half the average amount, you own a positive equity investment.

## Rebuy Tournaments

Rebuy tournaments are essentially elimination tournaments wherein the starters are entitled to buy more chips after the event starts, but only for a limited time, usually two or three hours. Normally, even if you do not rebuy during the rebuy period, you are allowed to make an *add-on*.

Typically, the additional chips are a better value, dollar for dollar, than your original chips—sometimes much better. For example, in a Pot-Limit Omaha tournament with rebuys, the original buy-in might be $500 and the entry fee $40. For that, you get $1,000 in no-cash value tournament chips. You're allowed to buy more any time your stack is $1,000 or less, so you can rebuy before the first hand if you like. You'd get another $1,000 in chips for another $500. These chips are a better "value" because they cost $500, not $540.

In some rebuy events, the extra chips are a *much* better value. For example, you might get $1,000 for only $300. Rebuy tournaments tend to be wild affairs before the rebuy period ends. People make all kinds of wild plays, knowing they can buy more chips.

## Perilous Play

Just because rebuys are available, inexpensive, and/or are a good value doesn't mean you should play crazy poker during the rebuy period. You'll see players moving all-in without even looking at their cards, hoping for a cheap double or triple-up, but usually they are just throwing money away. Often in less expensive events, some players will invest incredible sums trying, in effect, to buy a trophy.

As a result, you should take a long hard look at a rebuy event's structure before deciding to play. If the event costs $540 to enter, but has unlimited $300 rebuys, you simply can't attend with $540 in your pocket. This is an $840 event minimum and the average player will probably be in for about $1,500.

Sometimes rebuy tournaments are extremely inexpensive. Such an event might cost $11 to enter ($10 buy-in, $1 entry fee), for which you get $200 in tournament chips.

With unlimited rebuys for the first two hours and each rebuy getting you $200 in tournament chips, it isn't uncommon in no-limit events to see people making 20 or 30 rebuys.

If you already have a huge stack when add-on time comes, the add-on may not be a good value. Generally, the smaller your stack, the more each chip is worth, but you can hit a point of diminishing returns. In an event with one optional rebuy and one optional add-on, if you have $100 in tournament chips left at add-on time, you might decide it's not worth investing another $500 in real cash to get a stack that's a small fraction of *par*.

> **Perilous Play** ___
>
> With rare exception, information you gather during the rebuy period, even on apparent tells, is meaningless after the rebuy period. You certainly can't make assumptions about a player's style. A wild player may look tight because he's decided his strategy is to survive until the good-value add-on and many tight players look wild.

> **Table Talk** ___
>
> **Par** is the average number of chips the average player has at any given point. For example, in a nonrebuy tournament that had 100 starters who each began with $500 in tournament chips, there was $50,000 in play when the event started, so when 50 players remain, a par stack is now $1,000. As long as your stack remains near or above par, you are in relatively good shape.

I won't discuss every possible rebuy or add-on permutation here, but try to remember a few basic points:

- When making add-on decisions, ignore how much you've already invested. Make your decision based on how much you have to spend to get a stack of what size. Ask yourself whether it's worth that much to play that size stack. This is a variation of the classic poker advice, "Don't throw good money after bad."

♦ Rebuy tournaments are probably not ideal uses of your tournament dollars when you are first learning tournament strategy. After you've developed a feel for how well you play with small and big stacks (the techniques are quite different), rebuy tournaments will be better values.

♦ How tough is your table? If it isn't going to break for a long time and six of the ten toughest players in the field are at your table, this isn't a good tournament to invest lots of money in. Remember to check the table break list, though! If your group won't be staying together for long, its relative strength or weakness isn't too important.

♦ How are you playing? Some days you know you're on your game and some days you can tell you just aren't sharp. When you're playing poorly, cut your losses by avoiding rebuys.

♦ Be honest with yourself. If it would really mean a great deal to you to have a poker trophy, you can make what are poor financial rebuy investments. If you live somewhere where you will rarely have a chance to play in a tournament, you can make more rebuys than if you live in Los Angeles, where you could play a tournament 365 days a year if you really wanted to.

## Heads-Up Tournaments

A fairly recent phenomenon that is impractical for large numbers of players in B&M cardrooms (because each two players need a table and a dealer), heads-up tournaments are nonetheless growing more popular and prestigious. Many players consider them the most skillful form of poker and the ultimate test of poker talent and they tend to feature large buy-ins. For those reasons alone, beginners should probably stay away, but consider them as you progress.

Remember, if you want to win conventional tournaments, it's important to develop heads-up skills, because almost every single elimination event eventually gets heads-up.

## Supersatellite Tournaments

Supersatellites (or supers) got a lot of publicity when Chris Moneymaker parlayed $40 into $2,500,000, but too many players invest too much money in them.

The typical supersatellite resembles an unlimited rebuy tournament. Your initial investment isn't large and if you're a typical player, you'll probably have made a rebuy or two and an add-on by the time the rebuy period ends. The only significant difference is that you aren't shooting for a typical final table payout schedule.

Instead, the host casino is using the supersatellite to fill up the field for an expensive championship event. Let's suppose that the title event costs $10,000 (the tournament announces that it puts $9,700 from each player into the prize pool and keeps $300 as the entry fee). Not too many players want to pull $10,000 from their pocket to enter. Instead, they plunk down $225 and enter a supersatellite that offers $200 rebuys and a double $400 add-on. They spend $825 trying to win a seat.

### The Inside Straight _____

You would be hard pressed to find a situation in poker where it is more important to keep track of exactly how many chips you and your opponents have than at a supersatellite final table. You want to take the absolute minimum risk necessary to lock up a seat. Anything more risks giving someone else a better chance than he deserves, and anything less wastes your investment.

Suppose that 77 players do just that, creating a prize pool of $61,600 (800 × 77). (In reality, some of those 105 players would be in for the minimum, while some might be in for $2,025, but pretending our field members all invested the same amount gets us the same result as if they averaged that amount.)

In this super, six players will eventually win seats in the main event and the seventh-place finisher will be awarded the other $1,600. Normally, the rule is that you must play a seat won in a super. You can't sell it unless you win more than one or have already bought in for cash.

When the final nine players arrive at the final table, five happen to hold huge stacks and four have relatively tiny ones. Play will halt the moment player seven is eliminated. The top six win exactly the same thing. The five players sitting on the big stacks would have to be  terribly inexperienced to get involved in a big pot even if they started with pocket aces. Until two of the short stacks build up enough chips to start to become a threat to finish in the top six, there is no reason for the big stacks to gamble away what they probably already have clinched.

The strategies can be fascinating. If when player seven is eliminated, players one through five all own huge stacks and player six owns a single $100 chip, he wins the same $10,000 seat that the rest do. When something like that happens, it usually means that player seven or player eight (possibly both) made a terrible mistake on the final hand.

### The Inside Straight _____

Money management is crucial in supersatellites, and it takes awhile to get a feel for these situations. You'd do well to watch several supersatellite finals before entering a super yourself.

# Some Perfectly Honest Sneaky Supersatellite Timing

I really hate to give this next one away because it used to be one of my favorite tricks, but I don't play too many supers anymore.

Championship events that offer entrance via supersatellites usually come at the end of tournaments that run for several weeks (with a new tournament starting each day). For example, a hypothetical tournament schedule might be:

January 5: $330 Limit Hold'em

January 6: $330 Seven-Card Stud

January 7: $330 No-Limit Hold'em

January 8: $540 Omaha eight-or-better

January 9: $540 Limit Hold'em

January 10: $540 Pot-Limit Omaha (Rebuys first two hours)

January 11: $540 No-Limit Hold'em

The schedule would continue throughout the month with $1,060 tournaments starting in the third week, and eventually a championship No-Limit Hold'em event that would cost somewhere between $5,000 and $10,000 to enter (although with the Bellagio now offering a $25,300 event, who knows where the ceiling may go?).

**The Inside Straight**

If you review the names of players who make final tables at major tournaments, you'll notice a significant phenomenon. Usually more "name" players make it to the finals in no-limit and pot-limit than in limit events. There is more luck in limit poker. For related reasons, you should probably focus on limit events when you are a tournament novice.

Supersatellites for the Championship Event would run throughout the month, often twice a day, once in the afternoon and once in the evening. Now, if you wanted to avoid the superstars in the supersatellites, when do you think you might choose to play?

Do the dates January 7 and January 11 offer any intriguing possibilities to you? They should. It's a pretty fair guess that the best no-limit hold'em players are going to be occupied elsewhere during the afternoon super on those days (a condition that will be even more likely during the $1,060 no-limit hold'em day because the fields get tougher as the buy-ins get bigger). Often the better players don't arrive in town for a month-long tournament until the last week or two when the big events run.

That doesn't mean there won't be quality players in the supersatellite, but it's practically a certainty that the fields will be weaker on days when an expensive no-limit hold'em tournament is being played.

## Multistage Tournaments

As expensive championship events proliferate, casinos are becoming more and more creative in ways to draw players into these fields. The multistage tournament is a relatively recent phenomenon (more popular on the Internet than in B&M casinos, but available in both) and is a perfect example of this creativity.

Basically, the idea is that you're trying win (or place high in) a tournament that gets you into a second tournament. If you win that second tournament, you now either have a chance to compete against top players in the third, big money tournament, or (depending on how small you started) you might have to win a third tournament to get into the fourth tournament.

For example, you might pay $55 to enter such a multistage tournament. Ten players compete and the top two finishers move on to the next round (now owning $250 worth of equity). In the second round, those two players each go to tables that, if they win, get them in position. They now have $2,500 worth of equity. They then might play a four-person "final table" to win a seat in the main event. The three high finishes have earned them the right to compete for big money.

### The Inside Straight

There's nothing wrong with taking a few shots at these unlikely parlays, but remember the odds against pulling it off border on lottery-like. Remember that winning a seat doesn't earn you a penny. You still have to cash in the big tournament even after your unlikely parlay. The world's greatest players rarely cash in the big tournament (much less win!) even though they play it every year.

The possibilities are endless, especially because Internet cardrooms use multistage tournaments so frequently as promotional events and the number and variety of such tournaments will continue to proliferate.

## Freeroll Tournaments

Both B&M and Internet casinos like to reward frequent players with free tournaments. It only costs half as much to award $10,000 in freeroll tournament prizes to

1,000 entrants than it does to give every one of those 1,000 customers a $20 gift certificate ... but while your customers won't get very excited about a $20 gift, they will get very excited when they read the words "ten thousand dollars."

> **Perilous Play** _____
>
> The key letters in the phrase "freeroll tournament" are f-r-e-e. If your cardroom offers you a true freeroll, take your chance if you have the time. If you have to buy something you normally wouldn't have had to buy to get your freeroll, you've just entered the same arena as people who wrongly buy magazine subscriptions to increase their chances of winning sweepstakes.

The varieties of freeroll tournaments available are too numerous to discuss. Because they are so different, take a little time making sure you understand the qualifying rules.

Astonishing numbers of players are winning seats and trips to tournaments like the World Series of Poker in freeroll tournaments, although most of these are Internet cardroom promotions.

# Internet Tournaments

These days, you can find almost any kind of tournament on the Internet that you can find in a B&M room. There are also quite a few that you can't find in B&M rooms because no one has a casino with enough tables and dealers for 8,000 simultaneous players.

Single-table Internet tournaments deserve special mention, because these sit-and-go affairs allow players to gain hugely valuable shorthanded tournament experience. If you normally play tournaments entered by 200 or more players, you won't reach many final tables. If you enter lots of Internet single-table tournaments, you are in essence playing a final table every time you play (albeit without the huge money pressure or the need for a poker face).

# Nonmutinous Bounty Tournaments

*Bounty tournaments* (with or without the seafaring pun) are variations on conventional tournaments (most commonly the elimination kind) wherein certain players have "bounties" placed on their heads. If you knock out a player designated as a bounty player, you win something immediately even if you don't go very far in the tournament.

By far the most famous and important bounty tournament is the Bay 101 Shooting Stars Tournament, which this year became a World Poker Tour Event. Twenty famous players are given free entry into this event, one per table (entry is currently limited to 200 players). It costs mere mortals $5,200 to enter, so this is a great deal for the Stars. The catch is that the Stars have $5,000 bounties placed on them and anyone who knocks a Star out has paid his entry fee and is freerolling for other prize money.

> **The Inside Straight** _____
>
> Players invited to be Shooting Stars (or players in other bounty tournaments) aren't stupid. They know they might as well have targets painted on their chests, but it's hard to complain when entry costs them nothing. They tend to play a bit conservatively in the early going. Many players make overly optimistic calls against bounty players, hoping to win the bounty, and instead increase the bounty player's stack, making it much harder to knock him out.

Because of the bounty's obvious value, it becomes more worthwhile to make certain all-in calls against Stars than it does against other players. The pot odds change when winning the pot means that not only do you increase your chip stack, but you also collect cash. The best time to try something like this is when you have an excellent drawing hand. A bounty player is unlikely to get his whole stack in without a fairly strong holding, but if you have a draw to the nuts, the bounty's value can make your draw worth playing when it otherwise wouldn't be.

## The Least You Need to Know

- There are many different kinds of poker tournaments with the elimination tournament being the most common.

- Many players engage in one-table satellites for the wrong reasons: play them for profit or for experience, rather than as a cheap entry into another event.

- Understanding when and when not to rebuy or add-on is the real key to success in rebuy tournaments.

- When playing in supersatellite tournaments, don't try to finish first—just try to win a seat.

# Chapter 23

# Endgame: Where the Money Awaits

## In This Chapter

◆ Exercise strategy to reduce your need for luck

◆ Shift betting gears and accelerate past your opponents

◆ The blind structure affects optimal strategy

◆ The meek don't inherit the chips

◆ When it comes to chip stacks, size matters

◆ Good negotiators can increase their winnings

By now you understand that in the long run the cards break even and those players who employ superior strategy take the money. This is never more true than during the last few rounds of a tournament when the tacticians wheel and deal their way past their inexperienced opponents just when it matters most. This chapter will show you a number of key strategies, including how you should take advantage of larger blinds and inexperienced players.

# Tournament Tacticians Trump the Timid

Many players fantasize about catching an incredible run of cards right at a tournament's end, when the big money is on the line, and better still if they catch their super-strong hands when an opponent has a strong hand: If you make a full house when an opponent makes an ace-high flush, you're going to collect a lot more than if you're full and your opponent has a pair of twos.

People fantasize about winning the lottery, too, but wishing doesn't make it so. Consistent winners make their own luck at the end by employing a variety of tactics that don't rely on luck.

## By Shifting Gears You Instill Fears

What skilled players fear more than anything except perhaps a horrific run of cards is an opponent whose style makes him unpredictable. Poker is a game of incomplete information and if you're predictable, information about your hand isn't very incomplete.

> **Table Talk**
>
> When a veteran player says he's tired of folding to your many raises and is going to **look you up**, it means he's going to call you with even a modest holding because he believes you're bluffing.

If you play conservatively for twenty minutes and then suddenly raise six pots in a row, your opponents can't be sure whether you've decided to change tactics, have consumed too much coffee, or whether you are really catching cards. Conversely, if you've been raising two out of three pots for the last hour, your raises lack an intimidation factor: No one catches that many good cards and your opponents will *look you up*.

## How Tournament Structure Affects Betting Pace

Your decision to change betting gears comes in part from your sense of recent history ("I've been folding a lot lately and have a tight table image, maybe I should try to steal a pot or two"), the size of the blinds and/or antes will also impact your decision, particularly if a round is ending and the blinds are about to go up.

If, for example, you have $12,000 in chips remaining and the blinds are about to jump from $2,000-$4,000 to $4,000-$8,000, you don't have the luxury of waiting for a strong hand. If you don't make a move quickly, you'll be forced to post all of your remaining chips as blinds the next time the button approaches you.

If you see that you'll be forced to post the blinds in two more hold'em hands, you would be correct to raise all-in with a mediocre hand like A-2 offsuit. It's better to get your money in while you at least hold an ace than to post it as a blind and risk trying to survive with whatever weak random hand might show up next.

**The Inside Straight** _____

Although sophisticated opponents know that short-stacked players must raise with any decent hand, it's still better to get your last chips in raising than as a blind. No one may have the cards or desire to play Sheriff and you have some chance to win without a showdown. Experts take extra risks to avoid this position. They'll take their shot raising when they still have enough chips to be viewed as a threat.

## How Long Are the Rounds?

Don't assume that a tournament whose structure calls for blind increases of only 30-40 percent each round will give you more time to pick your spots than a tournament where the blinds double each round. Increases of thirty percent every fifteen minutes will send the blinds skyrocketing much faster than one hundred percent increases every ninety minutes. When assessing how fast or slow a tournament structure is, you must examine both the round length and the average blind percentage increases.

**The Inside Straight** _____

Do you want rapidly increasing blinds? The expert player wants the skill factor to dominate a tournament, while the novice should want luck to play as large a role as possible. Rapidly increasing blinds level the playing field because they require players to gamble more and maneuver less. While you're learning, you should seek out fast tournaments that experts would shun.

## Ladder Climbs

With the exception of a tournament that began with a very small field, the top nine finishers in every tournament each receive different payoffs. Unless the tournament sponsor is guaranteeing a special prize for first, the actual dollar payoffs are usually calculated after entries are closed, and are awarded as percentages of the total buy-in money (the buy-in goes back to the players, while the entry fee is kept by the house).

Although the percentages will vary by a point or two from tournament to tournament, the figures indicated in the following table should be fairly close to anything you are likely to encounter.

| Common Percentage Payoffs for a Nine-Player Final Table | |
|---|---|
| First: | 40% |
| Second: | 20% |
| Third: | 12% |
| Fourth: | 8% |
| Fifth: | 6% |
| Sixth: | 5% |
| Seventh: | 4% |
| Eighth: | 3% |
| Ninth: | 2% |

Naturally, if more than one table is being paid, some of the percentage money indicated will be shifted to the extra tables. Usually tournament officials pay roughly one table for each hundred players, so a tournament in which 120 players started might pay one table, while a tournament in which 170 players started would probably pay two tables. Payoffs are almost always made in multiples of one table, so 9, 18, or 27 players (or more, if the field is large enough) get paid in hold'em events, while 8, 16, or 24 players get paid in stud events).

As you can see, each time a player survives while another player gets knocked out, the survivor is ensured of earning a bigger payoff.

For this reason, players who are sitting with very short stacks sometimes go into an ultra-conservative mode, hoping that two larger stacks go to war with one knocking the other out. Even though this means that the winner of that hand now has a much better chance to win the tournament (or at least to get one of the top payoffs), the short-stacked player has managed to inch his way up the payoff ladder.

As a result, experienced players remain constantly aware of how many chips all opponents own. Although players who are more focused on winning than on relatively small incremental payoff increases will often take chances while one or more players are short stacked, most players remember the Legend of Glen Cozen and do what they can to remain alive until the short stacks are out.

---

> ### Poker Lore
>
> The most famous ladder climb in poker history came at the 1993 *World Series of Poker*. Jim Bechtel and John Bonetti each owned huge chip stacks ($1,150,000 and $935,000, respectively). Relative unknown Glenn Cozen was the third player left, but he had a relatively insignificant $95,000 in front of him.
>
> First place was to pay $1,000,000, second $420,000, and third $210,000. With such a huge difference between second and third place, observers assumed that the leaders would wait until one had knocked out Cozen before risking a major confrontation.
>
> On the fateful hand, Bechtel was dealt 6-6, and Bonetti *A-K*. The flop came K-6-4, giving Bechtel three sixes and Bonetti top pair, top kicker. All the chips went in with Cozen cheerily awaiting the outcome. Bechtel's set of sixes held up and Cozen's tiny stack of no-cash value tournament chips had suddenly become worth a very real $420,000.

There's no absolutely correct way to approach these situations. In the Bechtel-Bonetti confrontation, if Bonetti had held K-K instead of A-K, each player would have been completely correct to risk his entire stack, even with Cozen still loitering around. Three of a kind is a hugely powerful hand with only three players remaining. Final tablists must simply stay aware of the risk-reward ratio and balance a possible missed ladder climb against an outstanding opportunity to collect enough chips to ensure a huge payday.

## Rock Blunts Scissors and Aggressive Players Cut the Passive Players

Near the end of a tournament, the players in the money are (or should be) acutely aware of how much money they stand to make with each ladder climb. While this is a financially prudent approach, it nonetheless creates an opportunity for the aware and alert player.

If you notice that a player has gone into a holding pattern, refusing to play a hand until someone has been knocked out, you can take advantage of the situation by raising this player's blind with any two cards.

Your hand doesn't matter because your cautious opponent isn't going to play with you until or unless he picks up a big hand and that just doesn't happen very often. The odds against getting dealt pocket aces, kings, queens, or jacks—*any* of the four hands—are 55-1 against, and as you see in the table, the odds against hitting any single one of these hands are much higher.

**The Odds Against Getting Dealt Good Starting Hands**

| Hand | Odds against |
| --- | --- |
| A-A | 220:1 |
| Any single pair | 220:1 |
| Any high pair | 55:1 (jacks through aces) |
| Any pair | 16:1 |
| A-K suited | 331:1 |
| A-K unsuited | 110:1 |
| Any A-K | 82:1 |

Although calculated, sensible aggression is usually the right approach at any stage of a tournament, it becomes particularly important at the final stages. At this point many players will feel that their chip stacks are inadequate to win and they change their goal to hanging on long enough for some ladder climbs. If you've been paying attention to the way your opponents are playing (tightly, loosely, aggressively, passively), you'll know whom to target and whom to stay away from.

## When to Try a Steal

The art and science of knowing when you should try to steal a pot with a bluff could probably fill an entire book by itself, but I'll give you a good running start here.

Why is this art/science (and there are indeed elements of both, as you'll soon see) so important? Although there are certainly many things poker players can do to improve their chances of winning and losing outside of bluffing/stealing (for example, extracting extra bets from your opponents by trapping them with a check-raise, slow-playing a hand, setting up false tells, finding other players' tells), stealing is numero uno. When you get to the bottom line, you find that the only consistent way to get to final tables and win poker tournaments is by winning a fairly high number of pots to which your cards don't entitle you!

If you think about it, you'll soon see that this has to be true. If the player with the best hand always won the pot, the player who caught the best cards on tournament day would win the event. Poker would be a game of pure chance, no more difficult than betting on a coin flip.

The beauty—and danger—of poker lies in just how much skill is involved. There's far more skill involved than most players, even most very good players, realize.

This is "beautiful" because many players who aren't good enough to play against you will do so, figuring either that the game is mostly luck or hoping that they will get lucky enough to overcome their underestimated skill deficiency.

The danger comes in because it can happen to you too!

**Perilous Play**

One of the single biggest reasons why most players lose is that they overestimate their abilities. It does you no good to be the tenth best Seven-Card Stud player in the world if you take the eighth and final seat in a game featuring the world's top seven players. You can't choose to change tables in a tournament, but you can choose to avoid tournaments that feature too many star players (usually the more expensive events).

You'll almost certainly have to steal a fair number of pots to make it into the last two tables, but it becomes more important as you near the end for two reasons: First, there's more on the line. When you enter a $100 buy-in tournament, you never like to lose, but if you get knocked out early, you feel like you've lost only $100.

If you last much longer and get knocked out eighth, you (at least temporarily) feel like you've lost out on more than that even though you've actually won money by finishing eighth. By this time, the money for first or second has gotten into sight and a payoff of $1,500 for eighth place doesn't feel that great when you've been thinking about a real chance at $22,000 for first.

The second reason is that near the end, if you don't start stealing, you're going to find your stack shrinking rapidly because your opponents will steal more. This happens partly because your opponents are feeling more confident. They've lasted far into a tournament and probably have been catching a lot of good cards—partly because your opponents will, like you, be trying to take advantage of people who grow too cautious, and partly because the hand values change when the game grows *short-handed*.

Short-handed play is really an art form and many tournament players, especially beginning

**Table Talk**

A full hold'em table usually has nine seats and in stud it's usually eight. When more than two seats are empty, you are starting to play **short-handed** poker. If the players are experienced, their style will change. It's easier to be aggressive because it's less likely that someone else has a good hand and you don't need a strong a hand to win the average pot.

players, lack experience in it. They play well until there are five players left and then suddenly they feel uncomfortable. Players start raising and re-raising much more often, weak hands win pots, and by the time the player has started figuring out what adjustments he must make, his stack is almost gone.

The cure for this lack of experience is obvious: Play more short-handed poker. Many money game players quit if a game gets short-handed. They don't like the game's different nature. If you want to win tournaments, don't be one of those quitters. Stay in the game and enjoy the opportunity to play for a long stretch with only three or four opponents.

Another way to gain this experience is to play a lot of one-table (also called single-table) tournaments. These are usually satellite tournaments in brick and mortar card-rooms, but many online poker sites offer regular one-table tournament starting at all hours of the day and night. The advantage here is that you don't have to wade your way through 195 opponents to be 1 of the 5 players left: You only have to get through 4.

**CAUTION**

**Perilous Play** _____

If you play one-table tournaments in order to gain shorthanded tournament experience for bigger events, stay aware of one critically important difference. Almost all one-table tournaments use very fast betting structures. The blinds go up rapidly and players are forced to adopt an extremely fast, aggressive style. In larger tournaments, the betting structure will be slower, so you don't need to (and should not) play at ultra-sonic speeds. One-table experience will help, but remember this key difference!

Now you know that stealing becomes more important near the end of a tournament, but you can do even better in finding the right time for a steal. You've already learned that position is important in almost all forms of poker and it's far easier to try a steal when you have position than when you don't. If you try to steal from early position, you must run the gauntlet of many players who could wake up with a hand behind you.

If, on the other hand, you try to steal from late position, there are fewer opponents to deal with. The only problem is that the players whose money you are trying to steal are likely to be aware that your raise has a better chance to be a steal raise because you have position.

Unfortunately for them, you're still going to have a positional advantage on them for the rest of the hand. If they think you're stealing and want to play back at you, they're going to be forced to act first for the rest of the hand.

As a result, you want most of your steal attempts to come from late position. You should throw in an early position steal attempt occasionally so you don't become predictable. The other advantage of trying to steal from early position is that players won't expect it. They'll *give you credit* for having a good hand and will only play with you if their own hand is strong. This makes it much easier for you to know when you should give up your steal attempt and fold.

> **Table Talk**
>
> Although players sometimes ask their opponents for loans, usually when the phrase **give you credit** comes up at a poker table, it means "I believe that your bet isn't a bluff; you actually have a strong hand." It's common for players to give a bettor credit for a good hand when the bettor has raised from early position or has re-raised more than once.

## Chip Accumulation vs. Conservation

Although all tournaments use special "no cash value" tournament chips for their events, your tournament chips do indeed have value because you need to accumulate them to win or cash in an event. Because the chips merely serve to indicate who has more than whom, it would be accurate, technically, to think of your chip total as a "point total." Nonetheless, players are used to thinking of chips as being worth dollars, not points. The play seems more fun and exciting that way too, so casinos keep the harmless fiction alive.

Even though the "no cash value" chips do have value, their value is often different from the numbers marked on them: A $1,000 chip can be worth very different amounts to you at different stages of a tournament.

Let's suppose you've entered a $100 tournament where they give each player $1,000 in tournament chips to begin. If you get hot early and within the first half hour of what is expected to be a ten-hour event, you find yourself with $2,000 in chips, your thousand-dollar chip is very valuable. It's half of your stack and it represents a big lead over *par*. If you got involved in a big pot and lost $1,000 here, it would be a catastrophe.

In comparison, suppose you are now in the ninth hour of that same tournament and have a $100,000 stack. Winning or losing $1,000 at that stage barely matters. It's only 1 percent of your stack, rather than 50 percent of it.

That's only the first level of thinking about the changing value of your chips as an event progresses, though. Because you still have a chance to win even with only a few chips in front of you, your last few chips are worth much more, dollar for dollar, than the chips owned by someone who has a big stack.

If you're near the end of a tournament and you have $5,000 in chips while your one remaining opponent has $95,000, your position is bad, but not hopeless. If your opponent proposes a *deal* to split up the remaining prize money based on chip count, you would be foolish to accept only 5 percent of the money ... whereas if you had $40,000 and he had $60,000, accepting 40 percent would be reasonable.

> **Table Talk** _____
>
> In a typical tournament the winner takes roughly 40 percent of the prize pool. The runner-up gets about 20 percent, and the third-place finisher about 12 percent. In large tournaments, these differences can be worth thousands of dollars. Because the blinds are often very high at the end, the luck factor increases, motivating the final three to make a **deal** to redistribute the payouts based on chip totals and each player's perceived skill level.

For this reason, chip conservation is usually more important than chip accumulation even though you must accumulate chips to win an event. Let's use an impossible hypothetical situation to demonstrate. It's the start of a tournament where everyone gets $1,000 in tournament chips and just before the first hand gets dealt, the tournament director comes over to you and says "Tell you what, I'll let you flip a coin for $800 of your stack. If you win the coin flip, your starting stack will be $1,800, and if you lose, it will be $200."

Tournament directors can't do this sort of thing, which is what makes the hypothetical impossible, but if they could, you would be making a very big mistake to accept the bet. The $800 you would gain if you win wouldn't do nearly as much good toward your chances of winning the event as the $800 you would lose would harm your chances of winning. Someone who quickly increases his stack to $1,800 has improved his chances of winning, no question, but there is still a very long way to go. That extra $800 won't be very important in a few rounds.

On the other hand, if your stack takes an $800 hit right away and you're sitting there with only $200 in front of you, you're instantly in big trouble and probably have to win the next moderately size hand you get involved in.

This concept applies in much the same way near the end of an event. You always want to be looking for ways to increase your stack size, but you want an advantage when you try it. A 50-50 chance isn't good enough. The closer you get to having all of your chips committed to one hand, the less acceptable a 50-50 chance is. Those last few chips are just worth too much to risk casually.

# The Power of a Big Stack

Having a big stack well above par helps your chances of winning an event in several different ways. First, it allows you to bully the short stacks (as with all comments about big stacks, this is more true in no-limit than in pot-limit or limit, and more true in pot-limit than in limit poker). When you raise a short stack, its owner has to worry about losing those extra-valuable last few chips. The hand becomes critically important to him. It isn't vital to you because the short-stacked player doesn't have enough chips to damage the big-stacked player.

If you think that "bullying" sounds a little bit like "stealing," you're exactly right. Players don't like to "mess with" big stacks. Whenever someone has a bigger stack than you, he can break you but you can't break him. Indeed, if your stack is small enough, you can't even hurt him.

As a result, if you have a big stack, you should add "pick on the little guys" to your usual poker strategies.

An important corollary here is that a big stack should be cautious in getting involved in a hand with another big stack. If there is only one player at the table with enough chips to bust you, why play against him? Naturally, if you have a great hand, the chance to double your big stack can make it worthwhile, but otherwise, you're taking unnecessary risks.

---

### Poker Lore

In the 2002 World Poker Open, a $10,000 buy-in event that was paying $500,000 for first, there were 23 players left when a collective groan hit the room. Humberto Brenes, one of four players who owned a huge stack, got into an all-in hand with one of the other three: me. Why a groan? The other competitors realized that whoever won that hand could bully everyone else left. Brenes won the hand and eventually the tournament, which is why I'm writing this book instead of sunning myself in Hawaii.

# Short Stack Tactics

There's no way around it: Big stacks have an important advantage over short stacks. That's one of several reasons why many tournament experts feel it's worth taking risks early to accumulate a big stack that can be wielded like a weapon.

If you find yourself owning a short stack, you certainly shouldn't give up. There are hundreds of stories about players who had very few chips left and who came back to win tournaments. How did they do it? More important, how can you?

First, don't panic. A surprising number of players are so uncomfortable playing with short stacks (there's no clear definition of what makes a stack "short," but in most situations you'd be safe claiming that a stack was short if it amounted to 25 percent of par or less). These players tend to give up and casually push their last chips in with any sort of decent hand, not wanting to endure the hardship of short-stack ownership. "*Double me up* or get me out of here," they often say when their money goes in.

**Table Talk**

You hear the phrase **doubling up** a lot in tournaments, especially in no-limit events where it is easy to get your entire stack involved in one hand. In blackjack, players often get excited about the chance to double down, but in poker, they want to double up. The phrase means just what it sounds like—the bettor doubles his stack size in one hand, getting "back into the game" with one mighty, or lucky, blow.

You don't want to be one of those panicky types because all it takes is one or two double-ups or a short winning streak for smaller amounts to get you right back into the game.

Although you don't want to have a short stack you might be surprised to find that occasionally you can use your short stack as an advantage.

Remember that when you bet, you have two ways to win: Either via everyone else folding (an uncontested win), or you can get called and wind up having the best hand at the end. If you call in an all-in situation, there's only one way to win: You'll need to show down the best hand.

Because of this, if you take your short stack and push all of it forward, you put your opponents in a bit of a bind. There is no way they can raise you out of the hand or later outplay you with some great acting job. The only way they can take that money from you is by calling you and then showing down the best hand.

Unless you've been playing recklessly, your opponents will understand that you're probably not willing to risk your whole stack with a mediocre holding. Therefore, there is a decent chance that your all-in move will allow you to win the blinds and/or antes uncontested.

Also, because you have no more money your opponent can claim, he might not want to play the kind of drawing hand that can create a big payoff when he hits.

In hold'em, for example, a player might be willing to call a decent bet with the 6♠-6♣ because that hand can make a set if a six hits the flop. If its owner does make the hard-to-make set, he can probably extract lots of bets from players who hold strong hands like top pair or two pair (remember, Jim Bechtel beat John Bonetti in just this kind of confrontation). Because the short-stacked player is all-in, though, there will be no extra payoff for making a big hand.

As a result, a player who might call a $7,000 bet from someone who had another $100,000 in his stack might easily not call the same bet from a short-stacked player, even though his own cards were the same. Against the short stack, there's no chance to bluff, no chance to make a brilliant move, and no chance to make extra money if one makes a strong hand.

Try to avoid becoming a short stack. If you become one, try to climb out of the hole as quickly as is reasonable, but don't give up the ship.

# Deal Making

Most cardrooms hold tournaments in part for the money they make the house directly (the entry fee), but in equal or larger part because of the money they make from players who bust out of tournaments and then go play *side action*.

Because the side action is lucrative for the casino and because the casino tournament employees usually prefer not to work all night, the house has a vested interest in tournaments ending relatively quickly—in essence, as quickly as the players will let them "get away with."

In small buy-in tournaments, the rounds are often quite short with the blinds increasing

**Table Talk**

Almost all tournaments offer players the chance to participate not merely in a given day's tournament, but also in money games of all shapes and sizes where the chips do indeed have actual cash value. These money games are called **side action** when a tournament is going on; the rest of the year, they are just called regular ring or money games.

every twenty or thirty minutes. As buy-ins grow bigger, the rounds usually get a bit longer. Even then, the casino can make the event end relatively quickly by having large blind increases.

It is not at all uncommon to see the blinds double each round at the end of a tournament. When the game is short-handed (let's use a three-player situation), the players must pay a small blind once every three hands and a big blind once every three hands, instead of once every nine.

If the blinds increase from $5,000-10,000 to $10,000-20,000 to $20,000-40,000 and the players have to post these huge sums so often, you can start to see why the players must play less tactical poker and have to do a lot more gambling when the really big money is on the line. They can't wait for a strong hand: The blinds would gobble their stacks up.

---

### Poker Lore

The 2003 World Series of Poker proved that a tournament's betting structure has a major impact on the results. Tournament Director Matt Savage decided that the old structure involved too much gambling at the end, so he changed the structure so that the blinds doubled for the first three levels, but then moved up much more slowly at the end. A record shattering *six* players won two tournaments each at the event (the previous record was three).

---

Because there is more gambling and less skill involved at the end of an event and because the differences in the prize money for first-second-third are so great, the players often want to make a deal to reduce their risk (sometimes called reducing their fluctuation).

It's important to remember that unless *everyone* is willing to make a deal, the casino will not allow a deal. This is not a "majority rules" situation. Everyone must be okay not just with the concept of making a deal, but also how the splits come out, or else the players just keep playing. If you're new to a final table and are not sure if the deal being offered to you is fair, just keep on playing. That way you know that whatever happens will be fair, even if you aren't happy with where you finish.

The final three might decide, for example, that because they all have relatively equal stacks, they will just divide the prize money into three equal shares. Usually the players will leave at least a little money at risk and will play on for the trophy.

Equal splits aren't the only possibility, of course. In fact, they're rather rare because usually the chip counts aren't equal. In addition, if one famous player is left against two unknowns, the famous player may insist on a little something extra because of his supposed skill edge. Whether his opponents are willing to grant it is another question. Some of the best "bluffing" you'll see in a poker tournament occurs during deal negotiations.

Curiously, although they are in the worst position, short-stacked players should demand more than their chip percentage. With big blinds and a lot of luck in the air, a short stack can get big in a hurry and there is little incentive for someone to settle for five percent of the chips in play. Examined another way, someone who owns five percent of the chips in a three-player situation should win the event more than five percent of the time.

Excluding bonuses for short stacks or for famous players, the proper formula for making a deal is relatively straightforward, although it's a good idea to have a calculator handy. It's an even better idea to make sure that the host casino will ensure that the money gets paid out according to the deal terms; there's no reason you should trust a stranger to stick to a deal that forces him to pay you $12,000.

I'll give you the formula for a three-player deal and you can interpolate it for other numbers of players. The assumptions are:

- ◆ $40,000, $20,000, and $10,000 paid to final three finishers.

- ◆ Chip totals are: Player A, $50,000; Player B, $35,000; Player C, $15,000.

These players are dividing up $70,000 in prize money, but you don't just give Player A $35,000 in cash. Why? Because no matter what happens, everyone left is guaranteed to finish no worse than third. As a result, you take the $10,000 third-place money out of the calculation for each player and you work on dividing the money that is not guaranteed: $40,000.

Player A, who has 50 percent of the chips, gets 50 percent of $40,000, which is $20,000, plus his $10,000, for a total payout of $30,000.

Player B, who has 35 percent of the chips, gets 35 percent of $40,000, which is $14,000, plus his $10,000, for a total payout of $24,000.

Player C, who has 15 percent of the chips, gets 15 percent of $40,000, which is $6,000, plus his $10,000, for a total payout of $16,000.

Instead of payouts of $40,000, $20,000, and $10,000, we get a revised structure:

- ◆ 1st: $30,000

- ◆ 2nd: $24,000

- ◆ 3rd: $16,000

Unless there is a trophy to play for, play ends. This is rather anticlimactic, especially if there are spectators, so the players often decide to leave some money in play and to play on for that and the title. At the WSOP, a deal cannot end any event. The competitors must play at least for the bracelet, and deals where someone takes additional money and someone else gets to take the bracelet and be listed as the title winner are strictly forbidden.

Alternatively, three players who were quite close in chips might say something like "Hey, we want to keep playing this event, but we don't like the big spreads between first and second. Mr. Tournament Director, we want the payoffs to be $30,000, $24,000, and $16,000 (or whatever other numbers the players decide on—they could even make it winner take all if everyone agreed)." The tournament director would okay it and the tournament would continue with a new payoff structure.

Now you see why deal-making is considered a way to reduce fluctuation. The number of chips each player had in front of him bore a close relationship to his estimated winning chances. What usually winds up happening is that some money gets shifted out of the first place payoff and moved down into second and third.

Deal-making has been a common part of tournament poker for many years. Now that poker is starting to become a big television sport and sponsorship is starting to come in (meaning the players are now no longer just re-dividing money they put up themselves), deal-making may have to go away.

I mean, if Tiger Woods and Ernie Els were walking up the eighteenth fairway of a major tournament tied for first place and had a little chat that went something like this:

Tiger: Hey, Ernie, this tournament pays a million for first and $600,000 for second, why don't we just take $800,000 each?

Ernie: Fine by me, Tiger.

Wouldn't that take just a bit of the drama out of those ten-foot puts at the end? Of course, in golf, the players don't put up any of the prize money and it's televised live ("time outs" to talk about a deal can easily be cut out of tape-delayed broadcast), but as tournament poker gets bigger, deal-making will have to go away, at least at the major events.

## The Least You Need to Know

- ◆ Chip conservation is often more important than chip accumulation.
- ◆ Although big chip stacks have a significant advantage, players who own short stacks shouldn't give up hope.

◆ It is wise for players who own large chip stacks to eliminate small stacks before risking all their chips.

◆ As long as the players have created the entire prize pool with their own buy-ins, deal-making is an acceptable way to reduce fluctuation.

# Part 5

# The Psychological Side of Poker

People play poker for many different reasons and you'll probably find yours discussed here somewhere. Part 5 teaches you why mere mathematicians or those gifted with perfect memories stand very little chance of winning consistently in poker unless they can bring something else to the table (with the possible exception of games at the lowest stakes against the weakest players).

You'll learn why honesty with yourself is a powerful weapon and why learning how to understand how your opponents think can be even more important than an illegal glance at their cards. Some of the hints you'll receive about reading body language and betting patterns will come close to being as dependable as that illegal glace, too! You'll also learn the classic poker personality archetypes and which are more successful than others.

BE CAREFUL. THIS GUY HAS A REAL GOOD POKER FACE.

# Chapter 24

# Classic Poker Style Archetypes

## In This Chapter

- ♦ All poker players who employ a consistent style can be placed into one of four admittedly artificial categories.

- ♦ By understanding player personalities, you may be able to predict how a player will react in a given situation.

- ♦ Although generalizations about personalities can be useful they are no substitute for empirical data.

Most players can be characterized as either loose or tight, and also as either aggressive or passive. By combining the labels, you can place everyone into one of four groups: loose-passive, loose-aggressive, tight-passive, and tight-aggressive.

Although you will find those experts who insist on subdividing the poker population into many more subcategories—not an unreasonable position because there are many other kinds of groups into which you could divide the poker population, such as analytical vs. intuitive—there are only so many labels one can apply before the number of labels creates an impractical learning tool.

Let's examine these four subgroups. Later in this section and in the upcoming chapters, we'll look at personality traits that tend to create the individual styles.

# Loose Players and Passive Players

Loose players tend to get involved in a lot of pots. Because everyone gets roughly the same number of good cards over the long run, by definition a loose player plays many more inferior starting hands than a tight player. To use some artificial numbers purely for demonstration purposes, let's say that out of a hundred hands you'll get 20 good hands, 50 mediocre hands, and 30 bad hands. A loose player would probably play 70 hands, avoiding only the bad ones.

A tight player waits for quality starting hands. He would play only the 20 good hands, although a very tight player might play only a dozen, and a moderately tight player might play 30.

There's a middle ground for players who choose to play 50 or so hands. Some people want a third label for "average" players, while others want just to use "slightly tight" or "barely loose." When you start arguing about points like this, you're starting to lose the forest for the trees. Labels are only a tool and one has to think to use that tool. The thinking can happen when you create the labels, but it's probably wiser to do it later in the process when you actually need to make judgments and decisions about how to play hands.

# Aggressive Players and Passive Players

Aggressive players do a lot of raising. Although they will call if a situation truly demands it, they tend to prefer to fold if they can't raise. Often they will raise with hands that most players will fold, figuring that their aggression may earn them pots that their cards never could. The more aggressive a player is, the more difficult it is to *put him on a hand*. Super-aggressive players can raise with any hand.

**Table Talk** _____

When you **put someone on a hand**, you are making an educated guess as to what cards he is holding. Good players use many tools to do this: historical data on prior tendencies, betting patterns during the hand, body language, and more. Such educated guesses are extremely valuable when accurate, but it is important not to cling to an early projection. Keep looking for later clues that might call for a reevaluation.

Passive players do a lot of calling often with hands that other players would consider easy raising hands or easy folds. As with ultra-aggressive players, this trait can make it difficult to put them on a hand. They rarely initiate action, preferring to go with the flow. Just what caliber hands a passive player will call with depends on whether he is loose-passive or tight-passive. Now that we've looked at loose, tight, aggressive, and passive individually, it's time to start studying the four subgroups, which are, once again:

- Loose-aggressive
- Tight-aggressive
- Loose-passive
- Tight-passive

# The Loose-Aggressive Player

A loose-aggressive player is going to get involved in a lot of pots but he won't be limping in. He's often called (both in the literature and at the table) a maniac because he's raising and re-raising hold'em hands with small suited connectors from early position, re-raising stud players who have open pairs with apparent underpairs, and in general, just raising and re-raising the hell out of everyone, whether he appears to have the best of it or not.

If a loose-aggressive player catches a lot of cards, he's going to make a fortune—far more than players in any of the other three groups would make with the same cards. This happens because players correctly do not give him credit for having the kind of hand that his re-raises imply.

Because all players catch roughly the same number of good cards over the long run, you're usually correct to conclude that someone who raises six hands out of ten is bluffing some of the time; indeed, he's probably bluffing most of the time. That's why players don't give loose-aggressive players credit for strong hands, and why, if they do happen to pick up a big hand, they will get paid off handsomely.

The problem for the loose-aggressive player arrives when he doesn't catch above-average cards because in most games, he will then get clobbered. He will invest large sums in multiple pots, but he doesn't get the vitally important "two ways to win." He won't often win with his bet. He can only win with his cards and he's involved with too many substandard ones.

Some players adopt this style when they face weak opponents in their early days. If the opposition routinely folds in the wake of ferocious attack after ferocious attack, why stop attacking? Unfortunately for the loose-aggressive player, even weak players eventually learn to adjust.

Two other reasons why players adopt this inadvisable style come from envy and inter- mittent reinforcement. If in your formative days as a player you see a loose-aggressive player *book several large wins*, you might decide to mimic his style so that you too can enjoy such a session.

### Table Talk

When you **book a win**, you've left a game as a winner, but that shouldn't be your focus. If your goal is instead to spend time in good games (weak and/or tilted opposition) and avoid bad games, your long term results will be better than if you focus on booking wins. It can be tempting to book a win even in a good game to break a long losing streak, but recognize you're probably paying a price for your emotional healing.

If you try the loose-aggressive style and it happens to work once, you may find your- self unable to abandon memories of that one huge win even in the face of loss after loss.

Assuming that you're not getting clobbered, the loose-aggressive style is a fun way to play. You become the center of attention, the chips flow in, and players who don't know you watch in awe. The problem is that most of the time it doesn't work. You pay a very heavy price for the intermittent reinforcement you get on the nights when you catch cards.

People sometimes adopt the loose-aggressive style because they watch it work for someone in a tournament. The style is more effective in tournament play than in money play because there's no tournament payoff for grinding out one or two big bets an hour. Winning one big bet an hour might let you finish 30th or 40th out of 100, and while it might feel good to tell your friends you did that when you're first starting out, eventually you'll realize that in a 100-player tournament, there's no financial difference between finishing 100th and finishing 20th. You get paid nothing either way. This doesn't mean you should adopt a loose-aggressive style in tourna- ments (tight-aggressive is better for most people), but at least it can work there; it can't work in money play.

**Perilous Play** _____

When you watch televised poker, you are almost always watching an edited version of a much longer game. You see players make raises that steal pots and it's easy to assume that this is the correct way to play all the time. Usually, you've missed seeing the thief fail to play a hand for half an hour before his steal works. He got away with it because his table image was tight—but you never got to see that image develop.

Railbirds (and now, in the age of televised poker, national audiences) see the world's most famous and skilled players adopting what appears to be a loose-aggressive style and they try to apply it to their own money games. It doesn't work, partly because the situations are so different, and partly because the watchers don't have the talent to time their loose-aggressive play. There's a difference between loose-aggressive and insanely aggressive.

It's important to spot the loose-aggressive players in your game and choose the correct seat relative to their location. That seat is on their left/your right—no matter what your own style is! Let's see why.

If your own style is aggressive, it's good to have the loose-aggressive player on your right because when he raises, you can re-raise.

Even if you have a bit of a loose-aggressive reputation yourself (and hopefully after reading this you won't, because it _really_ is a bad way to play), other players will be hesitant to come in for three bets _cold_.

**Table Talk** _____

If you limp in and then later in that round must call a raise, it's fairly easy to call because you already have one bet committed and you're probably getting good pot odds. However, when there has been a raise before the action reaches you, you have to call two bets **cold**. The pot odds are worse, so you need a stronger hand. Most good players won't call two bets cold. If their hand isn't strong enough to make it three bets, they'll fold.

This lets you play heads-up against someone who often doesn't have a strong hand and you'll have position on him. If your style and reputation is tight-aggressive, you will get to isolate the loose-aggressive opponent much more because your re-re-raise will get more respect than a loose player's re-raise.

If you are loose-aggressive, other players may decide to come in for three bets, figuring that one bluffer has raised another. Don't be too concerned if someone behind you goes ahead and makes it four bets (capping it). He probably figures that the first loose-aggressive player would put the final raise in anyway, and this way he can seize the initiative. Indeed, if you have a hand worth playing for three bets cold, capping it to seize the initiative probably does make sense.

If you are a fairly passive player, it can be difficult to have an aggressive player on your left. When you passively limp in for one bet, the loose-aggressive player will raise behind you. Because the other players may not respect his raise, it may well be two more bets to you by the time the betting has worked its way back around (and the loose-aggressive player might put in the fourth bet if you decide to call bets two and three).

If it is starting to sound like it's difficult to have a loose-aggressive player in the game if you're passive, you're right. These problems help explain why loose-aggressive players can succeed against certain player line-ups. Loose-aggressive isn't the best of the four styles, but because passive players often can't adjust, it isn't the worst of the four either.

By having the loose-aggressive player on your right, you can at least make your passive decision to call for two bets with more information available to you, which will probably make it a bit more likely you'll be doing battle with a reasonable hand.

# The Tight-Aggressive Player

Tight-aggressive is, by a wide margin, the best of the four playing styles. You don't play a lot of hands, so you get the benefits that selectivity brings. When you do get involved you play aggressively and get the benefits that aggressiveness offers.

Loose-aggressive players don't get full value for their aggression because they're involved in too many pots for their raises to earn respect. As a tight-aggressive player, you will be able to steal a number of pots when your respectable starting hand doesn't improve.

For example, suppose that in hold'em you start out with K♠-Q♠. This is certainly a reasonable raising hand from middle position and later. You make it two bets and because of your tight reputation, no one behind you calls two bets cold. You do, however, get calls from the big blind and one player who had limped in before you.

The flop now comes A♠-10♦-4♥. This is the poker equivalent of shooting an air ball. You have chances for a gutshot straight and a backdoor flush, but because you will need to catch two perfect cards for the flush and one unlikely one for the straight, your chances of making a strong hand are slight.

Because you raised and an ace hit the flop, though, you have a pretty good chance to take the pot right away. So many people raise with hands containing an ace that it will be difficult for anyone to call you without one, even if, while playing a hand like J-10, they have flopped middle pair. Someone holding J-10 would call a loose-aggressive player very quickly here, but might decide to let it go against a tight-aggressive player.

Even if someone with J-10 calls on the flop, if the turn card doesn't help his hand and you bet again, he might decide to give up. Whether this will happen depends a great deal on your playing style, your opponent's playing style, and whether your opponent is aware of your playing style. It's harder to steal this pot against a loose player (which means it's harder to steal this pot in an Internet game!).

### The Inside Straight

If you're going to bet on the river, you should usually either have a very good hand or nothing. If you bet with a mediocre hand and everyone folds, you can safely assume that your mediocre hand would have won a showdown anyway. With a mediocre hand, you're much better off checking and calling; you'll pick off some bluffs from players who never would have called if you'd bet out. Betting with nothing (bluffing) is okay because you have a chance to win with your bet, especially (and here is where most amateurs struggle) if your betting pattern throughout the hand showed strength.

For the reasons you've read here and the weaknesses you're about to read about in the next two sections, the tight-aggressive style is definitely the best approach to money poker and usually the best to tournament poker.

# The Loose-Passive Style

You might have thought I disparaged the loose-aggressive style, but compared to the loose-passive style, the loose-aggressive style is championship level poker.

Loose-passive is easily the worst of the four approaches, leading to poor results unless you have both good cards and bad opponents. Even then, the loose-passive style wins less than it should. With *great* cards, loose-passive will probably do better than tight-passive and possibly even better than tight-aggressive simply because the loose-passive player gets involved in a lot of pots. Logically, if you're involved in a lot of pots with great cards, it's practically impossible not to win a lot.

Even with great cards, the loose-passive player does far worse than the loose-aggressive player would do. Just say no. This style doesn't work.

Remember, you want to have those two ways to win going for you in poker: You want a chance to win either with your bet or with your hand. The loose-passive player doesn't get a chance to win with his bet because he just calls. He doesn't raise very often (perhaps occasionally, when he has the nuts or something very close thereto), and he puts no pressure on his opponents.

**Perilous Play**

Another name for the loose-passive player is a *calling station*. One of the most widely accepted pieces of poker wisdom is "If you can't beat a calling station, you can't beat anyone." Loose-passive poker is losing poker. You're playing lots of pots meekly with substandard hands. It doesn't get much worse than that.

Loose-passive players stick with their weak approach because it occasionally provides intermittent reinforcement. They don't ever get bluffed out and whenever they pick off a bluff, they lean back sagely and congratulate themselves for their conservative intelligent play. They also shake their heads with disapproval when they see an aggressive player lose a pot he'd bluffed at from the start: *They* would never have lost chips like that!

Loose-passive players also congratulate themselves on the mystery in their games. Their opponents can't read them because they don't "give away" their hand's strength by raising. They'll trap players for bets that a raising player would have driven out.

Of course, they'll also allow players who have drawing hands to stay in at the right price to hit their draw and beat them, but the loose-passive player just figures that's poker—a classic form of gambling where one wins when one gets lucky and loses when one gets unlucky. The concept of "making one's own luck" just isn't part of their thought process.

**The Inside Straight**

*The Price is Right* isn't merely a long-running TV show. It's also a key element to winning poker: finding situations where your pot odds and/or implied odds are right. A loose-passive player who holds a great hand but who doesn't raise because "he wants to keep everyone in" will often find that in accomplishing his mission, he has kept someone in who winds up beating him. Sometimes it's right to slowplay a big hand, but the loose-passive player does it far too often.

They can also have winning sessions because if they get hit with the deck, not only will they be in there to catch the lucky draw-out, but their apparently weak (no raising) style may encourage other players to bet or raise, figuring they can either bluff the loose-passive player out (this line of thinking proves they haven't been paying attention: You don't try to bluff a loose player) or that he must be in with something weak.

When you break loose-passive down to its essential elements, it amounts to playing far too many weak hands (loose play) without ever winning a hand by pushing someone out (passive play).

# The Tight-Passive Style

The tight-passive player is also sometimes called a "weak tight" player, which should tell you most of what you need to know about the style.

Tight-passive players tend not to have big fluctuations. They win a little or they lose a little, although they lose a little much more often. They don't get clobbered because they are selective about their starting hands and they are not investing huge sums in dubious propositions.

The problem is that when they do invest, they don't invest enough. You only get so many good hands a night and in order to make up for the money you lose on your bad or weak hands, you need to earn reasonable profits on the good ones.

If, when you get one of your good hands, you meekly call, the pot won't be very large when you win. Worse still, if you're tight enough, you may back off at the wrong time. By not initiating action, the tight-passive player encourages others to attack. It's much easier to raise someone when you don't have to worry about a re-raise. If you're tight and you get attacked, you often fold.

### The Inside Straight

Another problem with tight-passive play is that in the modern game, players have grown to expect so much aggression that when they don't find themselves on the end of it, they grow more confident and attack not merely to be aggressive but because they've been fooled into thinking they are betting the best hand. This can pay dividends for the tight-passive player if he hangs in until the end, but he'll probably need a strong hand to do that.

Sometimes the tight-passive player won't take a stand, even with his better hands, and releases them in the face of pressure from players who own weaker hands.

Although "tight-passive" and "weak-tight" aren't perfect synonyms, they're close enough for your purposes. Casino and Internet players are accustomed to running into this sort of foe, in part because home game players are often a bit intimidated by the more formal cardroom atmospheres, but in larger part because many home game players are accustomed to playing in such ultra-loose games that all one need do to start winning is to tighten up. That really is a good adjustment for many losing home game players to make—at home.

Tightening up thus becomes these players' response to any unfavorable situation. It has worked before, so why not now? It doesn't work now because they have finally encountered more able opponents and tightening up just isn't enough there.

## A Style Summary

Although your personality may dictate how you play at first, hopefully what you've read here will help you change your approach. Ranking the styles from most effective to least, they are:

1. Tight-aggressive (best by far)

2a. Loose-aggressive (Near tie: wins more on good days, loses more on bad days; whether better or worse than T-P depends much on opponent styles and cards. Also depends on just how loose and how aggressive. Better in tournaments, worse in money games.)

2b. Tight-passive (Near tie: smaller upside, smaller downside; whether better or worse than L-A depends much on opponent styles and cards. Also depends on just how tight and how passive. Worse in tournaments, better in money games.)

3. Loose-passive (worst by far)

# Projecting Your Values onto Other Players

One of the more elementary psychological principles states that we tend to think that others perceive the world the way we do. If you have no honor, you don't expect others to have any (or at least, not much). If you're truthful, you expect others to be.

In poker terms, that means that

- Frequent bluffers tend to think other players bluff frequently (and so call people down with weak hands).

- Tight players tend to think other players are also tight (and so lay down hands to raises).

- Aggressive players tend to think their opponents are also aggressive (and don't respect re-raises).

- Competent players tend to think other players are competent (and so often give opponent plays more respect than they deserve).

Actually, there is some question about the last item on that list because of the earlier-discussed reasons about why players of comparable skill levels tend to consider themselves superior opponents.

Regardless of your view on the competence issue, it thus becomes vitally important that you understand yourself. First and foremost, your self-analysis will tell you much about how you are approaching your opponents' play … and perhaps suggest some changes to your approach when you realize that while it is indeed a common assumption, the reality is that we don't all act and think alike.

## The Least You Need to Know

- Because personality traits can predict the way many people will play, learn as much as possible about your opponents.

- Generalizations based on personality are helpful, but not as helpful as specific observations of playing tendencies.

- The tight-aggressive style is the most effective.

- The loose-passive style is the least effective.

- The tight-passive and loose-aggressive styles fall somewhere in between in effectiveness, and their effectiveness is more dependent on external factors than either of the other two.

- Because we tend to project our own values and styles onto others, it is important to understand our own values and styles.

# Chapter 25

# The Biggest Roller Coaster This Side of Wall Street

## In This Chapter

- ◆ Money management
- ◆ Reasons why you should and shouldn't leave games
- ◆ Reasons to bet and raise
- ◆ Why players overrate themselves and underrate opponents
- ◆ Winning and losing streaks

If by now you're not wondering how much of a bankroll you need to play poker, you should be! You've probably also thought about what effect a winning or losing streak will have on that bankroll. Let's investigate.

## Money Management: Part Vital Subject, Part Nonsense

Depending on how one defines "money management," it is either vitally important or complete nonsense. Most of the nonsense has been written about money management stop-loss and stop-win schemes. The useful material involves understanding what sort of fluctuations even a very good player is likely to go through, and so enables such a player to define what stakes he wants to play at to have a reasonable assurance of not *going broke*.

### Table Talk

When an intelligent poker player **goes broke**, he isn't selling his car or declaring bankruptcy. Although this does happen, normally "poker broke" means that a player has lost the money he'd set aside for playing poker. If he has been playing with rent or food money and is broke in a conventional sense, he has a gambling problem and should quit playing – probably forever, but certainly at least until he's both assembled a poker bankroll and developed more discipline.

## Stop and Go "Fish"

When some alleged experts talk about money management, they are referring to stop-loss and stop-win schemes. These charlatans (if they are intelligent) or well-meaning fools (if they aren't) claim that the successful player should never lose more than a pre-set amount and should always leave to lock up a win if he gets ahead a certain amount.

Life, as you have already learned, is one long session and by advocating a strategy that requires stopping and leaving when winning or losing regardless of the circumstances, a speaker proves that he hasn't the slightest idea what he's talking about. The game doesn't go away when you get up from the table; it's still there when you get back and has no idea that you took a break.

You will indeed run into many situations when leaving for the night while losing will make sense and many others when leaving while winning will make sense, but these situations arise in the *context* of several key elements:

- ◆ How well are you playing and are there reasons why the answer to that question is likely to change soon?

- ◆ Are you facing one or more players who will likely lose considerable sums before leaving for the night?

- ◆ How many of your opponents are playing better than you now and figure to continue doing so?

- ◆ Historically, how do you tend to perform once you have already won or lost large sums?

- ◆ What is your current table image?

- ◆ What is your current emotional status?

- ◆ What is your current physical status?

- ◆ How important is it to you that you finish the session a winner?

Let's look at some examples to see why absolute stop-loss and stop-win rules are absolutely wonderful ways to ensure that you will stop ... winning.

## A Bad Night for a "Stop-Win" Policy

You're in a terrific $20-$40 hold'em game (several weak players and the good players are temporarily on tilt). Your luck runs well. Your policy calls for you to depart whenever you get ahead $1,000. You win several pots and reach your magic number. You pick up your three *racks* of $5 chips (two of them profit), thanks in no small part to the presence of a guy who comes in maybe once a month and usually goes off for about a $3,000 loss (75 big bets is a lot to lose even for a bad player, but it can be done). He was down $1,200 when you left.

The next day you hear that he achieved a new "personal best" by dropping $6,500 and that the other players in the game were smart enough to remain at the table until he had cashed out and gotten his car from the valet (it's a bad idea to let someone know his presence is keeping a game going).

When someone loses that much money, it's probably because he's trying to punish himself, has had too much to drink, or is somehow otherwise playing under circumstances that make him almost fated to get clobbered.

**Table Talk**

Chip **racks** are almost always clear or opaque plastic and hold 100 chips in 5 columns of 20 chips. If a casino's chips are new, you can usually depend on a full rack containing exactly 100 chips. If the chips are old and worn, double-check, because you might find 21 chips fitting in a column.

Someone who regularly loses 75 big bets in one session is way past bad: He's horrible. Had you stuck around, you probably would have gotten your "fair share" of the full $3,000 he usually loses, to say nothing of what he wound up going off for. If you know how to adapt to a tilted loser's style, you might have walked off a $3,000 or $4,000 winner.

You locked up your win by leaving when you had your thousand dollars, but you left a game that was good in more than one way. You had a likely major contributor sitting there and you were probably playing well and/or also the beneficiary of a good table image because you were already winning.

Now, let's turn the previous situation around. Your stop-loss policy ensures you never lose more than $1,000. You're playing with the same players in the same game and you're playing well. This time you run into some bad luck in several of the huge pots the *fish* never belonged in. You're down a grand and the fish is winning $1,700 and raising every pot, thrilled to finally be catching the cards the "law of averages" tells him he knows he's entitled to.

"Twenty-five big bets," you think, "that's a lot and that's my limit. It's going to get even more expensive because the fish is raising every hand. Tomorrow is another day. I can always get even then, but if I take a big loss now, I may never get it back."

You get up and go home satisfied that you've protected your poker bankroll. Later, you learn that the fish temporarily got ahead $2,800, three-betting pots without even looking at his cards, ordering double-shots with beer chasers, and was generally enjoying the hell out of inflicting painful beat after painful beat on his old tormentors.

Unfortunately for the fish, the long-term expectancy caught up with him rather quickly. After catching every card he wanted for two hours, his luck changed to below average, but his already bad play turned horrendous. Not only did he give the $2,800 back, he lost another $8,000 on top of that.

There was $10,800 pumped into that game after you lost your $1,000 and left. Purely average luck and play would have made you a winner for the night and who knows how much you might actually have won. You left a good game, and you probably paid for it dearly.

**The Inside Straight**

Unless most or all of your bankroll is gone (a circumstance that suggests you are playing in too big a game), the only *financial* reason to quit any game early is if the current circumstances suggest you're unlikely to win (the bad players have left and have been replaced by good ones, your own play or image is sub-par, etc.). Unless you are playing poorly, stay in good games and leave bad games.

If a game is good but you're playing badly, for whatever reason, your expectation has become negative and it's time to quit. You might be ill or tired. You might be angry about a nonpoker matter. You might know of a flaw in your game: Some players, for example, know through painful experience that they play poorly once they get down about 30 big bets. While it might be worth investing a *little* money in a conscious effort to avoid the mistakes you inevitably make when losing, until you've figured out why a 30-big bet loss inevitably becomes a 50-big bet loss, you should honor your experience.

> **Perilous Play** _____
>
> If you fall apart when losing, try exchanging any large denomination chips or cash already on the table for the smallest legal size (for example, exchange your $100 chips for $5 chips). This might help you feel like your situation isn't so bad without putting more money at risk. Beware of pulling lots of extra cash from your wallet just to reestablish your chip mountain when losing. If you're on tilt, you may have made it too easy to throw more chips away.

If you find that your game worsens when you get far ahead *or* behind, you may be counting your chips too often. Try focusing on each hand.

Similarly, some players cannot stand success. Once they get ahead 40 big bets, they get giddy and play too many pots. Before they know it, most of their win is gone. Although learning how to stop making this mistake is your best long-term move, if it happens again and again, you probably should accept this flaw in your game and get out.

> **The Inside Straight** _____
>
> If you treat chips disrespectfully when winning heavily, try "coloring up" (exchanging three racks of $5 chips for three $500 chips). Even though you'll have the same dollar amount in front of you, you won't be sitting behind a physical mountain of money and that may help you control yourself.

Notice that the stop-win and stop-loss suggestions here are not based on some abstract mathematical theory. They are based on a great deal of unfortunate empirical evidence. You should try to figure out how to change your natural weaknesses, but until you do, why ask for trouble? The game has grown worse, not because your opponents have grown stronger, but because *you've* grown weaker.

As long as you're playing well, as long as you're not tired or have a pressing engagement, you should stay when your expectation is positive.

# What Kind of Winner Are You?

Many professionals strive for a win rate of one big bet per hour, but that goal isn't very helpful in a vacuum. The bigger the game, the harder this is to achieve. Someone who regularly plays $1,000-$2,000 probably would be content earning one quarter of a big bet per hour ($500), although he'd be putting a lot of money at risk to earn that.

Worse still, his fluctuations would be much higher than someone making a full big bet per hour at $80-160 (still a big and rough game) because as the stakes grow higher, the players grow more aggressive. More aggression leads to greater variance. Skillful players achieve much of their success by taking advantage of small edges.

You probably need more than 500 hours to determine your expected win or loss rate with any accuracy. If after that time, you are averaging a win of half a big bet an hour or more, you can probably feel sure that you rate to remain a winner in that game.

> **The Inside Straight** _____
>
> Is a winner a great player? It depends. Someone who beats $2-4 games for one big bet an hour could be a *terrible* player if he's playing against an even weaker group. If you can beat $15-30 for one big bet an hour, you're a good $15-30 player, but until you prove otherwise, you can expect to get chewed up at $200-400 (and a good $15-30 home player might get slaughtered in casinos). Before you label your play, either consider against whom you're earning your reputation, or use a narrow label ("I'm a winning $2-4 player").

# Other Ways to Judge Your Play

Poker is a very bottom-line oriented game. Your results are your results and excuses are just margin notes. It's pretty hard to call yourself a great player if you lose consistently.

Nonetheless, you can consider yourself on the *path* to superior play if you can cite a reason for most of the plays you make. Merely betting "because you have a good hand" is not a good reason. Context is king in poker. Four kings constitute an absolutely terrible hand if someone else has four aces.

Good reasons to bet or raise in poker include:

♦ To add money to a pot you *know* you are going to win.

♦ To increase the size of a pot in which you have a draw to the nuts so that if you make your hand, the pot size will force players with good but not great hands to make losing calls.

◆ To *isolate* another player (drive out a third player who had a chance to win or who might be a superior player).

◆ To encourage other bets and raises that will create the proper pot odds for you to draw to the hand you are trying to make.

◆ To cause players who might outdraw you to fold.

◆ To get a free card on a later (more expensive) betting round.

◆ To drive out players who would otherwise have position on you.

◆ To establish an image or reputation that may pay dividends later.

◆ In seven-card stud, when your cards are extremely live and/or your opponents' cards are mostly dead.

◆ You have made a read on an opponent (either through a betting pattern or a tell) that informs you your bet can make him lay down a superior hand.

As you can see, someone who approaches poker with an "I bet when I have a good hand" approach has far too few weapons in his arsenal. He might be able to beat other amateurs, or he might be able to beat good players for a short time if he *gets hit with the deck*, but over the long run, this simplistic approach is hopeless.

There are a host of other reasons to bet and raise, just as many to check, and even more to fold. If you do not have a specific, valid reason for each and every action you take (or fail to take), you have considerable room to improve, no matter your short-term results.

> **Table Talk**
>
> Start counting your money when you **get hit with the deck** (or as some players say, when you get hit in the face with the deck). This means you have been catching (receiving) virtually every card you've been hoping for. It's common when visiting a poker room to hear something like, "I was helpless: The deck hit him so hard that I thought his brother was dealing."

## I'm Better Than You Are!

One of the most common phenomena in almost all forms of gambling that involve a mixture of luck and skill is for players to overrate their own abilities and to underrate their opponents' skills and it's not because gamblers are delusional (many of them are delusional, but that's not the operative reason here).

Most complex games, like poker, backgammon, and gin, require a wide variety of skills to be mastered before one can be considered a great player. Sticking with poker for our example, the number of skills required for greatness might be 50 or it might be 500, depending on how narrowly we want to define "skills." Let's define the term narrowly and say that there are exactly 500 different skills available to master in poker.

Now, let's take two local club players, each of whom is pretty good—not duffers but no threat to win the World Series of Poker, either. Let's further say that these "advanced intermediate" players have attained that status because they have each mastered 300 of the 500 necessary skills.

This might make the two players equally talented and might mean that against equal opponents, they rate to achieve equivalent results over the long run, but it would take an astounding coincidence for each player to have mastered precisely the same 300 skills. They're probably good at different things. Let's say that Player X has mastered skills 51 through 350, while Player Y has mastered skills 176-475.

What happens when these two players square off? Player X sees Player Y consistently make errors whenever skills 51-175 come into play and grudgingly acknowledges that despite these shortcomings, Player Y can play a little because he can indeed handle skills 176-350.

**Perilous Play** _____

By definition, players are unable to spot their own blind spots, but players who focus on what they don't know will lack self-confidence and be easily intimidated. Former all-time great UCLA basketball coach John Wooden had a saying that helped his players battle this paradox: "Do not let what you cannot do interfere with what you can do." Translation: Utilize your strengths and keep learning. As long as you don't allow a lack of perfection to paralyze you, you can win.

At the same time, Player Y can barely contain his laughter whenever Player X tries to make a play involving skills 351-475. He concedes that Player X does at least understand the concepts behind skills 176-350.

The result? Each player is able to recognize his opponent's errors because he knows he would never have made that error. Neither player is able to recognize his *own* errors, though, because if he could recognize them, he would never make the errors in the first place.

In each case, the equally-matched advanced intermediates have big blind spots for their own weaknesses, but can spot their opponent's errors in a heartbeat. They walk away from their heads-up session each convinced that the other player is very lucky indeed to have come close because each believes himself far superior to his opponent. The reality is that the duo is equally matched.

The paradox is that it's vitally important to have self-confidence in poker. If you walk up to a table thinking you have no chance, you probably don't. At the same time, if you walk up to a table thinking you don't need your "A" game because you're so much better than your opponents, you probably don't have much of a chance, either. Learn to walk the fine line between a desire to grow and confidence in what you've learned so far and you'll be a dangerous opponent.

## How's Your Bankroll?

The only real money management you need as a poker player is to ensure that you maintain an adequate bankroll.

How large a bankroll you need depends on several factors: the type of game, the size of the game, how well you play, and how well your opponents play.

The starting point in any bankroll discussion is simple. If you are a losing player, no bankroll is adequate. Eventually, you will lose all the money you are willing to lose. What you are trying to learn here is how large a bankroll you need to avoid going broke through unfortunate runs of bad luck.

If you possess the skills to win long-term, it's crucial to avoid suffering "gambler's ruin" (loss of the bankroll that allows you to win money). The loss of your bankroll is ruinous not just because of the money you have lost, but because it keeps you out of action, and leaves you unable to make later winning bets.

In general, the better you play, the smaller the bankroll you need. For most games, authorities recommend a bankroll of somewhere around 300-400 big bets for winning players. Your

> **The Inside Straight**
>
> Draw poker and lowball require a smaller ratio of big bet to bankroll size. This is because there are only two betting rounds and because the games offer more complete information than flop and stud games. The more information, the lesser role played by luck and the greater the role played by skill. Fewer bets per pot lead to a smaller variance.

> **The Inside Straight**
>
> If you run into a bad streak and your bankroll shrinks noticeably, to avoid gambler's ruin you should move to a lower limit. If you are a great player playing $20-$40 on that recommended bankroll of $12,000, and have a bad run of luck that brings you down to $6,000, consider playing $10-$20 or $15-$30 until you bring your bankroll back up.

bankroll needs to be larger for Seven-card stud than for hold'em because seven stud has more betting rounds and more situations wherein "chasing" is correct. This leads to larger fluctuations.

The larger the game (that is, the higher the stakes), the larger your bankroll needs to be. That may seem self-evident, but this doesn't mean you need ten times more money to play $20-40 than $2-4. Fluctuations become larger in the $20-40 game because of the opposition's greater aggressiveness and talent.

The lesser your skills, the larger your bankroll need be. If you are a good player, instead of a great player, to weather the dry spells you might need a bankroll of 600 big bets, while as a great player, you might need only 300.

> **Table Talk**
>
> A **value bet** is made with a good but not great hand. It will win slightly more than it will lose.

If your bankroll is limited, you want to lessen the effects of variance. You should eliminate certain plays from your arsenal. Avoid marginally profitable plays until your bankroll grows. This may mean less *value betting* and playing fewer marginal hands, but beginners would do well to avoid playing marginal hands anyway.

## Moving On Up

When is it time to move to a new limit? If you double your bankroll, it is time to consider playing higher. Just recognize that the competition generally is better the higher you go, so you shouldn't double the stakes you're playing just because you've doubled your bankroll, at least not as a long-term plan.

Suppose you are a $10-$20 player and started with a bankroll of $8,000 (400 big bets). Over time, you have doubled that to $16,000. You could decide to experiment with a night or two of $20-40, and if your results are good, you can stay there until or unless things start going poorly. If you wanted a long-term experiment at higher stakes, though, you'd probably be smarter to try $15-30. This isn't because $20-$40 players are better than $15-30 players. Rather, it took you a long time to win that $8,000, and you want to give yourself awhile to get emotionally accustomed to bigger swings on a given night.

If you find you lose back a third of your new, increased bankroll, you should consider going back to the level in which you were doing so well. Don't fall into the poker snobbery trap of moving up to "elite" levels and then be afraid to be seen in the less expensive games.

**Perilous Play** _____

The business Peter Principle states that people advance through promotion to their level of incompetence and then stay there. Sadly, many poker players do the same. They succeed at lower ranks, sit down proudly among the $15-30 players and can't quite keep their heads above water. Rather than be seen back at the "lowly" $6-12 game, they fight on at $15-30 and turn a profitable hobby into an unprofitable one solely from pride.

What about moving down? It can take a *long* time at a lower limit to build your bankroll back up to where you can play comfortably at the higher limit. If you lost your money playing $40-80 and didn't back off in time to slow to $20-40, it can take a long time at $5-10 to work up enough money to play in your old game again. If things start going badly, consider applying the brakes before you have to play at such a low limit that it will either take years to build up a sufficient bankroll for bigger play, or you have to dip into nonpoker capital to give it a try.

## Keep That Bankroll

When you make a nice tournament score or series of money wins, you will be tempted to go out and buy a new car or home theatre system. Resistance is not futile! *Your poker bankroll should be kept separate from your living money.* If you have an unusually profitable run, one that you know can't be explained by your skill but which has come because you've been unusually lucky for awhile, realize that it's possible things could swing the other way. If you've gone out and blown the poker money on luxuries, you won't have the bankroll to handle the inevitable swings.

If instead you hang onto your bankroll and let it grow, you'll be able to weather the inevitable bad times and to consider moving up.

This next point should seem obvious, but unfortunately it isn't to many players. If things are going poorly for you at your normal limit, don't trying playing higher as a way to change your luck. The players are tougher, and if you've really established a poker bankroll and it has been shrinking, one or two bad sessions at the new higher limit could wipe you out. Many players have a hard time resisting the "get it back in a hurry" attitude that one often sees in craps or blackjack players, but it's a bad mistake.

I have seen losing players move up because they claim they are playing too loosely at the lower limit and they know the higher limit will keep them in line. There's just enough truth in this line of thinking to make it dangerous. You shouldn't have to rely on game size to make you play well. If you have so little self control that you can't keep yourself from playing weak starting hands unless you are playing for uncomfortably high stakes, some other kind of error will almost certainly doom you in the bigger game.

# Winning Streaks and Losing Streaks

You might hear a player moan, "I just had my twentieth losing session in a row." What can you conclude from that?

Although players are more likely to exaggerate wins than losses, they aren't above exaggerating the tough times to elicit sympathy. Poker players have very selective memories. Maybe he's lost 15 out of the last 20 plays and doesn't remember the wins or discounts them because they didn't add up to as much as he lost.

If you were in a very volatile game and you played in a high-variance way, it's quite conceivable that you could lose on average three times out of four and still be a big winner in the long run. As long as your losses are smaller than your wins, you can lose more than half the time and still be a winner.

It is quite possible for someone to win as much as 90 percent of the time and still be a big loser.

---

### Poker Lore

Every cardroom has a player like Tom. Tom comes in at noon and buys in for the minimum, usually one stack, say 20 $5 chips in a $5-$10 game. He starts out playing tight and that's usually enough to win in this game. If he doubles up, he leaves. He might not even stay past the first round. The night players hardly ever see Tom. But if he gets stuck, his play changes and he starts playing a lot of hands. He buys stack after stack and keeps playing.

If anyone in the night crew sees him in the game when they come in to play, they say, "Tom must be stuck; he's still here." Tom stays until he runs out of borrowing ability on his credit card, the game breaks up, he falls asleep, or he gets even. That last is the least likely. When he has a disastrous session like that, the players don't see him for a week or two. Tom wins 90 percent of the time and he's one of the biggest losers in the club.

---

Winning streaks and losing streaks are not at all unusual. In fact, the only thing a mathematician would find unusual would be if streaks did *not* occur.

Losing streaks can be very demoralizing. They can also affect your play. Most people play better when winning and worse when losing. Especially at the higher limits, your opponents can sense weakness and tend to play more inspired poker against you when you're on a losing streak, so don't advertise the fact that things haven't been going well lately. They also tend to play more timidly and less aggressively against you when you're on a winning streak.

**The Inside Straight** _____

A great player plays the same when he's losing as when he's winning. If a player's game doesn't lose aggression, if he doesn't whine or blame the world for his troubles, and especially if he doesn't sarcastically explain his superiority to the game's weaker players, watch out! This player's losing streak won't last long and when he starts winning, you should see if a table change is available.

You can do several things to turn around a losing streak. The oldest and still best solution is to take some time off. The games may not be good, you might not be good, or both might not be good, so it's as good a time as any to go on a vacation. When the games are bad or your performance is poor, take a break. At least you won't have to recite the *Gambler's Prayer* (sometimes called the *Horse Player's Prayer*): "Oh, Lord, please let me break even today, I need the money."

Another way to turn around a losing streak is to play at a different cardroom, particularly if you now patronize one cardroom almost exclusively. The new venue may force you to be more observant and probably play better. Maybe you've fallen into bad habits and play on autopilot. Maybe you have a tell that it will take new opponents a while to learn. If your opponents don't know you and aren't aware you're doing poorly, they may play uninspired poker against you. That may be all it takes.

## The Least You Need to Know

- Realize that stop-loss and stop-win schemes hurt your results.
- Play when a game is good and when you're playing well; quit otherwise.
- Have an adequate bankroll for the game.
- Segregate your bankroll for poker uses only.
- Realize that winning and losing streaks are normal, and don't make panic moves in reaction to them.

# Chapter 26

# Understanding Your Opponents

## In This Chapter

- ◆ You are your toughest opponent
- ◆ Your opponents' actions speak louder than their words
- ◆ Certain personality traits tend to lead to certain playing styles

Because the human element is such an important part of poker and because it grows more and more important as the stakes get higher and your opponents get tougher, it becomes more and more important to become a student of human nature as you develop your poker skills. Sometimes when we study others, we forget that the most important human being at any poker table is the one sitting in your own chair.

# Your Toughest Opponent: Yourself

Eastern philosophers recognize that if we can't understand the subject to which we have the most access (ourselves), it's hard to imagine how we can understand subjects to which we have considerably less access.

These same philosophers also understand that we are, all of us, more alike than we would often care to admit. If we can understand ourselves, we have a better chance of understanding others.

Literally tens of thousands of books strive to help us understand the human condition—some fiction, some not. It should go without saying that if all those books and authors haven't settled all the key questions, we're not going to solve the Mysteries of the Universe in a chapter here. We can get started, though, and give you some questions to work on.

## How to Learn About Yourself

Probably the single greatest hurdle most of us have to overcome in the search for self-understanding is our unwillingness to open old assumptions. It has taken us years to develop a picture of how the world works and whether we're comfortable with that picture or not, reshaping it can be an unsettling experience.

Before you bother spending much more time with this chapter, ask yourself if you're willing to reexamine old assumptions or beliefs you have about both yourself and the way the world works. If the answer is yes, please keep reading. If the answer is no, you might do well to abandon the idea of playing poker for all but the lowest stakes because the odds of your succeeding aren't great.

## Your Most Valuable Self-Assessment Tool: Honesty

Most human beings lie from time to time and poker players probably lie away from the tables no more or less than the average person; on the one hand, they've been drawn to a game wherein lying is, to a certain extent, not only allowed by the rules, but encouraged as part of good strategy. On the other hand, the poker world is a close-knit community where word of untrustworthiness both spreads rapidly and can be damaging.

At the tables, the player who cannot or will not bluff (lying, if you will, with his bets) won't be very successful. Neither will the player who can't use a poker face (lying, if you will, by disguising his emotions).

**Perilous Play** _____

Don't assume that poker players are liars away from the game. One of the reasons I love poker is that I believe strongly in honesty and integrity in personal and business relationships, but I also have a "sneaky side" that I like to indulge and one can play only so many practical jokes. Poker allows me to play little games within the rules and to get my sneaky side out of my system.

Perhaps it is this undercurrent of deception at the tables that accounts for the easy way that so many players tell "white lies" about their results. A "big win" is often just a decent win, a "won a little" means the player broke even, an "I broke even" means a small loss, and "I lost a little" means it wasn't a pleasant night. Only results at both extremes seem to be reported accurately: "I set a new personal best for one night" tends to be trustworthy, as does an "I got my butt kicked so bad, I'm going to have to play standing up for the next month."

I dislike this sort of fibbing because it only leads to trouble. Lies, even of the relatively minor variety, aren't good for relationships and have a way of blowing up in one's face. Lies told to one's friends that inflate one's results might encourage those friends to go play more ("If John could beat that game, I sure could") when they should be playing less.

There is one kind of lying that spells disaster for almost any poker player. If you're prone to it in other areas of your life, you should probably avoid poker as a hobby for anything other than purely social reasons because your chances of becoming a good player owning this vice are small. The disastrous vice is lying *to yourself*.

**The Inside Straight** _____

"Sure I can be honest with myself when I play," you might say. "I know when I run over those fools, it's because I've outplayed them. Every once in awhile they get lucky on me, but I know how to take responsibility for a win." Yep, you and just about everyone else. While accepting responsibility for a win can help your self-confidence, it means almost nothing unless you can accept responsibility for your defeats, too.

If you cannot be honest with yourself, you won't admit your mistakes to yourself. You'll blame luck, the dealer, the cards, your astrology chart, your biorhythms, and/or the valet before you blame your own bad play for a losing session. If you cannot accept responsibility for bad results, you have virtually no chance to improve and unless you're a one-in-a-million savant, you're going to have to work to improve as the games you play in get tougher over time.

If, on the other hand, you can accept some responsibility for your results, you have a chance to improve. This doesn't mean you have to (or should) beat yourself up for every mistake or blame yourself for every losing session. Sometimes the cards do play cruel tricks on us and everyone makes mistakes. The key is not making many of them twice.

## Other Ways to Be Your Own Worst Enemy

A few ways you can lead yourself to defeat:

- ◆ Poker tables are dangerous locations for those who believe that justice will and should prevail. Unlikely events happen all the time and if you let them get to you, your subsequent actions will cost you dozens of times as much money as that single unlucky card did.

- ◆ If you sit and moan about your bad luck and inspire your opponents to attack, they will do it for several reasons: The superstitious ones will think you're running bad, the wise ones will suspect you're on tilt and/or not thinking clearly, and the unlucky ones will think it's finally someone else's turn. Just who is responsible for your defeat?

- ◆ If you sit in on a game where stakes are too high, causing you to play too tight, or a game where stakes are too low, causing you to play too loose, whose mistake is that?

- ◆ If you eat a gigantic meal before playing and feel kind of groggy and/or sluggish when playing, whose fault is that? Whose fault is it that you haven't exercised in a year or eaten a healthy diet in three?

If you make a final table at a tournament but flounder when the game gets short-handed because you didn't play 50 one-table tournaments like your opponents did, whose fault is that?

I could go on for 40 more pages with similar examples, but the idea isn't to depress you. The idea is to show you that although you hate to admit it when things aren't going your way, your overall commitment to the game and the effort, energy, and focus you bring to the game on any given night have a great deal more to do with your results than most players are willing to admit.

If you take the time to study yourself and learn your strengths and weaknesses, remain honest about both, try to avoid situations where you know you're weak and seek out situations where you know you're strong, you're quite naturally going to perform better.

Every opponent you face at the poker table will try to take your money, but it's impossible for them to take it as fast as you can give it to them. Study yourself with brutal honesty, try to improve where you need improving, don't beat yourself up for playing less than perfectly your first time out, and pretty soon you'll find that you won't lose. Sometimes you'll get beaten, but you won't lose and there's a huge difference in those two conditions.

# Your Other Opponents

Certain personality traits tend to be good predictors of certain styles of play. If someone is talking about himself, he may provide you with personality clues that teach you about his poker even faster than his actual poker play does.

If someone is an "action guy" away from the poker tables, he's probably a loose player at the tables. Loose players stay in on the action in part because they can't stand being left out. Lord help the friend who doesn't invite the action guy to a party that he got invited to by a friend of a friend. He's probably an extrovert because if he were comfortable in his own head and with his own thoughts, he wouldn't need so much involvement with other people.

---

**CAUTION**

**Perilous Play** _____

It's an apparent paradox—while making assumptions and generalizing are often two of the worst possible mistakes, *failing* to do either can also be a huge error. It's all a matter of timing. When new to a game or player, you ignore often-true assumptions at your peril. After you have time to collect more accurate, specific data, continuing to rely on assumptions is foolish. Consider generalizations to be crutches that must be cast aside as soon as possible, lest you risk permanent damage.

---

If a speculative new investment comes along, the action guy is a decent candidate. Just think, he might be missing the next Microsoft! He likely talks more than he listens because by talking he's assured of being in on the action. As a listener he might get ignored. Name-dropping all the famous people you allegedly know will certainly keep you in the middle of the action, too.

Flashy clothes and flashy jewelry also call attention to oneself. What extrovert wants to be dull or drab? If he can afford it, a Lexus or BMW sure makes a lot more sense than a Honda. His job is probably people-oriented, at least if he's been in the workforce long enough to find something he's happy with.

All of these clues may help you more than an hour or two of observations. The cards he's catching may be overpowering his natural tendencies.

After all, if you deal the world's tightest player big pocket pairs six times each round, he's going to look loose, especially if coordinated boards show up that convince him that his pocket pair isn't any good (as a tight player in that situation, he'll fold after the flop so you won't get to see that he started with a great hand).

You can also learn something about an opponent by the way he handles his chips. If they are all stacked in neat piles of 20 (the number that fit in one rack row), that's a "tight" clue (even stronger if the stacks themselves are arranged neatly and/or geometrically, like in a triangle). Tightness and orderliness go hand-in-hand.

Neat 20-chip stacking is a particularly useful sign because it makes it so easy for a player to count how much he has won or lost. Generally, it's the tight players who always want to know exactly how much they're ahead or behind.

### The Inside Straight

The manner in which a player stacks his chips isn't the only way he handles them. Shuffling chips (using one hand to turn two stacks into one) is a common trick. Players perform such tricks to intimidate opponents ("Oh, look at that, he must be very experienced"). It's possible your opponent is experienced, but he might also be a former cashier or dealer. Getting intimidated rarely helps, unless it scares you out of a game you don't belong in. Don't let chip tricks frighten you.

If, on the other hand, your opponent leaves his chips strewn about in a haphazard fashion, it's more likely he's a loose player.

Sometimes the verbal clues your opponents offer don't match up with what you observe them do. They may talk about how tight they play but act like loose players. Life lessons apply well to most forms of poker. Actions speak louder than words. It's fairly easy for someone to try to delude you about his style through a planned speech. Exhibiting a consistent pattern of false actions is much tougher.

How much of this information is available to you at a poker table? In a home game assembled by friends, you should have quite a few clues available. You know your friends' jobs, social habits, and cars, and you may be able to adjust your play to the individual the very first time you sit down against him. In a cardroom, you probably wouldn't know that much when you first sit down, but if you can get the other fellow talking, you'll soon learn quite a bit about most people's favorite subject: themselves.

You can certainly check out clothing and jewelry in a cardroom, but be careful about drawing absolute conclusions. A shabbily dressed man might have just come from helping a friend build a carport for his Jaguar; a well-dressed man might have to wear a suit to work, but hates it, and might have stopped off to play right after work. Even an expensive suit doesn't prove a thing. The player might have used most of his available cash to buy it as an interviewing suit.

You certainly can't draw any absolute conclusions about likely style of play from someone's actual wealth, let alone his apparent wealth. A person short on cash might play tight, knowing that he can't afford to indulge his desire to gamble; it's almost as likely that he'll play loose, figuring that his only chance to dig himself out of the hole is to take changes.

Similarly, many wealthy people get that way by watching the expense bottom line. Someone who attributes his success to that style will probably play tight. Someone who got wealthy as a risk-taking entrepreneur will probably play differently. *Actual data trumps generalizations every time!*

Information you know, or collect, about an individual's personality traits may help you label him as "likely tight" or "likely loose," but this information is only a tool. If you collect actual data based on poker play, that's a much more useful guide to your opponent's likely future play than what kind of wristwatch he wears.

Finally, note that someone who loves to gamble in other arenas probably likes to gamble in poker, too. If you hear someone talking about his sports and/or horse bets, or casino action, it's a fair guess that he likes to gamble in poker, too. That almost certainly means a loose style. People who love getting money into action in near-certain loss pit games aren't candidates for ultraconservative poker play.

## Tight Players

Tight players don't get involved in a lot of pots. They don't need to be in action all the time. They're willing to wait for strong hands. They might use the time in between hands to study their opponents, or they might use it to watch television. Learning which tight players fall into which of those two groups can be very helpful. The guy who has been watching TV won't be making many plays based on recent table trends.

What kind of personality traits would lead to tight play? You can, of course, invert most of the characteristics previously for loose players and have a good tight play hint, so I won't go through all those again. Still, there are a few special traits worth mentioning (and yes, their opposites are usually good clues to looseness).

If someone is immaculately groomed and/or dressed, he's probably not going to be that sloppy about the way he plays poker. Someone who neither drinks too much nor smokes at all is probably a decent bet to be a tight player. Part of the drinking equation is obvious. There aren't too many drunks who play conservative waiting games. Even one or two cocktails offers a clue, though. Most serious players won't touch a drop of alcohol when playing. They don't want their judgment impaired.

> **Perilous Play** _____
>
> Make sure you observe your target actually *drinking* his beer, rather than *nursing* it. Many players like to create a false image as moderately drunk gamblers who don't notice or practice subtleties, when actually just the opposite is true. If you spot this, don't let the actor know you've blown his cover. Indeed, you might profit if you're a good enough actor yourself, from appearing to fall for it.

Just how carefully smoking, or the lack thereof, should be considered part of someone's poker personality profile is a bit controversial. On the one hand, it's an addictive behavior and someone who has one addiction is more likely than a randomly selected second person to have one or more other addictions. Gambling can certainly be an addiction and poker players who are also gambling addicts (a minority, certainly) will tend to be loose players.

What this does make clear is that if you learn someone had the willpower to *quit* smoking, you're more likely to have a tight player on your hands. It takes a lot more willpower to quit smoking than it does to fold Q-J in early position.

If you learn about other addictions—to drugs, food, shopping, you name it—then you're probably safer guessing you might be playing with a gambling addict. You may feel badly that he is a gambling addict, but your refusal to play with him isn't going to cure him. He's going to lose his money to someone and it might as well be you.

If you know you're playing with someone who can't resist getting into action, wait until you have something and make him pay. He won't stop just because you probably have the best of it.

If your conscience bothers you, consider donating a significant share to Gambler's Anonymous or other useful social service organizations. Unless you're a qualified therapist, you're out of your element trying to cure someone with a real problem. Fortunately, poker players are underrepresented among problem gamblers (video poker, an entirely different game, leads the way).

## The Least You Need to Know

- Because you are your own toughest opponent, a thorough understanding of your own skills, motivations, strengths, weaknesses, and fears is necessary to succeed.

- You must be honest with yourself to understand yourself.

- You can sabotage your efforts far more easily than any other opponent can.

- Certain personality traits offer clues about how your opponents will play.

# Chapter 27

# Put On Your "Reading" Glasses

## In This Chapter

♦ Looking behind the poker face

♦ Most players couldn't make it in Hollywood

♦ Giving yourself away through your body language

♦ "Reading" an opponent is part sixth sense and part analytical

♦ Giving opponents what they want—tells

Poker would be a fairly simple game if we could either read our opponents' minds or the backs of their cards. Fortunately for the spirit of fair competition (although perhaps unfortunately for our bankrolls), we have neither the mind-reading abilities of a *Star Trek* Betazoid nor the x-ray goggles that so many adolescents fantasize about. (Sometimes cheats can read the backs of cards, but that has been discussed elsewhere.)

Fortunately, the skilled player has multiple tools at his disposal that, while not perhaps quite as accurate as mind-reading skills, often come remarkably close. We'll examine some of those skills here.

# Poker Faces

Even people who have never played poker have heard of "the poker face." It's one of the many poker expressions that has worked its way into mainstream English. Someone who has a poker face is capable of hiding his emotions, be they at a poker table (when we hide delight holding four kings, or anger at missing our flush draw), or in a business negotiation when the other side's first offer exceeds what our side was willing to take as a final offer.

Rather than celebrating and immediately shaking hands, we frown and indicate they'll have to up their offer if they want to have a chance—an exercise not merely of a poker face, but of a bluff. Indeed, business negotiations so often resemble high stakes poker games that some players have started offering their services as negotiation consultants. Businesspeople want to extract every possible dollar from a negotiation, just as poker players want to extract every possible dollar from a pot.

Some people have natural poker faces. For reasons that probably go back to their childhoods, you can't tell when they are happy or sad, tired or energetic, nervous or calm.

Such a natural shield doesn't often help us socially—many people distrust those who don't let the world know what they are feeling—but it can certainly be a tremendous asset at the poker table, especially when our opponents stare us down.

Although sometimes called "the evil eye," there's nothing evil about a stare-down, of course. It just feels that way when you've pushed a significant bluff out there and your opponent sits and stares at you for a minute or two to see if you stop breathing.

### The Inside Straight

For the most part, a player faces no time limit in making his decisions and usually opponents are willing to give him several minutes if a decision is important and he hasn't often used lots of time. At any point, though, any player at the table may call for a clock, which gives the thinker one minute to make a decision. After the minute runs, the director (or floorman, in a money game) counts down 10 more seconds. If the player hasn't yet acted on his hand, it's dead.

For most people, the longer you have to hold your poker face when you're bluffing, the tougher it becomes. Mouths get dry, lips get dry, and breathing often becomes labored. Frequently players who suspect a bluff will stall with their medium-strength hands, knowing that they can beat a bluff but not a strong hand, and hoping that time pressure will cause a player's poker face to crack.

---

**Poker Lore**

Two-time World Champion Amarillo Slim Preston, for many years poker's most colorful character, had a favorite comment he'd like to drawl out when someone went into a long study after a big bet, although out of respect for his fellow combatants, he wouldn't say it until the hand was over.

"What was you a doin', a waitin' fer him ta faint?" Slim would ask.

The line invariably got a laugh, but Slim wasn't that far from the truth. The staller wasn't really expecting his opponent to faint, but he was hoping for some other giveaway sign almost as useful.

---

If you naturally have a great poker face, congratulations. It's a difficult thing to develop. People spend their entire lives developing personalities that are either expressive or not and it can be hard to change just when you become a poker player.

If you don't have a natural poker face, there are a few steps you can take. The first is, in effect, hide. The 2000 World Champion, Chris "Jesus" Ferguson, wears a heavy beard, mirrored sunglasses, and a trademark cowboy hat. The combined effect of all three leaves an observer almost nothing to look at. Chris doesn't always use both glasses and hat, but when he "gives it the full Ferguson," his opponents had better hope they can read his breathing or his betting patterns, because there isn't much left.

Few players employ "a full Ferguson," but baseball caps (and to a lesser extent, cowboy hats) and/or sunglasses are quite common. Sunglasses are extremely popular because "the eyes are the windows to the soul," and most people cannot control an involuntary dilation (widening) of the pupils when they see something they like. This has been proven by any number of scientific studies.

If you don't have a good poker face, you don't have to abandon hope of a quality poker career. At lower stakes, players rarely look for the clues offered by facial gestures or their absence, and if you can afford high stakes poker, you should be able to afford sunglasses!

# Grade B Actors

Although a great poker face is probably ideal, few of us can hope for perfection. Those of us who withhold information can give away misinformation. In essence, this is acting.

---

### Poker Lore

Recently I had a chance to interview Hollywood legend James Woods, who, while better known as an actor, is also a director and a promising poker player. I was curious how much he thought *real* acting ability helped his poker playing, but he came back with an unexpected reply.

"Acting helps, of course," Woods said, "but my directing helps more. When I sit in the director's chair, I'm studying the actor and asking myself 'Am I buying what he's selling? Is his performance credible?' That experience helps me more than any acting I might do at the table myself."

For the 99.99999% of us who can't act as well as Woods, but who have spent endless hours watching movies, that's probably a comforting analysis.

---

As any Hollywood casting director can tell you, there are a great many more people walking around who think they can act than there are those who actually *can* act. The casting directors are dealing with would-be professionals, not poker players who are trying to act as a kind of sideline.

For this reason, many professional poker players have a label they apply to the vast majority of people who try to give out disinformation: *Grade B actors.*

The "B" grade is probably rather generous, but comes from bad movies, which are often called "B" movies. Frankly, the few poker players who are good at giving out disinformation—false tells, apparent nervousness when calm, apparent calmness when terrified—should probably be wearing those t-shirts that say "I am a professional, do not try this at home." Most players are better off using a hat and sunglasses than trying to pretend they could have been Al Pacino if they'd focused on their acting skills earlier in life.

---

### Poker Lore

If you've heard a rumor that at least one reasonably well-known tournament player and author has been able to train his pupils to dilate on command, don't believe it. I mean, why would I, er, I mean he, want to be able to do something like that? Because it could convince someone to fold by creating the appearance of a good hand? Of course, it wouldn't be a useful skill if he couldn't do it in reverse, too, so he must be lying about it.

That's really a shame, because it sounds like a darned useful skill.

---

Curiously enough, there were a fair number of SAG (Screen Actors Guild) members who were poker players even before poker started becoming popular on TV. Actors spend a lot of time sitting around and waiting, and the successful ones often have a little extra cash floating about. Although a few really big-name actors have developed a taste for tournament poker recently (I'm tutoring one; we'll see how that comes out), none of the really big names has yet broken through as a legitimate star player, which should tell you a little about where the need for acting skills falls on the pecking order of important poker talents.

There are several professional poker players who are also actors, but as of this writing, none of them is in the $1 million (or higher) movie paycheck category.

## The Best Ways to Lie

If you're going to try your hand at acting during a poker game, try to follow the K.I.S.S. ("Keep It Simple, Stupid") method. The more complicated the lie, the tougher it is to pull off.

Although not world famous for either his lying or acting skills, the famous science fiction writer Robert Heinlein once had one of his most enduring characters explain the two best ways to lie:

> "The second best way to lie is to tell the truth, but not all of it," explained character Lazarus Long (*Methuselah's Children, Time Enough for Love*). "The best way to lie is to tell the truth, but in an unconvincing manner."

# Tells

You've heard tell of tells throughout this text, because they're so important. A thorough study of tells can and has taken more than an entire book, and I can't hope to cover it in depth here. Instead, let's look at a few of the more reliable ones— although be warned, the more reliable the tell, the harder good players have worked either to eliminate it, or to mimic it whenever they want to.

## The Trembling Hand

An oldie but still a goodie. Suppose you saw someone's hand tremble ever so slightly as he released his chips into the pot. You've caught a bluffer dead to rights, right?

Nope. In fact, this is one of the more reliable tells in the *other* direction. The tremble comes from a *release* of tension, because the bettor knows he's going to get paid off on his big hand.

It is most certainly true that good players have learned how to mimic this tell—doing so is far easier than learning how to control one's eye pupils. No "general" tell is 100 percent reliable. This is a pretty good one, though, especially when dealing with intermittent, intermediate-level players.

## I Am Strong Bet, Hear Me Roar!

Almost without exception the first act of deception any poker player tries in his life is the old "act strong when you're weak or weak when you're strong" play. If you've got a busted flush, you slam your chips into the pot like you've got a royal flush; if you've got four kings, you put your chips in the pot hesitantly, almost apologetically.

When you're new, every trick, even an elementary one like this, seems brilliant and crafty, and it doesn't hurt when the weak players in your early games fall for it.

What happens as you move up in class is that poker starts becoming a game of I know that you know that I know that you know that I know that you know that I know (got a headache yet?). Against more experienced players, you have to decide if:

♦ Strong means weak (first level thinking)

♦ Strong means strong (second level thinking)

♦ Strong means weak again (third level thinking)

♦ Strong means strong again (fourth level thinking)

… and so on, and so on. Many times, the play doesn't mean as much as how well you've set it up. How have you acted before with strong hands? Do you vary your play? Do you show an awareness of varying your play and of tells? Do you think they're paying attention? Do you think they think you think they're paying attention?

It really is enough to give you a headache, but it sure is fun when you're right.

## The Old "I Couldn't Care Less" Play

The action is moving around the table and your eyes are everywhere but the green felt. You appear to be watching the TV, the cute waitress or busboy, or maybe listening to the argument a couple tables away. Obviously you're not interested in what's going on at your table; if you do stay it, you'll be handicapped by a lack of knowledge about who did what.

In a pig's eye, you will, because actually you were exercising the same skills you practiced in high school when you spent every moment studying the girl or boy of your dreams but had to be sure she or he couldn't notice you were watching.

Sometimes not paying attention means paying very close attention surreptitiously and sometimes it means you're not paying attention. It's a good idea to spend some time carefully studying your opponents on hands in which you have absolutely no interest, because that way, if you study them later when you are interested, they don't know if you're sending another false signal or not. Perhaps more important, if you study someone and he doesn't realize you're studying him (yet another use for your sunglasses), you're more likely to pick up reliable information.

## Take a Deep Breath

Players who hold their breath for a while and then inhale deeply tend to have strong hands, rather than weak, but this is only a tendency; you have to know your man. Breath is easier to control than most other physical displays. Most of the time, a heaving chest means a big hand, but this is just too easy to fake or control to put much stock in without some history on your player.

Tells are a fascinating subject, but as knowledge of common tells becomes more common, it becomes less useful. The information remains valuable against relative novices, but isn't particularly valuable against more experienced players without empirical and player-specific research.

Televised poker is going to make it much easier to pick up tells on players, because we're all going to get to see faces and hole card simultaneously. I can tell you from first-hand experience that players are working on sending false tells to TV audiences. When I knew prospective opponents might be studying videotapes of me, I made quite sure I included some meaningless repetitive motions.

# Betting Patterns

Tells are physical clues. They seem glamorous and like real inside secrets, so players spend a lot of time looking for them. Every once in a while, that study pays off. Although world class players rarely display the more common tells, almost any action, sound, or motion (or the lack thereof) can be a tell if you use it in only certain situations.

World-class players tend to learn how to avoid them, but they still happen and when they do, players guard the secrets like gold. You don't even tell your friends. I have a tell on a very famous player and he has a very hard time with me, even though he's a better player in the abstract. I usually know when he has a strong hand, and so would rather see him at my table than someone with a tenth of his talent. If you have consistent trouble with someone, especially if he's someone you can't ever bluff successfully and/or can't get to "pay you off" when you have a big hand, there's a good chance he has a tell on you.

There is another class of clues that are easier to find and more reliable than tells: betting patterns. They're more reliable because they are based on logic and to avoid logic a player must make mistakes earlier in a hand.

As you gain experience, you'll learn more and more about how certain actions early in a hand tend to mean certain types of hands are more probable later in a hand. Many a hand has been won or lost because someone did or didn't keep track of how an opponent bet a hand throughout.

> ### Poker Lore
>
> I successfully "called" Chris "Jesus" Ferguson's cards on the final hand of the 2000 WSOP. I whispered to an onlooker that "Chris has A-9." (See page 327 of James McManus's best-selling *Positively Fifth Street*, the 2004 paperback edition, for confirmation), I didn't have a tell on Chris (sure wish I did: he's one of the most talented players on the planet); there was just a very narrow group of hands that made sense, given the betting patterns and the time he was taking to make the call.

Especially when you combine knowledge of exactly who raised when with how a player tends to play certain hands (is he a trapper, a check-raiser, an all-out aggressor with strong hands ...?), it becomes much easier to figure out whether that raise on the turn is a level one thinking "I'll wait until the turn to show strength, because that's where I can collect doubled bets," or a level two "by betting on the turn, it looks like I'm weak because I would have shown strength earlier."

You don't have to choose between learning about tells and learning about betting patterns, but if you did, learning about betting patterns would be much more profitable over the long run.

# As Ye Sow, So Shall Ye Reap

I've already discussed how people tend to project their own values onto others. You can take this a step further in the psychology of reading other players hands, and in how they read yours. If you're up against a level one "strong means weak" player, he will probably think you employ the same "clever" strategy.

To play poker at a strong level, you need to study yourself, your opponents, your opponents' view of you, and (if you still have any energy left) what you think your opponents think you think of them.

To do that, you need to study and remember everything that happens at the table. In online poker, this is fairly easy: Almost every site now has a note-taking feature that allows you to store useful notes like "Likes to overbet pre-flop with small pairs."

In conventional poker, while technically there are no rules against keeping notes at the table (there is a rule about paper and pen *on* the table, but technically you could keep a journal behind you and write in it between hands), you'll almost never see anyone do it. Even though the information is valuable, it puts your opponents on notice that you are playing seriously (which makes them play more seriously), and it practically begs them to try to create false tells. It just focuses your opponents too much, and in a macho crowd, it looks a little geeky, too.

With "in the moment" written notes only practical online, it's an excellent idea, unless you have an eidetic (photographic) memory, to write down B&M notes when a session is over so that you can keep a book on opponents for later.

---

### Poker Lore

Although he doesn't claim an eidetic memory, poker legend T.J. Cloutier knows the value of experience. "I might not remember everybody's name," Cloutier says, "but if I played with you five years ago, I remember exactly how you played." With more than 50 major tournament wins on his resumé, even if Cloutier is bluffing on this one, it isn't by much!

---

Do not forget to include in that book how you have played, because of the "we project our values onto others" concept. How you played tells others a bit about how you think they play, and if you know they have an impression of how you play, you can take advantage of that. It won't help as much as your record of what your opponents do because if they do something once, they'll probably do it again. Even if they intentionally try to vary their play, they will still probably tend to take a certain approach—slow playing big hands, for example—most of the time.

Remember what your opponents do and you'll know what they'll probably do in the future. Remember what you do, and if your opponents are paying attention, you'll know what they expect you to do in the future. That's not quite as good as being able to see your opponents' hole cards, but sometimes, it can come pretty close.

# A Final Note

The book isn't "over," because some very useful information appears in the appendices, but this is the last chapter, so I want to finish with my top tips for a beginning poker player. Some of these clearly spill over into the category of tips or guidelines for life. That's not strange. If you keep your eyes and mind open, poker can teach you much about life, and vice versa:

♦ Make sure you enjoy yourself … but don't forget that winning is usually more fun than losing!

♦ Unless you hate yourself or your money, stop playing the moment you realize you're on tilt.

♦ No single book or even single author can teach you everything you need to know; to my knowledge no single book even tries. Read a wide variety of books, and don't hesitate to question an author's opinion.

♦ Alternate your reading with playing experience. Too much of one without enough of the other will leave your education incomplete.

♦ Learn the odds. You can ignore them to go with a feeling if your feeling might be based on the subconscious assembly of data you can't explain or even see; if you ignore the odds just because you want to ignore the odds, you've started down a path that may be difficult to leave.

♦ Tournament poker and money poker require different skill sets to excel. The overwhelming majority of players eventually own skill sets that are better suited to one form than the other. Your emotional makeup is part of that skill set.

♦ There's an immense difference between experience and intelligence, or between education and ability. Don't assume that skill in poker (or the lack of it) proves anything about your ability to do anything else, at least not until or unless you've decided to spend years studying and practicing the game. A poker neophyte neurosurgeon who makes a weak play is not "an idiot," although someone who has spent his entire life playing poker and who calls that neurosurgeon an idiot might be one.

♦ Play your best and hardest against everyone, even your friends. Indeed, you should play your absolute hardest against your friends. Not only do ethics demand that in situations where third parties are involved, you're cheating your friend out of the chance for an honest triumph if you play soft. If you're in a home game where the social mores dictate otherwise, do what's expected, but realize you're not playing poker, no matter what they call the game.

♦ Don't believe anything you hear about cards you don't see.

♦ Even though bluffing and certain kinds of lies are expected, acceptable, integral parts of the game, play honestly, fairly, and with integrity at all times. Honor should be its own reward, but if it isn't, remember that dishonor has a way of sticking to your shoes for life—even if you change your shoes.

- Neither a borrower nor a lender be, and don't forget, stay out of debt.

- Don't expect too much or too little of yourself when you are starting out … and keep it that way for the rest of your poker career.

- Accept the fact that there is luck in poker; sometimes it will even run your way. Don't expect "justice" at a poker table.

- In most situations, your best play is to fold, your second best is to raise, and your worst is to call.

- Private lessons are usually not cost-effective for beginners or even intermediates: there's too much free or inexpensive information available to you. Private lessons are for the rich, the lazy, or for those who don't have enough time to play poker!

- If you play with money you can't afford to lose, you will.

- Focus on making correct decisions, rather than on your results; eventually the results will take care of themselves.

- Position, position, position.

- Life is one long session.

- If you get lucky and win a hand with a bad play or with weak starting cards, accept your winnings. Don't give them back by insisting on making the bad play again or playing the same weak starting cards again.

- Logic is the beginning of understanding, but not the end of it.

- If something keeps happening, it's probably happening for a reason, even if you can't figure out what the reason is. Don't swim against the current unless you have to.

- The true definition of cheating is much broader than most people think. If you think there's any possible way that someone who knew the true facts could interpret your actions as cheating, they probably were.

- Every once in a while, ask yourself if the time you're investing in learning or playing poker might not be better used elsewhere. That doesn't mean everyone should quit poker so they can save the whales. Poker is a lot of fun, and it's easy to get so caught up in it that you ignore activities that, or people who, deserve more of your time.

◆ Luck is the residue of design. Put another way, the harder you work, the luckier you'll be.

◆ If you study people, your poker will improve, and so will many other aspects of your life.

◆ To thine own self be true.

Thanks for listening. I hope that this book has helped, and that you return to it for second helpings after you've taken some of its advice out for a test drive. Space considerations have occasionally limited what I wanted to write about certain topics, but there are more books and articles on the way. For the nonce, may the Force—and the flop—be with you.

## The Least You Need to Know

◆ Most of us can't act as well as we think we can.

◆ "Classic" tells are useful mainly against beginners.

◆ Even world-class players can inadvertently give away information, if you pay close attention.

◆ Analyzing betting patterns logically can provide information just as valuable as tells.

◆ Keeping notes on player tendencies can help tremendously when you face someone a second time.

◆ Review this book, especially my "top tips," periodically.

# Appendix A

# Poker Books

Given the huge impact that the Internet and television have had on poker, there can be little argument that from an educational point of view, the single greatest change in the game of poker over the last 30 years is the quality of poker literature, more specifically, poker books.

Before Doyle Brunson and his team of all-star contributors created *Super/System* in 1978, most poker books were aimed at beginners and gave away little in the way of "secrets" or advanced advice. Before *Super/System*, if you wanted to become an advanced player, you acquired your poker education the old fashioned way: by playing (and in all likelihood losing for a substantial period of time) against superior players. The only shortcuts that were available were those players who were willing to mentor or teach friends or paid students. Top players would exchange information on an informal quid pro quo basis, but the route for beginners into poker's higher levels was usually long, difficult, and costly.

*Super/System* changed all that, and for a while, many of Brunson's contemporaries were not happy that he'd written the book. Too many people now had too much easy access to information the existing professionals had acquired at great expense.

Eventually, most of the pros came around. Just because something is written in a book doesn't mean just anyone can apply it and the book encouraged many new players to try the game.

Since then, a great many poker books have been written, some excellent, some good, some mediocre, and some downright awful. It's our tendency to assume that if something is printed in book form, it must be valuable and/or correct, but that isn't necessarily the case with poker books—in some cases because their editors/publishers had no easy way to verify the author's theories, and in some cases because the books were self-published (don't automatically damn self-published books: There are some terrific ones out there).

This appendix teaches you a few things about poker books, as well as giving some recommendations.

# Penny-Wise and Pound Foolish

I've never ceased to be amazed how otherwise bright individuals could regularly risk sums as small as $30 a week, let alone participate in games where ten, a hundred, or even a thousand times that much was regularly at risk, and yet be unwilling to invest $10 to $50 on a poker book. The majority of poker players can recoup in *one pot* the cost of any poker book and quite a few players participate in games where they can recoup the cost of *an entire poker library* in one pot, let alone one session.

> **The Inside Straight**
>
> Good poker books are the smartest investment a regular player can make. Even if you're a social player, it's more fun to win than to lose. What's more, many of the lessons you'll learn in a good poker book will carry over to other areas of your life.

As someone who depends on poker for part of his living, I'm delighted by this extraordinary example of "penny-wise, pound-foolish" living. As a teacher (and, I freely admit, as an author), I'm stunned.

I've heard people with six-figure incomes who regularly play in games where an average, nothing to write home about win or loss was $500 say "I'll buy so-and-so's book; it costs $19.95. But I won't pay $35 for Joe Blow's book. That price is outrageous!"

Of such thinking are golden poker opponents created. If you're going to play once a week in a friendly $1-2 game, buying one good beginner's book and stopping there isn't unreasonable (although it's probably still a mistake).

If you're going to play $5-10 or higher on a regular basis, you should probably buy every recommended poker book in existence. It's pretty hard for just one good idea in a book to fail to pay for the book all by itself, but fear not, many of your opponents will "wisely" save money on poker books, thus giving them both the capital and the lack of ability necessary to hand their money over to you.

# The Best Poker Books

Different players have different needs. A beginner needs a different book than an experienced player does, and someone who wants to learn hold'em doesn't need a book that focuses on five-card draw.

As a result, I am including recommendations across a wide range of areas of need and interest, and, where appropriate, including reviews.

If a book isn't on my recommended list, there's a pretty reasonable chance that it's missing for a reason. Please don't assume that exclusion means I think a book is worthless. I've read widely, but I haven't read every poker book in existence, and it's possible that I missed some good ones. Also, new poker books are coming onto the market all the time, and a "missing" book may have been published after this book was written. Check out continual updates of this list at my web site at AndyGlazer. com. The first time I ever wrote a comprehensive evaluation of poker books, I used four categories: Awesome/Must Read, Excellent, Good, and Mixed. I omitted a fifth but tempting category, "Avoid." This time around, there are just so many good books now available that I have dropped the "Mixed" books from my ratings.

In the sections that follow, I group books together in the remaining three categories, to avoid picayune debates about whether one book in the "Excellent" category should be #2 or #3:

Category I:     Awesome/Must Read

Category II:     Excellent

Category III:     Good

# General Books

The following books are not necessarily focused on one particular brand of poker:

### Awesome/Must Read

*The Theory of Poker*, by David Sklansky, Two Plus Two Publishing LLC; 3rd edition (July 1999). Sklansky is one of poker's top theorists. Although he's not a feared tournament player, his books are a reference for any player who is learning the game, and The *Theory of Poker* is his best work, because it describes many fundamental poker principles. One caveat: If you are a beginner, you will probably find the book a bit difficult to follow in places. Also (might as well get it all out of the way at once), Sklansky is, by his own admission (see page nine of

*Hold'em Poker for Advanced Players*) not a "professional writer." He writes great poker books, virtual must-reads that will teach you a lot, but he won't dazzle you with his prose. So what? If you're feeling empty afterwards, read some Shakespeare.

*Super/System*, by Doyle Brunson, Cardoza Publishing (1979). When it was written in 1978, *Super/System* was certainly the greatest poker book ever written. *Super/System* is still a must-read, even though some of the information is now out of date. Brunson is one of few players who has achieved true greatness both as a money player and a tournament player; usually, someone who is "great" in one arena is only "good" in the other. His style is entertaining, he taps several other poker greats to contribute chapters, and the book covers most of the more popular poker games. Beginners will probably find the book a bit tough to follow, but it's worth the work. By the time you read this, a revised edition will probably be on the market, and I will be standing in line to get a copy, I assure you.

*The Body Language of Poker*, by Mike Caro (2003 Edition), Simon & Schuster; (March 15, 2003). Caro, poker's self-styled "Mad Genius," broke new ground with this book. I recommend it strongly, but with one important caveat: Don't take every word as gospel. Caro often reduces information about tells to percentages that are far too precise for my liking. Perhaps even more important, the book's mere existence has made some of the information less reliable, because good players have read it and taken steps to avoid giving away information in the manner Caro describes! Generally, the higher up the poker ladder you go, the less useful the book will be, but you ignore this book at your peril.

## Excellent

*The Psychology of Poker*, by Alan Schoonmaker, Ph.D., Two Plus Two Publishing LLC; 1st edition (May 2000). Although many readers claim they feel this book is more useful for beginners than for experienced players, I disagree and consider it a vital part of any poker player's arsenal. Although this becomes truer as the stakes grow larger, at virtually any level, poker is a people game that happens to be played with cards, rather than a card game played by people.

*Inside the Poker Mind: Essays on Hold 'em and General Poker Concepts*, by John Feeney, Ph.D., Two Plus Two Publishing LLC; 1st edition (May 2000). I've heard some people call this "The advanced player's version of *The Psychology of Poker*," but the books are quite different and there was so much information on hold'em in here, I was tempted to list it among the hold'em books. Nonetheless, it's an important work, although a bit rough going if you're a true beginner.

*The Art of War*, by Sun Tzu, Dover Pubns.; (November 13, 2002). Not a poker book at all, but poker is warfare, at least once you get beyond the friendly kitchen game for matchsticks, and anyone who doesn't realize that will be a losing player. You'll need to be a bit of a philosopher to translate the lessons into poker applications. Save this one until after you have read the technical books and played a lot of poker, but then read it to take your game to another level. If it sounds familiar, actor Michael Douglas mentioned it in the movie *Wall Street*, while playing Gordon Gecko. The Gecko character wasn't a good guy and his immorality eventually did him in, but he was one tough competitor.

*Poker Essays, Volumes I, II, and III and Gambling Theory*, by Mason Malmuth, Academic Press; Revised edition (March 10, 1995). Like his frequent writing partner Sklansky, Malmuth is better known as a theorist than as a successful tournament or high-limit player, and as I've said about Sklansky, that shouldn't even slow you down from eagerly devouring his essays. It's inconceivable to me that Malmuth could write a bad poker book. My only reservation about his work is that he tends to talk too much in absolutes for my liking. Malmuth's opinions are very useful and usually right, but many times he makes statements that are opinions with such confidence that he makes it seem as if they were facts. Malmuth's work is really meant for advanced players. It's not the kind of book I could write: I don't have his mathematical background. Nonetheless, once you have progressed to a certain point in your general poker studies, it's worth a look, even if occasionally you will have to decide whether you want to skip over an equation or risk a headache.

*Zen and the Art of Poker*, by Larry Phillips, Publisher: Plume; (November 1999). Probably a surprise entry for those familiar with the more famous poker books, but in poker, as in so many other parts of life, mastering and understanding yourself is something you have to do before you can hope to conquer others. A large percentage of poker players play very well when things are going their way, only to fall apart when trouble arrives.

### Good

*The Tao of Poker*, by Larry W. Phillips, Publisher: Adams Media Corporation; (March 2003). "Wayno," as his friends call him, is starting to annoy at least one of those friends, taking all the good book titles and then stuffing good books inside the covers before I can either take the title or write the book. If you believe your most dangerous foe is yourself—and you should—you should also be reading Larry's latest. Wayno's books don't review many hands, but they do help you philosophically and they are consistent. Don't get them confused, though. That was Zen, and this is Tao.

*Improve Your Poker*, by Bob Ciaffone, Bob Ciaffone; (October 1997). A lot of excellent advice for both the beginning and experienced player, from a respected teacher and player. A surprisingly small number of poker authors can regularly beat the bigger side games, but "The Coach" is one of them.

*Casino Gambling the Smart Way*, by Andrew N.S. Glazer, Career Press; (March 1999). Okay, so I'm more than a little biased … and let me make one thing clear, *Smart Way* isn't a poker book; rather, it's a philosophical guide to casino gambling that tries to get you to look at your motivations for gambling, and then, once you've established those motivations, helps you figure out the best way to accommodate them. I'm comfortable listing it here because most of the lessons that I try to teach people about psychology in conventional gaming apply to the emotional and psychological aspects of poker. And if you go get your copy at casinoselfdefense.com or AndyGlazer.com, it will come autographed.

*Caro's Fundamental Secrets of Winning Poker*, by Mike Caro, Simon & Schuster; 3rd edition (November 19, 2002) and *Poker at the Millennium*, by Mike Caro and Mike Cappelletti, Mike Caro University; (2003). *Fundamental Secrets* is more of a booklet than a book, and *Millennium* is a potpourri of Caro hold'em thoughts and Cappelletti Omaha thoughts. Basically, if Caro writes it, you have to buy it.

*Sklansky on Poker*, by David Sklansky, Two Plus Two Publishing LLC; 2nd edition (January 1994). Like just about everything Sklansky writes, this book has value, but I think a more accurate title would have been "Half a book on matters I've already written about elsewhere and half a book on Razz." It certainly doesn't hurt to re-read Sklansky, but if you've read his other books, the only reason you should buy this one is if you want to learn Razz. The only people who want to learn Razz are high stakes players who sometimes play it by itself, but much more commonly play it as part of the rotation games (like H.O.R.S.E.) that become popular at high stakes, or in tournaments. If you ever want to be part of the high stakes crowd, you'll save yourself a lot of money by learning some of the finer points of Razz, which is deceptively simple.

*Play Poker Like the Pros*, by Phil Hellmuth, Jr, HarperResource; 1st edition (May 6, 2003). When a guy is one of your best friends and you wrote the book's introduction, no one believes a great review anyway. So, I'll list it in the Good category instead of the Great—which I was tempted to do anyway, just for the title, because although this book does a lot of things well, teaching you how to play like the pros isn't one of them. It teaches beginners and intermediates how to play better, but not at a pro level. It isn't aimed at advanced players: although they should read it, if for no other reason than insights they might get into Hellmuth (you need every edge you can get, especially if you find him staring across a tournament table at you), the book is really much more of a beginner-intermediate text.

# Books for Beginners

If you've been playing poker for a few years, you will probably find the books in this section a waste of your time. If you've just begun, not only will you find these books much easier to read than those listed in the first section, you will probably find them necessary to get to the more advanced books—unless, of course, you prefer to learn how to play by losing money to your opponents:

### Awesome/Must Read

*The Education of a Poker Player*, by Herbert O. Yardley, Simon & Schuster (Paper); (December 1970). Another oldie but goodie—enough of a goodie to still be in print, despite a 1957 original publication date. It helped launch me and probably a few hundred thousand other players. Come to think of it, a few hundred thousand might be a low estimate.

### Excellent

*The Official Dictionary of Poker*, by Michael Wiesenberg, MGI/Mike Caro University; (March 1, 2000). This book is just what it says: a dictionary. For that reason, it certainly should not be the first poker book you buy if you're only buying one. But, if you're getting started, the terminology you run into in many books and magazine articles can be baffling, so I would highly recommend this book if you are getting several others.

### Good

*Thursday Night Poker*, by Peter O. Steiner, Random House; (January 30, 1996). Most of the better poker books around focus on casino or cardroom poker, but that's not how most players start: They begin in home games and home games are a very different animal. Steiner's book helps the home game player more than most, but his lessons are useful to the cardroom player, too.

*Fundamentals of Poker*, by Mason Malmuth and Lynne Loomis Two Plus Two Publishing LLC; 3rd edition (January 2000). A very short, pocket-sized, non-intimidating book that does a good job of preparing the novice for his or her first poker efforts.

# Books About Specific Poker Games

This section outlines books that cover specific poker games.

## Hold'em

**Awesome/Must Read**

*Hold 'em Poker for Advanced Players (21st Century Edition)*, by David Sklansky and Mason Malmuth, Two Plus Two Publishing LLC; 3rd edition (October 1999). There's no disputing this work as one of the fundamental building blocks for taking your hold 'em game to the next level. Even though some players believe that the theories in this book have become so integrated into modern play that going against the text advice will produce more profits, I think you have to learn how to play by the rules before you start messing around with breaking the rules.

*Middle Limit Hold'em Poker*, by Bob Ciaffone and Jim Brier, Bob Ciaffone; (January 2002). One of the very best poker books around. Anyone who plays middle-limit hold'em ($10-20 through $40-80) would have to be extraordinarily foolish to know about this book and not read it. It provides terrific specific examples and analysis. I was so impressed by explanations of questions I "missed" that I stopped playing limit hold'em for a few months while I reassembled my game.

*Winning Low Limit Hold'em*, by Lee Jones, Conjelco; 2nd edition (November 16, 2000). Although the name implies that the advice will help only in low limit games, many players have found extremely loose and wild games at higher limits (especially in California and home games) where the advice in this text will be invaluable. I think it's an awesome "partner" to the HFAP (above), because between the two books, you will get good advice about the two main kinds of games you're likely to run into: tight and loose.

*Championship No-Limit and Pot Limit Hold 'em*, by T. J. Cloutier and Tom McEvoy, Cardsmith Pub.; (1997). Cloutier is a poker tournament legend and 1983 WSOP Champ McEvoy isn't far behind. If you're thinking about moving up into poker's big leagues, this is a must-read. It focuses more on tournaments than it does on live game play, but for Americans who (unlike their European counterparts) rarely find live pot-limit or no-limit games and who must learn via tournament play only, that's probably not such a bad thing. A new edition will be out by the time you read this.

**Excellent**

*Pot-Limit and No-Limit Poker*, by Bob Ciaffone and Stewart Rubin, Bob Ciaffone; 2nd edition (March 1999). A nice companion book to the Cloutier text because it doesn't focus as much on tournaments and gives one more tips on live play. I still think the ultimate text on how to play live (money, as opposed to tournament) pot-limit poker book has yet to be written, mostly because the people who really know how to win in live pot-limit games are making far too much money playing to give away their secrets.

**Good**

*Real Poker: The Cooke Collection*, by Roy Cooke, MGI/Mike Caro University; (October 1, 1999) and *Real Poker II: The Play of Hands*, by Roy Cooke, Mike Caro University; (2001). A long time Card Player columnist compiles some of his better columns in each book: As the names imply, it's really a "best of" collection of independent articles, rather than a book that moves from a beginning to an end. Cooke doesn't write solely about hold'em, but close enough to put the books in the hold'em category. He got a "good" rather than an "excellent" because even though his columns are excellent, one is often much like another. I'd like to see him stretch into some other areas. Some of the "good" books here were borderline inclusions; these two weren't.

*Hold 'em Excellence, and More Hold 'em Excellence*, by Lou Krieger, Conjelco; 2nd edition (September 8, 2000). Krieger, a mid-limit Southern California player, provides a lot of useful information for the intermediate player in an easy to digest, short-chapter style.

*Championship Hold'em*, by T. J. Cloutier and Tom McEvoy, Cardsmith Publishing; (April 2000). The first edition of this book was not the best work these two had ever produced. Happily, they realized that and in January 2002 they produced a revised edition that was more in keeping with their outstanding reputations.

*Hold 'em Poker*, by David Sklansky, Two Plus Two Publishing LLC; (December 1996). Hold 'em is certainly the poker game in casinos and cardrooms, and Sklansky gets novices off to a good start here. Advanced players will find this work a bit too mechanical and incomplete, but Sklansky makes it quite clear he didn't intend this book for advanced players: You've already seen that work in the "Must Read" list.

*Get the Edge at Low-Limit Texas Hold'em*, by Bill Burton, Bonus Books; (January 2003). Definitely a beginner's book, but well written and user-friendly. Not a bad way to get started with the game.

# Seven-Card Stud

### Awesome/Must Read

*Seven-Card Stud for Advanced Players* (21st Century Edition), by David Sklansky, Mason Malmuth, and Ray Zee, Two Plus Two Publishing LLC; 4th edition (October 1999). The name says it all and you've already seen all three authors' names on this list. One caveat: The book is really designed for those playing at mid-limits, such as $20-$40. A lot of the concepts don't work very well at lower "no fold 'em" limits, or in very high limit games. I have a lot of respect for Sklansky and Malmuth, and when you add Ray Zee (who has won a lot of money playing poker) to the team, you get a very good book.

*High-Low Split Poker for Advanced Players*, by Ray Zee, Two Plus Two Publishing LLC; 2nd edition (August 1994). High-low is a very different animal from straight high poker and this book, which is actually two books in one, with separate sections for seven-card stud and Omaha), does a great job of explaining just how different.

### Excellent

*Championship Stud Poker*, by Max Stern, Tom McEvoy, and Linda Johnson, Cardsmith Pub.; (January 1998). A useful guide for both mid-limits and tournament play, especially because the authors don't hesitate to disagree with one another. I'm very fond of the book for that reason: Too many poker authors write as if their recommended plays are the gospel that no sane person should dare challenge. Stern, McEvoy, and Johnson freely admit that there's more than one road to success.

### Good

*7-Card Stud*, by Roy West, Poker Plus Publications; (April 1996). West is a solid writer who aims his text squarely at low and mid-limit games, and I like his "lesson plan" approach. This book is well worth a look.

*Winning 7-Card Stud: Transforming Home Poker Chumps into Casino Killers*, by Ashley Adams, Lyle Stuart Hardcover; (November 2003). This book is definitely for beginners and intermediates, rather than advanced players, and worth a look.

# Omaha

### Awesome/Must Read

*Championship Omaha*, by T. J. Cloutier and Tom McEvoy, Poke & Plus Pubns.; (March 1999). It earned me 23 times the cover price the first time I played after I read it. 'Nuff said.

### Excellent

*Winning Omaha/8 Poker*, by Mark Tenner and Lou Krieger, Conjelco; (December 2003). An intriguing team: Tenner is a successful medium to high stakes side game player who hasn't written much, and Krieger is a lower stakes hold'em player who has written a lot. This means the book had a chance to be awesome or terrible. I'm settling on excellent.

### Good

*Cappelletti On Omaha*, by Mike Cappelletti. Mike's 1989 edition is a self-published book about high Omaha that is no longer in print, but it's worth hunting down. Cappelletti is more respected as a theorist than he is feared as a player, but if someone has to be stronger in one category than the other, that's the split you want when buying a book! Mike's point-count approach is a bit technical for my liking, but Omaha is certainly the most technical form of poker, and if a little math doesn't bother you, you might love it.

*How to Win at Omaha High-Low Poker*, by Mike Cappelletti, Cardoza Pub.; (December 23, 2003). This Cardoza book is in print (2003), and it's less technical and more anecdotal than his earlier book on high Omaha.

*Omaha Hi-Lo Poker, How to Win at the Lower Limits*, by Shane Smith, Poker Plus Publications; 1999 Edition (1999). A spiral-bound 1999 revision of an older text, it's user-friendly and is quite helpful for beginners. If you can already beat $6-12 games, you probably won't learn much new here, but most low-limit Omaha players don't beat any limit!

*Omaha Hold'em Poker: The Action Game*, by Bob Ciaffone, Bob Ciaffone; Reprint edition (June 1999). It's not a long book, but when Ciaffone speaks, I listen.

## Tournaments

### Awesome/Must Read

*Tournament Poker*, by Tom McEvoy, Cardsmith Pub. Unless you're some sort of natural poker savant, if you aspire to tournament success, you must read this book, beginning and end of story. Tournament play is very different from ring (money) play, and McEvoy does a fine job explaining how. This is very clearly numero uno when it comes to books on tournaments, and there were more than a few tournament pros who were not happy with McEvoy when he wrote it, feeling he gave away too many "secrets."

*Tournament Poker for Advanced Players*, by David Sklansky, Two Plus Two Publishing LLC; (April 2002). Because Sklansky is who he is, the book has quite literally changed the way many people play tournaments and the jury is still out on whether the change will be to their long-term benefit. For the moment, many "old school" tournament players are having trouble coping with the methods Sklansky disciples are employing, although many of them are misunderstanding Sklansky's message and taking his approach too far, to their detriment. You must read McEvoy's book to learn about playing tournaments. You should probably read Sklanksy's book for the same reason, but you must read it just to understand what all the Sklansky-ites are doing, and why some of them are doing it incorrectly. So far, none of them have shaved their heads and started chanting, but it might just be a matter of time.

### Excellent

*Championship Tournament Practice Hands*, by T. J. Cloutier and Tom McEvoy, Cardsmith Pub.; (April 2003). I'm not exactly sure why I need the book, since T. J. is at the final table of practically every tournament I see, so I get to watch what he thinks all the time anyway. For those of you who aren't tournament reporters and don't yet have a copy of *Tournament Poker with the Champions* (which is all of you, because it isn't out yet), open up your wallet, the way you're supposed to for all of T. J.'s books. Just try to avoid learning how to get horribly unlucky right at the end of major tournaments the way T. J. has been the last three or four years.

### Good

*Championship Satellite Strategy: How to Turn a Toothpick into a Lumberyard*, by Tom McEvoy and Brad Daughtry, Cardsmith Publishing; (October 2003). Two former world champs for the price of one. I've lately become more of a believer in the value of satellites for more than just cheap entry into bigger tournaments and these guys play a lot of satellites.

*Poker Tournament Tips from the Pros*, by Shane Smith, Cardoza Pub; (July 22, 2003). The book's cover is very honest: It says "Especially good advice for rookie tournament players," and that's exactly the group to whom I'd recommend it. I don't think there's much in here for the tournament veteran, but tournament strategy is very different from money game strategy. If you're thinking about trying out tournaments, this book is a very good place to start.

*Poker Tournament Tactics for Winners*, by D.R. Sherer, Poker Plus Publications; (November 1998). A pretty reasonable tournament primer, and when you're just getting started with tournaments, $24.95 is a lot better than $49.95.

*Poker Tournament Strategies*, by Sylvester Suzuki, Two Plus Two Publishing LLC; (April 1997). Like Buntjer's book and unlike the Smith or Sherer texts, Suzuki's book contains advice more useful to someone who has already played some tournaments than to a tournament rookie.

*The Championship Table: At the World Series of Poker (1970-2003)*, by Tom Mc-Evoy, Dana Smith, and Ralph Wheeler, Cardoza Pub.; (March 23, 2004). More of a trip down memory lane than an instructional text, but you'll learn a thing or three and it's worth it for the historical value alone.

# Anecdotal Books for All Players

Note: The following books aren't instructional texts, although occasionally you learn something about poker from reading them. They are good collections of poker stories that I think most poker players would like.

### Awesome/Must Read

*Telling Lies and Getting Paid*, by Michael Konik, The Lyons Press; 1st edition (December 1, 2002). Although the whole book isn't about poker, the title piece (it's a collection) is worth the price of admission by itself. If you like playing poker and you don't buy this book, you're making a mistake.

*Positively Fifth Street*, by James McManus, Picador USA; (March 1, 2004). I was there watching it happen; heck, I even helped it happen a little and McManus even got to immortalize my correct prediction of Chris Ferguson's exact hand on the final hand of the 2000 WSOP, when McManus came in fifth after coming into town to write a story and instead became part of it. There are a few minor technical errors that only a poker audience could possibly spot, but make no mistake, this book is a masterpiece. McManus neatly weaves his WSOP experience together with the Ted Binion murder trial and some courageous personal admissions. You're getting to read about sex, drugs, murder, and a first-person WSOP final table poker experience from a literary author all in the same book. I suppose you want your parking validated, too.

*Total Poker*, by David Spanier, Trafalgar Square; (March 2003). I'm sorry to say the poker world lost David Spanier in the year 2000, and it was a big loss. Spanier was a terrific writer, much more so than most of the poker-playing authors out there, and you should grab hold of this and all other Spanier books. Another nice one, published just about the time of his death, is *The Little Book of Poker*.

*Big Deal: One Year as a Professional Poker Player*, by Anthony Holden, Abacus; (October 2002). Holden, like McManus and Spanier, a writer first and a poker player second, does a great job of describing a good player's foray into the world of big-time poker. If you read it, you'll almost certainly get Big Tournament Fever and start playing a lot more poker. When you read *Poker Brat* (the book I'm working on with Phil Hellmuth, Jr., right now) sometime in 2006, your case of Big Tournament Fever will become critical.

*The Biggest Game in Town*, by A. Alvarez, Chronicle Books; (March 2002). Out of print at the moment, although you can probably find a copy in a poker-playing friend's library. Alvarez fits in with Holden and Spanier as a writer first and poker player second. If you like stories about Big Time Poker, you'll love this work, which many people consider the best book ever written about the World Series.

*The Man with the $100,000 Breasts (and other gambling stories)*, by Michael Konik, Huntington Press; (January 1999). Like *Telling Lies and Getting Paid*, this book isn't solely about poker, but I don't think you'd ever find any poker player anywhere who felt it wasn't a great read (except perhaps the players who read only menus). Konik is a great writer who is also a very good player. He lives in a house in Hollywood formerly owned by Ashton Kutscher (really). Unfortunately for Konik, a possibly better poker player lives in a house directly across the street from him, and that player has Kutscher's old hot tub. Unfortunately for Glazer, a possibly better writer lives in a house directly across the street from him, and Kutscher's old house is nicer than his old hot tub.

Rumors that Konik and Glazer have petitioned the City of Los Angeles to rename their street "The Oddly Overlapping Talent and Mutual Admiration Society Way" are totally unfounded.

*Bets, Bluffs, and Bad Beats*, by A. Alvarez, Chronicle Books; (June 2001). Really more of a "coffee table book" than most of the others here, but if you love reading about the game, you have to love that Alvarez wanders back into the field now and then.

*Amarillo Slim in a World of Fat People: The Memoirs of the Greatest Gambler Who Ever Lived*, by Amarillo Slim Preston with Greg Dinkin, HarperEntertainment; 1st edition (May 6, 2003). The title alone tells you something about Slim's talent for self-promotion. The book disappointed some people who had heard these tales and wanted more, but if you haven't heard these stories already, you'll want to.

*Poker Faces: A Girlhood Among Gamblers*, by Katy Lederer, Three Rivers Press; (August 24, 2004). On genetics alone, this book couldn't miss: Katy's dad is a noted author and grammarian, and her brother, Howard Lederer, and sister, Annie Duke, are both world-class players. If you thought your household was just a little different from the one most of your friends grew up in, you'll relate. Your household won't have been like this one, but you'll relate.

**Good**

*Poker Wisdom of a Champion* (Originally published as *According to Doyle*), by Doyle Brunson, Cardoza Pub.; (November 4, 2003). A very entertaining, and also informative, 2003 re-release of Brunson's 1984 collection of articles by one of poker's all-time great players and personalities.

*Tales Out of Tulsa*, by Bobby Baldwin, Gambling Times; (January 1, 1985). Baldwin, who was the youngest player ever to win the World Series of Poker until Phil Hellmuth broke his record, has proven that wisdom at the poker tables can translate into wisdom in the business world, having gone on to high-profile casino management success. A little wisdom here, a little humor there, and you'll be glad you picked it up.

# How to Use Poker Books

Assuming you actually do read your books, *the real key is to read actively, not passively*. If a hand is described, don't just nod your head and sagely agree that you'd have made the same decisions. Cover over the text to come and see if you can anticipate the next step or the right move, and if you didn't, read back through to see if you understand why you made the wrong choice.

Pause a lot as you read. I believe I'm a pretty decent teacher, thanks entirely to a teacher I had in the second, third, and fourth grades, who told her students "If you can't explain something to someone else, you don't really understand it." When you pause in your reading, think how you might try to explain the concepts you just read to someone else. If you can't do it without simply parroting the author's words, you probably have some re-reading to do.

Especially as you gain experience, don't assume everything an author writes must be correct. Challenge his assumptions. Most of the time, you'll probably decide he is correct, but you'll understand the subject much better for having tried to pull down your teacher's claims. When you can't find a hole in his logic, you probably understand his logic.

# When to Use Poker Books

Use poker books as early in your learning process as possible. You don't need to throw money away when learning, and you don't want to pick up habits you have to unlearn.

You should not, however, buy a collection of books and just bury yourself in your library for weeks without playing a hand. You'll learn best by reading and then trying to implement what you've read by going back and forth between your books and the tables.

Perhaps just as important, you shouldn't pass your poker books on to a friend when you've finished with them. Rereading poker books after a year or two is an excellent idea, at least with some texts. Once you have more practical experience under your belt, you may pick up subtle points that just blew right past you the first time you read a book. You also may find that quite by accident you have drifted away from a practice your book taught you to employ.

For example, you might have started playing starting hands in early position that you originally learned were only playable in late position. It may be fine for you to have made this shift, but you shouldn't do it unknowingly. Rereading your poker books may not only refresh lessons you've forgotten, but it may teach you some lessons you simply weren't ready to absorb on your first ... or second ... or third reading.

You probably won't have time to reread all your poker books, especially in an era when so many good ones seem to be coming out so quickly. You don't have to reread them all. You'll certainly have favorites, books that were clearly better than others, and it's easy to return to those.

You'll probably also have a few that just seemed too hard to understand when you first took a shot at them. If, when reading them now, the advice they offer seems perfectly reasonable and perhaps even obvious, you'll have concrete proof of the strides you've made, and anything that's good for your confidence is probably going to be good for your results, too.

# Internet Resources and Poker Software

## Internet Posting Forums: The Good, The Bad, and The Ugly

Online gambling discussion groups began with rec.gambling. That eventually spun off the poker discussion group rec.gambling.poker, widely known among participants simply as RGP. Participants are frequently called RGPers. RGP has always been an unmoderated discussion group and is discussed at some length in the main text, so I won't repeat myself here.

An unmoderated group has all the advantages you would expect to come along with freedom of speech and lack of censorship, and many of the expected disadvantages, too. There's a trade-off in access for the need to accept abusive and or irresponsible conduct.

### I Feel the Need ... The Need For Speed (Oops, Wrong Maverick)

RGP has been around a long time so I feel comfortable discussing it; I know it will still be around by the time this book hits the bookshelves and that it won't have changed much in character.

I discuss just two other posting forums here, and indeed just a few other Internet sites in general ...

When you go to AndyGlazer.com, you will find an updated list of valuable Internet resources for the poker community.

What follows is a brief list of sites that stand a reasonable chance of still being in operation when you read this book.

## Moderated Posting Forums

Probably the single most important poker forum of all can be found at twoplustwo. com, the website that is the home of David Sklansky and Mason Malmuth, poker's two most important theorists. It's also the home of Ray Zee, who I wish would write more books and articles, because his work is magnificent.

The site is more than a home to a serious moderated poker forum. You can buy great Twoplustwo books. Visit this forum when your self-confidence is strong so that you don't get upset by the writings of people who don't often have beginners in mind.

The forum is organized into several categories so you don't have to sift through hundreds of posts to find the few you want. The people who post there know what they're talking about, which can't be said about a lot of postings in forums.

The main downside is one shared by most posting forums: it's web-based, which means that if you don't have a fast connection, you'll go insane trying to follow a thread. A dial-up connection just won't cut it. You also have to be willing to live with occasional censorship and with decisions to take down threads which the site overseers deem as improper. Most of the time, these decisions aren't just appropriate, they're praiseworthy: Ads and personal attacks don't belong on an analytical posting forum. Every once in a while, the baby gets thrown out with the bathwater.

Keep in mind that there is a difference between opinions and facts. For the most part, though, most poker players would achieve much better results if they would follow The World According to S&M. I think that's where your poker education should start, although it should not end there.

The only other downside isn't really a downside so much as a set of features you can't use as a beginner. This is a *serious* poker forum. Beginners will be overwhelmed by much of the terminology they'll run into at the site and by many of the concepts the posters take for granted. Don't get frustrated.

Unitedpokerforum.com has Mike Caro and Roy Cooke, two great writers, behind it, and that's enough for me. The forum isn't as organized as Twoplustwo, but it feels more casual and relaxed and user-friendly. I suggest you visit both, and "lurk" (read without posting).

There are other forums, but these three should be enough to keep you busy for, at a rough guess, the next 42.042 years.

# Poker Information Sites

By the time I have finished typing this sentence, someone else will have started another poker information site. You can drown in the amount of poker information that's available on the Internet and drowning while working with electrical equipment is doubly painful.

Trying to keep things current is, as I've said, impractical without using the Internet itself, but some sites that should still be around and will likely be of use include (but are most definitely not limited to):

Cardplayer.com (Card Player Magazine's site)

Cardplayercruises.com (for nautical poker players)

Conjelco.com (lots of books and WSOP historical info)

FinalTablePoker.com (offers tournament reports and more)

Gamblersbook.com (lots more books)

Gambling-law-us.com (discusses gambling laws in many states)

Gamblingtimes.com/poker_player/ (Poker Player Newspaper site)

Liveactionpoker.com (a GenX potpourri)

Philhellmuth.com (guess really hard at the emphasis)

Pokerineurope.com (guess the emphasis)

Pokernetwork.com (Australian emphasis)

Pokerpages.com (an old potpourri)

Pokertop10.com (a new potpourri)

Worldpokertour.com (you'll never guess the emphasis)

As poker becomes more and more commercialized, some poker players' names are actually starting to acquire commercial value and so are their endorsements. Some websites have picked up on this and are playing a bit fast and loose, ethically, with who is supposedly "on their team" or "writing for them" or "endorsing them." Just because someone once wrote an article for a website or magazine (or let them reprint something written for someone else) doesn't mean he works there now, endorses them now, or indeed ever endorsed them in the first place.

## Lie Down with Dogs, Wake Up with Fleas

Going one despicable step further are the ever-increasing number of online magazines and/or newsletters that are just taking writers' work and stealing it by putting it on their site. When hit with complaints, they feign surprise and indicate they assume the writer would have been "pleased to get the exposure."

If you find out a site does this, do your best to ignore both them and their advertisers. Loose ethics in one area carry over to another. They may sell your name or private information, they may run worthless articles (one of the tricks designed to keep authors from finding out about stolen work is altering articles by rewriting a few lines or deleting titles and/or paragraphs; this practice sometimes ruins the article's point).

Their advertisers may or may not know what the rogue site is doing, but if you inform the advertiser the site's actions have cost the advertiser your business, the site will soon hear from someone with more clout than you or me.

Finally, I can't speak for the other writers, but anytime someone finds someone stealing some of *my* work, I offer the finder free lessons—or at least free answered questions—as a "thank you."

# Poker Newsletters

There are currently two printed poker publications: the slick-stock *Card Player Magazine* (where I am a tournament editor and a columnist), and the newspaper-format *Poker Player*, which is quite new and so has fewer known writers. If you live near a legal poker room, you can pick them up for free. If you don't, you can and should subscribe (information available at their websites).

As with book authors, the quality of the columnists is quite uneven, but you'll figure out who's good and who isn't, and who's writing about subjects that interest you and who isn't, pretty quickly. I have my favorites, but a lot of the columnists are my friends and the subsets "Andy's friends" and "the best columnists" aren't identical, so I'll just tell you my favorite *Card Player* writer whom I don't know: Rolf Slotboom. He's pretty new at the column writing game, but you wouldn't know it to read his work.

You can't always carry a laptop, so print magazines and newspapers will always have their place (remember all the people who thought TV would kill radio, yep, they were right about that one). There are, though, now e-periodicals available.

The biggest problem with poker newsletters is that while some of them contain useful poker information, others are virtually mere banner farms. There's a third group that are useful in limited ways: they're just "commercial" news, advising online players about current deals available at online cardrooms.

For four years I published a bi-weekly newsletter called *Wednesday Nite Poker*, but things change on the Internet and my old sponsor and I had a parting of the ways, albeit friendly enough. My newsletter should be back by the time you read this (under a different name, but using the same format). To find out where visit AndyGlazer. com. It's free.

Two of the sites mentioned previously, CardPlayer.com and PokerPages.com, also offer newsletters which are worth checking out. Beyond that, I'm not willing to speculate six months into the future. Check back at AndyGlazer.com.

# Poker Software

In the old days, truly industrious poker players would perform hours of mathematical calculations and spend many more hours dealing out hundreds of hands. You can now achieve all they did in about 12 minutes, using relatively inexpensive commercial software (and a lot of it using completely free software!). You can also perform hand comparisons, do other research, and test out what you think you've learned in books and articles in a few quick 10,000 practice-hand minutes.

The two commercial heavyweights are *Wilson* and *AceSpade*:

- **Wilson Software**'s Turbo series offers learning tools for hold'em (plus a tournament version), Omaha, Omaha/8, seven stud, stud/8. These programs play interactively within all betting structures, allow you to specify the skills of your opponents, offer advice on correct play, let you know when your play deviates from a specified strategy, and compare millions of hands and situations at high speed. Ordering information and free demos appear at www.wilsonsoftware.com.

- **AceSpade** offers learning tools (including tournament versions) within all betting structures for hold'em, Omaha, Omaha/8, seven stud, and stud/8. Crazy pineapple high and high-low also are also offered. Find them at www. acespade.com.

Wilson and AceSpade each offer quite a few different products and I would suggest trying one from each before ordering lots from either. It wouldn't be unreasonable to get and use everything from both of them, but you can probably get along with one or the other.

*Masque.com* still offers, as part of its "Deluxe Casino Pak," an inexpensive World Series of Poker simulation, but I always found it a little twitchy. At this point it's out of date compared to what Wilson and AceSpade offer. I mention it mainly because there is so little poker software available for the Mac and because it is so inexpensive.

Mike Caro's **Poker Probe** was a valuable groundbreaking tool, but therein lies the main problem. It was written for DOS (remember DOS?) and is still not available in a Windows version, which makes it inaccessible for the overwhelming majority of users.

If you still know how to use DOS, you can use Poker Probe to compare millions of poker hands in many different games (deuce-to-seven, ace-to-five with and without joker, seven stud high and high-low, draw high and high-low with and without joker, hold'em and high-low, Omaha high and high-low).

Poker Probe is not a game, but an analysis tool that you can use to compare specific hands against each other, or hands against random hands, in simulations that would take hundreds years of actual play to encounter. Find information at www.caro.com.

Check that site out even if the word "DOS" still sends shivers down your spine, because it will send you into the world of Poker's Mad Genius, Mike Caro, where you will be able to order *Everything You Ever Wanted to Know About Poker, But Were Afraid to Ask (for)*. Mike has written a lot and you should buy everything he sells, unless he starts selling used cars.

Finally, the Program for the Rest of Us …

Steve Brecher's **Hold'em Showdown** is one very handy little freeware program. It's astoundingly simple and lets you quickly examine the odds of any number of hold'em hands winning or tying, either before the flop, on the flop, or on the turn. Just go to www.brecware.com and download it. You'll figure out how to use it in about 45 seconds and it's a great learning tool if you're not sure about the equities in certain frequently encountered situations.

Play around with it for just a little while and before long you'll understand why that horrible beat you took wasn't actually so unlikely, and better still, you'll learn things that will make pot odds decisions a snap.

The really unbelievable part? There's a *Mac* version. That, aside from its marvelous usefulness, ease of use, and absolutely free status (*freeware* doesn't even carry the "moral" obligation to send some money in if you use it the way *shareware* does), makes it the program for the rest of us.

# Appendix C

# Glossary

**ace-to-five lowball**   *Lowball* in which the lowest hand is 5-4-3-2-A (*wheel*), with suits having no bearing.

**active players**   Those who have stayed in through the current betting round.

**ahead**   (1) In the position of acting before another player; that is, sitting to his right. However, if no one in between enters the pot, it may be so far to his right that it looks like he's on his left. (2) Leading a hand before the final card or cards have been dealt.

**all-in**   Putting all of your chips into play. Sometimes called *going all-in* or *moving all-in*, when done offensively, or *calling all-in*, when done defensively.

**anaconda**   *See* pass the trash.

**ante**   One or more chips put into each pot by each player before the cards are dealt. An ante is not part of a player's next bet, as opposed to a *blind*, which usually is.

**around-the-corner straight**   A nonstandard, private game poker hand: five cards in a series in which the sequence of cards is considered to continue from king through ace, for example, J-Q-K-A-2

**B&M game**   Brick & Mortar game.

**backdoor hand**   A hand made in hold'em or Omaha by catching two perfect consecutive cards on the final two cards. With a backdoor flush, for example, a player starts with two spades and only one comes on the flop. The other two come as the last two cards, on the *turn* and the *river*; catching two perfect consecutive cards is also called catching *runner-runner*. Also used as a verb, to *backdoor* a flush.

**back in**   (1) Win part or all of a pot or tournament by accident, perhaps because an opponent misplayed, fouled, or misdeclared his hand. (2) To take all or part of a pot in a declare game with an inferior hand because a two-way declarer failed to win both ways. For example, in a three way declare, one player declares high with a full house, one player declares both ways with a wheel, and one player declares low with a 6-4-3-2-A. If *backing in* is allowed, the pot is split between the players holding the full house and the 6-4; if it isn't, the player with the full house wins the whole pot.

**bad beat**   An unlikely defeat, often but not always suffered at the last moment (final card or penultimate card). For example, a hold'em player who starts with A-A and loses to K-K (or worse yet, A-K) has suffered a bad beat and the beat is even worse if it comes via the last card because the trailer was almost out of chances. For an example of a really bad beat, imagine you start with Q-Q against A-7, and the flop comes Q-8-8. Now all the money goes in and you can't lose, right? Now look what happens if the turn and river are both eights. 8-8-8-8-A beats 8-8-8-8-Q.

**bad beat story**   Any poker player's tale of his unlucky defeat. It is one of poker's near universal truths that almost everyone tells his own bad beat stories but doesn't want to listen to anyone else's.

**banker**   In a private game, the player who sells and buys the chips.

**behind**   (1) In the position of acting after another player; that is, sitting to his left. However, if no one in between enters the pot, it may be so far to his right that it looks like he's on his right. (2) Trailing in a hand before the final card or cards has/have been dealt.

**bet after the declare**   Have an extra round of betting in a *declaration game*. This rule offers a huge advantage to any player who is the only one who has declared in his direction.

**bet-declare-bet**   Bet after the declare.

**big bet game**   Usually *pot-limit* or *no-limit*, although sometimes used to refer to a limit game of extremely high stakes.

**big blind**   The blind to the left of the little blind. One full-sized bet for the first betting round in hold'em or Omaha.

**blind**    A forced bet put in by a player before he gets his cards. A blind is part of that player's bet if he comes into the pot, as opposed to an *ante*, which just "belongs to the pot."

**Big Cross**    A *widow game* in which each player is dealt two to five cards face down and nine cards are dealt face down in the center (widow), in the form of a cross.

**Big Squeeze**    Six-card high-low stud with a *twist*.

**board**    (1) The *community cards* in hold'em and Omaha. (2) A player's upcards in seven-card stud. (3) *Signup board*.

**boardman**    A cardroom employee who puts waiting players' names on a list of the games they're interested in.

**board cards**    The cards of the *board*.

**brick**    A bad or useless card most commonly used in reference to catching a nine or higher when trying to complete a low draw.

**Brick & Mortar game**    *See* B&M game.

**bring-in**    *Bring-in bet*.

**bring-in bet**    Forced minimum bet made on the first round by the holder of the lowest card in seven-card stud or stud eight-or-better, or the highest card in razz.

**bug**    A not-completely-wild joker, making a fifth ace in the deck or to fill straights and flushes.

**buried**    A card or cards hidden in the *hole* in a stud game.

**burn**    (1) To take the top card out of play, usually by placing it face down among the discards. (2) The card that is burned. Also called burn card.

**burn card**    *See* burn.

**button**    (1) Nominal dealer position in a game dealt by a house dealer or the player in that position. (2) An actual object, usually a plastic disk or puck, denoting that position and moved one position clockwise each deal.

**button charge**    A once-per-round fee charged to the player holding the button and collected by the house to serve as a game's rake. Most commonly used in middle-limit games.

**calling station**    Player who calls bets with questionable holdings (both too weak and too strong) and who rarely raises.

**cards speak**   In *split-pot games* that have no *declaration*, splitting the pot at the end among active contenders with half the pot going to the holder of the highest hand and half the pot going to the holder of the lowest eligible hand.

**check**   (1) Continuing in a hand without increasing the pot's size, but retaining the option to bet, raise, or fold later. (2) A chip.

**check-raise**   (1) Raising after first having checked. (2) The bet so made.

**Chicago**   Seven-card stud with the pot split between the high hand and whoever holds the highest spade in the hole. If no one has a spade in the hole, the highest hand takes the entire pot.

**chip runner**   Cardroom employee who sells chips to players for cash, either by carrying them in a specially constructed apron or by making a trip to the cage or a special chip runner's tray to get them.

**collection**   *See* time collection.

**come hand**   An incomplete straight or flush, usually one that needs one card to become complete.

**community cards**   Cards dealt face up to the center of the table in hold'em or Omaha. These become part of each player's hand. Sometimes called the board.

**complete the bet**   In stud games, the low card has a forced bring-in. The person who instead of calling that bet now makes a full-size bet is more properly said to complete the bet rather than to raise it. For example, in $30-60 stud with a $10 bring-in, the player who makes it $30 completes the bet. It's not merely semantics; the completing action does not count against the maximum number of allowed raises.

**consecutive declaration**   In which players *declare* one at a time, starting to the left of the dealer, rather than simultaneously. Because consecutive declaration offers a huge advantage to the final declarer, it is an ill-advised rule.

**consecutive replacement**   Players discard their *twist* cards one at a time, starting to the left of the dealer rather than simultaneously.

**counterfeited**   (1) In Omaha, when a low card from your hand has appeared on the board giving someone else access to that rank and therefore usually turning your previously leading low into a loser. (2) In hold'em, having a low pocket pair's value destroyed by two higher pair appearing on board, e.g., someone holding 5-5 is leading someone holding 9-2 until the final card hits in the board Q-Q-3-10-10, where the winning hand is now Q-Q-10-10-9. (3) In hold'em, a more general term for having a probable winner turned into a probable loser by the appearance of another card on the board.

**courcheval**   A form of Omaha in which players start with either four or five hole cards and the first flop card is exposed before the first round of betting.

**crazy pineapple**   A form of pineapple in which players discard their third hole card *after* the flop and after the second round of betting.

**curiosity call**   Call made by a player to "keep you honest" (make sure you're not bluffing).

**dangler**   Omaha hole card that doesn't coordinate with the other three cards.

**dead**   Pertaining to cards not available to be dealt or drawn. *See also* drawing dead and dead hand.

**dead hand**   A hand no longer eligible to participate in the pot because of a rule violation, such as a clock expiration or the hand touching the *muck*.

**deal**   (1) Distributing the cards prior to playing a hand. (2) Acting as a *dealer*. (3) *See* make a deal (tournament definition).

**dealer**   (1) The person who shuffles and distributes the cards to all players in the game. (2) The nominal deal position in a game with a house dealer.

**dealer-advantage game**   (1) Game in which the dealer always gets to act last like draw or hold'em. Different from Seven-card stud in which betting is dependent on a player's board. (2) Home game in which dealer always gets to act last, but where the nominal dealer position does not rotate through use of a button, thus forcing other *dealer's choice* players to either call similar games or yield an advantage.

**dealer's choice**   A form of poker, more common to home games but also gaining popularity in some cardrooms, in which the dealer chooses the form of poker to be played on his own deal (as opposed to playing one game exclusively for the entire playing session) or the next round. In home games, the dealer is often permitted to choose any game he wishes, no matter how unusual or disliked by the other players; in cardrooms, the dealer usually must choose from a relatively small list of possibilities. A better home game rule for dealer's choice is for each player to call a game which then gets dealt for an entire round, eliminating dealer advantages.

**declaration**   (1) Indication of which portion of a pot a player is contending for, usually done with a simultaneously revealed number of chips. (2) A statement of one's intention in a pot, as, "I raise," "I call," and so on. A verbal declaration of intent to bet is binding and overrules an inconsistent chip action.

**declaration game**   Split-pot variation in home games in which players indicate whether they're contending for high, low, or both by displaying a number of chips (as one for low, two for high, three for both ways), or verbally.

**declare**   Indicate which portion of a pot a player is contending for.

**deep**   A reference to how much money one has on the table, usually used in the form of the question "How deep are you?"

**deuce**   (1) A two (the card). (2) Deuce-to-seven lowball draw.

**deuce-to-seven lowball**   Lowball draw in which hands are the opposite of high hands. Aces are high only and straights and flushes count against you, so the lowest hand is 7-5-4-3-2 of mixed suits.

**deuces wild**   (1) A wild card game usually played as draw poker. (2) A popular form of video poker.

**dime $1,000**   If you win $7,000, you say "I won seven dimes."

**discard**   (1) Throw (gently toss or slide) one's cards in to the dealer in draw poker prior to receiving replacements. (2) The card so discarded. (3) Twist.

**doorcard**   A player's first upcard in a stud game.

**double-ace flush**   Nonstandard poker hand that beats any other flush (except a straight flush); it is a flush containing an ace and the joker.

**double fake**   Acting strong when actually strong in an attempt to make opponents think you have the opposite, that is, make them think you're acting.

**double reverse**   *See* double fake.

**double-flop hold'em**   Rare hold'em version with two boards.

**draw**   (1) High draw poker. (2) The act of taking cards in any form of draw poker.

**draw poker**   A form of poker in which players are dealt five cards face down and bet or fold based on those cards; those players remaining replace one or more cards (draw) or elect not to replace any (stand pat). Then they participate in a second round of betting, after which the best of the remaining hands wins the money in the pot. Forms are high draw, high-low draw, and lowball.

**drawing dead**   Trying to improve to a hand that cannot win if you make it, for example, drawing to a straight when someone else already has a flush.

**drop**   (1) Fixed amount taken by a cardroom out of each pot. (2) Slang for the amount lost in a session's play, as in "I dropped a thousand."

**drop slot**   A slot in a poker table with a receptacle underneath to accept the drop.

**early position**   The first two or three seats to the left of the big blind.

**eight-or-better**   Split-pot game with an eight qualifier for low.

**eight qualifier**   A low hand that is at least an eight low. In cardroom high-low games, low hands must "qualify" by being at least this low, or else the high hand takes the entire pot.

**five-card draw**   The high form of draw poker, unless one of the other variations is specified.

**five-card Omaha**   Omaha played with five hole cards.

**five-card stud**   Stud poker with one hole card and four upcards.

**five-card stud high-low with a twist**   A variant of five-card stud in which players replace one card at the end.

**five of a kind**   A ranking hand in games with wild cards that beats any straight flush.

**floor**   Floorman/Floorperson.

**floorman**   A cardroom employee who supervises several tables. Poker is one of sexism's last holdouts. The term floorperson is also used, but almost always in written documents. When someone needs a decision made, they yell either "Floor" or "Floorman."

**flop**   (1) The first three community cards. (2) Occasional misusage for all five community cards, which are more properly referred to as the *board*.

**fluctuation**   Up and down swings in a player's earnings, most commonly used with reference to session earnings but also correctly used to refer to longer time periods. Often confused with *variance*.

**friendly game**   *See* social game.

**give someone credit**   (1) Indicate (usually by folding) that one believes a bet isn't a bluff, that the bettor actually has a strong hand. (2) Lend money (usually a bad idea for a private individual). Some card casinos will set up players with lines of credit.

**going light**   *See* lights.

**go on tilt**   *See* on tilt.

**guts**   (1) Three-card poker variation (distinguish from the casino table game of the same name). (2) Guts to open.

**guts to open**   In cardrooms, referring to high-draw poker with no opening requirements (for example, not jacks-or-better).

**half kill game**   *See* kill game.

**high draw**   High-draw poker.

**high-low split-pot game**   In casino poker, high-low is always played with an eight qualifier. In home games, it can be played either with a qualifier or a declare.

**high-low split**   *See* split-pot game.

**hijacking**   Robbery by (usually) armed thieves of a private game.

**hit-and-run artist**   Someone who jumps into a game and then leaves after getting ahead a relatively small amount.

**Hog Scoop**   Winning an entire high-low pot.

**hold'em**   A form of poker with two cards dealt face down to each player and five community cards dealt face up in the center of the table. The game has four betting rounds, one after the first two down cards, one after the first three community cards (flop) are simultaneously dealt, one after the next upcard (turn or fourth street), and one after the fifth (river or fifth street). Each player forms the best five-card hand from among his two hole cards and the board. The "official" name of the game is Texas hold'em, but the game is more commonly called hold'em.

**hole**   *See* hole cards.

**hole cards**   Player's face-down cards in community card or stud games.

**home game**   *See* private game.

**hourly rate**   (1) What a player expects to win or lose per hour over a long period of time. (2) What a player actually wins or loses per hour over a long period of time.

**house**   Casino or cardroom, or its management.

**ignorant end**   Holding the low side of a straight in a community card game, as having an eight in the hole when the board in hold'em is 9-10-J-Q.

**implied odds**   The ratio of what you are likely to win on a particular hand if you make your draw (including money likely to be bet and won after you have made your draw) to what the current bet costs. Compare with pot odds.

**jacks-or-better**   A qualifier in a draw game, the minimum holding required to initiate the betting.

**joker**   The fifty-third card in the deck, either completely or partially (the bug) wild.

**Kansas City lowball**   *See* deuce-to-seven lowball.

**Kelly Criterion**   A mathematical principle that states that if you constantly overbet your advantage, you have a high likelihood of going broke.

**kicker**   (1) In hold'em, the "extra" card that accompanies a hand's primary value, as the 10 in the hand A-10. (2) In draw, a side card kept with a pair on the draw to improve chances of making a high two pair (as keeping 7-7-A and drawing two cards), or with trips to disguise the holding (drawing one card to 7-7-7-9 to make it appear you are drawing to two pair, a straight, or a flush).

**kicker trouble**   In hold'em, playing a high card with a smaller card causing your hand to be dominated by any hand that contains the same high card and a bigger kicker. For example, someone playing A-4 against A-J has kicker trouble. One does not have to play a small kicker to have kicker trouble. Someone playing A-Q has kicker trouble against someone playing A-K.

**kill**   Prior to the deal of a hand, adding chips to a pot such that the stakes increase for the next hand. For example, a $15-$30 game might become $30-$60 for one hand. Also called *overblind*.

**kill game**   Form of poker where stakes double if one player scoops consecutive hands of more than a certain minimum size. Such games are sometimes played in half-kill form, where stakes increase 50 percent. The player whose wins created the kill typically must post a special big blind at the higher stake and often (but not always, so check local rules) acts in last position for the first betting round.

**kitchen table poker**   A social game played for low stakes.

**ladder climb**   Advancement to a higher payoff level in the final stages of a tournament.

**late position**   The button and one or two seats to its right, in games like hold'em and Omaha, or the 2-3 seats immediately to the right of the highest hand in stud games (on all rounds after the first; in the first round, the low hand must bring the action in, so those individuals to the low hand's right have position for that round). Late position is immutable in button games but can change in stud games.

**lazy pineapple**   A form of pineapple in which players keep all three cards to the end.

**lights**   In a social game, when a player doesn't have enough chips on the table to continue playing a pot, he withdraws chips (lights) equal to the bet amount from the pot, rather than putting them in, and stacks them before him. Doing so is going light.

**limit**   (1) Structured betting game wherein all bets proceed in multiples of the limit for the game, as opposed to pot-limit or no-limit. (2) The actual betting increment size for a game; in a $2-4 game, all bets are in $2 increments in the early rounds and $4 increments in the later rounds.

**limp**   Enter a pot by calling the size of the blind (or bring-in in stud), as opposed to coming in for a raise.

**little blind**   The blind to the left of the dealer. More commonly called the small blind. Usually half of the big blind, but can range from one third to two thirds.

**live**   (1) Playing like a live one. (2) Pertaining to cards that should be available to be dealt or drawn. (3) Alternate expression (acceptable usage) for money game (as opposed to tournament). (4) Alternate expression (weak usage) for Brick & Mortar game (as opposed to Internet).

**live hand**   In seven-card stud, one whose chances of improvement have not been hurt by key drawing cards appearing in other players' hands.

**live one**   A very loose player, usually implying one who plays poorly and has a reasonable supply of funds available to lose, although live ones sometimes also make frequent trips to ATMs and credit card cash advance machines.

**lock**   A guaranteed winner for some portion of the pot.

**locksmith**   A tight player who only plays the nuts; similar to rock.

**look-at-two-and-kill**   In lowball, kill after seeing one's first two dealt cards.

**look-at-three-and-kill**   In lowball, kill after seeing one's first three dealt cards.

**look someone up**   Call someone, probably with a mediocre hand because one believes the player is bluffing.

**loose**   Descriptive of the play of a loose player.

**loose player**   One who plays many speculative hands and gambles a lot. Opposite of tight player, rock, or locksmith.

**lowball**   Five-card draw in which the lowest hand wins. Forms are ace-to-five and deuce-to-seven.

**lowball draw**   *See* lowball.

**make a deal**   Agree in a tournament to redistribute payouts based on chip totals and each player's perceived skill level. Deals must be agreed upon unanimously and involve all remaining players.

**mexican stud**   Five-card stud played with a stripped deck, one from which the eights, nines, and tens have been removed, and in which at each round players have a choice of exposing their hole card and getting a replacement, or having the next card dealt face up.

**middle position**   Somewhere between early and late position.

**Mississippi stud**   A form of seven-card stud in which the fourth and fifth cards are dealt successively without an intervening betting round and the last card is dealt face up.

**mixed game**   A format in which several forms of poker are played in rotation, usually half an hour of each or a round of each. A mixed game usually includes anywhere from two to five different forms of poker and is much more common at high stakes than at low or even middle stakes. Also called rotation game.

**nickel $500**   Unlike $1,000 dimes, normally used only in the singular (that is, a player who won $1,500 wouldn't say "I won three nickels" or even "I won a dime and a nickel." The term is more commonly used in sports betting.

**no-limit**   A betting arrangement wherein any player on his turn may bet or raise any amount from the current minimum to as much as his entire stack.

**Omaha**   A variation of hold'em in which players start with four hole cards, of which they *must* use exactly two in combination with three of the community cards.

**Omaha eight-or-better**   Omaha high-low, with an eight qualifier for low.

**on a draw**   Having four cards to a straight, a flush, or a low, but not yet a made hand, as opposed to already having some kind of hand that can win without improving.

**one-eyed jacks**   J♠, J♥.

**one-eyes**   The three one-eyed face cards (J♠, J♥, K♦).

**on tilt**   Suffering loss of emotional control, usually due to losing steadily or through one or more bad beats.

**outs**   Cards that will win the hand for you. If you are on a heart flush draw, the remaining hearts are outs.

**overblind**   *See* kill.

**pass the trash**   A variant of seven-card stud in which players are dealt seven cards, pass some of those cards to left and right, choose the best five of their resulting seven cards, and then roll'em.

**penny-ante game**   Low-stakes home game.

**pineapple**   A variant of hold'em in which players start with three cards instead of two.

**play back**   Raise or (usually) re-raise.

**PLO**   Pot-Limit Omaha.

**position**   Where one sits in relation to the others at the table, one player specifically, or to the button.

**position play**   Playing to take advantage of where one sits in relation to the button or another player.

**post**   In hold'em or Omaha, a new player can either wait for the big blind to reach his seat or he can join in the action immediately by posting a big blind. If a seated player gets up and misses the blinds, he can either wait until the big blind reaches him the next time, or post both the big blind (which stays in front of him and serves as a live bet) and the small blind (which goes into the center of the table as part of the pot).

**pot-limit**   A betting arrangement wherein bets fall in a range. The smallest bet is equal to the size of the previous bet or raise. The largest bet is equal to the size of the pot after the previous bet or raise has been called. A bet or raise may fall between the limits as long as it is equal to or larger than the previous bet or raise.

**pot odds**   Immediate return on investment, that is, the ratio of what it currently costs to call compared to the pot size.

**private game**   One not played in a public cardroom or casino.

**pulling the tape**   Removing and viewing the tape from the surveillance camera above a table for the purpose of determining whether an alleged rules infraction took place or resolving a dispute.

**qualifier**   (1) In split-pot games, a minimum holding required to win half the pot. Qualifiers are much more common on the low side (for example, an eight-low can qualify for the low side of a pot, while a nine-low can't), but occasionally you run into high qualifiers. (2) In a draw game, a minimum holding required to initiate the betting, as jacks or better.

**rake**   Money taken by a cardroom in return for providing players many services. The rake may be taken as a percentage of each pot (with a limit), a button charge (once per round fee), or a time charge (fee collected each half hour).

**razz**   Seven-card stud played for low.

**redraw**   Have one hand made that can improve to something better. For example, if you make a straight on the turn in hold'em, four cards of which are spades, you have a redraw to a flush. Redraws are particularly important in Omaha.

**reentry blind**   In lowball or draw, a forced kill a player who has missed the blinds must put up to get dealt in.

**replacement**   *See* twist.

**reverse hold'em**   Rare hold'em variant with flop and turn of one card each and river of three cards.

**rock**   An extremely tight player.

**rolled up**   Having rolled up trips.

**rolled up trips**   Three of a kind as one's first three cards in seven-card stud.

**roll'em**   Stud variation in which players arrange their five cards face down in a pre-determined order, then expose one at a time, each followed by a round of betting until four cards have been exposed.

**roll your own**   *See* roll'em.

**rotation game**   *See* mixed game.

**runner-runner**   Catching two consecutive perfect cards in hold'em or Omaha. For example, starting with two diamonds in your hand in hold'em, seeing only one on the flop, but catching diamonds on both the turn and river to make your flush.

**scarne cut**   A form of cut in which the cutter holds the cards in one hand, removes the bottom half with the other, places them atop the remaining half, pulls a packet from the center, and places those cards on top of the remaining cards. It is named after John Scarne, who lectured to servicemen of World War II and wrote later about gambling thieves. He introduced this form of cut as a means of foiling cheaters who had stacked the deck. The Scarne cut is not permitted in most public cardrooms where the deck must not be lifted from the table and must be cut with one hand.

**scoop**   In a split-pot game, hold both the highest and lowest hand, in which case you win the whole pot or you win the whole pot with a high hand because there is no *qualifier* for low. Sometimes called *hog* or (in noun form) a *scooper* or a *hogger*.

**serious game**   Home game in which the money is more important than socializing.

**session**   Amount of time you spend sitting in one poker game from the time you buy in until the time you cash out.

**setup**   Two decks of casino-quality cards in their box. When players ask for a deck change, they often want both changed and the dealer *calls for a setup*.

**seven-card stud** *Stud poker* played with seven cards, starting with two hole cards for each player plus one upcard dealt all at once, followed by a round of betting, then three upcards dealt one at a time, each followed by a round of betting, then one hole card, followed by a final round of betting and the showdown.

**short-handed** A game with more than two seats empty.

**shorts** Small pairs in draw poker, sometimes considered any pair smaller than jacks.

**showdown** (1) The point in a poker game at which the betting is done and the players show their cards to determine who wins. (2) A no-skill form of poker where each player bets, gets five cards, and then turns them over one at a time, frequently used as a "double or nothing" device, as in "Let's play one hand of showdown for the whole thing."

**side action** Money (nontournament) games that take place when a tournament is going on. Also called side game.

**signup board** A cardroom list of available games to which waiting players add their names for those they're interested in. Range from low-tech clipboard notes to blackboards/whiteboards (most common for large rooms) to high-tech computer-generated screens.

**slowroll** When holding the best hand at the showdown, wait until the last possible moment before showing that hand. Generally considered an extreme breach of etiquette and has been the cause of more than one literal fight.

**small blind** *See* little blind.

**social game** Friendly home game, often for small stakes.

**Southern Cross** *See* Big Cross.

**split-pot game** A game in which at the showdown the pot is split usually between the highest and lowest active qualifying hands.

**spread** To offer a particular game to one's customers, as in a cardroom ad that says "Now spreading $20-40 hold'em."

**spread-limit** A betting arrangement wherein bets fall in a variable range; something of a hybrid betting structure, combining elements of limit and pot-limit or no-limit. The smallest bet is equal to the lower limit and the largest bet is equal to the larger limit. A bet or raise may fall between the limits, as long as it is equal to or larger than the previous bet or raise. As an example, you might see a cardroom spreading $20-200 spread-limit hold'em.

**Steel Wheel**   A suited wheel: the lowest possible low hand and a straight flush for high. The ideal eight-or-better poker hand.

**stud poker**   A form of poker in which one or more cards are dealt to each player face down, followed by one upcard, with a betting round, more upcards, with a betting round after each. Then in seven-card stud, a final hole card, and a final betting round. The primary forms are five-card stud and seven-card stud, although many home game variations exist.

**table image**   How the other players view you and your likely style of play.

**take a card off**   Call a bet so as to receive another card even though you are certain you are trailing, because you are getting acceptable pot odds or implied odds.

**tell**   A mannerism, or change in or lack thereof, that gives a clue away about your holdings.

**Texas Hold'em**   *See* hold'em.

**throw a party**   Be the big loser at a table.

**tight**   Descriptive of the play of a tight player.

**tight player**   One who plays only premium starting hands. *Also* known as a rock or a locksmith. Opposite of loose player.

**tilt**   *See* on tilt.

**time**   *See* time collection.

**time collection**   Rental fee paid at regular intervals (typically by the half hour) by each player for the use of a cardroom's facilities and services. Time charges tend to increase as the stakes increase. Only a cardroom's higher stake games charge time. The other games use a percentage of the pot rake or a button charge.

**toke**   Tip.

**top section**   Area that contains the highest stake games in a cardroom, often roped off or otherwise separated from the rest. Sometimes literally on a higher platform or level, hence the name.

**triple-draw**   *See* triple draw lowball.

**triple-draw lowball**   Lowball with three draws and four betting rounds.

**trips**   Three of a kind.

**twist**   In a five- or six-card stud game, an optional card replacement at the end. A player receives a hole card for a discarded hole card and an upcard for an upcard. *Also* called reject or discard.

**variance**    (1) Deviation from expected results, measured mathematically as the square of the standard deviation. (2) More generally used to describe the width of potential results. For example, an above-average player who enters the Bellagio $25,000 event is making a high variance play because even if he got a chance to play the event 10,000 times he would be certain to show a profit, the chances of him making the money in any one given event are low.

**wheel**    Five-high straight, usually used in a low context.

**widow**    One or more community cards dealt to the center of the table in stud poker as played in home games only and available to be part of any player's hand. Some kind of geometric pattern other than one straight line is involved, such as a square or a cross.

**widow game**    One that uses a widow, as Southern Cross.

**wild**    Pertaining to a card that can take the value of any other card, as the joker, deuces wild, or low hole card wild. A wild card turns a pair into three of a kind, two pair into a full house, four to a straight into a straight, and so on. Wild cards are only used in home games, except for those varieties of draw that use the semi-wild bug.

**wild card game**    Any poker game played with wild cards.

**wrap**    *See* wraparound straight draw.

**wraparound straight draw**    In Omaha, a situation in which your four hole cards consist of three or four closely connected cards. In turn they combine with two flopped cards to create a situation where any of a large number of cards can give you a straight. Depending on the precise configuration, you can have as many as 17 outs to a wrap. For example, with a K-10-8 flop and Q-J-10-9 in your hand, you can make a straight with an ace (use your Q-J), a queen (use your J-9), a jack (use your Q-9), a nine (use your Q-J) or a seven (use your J-9). There are four aces and four sevens left in this configuration (eight outs), and three queens, jacks, and nines (nine outs, for a total of seventeen). Other "large number of outs" configurations are also called wraps.

# Televised Poker Tournaments

Poker is booming, more in the last year than ever in the past. This is due to three things:

♦ Televised poker tournaments that show hole cards

♦ The popularity of the *World Poker Tour* and its turning poker champions into semicelebrities

♦ The win of the most prestigious tournament of all, the Championship event of the *World Series of Poker*, by a relative newcomer, the improbably-named Chris Moneymaker. Chris initially bought into an online satellite tournament and turned that $40 buy-in into a $10,000 seat. That seat became a cool $2.5 million in an event that was later televised in a seven-part ESPN series.

Let's talk about televised tournaments and the possibility of corporate sponsorship.

# Televised Tournaments Now Show Player Hole Cards

Coverage of poker events has long been available. You can purchase *World Series of Poker* videos from as far back as 1973. The final event has been aired on several sports cable channels for many years. What was missing all along, though, was knowledge in most cases of what the players had, and that has made all the difference in the world. Unless there was a showdown, viewers did not know what the players were betting on and showdowns were infrequent. This made most of the events relatively uninteresting except to insiders and those who knew the players personally.

## Where It Began

Tournament-wise, everything changed in 2000, when Ladbroke's held the first *Poker Million* tournament on the Isle of Man (a golf haven and tax shelter that is located between England and Ireland). The innovation, borrowed from the UK's *Late Night Poker*, revealed the players' hole cards to under-table cameras.

John Duthie won a million pounds and put on a brave performance, shamelessly bluffing hand after hand in a live broadcast that claimed millions of viewers in Europe and more later in an edited version shown in the United States. He capitalized on a tight reputation he had earned earlier in the event and by the time the opposition realized he had switched gears, Duthie had too big a chip lead to overcome.

Some argue that this was actually the first major tournament to have corporate sponsorship, because Ladbroke's added 250,000 pounds to the prize pool. It was a rather unintentional £250,000, however, as Ladbrokes had guaranteed £1,000,000 for first place and didn't quite draw that much in buy-ins. In a classy gesture, the organizers added a bit more than was needed to reach the guarantee, so that someone other than the first place finisher could take home prize money.

The big time arrived in 2003 with the *World Poker Tour*, and its "lipstick cameras" and "live" commentary (although presentation of the actual hands was edited in later, as was relevant commentary). Each show featured the final table of a major stop on the international tournament circuit and was edited down to two hours.

Events were first broadcast months after they actually occurred. Adding to the interest was an educational tool: presentation of running odds on each hand as the hand was played out.

Some tournament players initially objected to showing their hole cards, not wanting to give away their plays. They changed their minds when they discovered that televised winners were becoming celebrities who could sell books and endorse products, although the WPT itself strictly forbade anyone from wearing any logos.

You might think that the poker greats disguise their play at the final table to prevent viewers from picking up patterns or tells. You'd be right to think so. On key hands they have to make the best available play, but they can and do certainly engage in a bit of acting for the TV audience.

Such tournaments allow viewers to get inside the heads of top players. Thousands of wannabe champions compete in satellites and tournaments, emulating the play they see at final tables. What many don't realize is that tournament coverage is edited to show exciting confrontations. All the boring instances of one player coming in for a raise and everyone folding are edited out, which has led to quite a few amateur players playing a reckless style as they learn. Some have argued that the WPT finalists should wear T-shirts saying "I am a professional: do not try this at home."

You can buy an entire season of the *World Poker Tour* on DVD. This is undoubtedly a good investment for prospective tournament players and for those who plan on competing in *WPT* events. These shows have become the equivalent of scouting videos that pro sports coaches show to their players.

Probably the best educational value comes for tournament players who are already fairly decent players; they understand tournament basics and how sometimes final table chip positions require players to make moves that startle amateurs. If you've never before seen a poker tournament, watching a *WPT* final table is not a good way to get ready for your opening rounds. If you are already a competent tournament player, these programs show you professional secrets worth incalculable sums. Only the endorsement and sponsorship money that these tournaments bring into poker can repay the top pros for the secrets these shows give away.

## Recent Programs

Major events that have been televised recently that are not just on cable are:

- **The World Series of Poker.** Seven-part series ran constantly for months on various ESPN affiliates. In 2004, ESPN added coverage of many of the preliminary events, with plans to show them throughout the year.

- **The World Poker Tour.** Twelve events in 2003, usually with buy-ins ranging from $5,000 to $10,000. The Tour reached its climax in the thirteenth, the Championship Final $25,000 buy-in event at the Bellagio in Las Vegas. The series ran on the Travel Channel.

    In addition to first prizes that sometimes exceeded $500,000, winners of individual events got an entry into the Championship Event. Each event was held as the culmination of a major tournament series at a sponsoring casino. Each event got its first airing on a Wednesday and replayed several times during the week. After the final event, the entire series then ran all over again several times. This series is making stars out of some of the great competitors.

In 2003, the reruns actually had more viewers than the first go-round.

The *WPT* had other specials, including a championship among the 13 champions of the first season on NBC right before the 2004 Super Bowl. There also was a women's invitational tournament, which awarded an entry into the $25,000 buy-in Bellagio Championship Event.

♦ **Showdown at the Sands.** The Atlantic City event was shown as a six-hour marathon.

♦ **Late Night Poker.** Nine-part weekly series from Cardiff, Wales that has run for several years now.

♦ **Bravo Celebrity Poker.** A weekly show featuring actors who compete for cash prizes for their favorite charities. The winners of each show compete in the finale. You might enjoy seeing the stars, but you probably won't be impressed by the quality of the poker.

♦ **The Jack Binion World Poker Open.** This event was jointly held at the Horseshoe and Gold Strike Casinos in Tunica, Mississippi, and has been televised the past three years; it just joined the *WPT*.

♦ **Poker Million.** British viewers watched six heats leading up to the invitation-only *Poker Million 2003*. The *Poker Million* itself was postponed indefinitely, but scheduled to run in 2004.

# Gamble On It

The aforementioned shows have proven so popular that they have given some added impetus to a plan for an all-gambling network on cable. There have been other groups who have announced similar plans in the past, so don't count on The Gambling Channel just yet, but its time appears to have come.

# Let's Not Make a Deal

When corporate sponsorship appears, tournament players will no longer be able to make deals. Previously, players used the quite reasonable argument, "We put up all the prize money via our buy-ins, so we should be able to do what we like at the end. The final results are too dependent on luck, and this evens things out."

Corporate sponsorship—more specifically, adding corporate money to prize pools—will necessitate awarding the prizes as originally offered. Viewers would question the integrity of a tournament if they discovered that the winner didn't actually go home with all of the announced $3,000,000 first prize. Deal-making will end, but as long as players see money come into poker from somewhere other than their own pockets, they'll be able to live with it.

# Appendix **E**

# Mentors

If you read this book, you likely want to improve your poker play. You're in the right place: Poker books are certainly among the most cost-effective educational resources you can find, right up there with magazines like *Card Player* and several free Internet information sites.

After you do your reading, you'll want to mix in some live play, but even with the right texts, this can be an expensive process. One of the best ways to combine what you've learned from reading with the experience you gain by playing is to get some personalized help in the form of a mentor.

## Finding a Mentor

Free advice is often worth what you pay for it. Don't look for a mentor in the wrong places. Friends from your local poker game can indeed help you improve your Pass the Trash, but if they haven't played casino or card room poker successfully, they aren't likely to be much help.

If your friends have ventured forth from their hometown to a card room somewhere and tend to come home with more than they leave with, you can certainly consider a friend a good free mentor source. A lot of people are willing to help you just from the kindness of their hearts. The real trick is to figure out if your friendly neighborhood mentor actually knows enough to serve as a worthwhile teacher. Free lessons can be very expensive if they teach you bad habits or concepts that you must unlearn.

Once you've decided you want to take it further than the friend who seems to do fairly well in your local games, you have some hard choices to make.

## Unpaid Mentors

Advice from those you play with regularly can help, but recognize that if they continue to oppose you, they have good reason not to be *too* helpful. It's not impossible for you to run into someone who does indeed want to help you—just enough so that you don't get clobbered in the local games, but instead lose slowly, perhaps just slowly enough to shear you as a sheep many times rather than kill you once. You probably won't get much actually misleading advice, but players don't usually share secrets without some incentive.

Don't forget, of course, the next time you are tempted to credit a mentor for teaching you everything you know, he might say softly, "Yeah, but I didn't teach you everything *I* know."

## Evaluating Potential Mentors

To evaluate the person you want as a mentor, think about the following:

- What limits does he play?
- What is the quality of his competition?
- What games does he succeed in?
- If you're interested in tournament mentoring, what tournaments has he made final tables in or won?
- If he's a writer, how well does he communicate?
- What do others think of his writing and teaching abilities?

Realize that someone who plays $80-$160 hold'em exclusively, or only no-limit tournaments, may not necessarily be your best teacher if you want to learn how to beat the smaller limits.

## Paid Mentors

Would you like to be taught tournament skills by a World Series of Poker champion? You can be. Don't be intimidated by their wins or reputations; many are accessible. How about authors you admire? You can contact them, too; many offer mentoring.

You can write to noted players and ask if they take on students. Many can be found online at various poker sites. Some have their own Web sites. Gambling magazines usually list contact information for contributors, or you can write the author in care of the magazine. You can usually write the authors of books in care of their publishers. Because many of the publishers of poker books have Web sites, you can find contact information there. Some teachers advertise in well-known poker magazines.

If you like this book, you can contact me regarding lessons. I have had great tournament success—particularly of late—and am a top-flight online and side game player, and also an excellent teacher and communicator. Find me in all my humility at www.AndyGlazer.com.

## The Online Experience Helps the Mentoring Process

With the explosive growth of online poker sites, a mentor can now watch you play online and give direct advice. This creates long-distance teaching possibilities that didn't exist before widespread Internet play.

In the typical scenario, your mentor logs on to the poker site of your choice, watches you play, and critiques your plays while they happen. This is the very moment that the input might make the most lasting impression on you. Sometimes the mentor watches for awhile, takes notes, and then discusses with you later about how to improve.

Sometimes mentors advise you how to play your hands in actual online money games or tournaments. For legal reasons, it is usually better to use a site's free games for these purposes. There is nothing unethical about a mentor helping you make decisions—after all, the mentor could be sitting there in your home office. The Internet merely gives you access to mentors at a distance.

This is generally not something you can do in a brick-and-mortar card room (B&M). Your opponents would not appreciate it if Phil Hellmuth or Andrew Glazer sat with you to give advice about how to handle your cards, even if they were permitted to sit there (many card rooms don't allow this). Discussing a hand in play would violate the card room's one-player-to-a-hand rule; discussing a hand afterward would likely disturb those at the table.

## Expect Miracles—Not!

When you engage a mentor, make sure you get what you want and need. Don't expect miracles, but do expect progress. Don't pay too much up front. First, make sure the price (this is usually an hourly rate) is reasonable. Occasionally mentors or teachers like to "gamble" with their students: They don't charge anything if the student doesn't have a winning year, but they take a percentage if the student does win. This clearly requires a certain trust level on the mentor's part and you shouldn't be insulted if a mentor who has never met you isn't interested in such a deal.

If what you seek is becoming a winner at low-level hold'em, it may not be cost-effective to engage the services of a former world champion. Aim a bit lower first.

Don't buy too many lessons at the beginning of your lessons. Try a few lessons, play some, and see if the lessons help. If they do, take a few more, and play some more. And all the while, read books—good ones. Keep applying the advice to your play. You should be able to sense how much better you're playing. If someone tries to sell you a package of 50 lessons, run, do not walk, in the other direction. Poker teachers haven't earned the reputation of dance studios, but the year is young.

Watch out for mentors who frequently use the words "always" and "never." Poker is not a game of absolutes: Context is king. After you master basic principles, you will find out there are times when it's right not to follow them. Using hand guidelines can help you when you start, but everything in poker depends on circumstances. Sometimes you need to deliberately violate guidelines. A good mentor will teach you those times.

If a potential mentor guarantees that you'll be a winner, find someone else. The mentor has no idea what your potential is. Guaranteed *improvement* is credible; guaranteed *winning* is not.

# Hand Values

Before playing poker, you need to know what beats what in all games. If you need to, practice in small games until you can just glance at multiple hands and immediately know which hand is best, which is second best, and so on. Online "play money" games serve this purpose well, as do any number of very inexpensive computer software programs, but just a little time with this Appendix and a deck of cards will do just fine.

## High Hands

Here are the high hands in high only and high-low split games, from highest to lowest. When examining hands, you will encounter ranks and suits. Card ranks are values, A-K-Q-J-10-9-8-7-6-5-4-3-2, with the ace highest and the deuce lowest: Single cards can outrank one another (as an eight outranks a five) and so can more complex hands (as a pair of jacks outranks a pair of nines). Suits (spades, hearts, diamonds, and clubs) never come into play in final hand values. In stud games, suit ranks occasionally determine who must make the bring-in bet. Suit ranks from highest to lowest are in reverse alphabetical order: spades highest, then hearts, diamonds, and clubs.

Any hand on the following list beats any hand that is described after it:

**Five of a kind:** Five cards of the same rank. This is a special hand, possible only when wild cards are used. In a deck with the joker used as the *bug* (for aces, straights, and flushes), the only possible five of a kind is five aces. Examples: A♥-A♠-A♦-A♣-joker, a hand called *five aces*. In a game of deuces wild: K♠-K♥-K♦-2♠-2♣, a hand called *five kings*. In a contest among players holding five of a kind, the hand with the highest rank wins. Q♦-Q♣-Q♥-2♠-2♦ beats 8♣-8♥-8♦-8♠-2♥.

*A five of a kind hand.*

**Straight flush:** Five cards in sequence with all five cards of the same suit. Example: 8♠-7♠-6♠-5♠-4♠. The highest straight flush, having an ace as the high card, has a special name, **royal flush**. Example: 10♥-J♥-Q♥-K♥-A♥. In a contest among players holding straight flushes, the hand with the highest top card wins. 10♣-9♣-8♣-7♣-6♣ beats 8♠-7♠-6♠-5♠-4♠.

*A straight flush.*

*The royal flush.*

**Four of a kind:** Four cards of the same rank. Also known as *quads*. Example: K♥-K♠-K♦-K♣-7♥, a hand called *four kings* or *quad kings*. In a contest among players holding four of a kind, the hand with the highest rank wins. J♦-J♣-J♥-J♠-5♦ beats 8♣-8♥-8♦-8♠-A♥. In a community card game like hold'em, it is possible for two players to hold the same four of a kind if the four equally ranked cards are on board. If that happens, the player holding the highest kicker wins. If their kickers are equal, or both lower than the fifth board card, the hand is a tie.

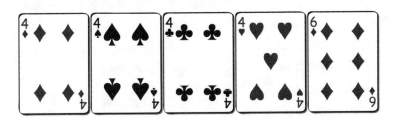

*A four of a kind hand.*

**Full house:** Three cards of one rank plus two cards of another rank. Example: 10♥-10♦-10♠-5♥-5♦, a hand called *tens full of fives* or simply *tens full*. In a contest among players holding full houses, the hand with the highest three of a kind wins. 6♥-6♠-6♦-2♥-2♠ beats 5♦-5♣-5♥-A♠-A♣.

*A full house.*

**Flush:** Five cards of the same suit. Example: A♥-10♥-8♥-7♥-2♥. In a contest among players holding flushes, the hand with the highest top one or more cards wins. When the top cards are tied, the next card is compared; when the top two cards are tied, the third card is compared; and so on. For example, A♦-9♦-8♦-7♦-6♦ beats K♣-Q♣-J♣-9♣-8♣, and 10♥-9♥-8♥-4♥-2♥ beats 10♠-9♠-7♠-6♠-5♠. If one player held A♦-9♦-8♦-7♦-6♦ and another A♣-9♣-8♣-7♣-6♣, they would split the pot.

*A flush.*

**Straight:** Five consecutive cards. An ace can be high or low, but cannot "turn the corner." For example: A♠-K♦-Q♦-J♠-10♠ is an ace-high straight (with a special nickname, "Broadway"; A♥-2♣-3♦-4♠-5♥ is a five-high straight. However, Q-K-A-2-3 is not a straight. In a contest among players holding straights, the hand with the highest top card wins. 9♥-8♦-7♣-6♣-5♠ beats 7♥-6♦-5♣-4♣-3♠.

*A straight.*

**Three of a kind:** Three cards of the same rank. Also known as *trips* or, especially in flop games, a *set*. Example: A♠-A♥-A♦-Q♣-3♠. In a contest among players holding three of a kind, the hand with the highest rank wins. J♦-J♥-J♠-3♦-2♣ beats 10♠-10♣-10♥-A♦-K♣. In games like hold'em, if trips are on the board, the player with the single highest kicker wins.

*Three of a kind.*

**Two pair:** Two cards of one equal rank plus two cards of another equal (but different) rank. Example: A♠-A♥-Q♦-Q♣-4♣, a hand called *aces and queens* or simply *aces up*. In a contest among players holding two pair, the hand with the highest pair wins. A♥-A♦-2♦-2♠-3♥ beats K♥-K♦-Q♣-Q♠-J♠. In a contest among players holding the same top pair, the hand with the highest second pair wins. 9♥-9♦-8♠-8♣-4♦ beats 9♠-9♣-7♠-7♥-A♦. In a contest among players holding the same two pairs, the hand with the highest *kicker* wins. 10♥-10♦-9♣-9♠-4♦ beats 10♠-10♣-9♥-9♦-3♠. Note that a poker hand always consists of five cards, so there is no such hand as "three pair." If one seven-card stud player has 5-5-4-4-3-3-A, he loses to someone who holds 9-9-8-8-4-3-2. In that showdown, nines and eights with a four beats fives and fours with an ace; the pair of threes is irrelevant.

*Two pair.*

**One pair:** Two cards of the same rank. Example: 9♠-9♥-A♠-K♠-Q♠, a hand called a *pair of nines*. In a contest among players holding one pair, the hand with the highest pair wins. A♠-A♥-6♦-5♣-4♥ beats K♠-K♦-A♠-Q♦-J♣. In a contest among players holding the same pair, the hand with the highest one or more side cards wins. 10♠-10♥-9♦-8♣-4♥ beats 10♣-10♦-9♥-8♠-3♠, just as J-J-A-2-3 beats J-J-K-Q-10.

*A pair.*

**No pair (High cards):** None of the preceding. Example: A♠-K♥-7♠-5♦-4♣, a hand sometimes called *ace high* or *ace-king high*. If no hand is better at the showdown, the hand topped by the highest one or more cards wins. When the top cards are tied, the next card is compared; when the top two cards are tied, the third card is compared; and so on. A♠-9♥-5♦-4♣-2♠ beats K♠-Q♥-J♦-10♠-8♥, and Q♦-J♥-10♣-8♣-4♦ beats Q♠-J♣-10♥-8♠-2♦.

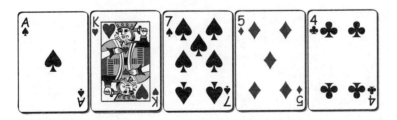

*The high card is the ace.*

# Low Hands

Lowball and razz are games in which the lowest hand wins. These are games of pure numbers, because straights and flushes have no bearing and the ace is low only and is the lowest low card. The lowest hand is A-2-3-4-5; it doesn't matter if the suits are different or all the same. The hand is called a *wheel* or occasionally a *bicycle*. Lowball hands are ranked by the top card, sometimes the top two. For example, the second-best hand, 6-4-3-2-A is called a six-four. The next hand, 6-5-3-2-A, is called a six-five, and so on.

The key to understanding low hands is to focus on the highest card in the hand until the tie is broken. A 7-6-5-4-2 is lower than an 8-4-3-2-A; this confrontation would be called an eighty-four losing to a seventy-six, or an 8-4 losing to a 7-6.

This is the hand-ranking system used for *ace-to-five* lowball and razz, and also for high-low games as usually played in cardrooms. These games feature an *eight qualifier*.

When comparing lowball hands, first the top cards are examined, and then, if necessary, the second, and succeeding cards. For example, any hand topped by an eight beats any hand topped by a nine. 8-6-5-4-3 beats 8-7-3-2-A; 7-6-5-4-2 beats 7-6-5-4-3; and so on.

Pairs are bad in lowball, so a hand like K-Q-J-10-9, while not one that would normally be played, is better than the result of an A-2-3-4 in which you catch an ace.

Worse hands than pairs are in reverse order from the ranking of high hands, except that straights and flushes are excluded. That is: Any pair beats any two pair, which beats any three of a kind, which beats any full house, which beats any four of a kind. Among hands of the same rank, the lower wins. Examples: A♠-A♥-K♠-Q♥-J♦ is a lower low hand than 4♥-3♣-2♠-2♥-A♦, because a pair of aces is considered lower than a pair of twos in pure low games (in high-low games, a pair of aces is considered the highest pair, even though a single ace is the lowest card). 3♠-3♥-2♠-2♥-K♠ is a lower hand than 4♠-4♣-3♦-3♣-A♠, because two pair, threes and twos, are lower than two pair, fours and threes.

Variants of lowball rank hands differently. Rankings in *Deuce-to-seven* (often just called *Deuce*) are almost the exact opposite of high poker. The best hand is 7-5-4-3-2. Can you guess why? A six-low hand must either be a straight, or contain an ace. In Deuce, the ace is a high card. A five-low is a straight, leaving 7-5-4-3-2 (with at least two different suits represented, so it isn't a flush) as best, with 7-6-4-3-2 next, and so on.

Good drawing hands are quite different in Deuce. In most low or high-low games, a draw to 3-4-5-6 is extremely strong. In Deuce, the aces, deuces, and sevens that would be great catches in the other games are ruinous.

The one exception to deuce-to-seven hands being the exact opposite of high poker is the hand 5-4-3-2-A of mixed suits. Because the ace is high only, that hand is not considered a straight. It is the best-possible ace-high hand, and beats A-6-4-3-2, but is worse than K-Q-J-10-8.

There are a few localized versions of lowball that use aces low, but straights and flushes counting as high hands. In this game, the best hand is 6-4-3-2-A of mixed suits. The worst six is 6-5-4-3-A. The hand 6-5-4-3-2 is not a low hand, so the next best hand is 7-4-3-2-A. Various forms of *London lowball* use this ranking. Otherwise, this ranking is seen only in private games, where, as you have seen in this book, far stranger rules than this are sometimes employed.

# High-Low Hands

In high-low poker, lowball rankings are usually ace-to-five. Most games have an *eight qualifier*. That is, to win half the pot, the low hand must be an eight high or better.

The big thing to watch out for in high-low poker is the local rule for two key questions:

- What is the best low hand?
- What happens in high-low declare games when there is a tie on the low side?

It is not unusual for private games to play some games in which the best low is the wheel, but others in which it is the 6-4, and I'm not discussing a game where they play Deuce occasionally. Often the more creative "invented" home games are high-low games, and the inventor gets to make up his own rules.

It is a bad policy to shift back and forth for no apparent reason; it leads to confusion, especially for new players. This policy at its worst leads to unfortunate errors costing players entire pots; at its best, it slows the game down as players continually request reminders about which low is the best low in "Omaha Soweto" or "Yellow Brick Road" or "Harvey" (all bizarre games I have come across at one time or another).

By far the more common problem occurs in the situation in which there is a tie on low hands in declare games. In eight-or-better poker, the games are played in *cards speak* fashion and ties result in splits. In declare poker, someone who declares both ways must win both ways (or else there would be no reason not to declare both ways every time).

Although it is possible for ties to occur on the high hand (and when these occur, the same problems come up as when ties happen on the low side), high ties are far less frequent. Every once in a while two players will hold the same straight, and even less frequently the same flush (remember, only suits can create flush ties; if one player holds A-K-Q-9-3 suited and another A-K-Q-9-2 suited, the first player wins).

On the low side, though, it's fairly common, especially in high-low games where players see many cards, to get ties on low hands. Someone who owns a wheel can face a difficult decision. He can't be beaten low, but he certainly can be tied for low, and if he *swings* (declares both ways) when someone else also has a wheel, all kinds of unusual situations can arise.

Suppose that the rule is if you go both ways, you must win both ways; a tie is considered a loss. With two players in at the end, each with a wheel, if one swings and the other doesn't, the nonswinger gets the whole pot (if they both swing, they split). If the rule is that you can tie, the swinger would get three quarters if his opponent declares low-only or high-only, or half if his opponent swings.

Suppose the situation gets more complex; now we add a third player who declares high only with his trip jacks. Two players with wheels both swing. If you must win both when you swing, the player with the trip jacks would get the entire pot in many games! In other games, the player with the jacks would get the high and the players with the wheels would split the low, while in others, the player with the jacks would get shut out, with the others splitting the pot.

It can get even worse. Suppose now the three hands are a wheel, a 2-3-4-5-6 straight, and trip jacks. If you must win both ways, backing in is allowed and the two low straights each swing, the trip jacks get the whole pot in many games because the low straights have each lost in one direction. In some games, the wheel would get shut out because it has been beaten for high, but the player with the 2-3-4-5-6 would get the whole pot because "the jacks can't back in" to win the high end when the six straight beat him in his direction. In other "no backing in" games, the wheel would get half the pot and the six straight half the pot because that's what would have happened if the jacks weren't in.

The problem is that there are reasonable arguments in favor of each of these approaches. Some are more reasonable than others, but none are irrational. It becomes vital to discuss and agree upon what rule will be used before a hand is played because hard feelings will result if someone has to make a decision after the fact.

In my opinion (and that's all it is), I like the idea of rewarding good play (playing wheel cards that can turn into small straights) and avoiding harsh penalties when a player has a good hand like a wheel. Players who swing should be allowed to split the low (or high) end when they tie there. This certainly doesn't make swinging a wheel an automatic play; wheel owners who suspect a better high hand might be out sometimes must opt to declare low only. It just seems wrong that someone who owns a steel wheel (A-2-3-4-5 suited, the best possible low and a straight flush for high) could wind up with nothing if he swings his hand and someone else has a regular wheel.

Naturally, if one player has a six-straight and the other a wheel, and the wheel swings and the six straight just goes high, the six-straight must win the whole pot; he's won the only direction he went in, and the swinger got beaten cleanly in one of his directions. I also like the "no backing in" rule that doesn't let the owner of an inferior hand take part or all of a pot because two players who both had better hands than him for high also swung their hands. But any of the possible rules is fair, as long as everyone knows it in advance. If the players have tried to develop rules that cover every possible situation, but fail to anticipate one, a rule that splits the pot seems to create fewer hard feelings.

# Index

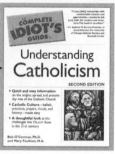
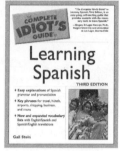

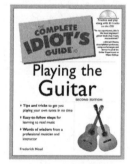

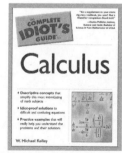